from the library of:
    Tom Simpson
    (BMHS '74)

THE MARYLAND LINE

IN THE

CONFEDERATE ARMY.

THE PARTING OF GENERALS LEE AND JACKSON AT CHANCELLORSVILLE, MAY 2D, 1863

THE MARYLAND LINE

IN THE

CONFEDERATE ARMY.

1861-1865.

BY

W. W. GOLDSBOROUGH.

⚜

PUBLISHED FOR THE BENEFIT OF THE MARYLAND LINE CONFEDERATE
SOLDIERS' HOME, PIKESVILLE, MARYLAND, UNDER AUTHORITY
OF THE BOARD OF GOVERNORS OF THE ASSOCIA-
TION OF THE MARYLAND LINE.

1900.

New Materials © Copyright 1983 by
BUTTERNUT PRESS
12137 Darnestown Road
Gaithersburg, Maryland 20878

ISBN 0-913419-00-1

NOTE.

The article on the Second Maryland Cavalry is contributed by Gen. Bradley T. Johnson, and that on the Third Maryland Artillery by Capt. W. L. Ritter.

PRESS OF
GUGGENHEIMER, WEIL & CO.
BALTIMORE, MD.

CONTENTS.

	PAGE.
Introduction,	1-5
First Maryland Infantry,	9-81
Second Maryland Infantry,	85-159
Company B, Twenty-First Virginia Infantry,	160-162
First Maryland Cavalry,	165-236
Second Maryland Cavalry,	241-248
Company K, First Virginia Cavalry,	249-256
First Maryland Artillery,	259-271
Second Maryland Artillery, (Baltimore Light)	275-295
Third Maryland Artillery,	296-318
Fourth Maryland Artillery, (Chesapeake)	319-328
Marylanders in the Confederate Service,	329-333
Confederate Soldiers' Home,	337-371

INTRODUCTION
to the
BUTTERNUT EDITION

Maryland has always been rather an anomaly, even for a border state. Caught between, and close to, both an industrial North and agrarian South, at no time was this geographical dilemma more poignant than during the War Between the States. With the eastern and southern sections of the state, particularly around the great port city of Baltimore, solidly secessionist in sympathy and the northern and western sections just as solidly opposed to leaving the Union, many of Maryland's sons must have faced with dread the choices forced by impending Civil War. Such would have been the case, in 1861, with a young printer and journalist, W. W. Goldsborough, as he and his physician brother, Charles, disagreed over their own political paths as the sectional crisis deepened. Their emotional predicament, and eventual pain, as well as that of all Marylanders, would soon be capsulized when, on May 23, 1862, at Front Royal, Virginia, Captain W. W. Goldsborough of the 1st Maryland Regiment, C. S. A. would capture Surgeon Charles Goldsborough with the 1st Maryland Regiment, U. S. A.

William Worthington Goldsborough was born in Frederick, Maryland, in 1831, the son of Doctor and Mrs. Leander Goldsborough. Growing up in Frederick, he learned the trade of printer and continued in that business after his family moved to Baltimore in the early 1850's. Joining a local militia unit, the Baltimore City Guard, Goldsborough, in 1859, got his first real taste of military life, as well as a vivid preview of the coming crisis, when his Company was called to assist in retaking the Harpers Ferry engine house seized by John Brown and his fanatics. Two years later, when political invective, so steadily fueled by the madness at Harpers Ferry, degenerated into a shooting war, Goldsborough quickly enlisted under the Southern banner.

Initially joining Company C of the new 1st Maryland Regiment as a private, Goldsborough did not remain long in the ranks. In June of 1861, he was elected Captain of Company A, which he led with distinction through first Manassas, the Valley Campaign, and Seven Days battles. When, as a result of the Confederate conscription laws, the 1st Maryland Regiment was disbanded on August 17, 1862, Goldsborough and other now supernumary officers, offered themselves as volunteer aides to Lieutenant General Thomas J. Jackson. While serving in this capacity on the staff of a Virginia Brigade, he was wounded on August 30th at the second Battle of Manassas.

Upon his recovery, about October of 1862, Goldsborough went to Richmond and there accepted a staff commission. Quickly dissatisfied, he resigned within two weeks and secured permission to raise an infantry company from amongst the many young Marylanders who continued to trickle south throughout the war. By the end of December, he lead his new unit out of Richmond to New Market, Virginia, where the newly organized 2nd Battalion, Maryland Infantry was encamped. There, his men were mustered as Company G of this successor to the old 1st Maryland and Goldsborough himself, on January 26, 1863, was appointed Major of the battalion.

After wintering in the Valley, the 2nd Maryland participated in the Pennsylvania campaign as part of Steuart's mixed brigade of North Carolineans, Virginians, and Marylanders. At Gettysburg, in their first real test of combat, the 2nd Maryland, while advancing up the fire-swept slopes of Culp's Hill on July 2nd, penetrated almost a hundred yards into the Federal lines. There, Goldsborough was desperately wounded in the side and left for dead on the field. First imprisoned at Fort Delaware, he was later one of those Confederate officers — the so-called "Immortal Six Hundred" — taken to Charleston, South Carolina and placed in an exposed stockade masking a Union battery and within range of Confederate guns. Released on parole on June 13, 1865, he returned to Baltimore and resumed his career as a printer and journalist.

While Goldsborough had been in prison, a little-known incident occurred which serves to graphically illustrate the fiercely independent nature of the Marylanders in the Confederate Army. This curious episode had its origins in 1861 when a 33 year old southern Maryland tobacco planter named William Fendly Dement, disgusted at Maryland's refusal to secede, led a group of neighbors, all Catholics from Charles County, south across the Potomac. Landing in Fredericksburg, Virginia, they planned to organize a cavalry company but, when the promised horses and mustering officer did not arrive, a young Baltimore architect, R. Snowden Andrews, persuaded them to form an artillery unit. Known as the 1st Maryland Battery, with Andrews as Captain and Dement as 1st Lieutenant, this unit would become conspicuous on many of the hard fought fields of the Army of Northern Virginia. Though the temptation to visit nearby home resulted in much "French Leave", the men remained consistantly loyal to the cause. According to family tradition, even Dement, shortly promoted to Captain would periodically return to his farm near Pomfret, Maryland to check on his crops and balance the accounts. In 1864, the Confederate Congress passed a new conscription act which compelled all able bodied men, between the ages of 17 and 50, residing in the Confederacy to serve in the Armed Forces for the duration of the war. Those presently serving thus had their enlistments effectively extended until war's end. For Dement's men, whose enlistments were up in July, the congressional act created one of those legalistic impingements on their rights so bitterly resented in the 19th century South. Reasoning that they were not residents of the Confederacy, but native sons of a soverign — and foreign — state, they believed reenlistment was legally theirs', and not the government's, choice. Accordingly, Captain Dement so wrote to Jefferson Davis who forwarded his letter to the Secretary of War. That official ruled that by leaving their home state to fight for the Confederacy, the Marylanders had effectively chosen a new domicile and were thus bound by the laws of the same. Dissatisfied, Dement and his men hired an attorney and sued. When the case was eventually heard in a Confederate Court, the attorney for the Marylanders argued that Dement's men intended to return to their home state after cessation of hostilities and, therefore, never planned to become residents of a Confederacy which did not include Maryland. Thus, they were neither citizens nor residents of the Confederacy and, therefore, could not be subject to her conscription laws. When, after tortured and exhaustive legal argument, the Judge found in favor of the Marylanders claim, all of the men, except one, promptly reenlisted.

In 1869, Kelly, Piet & Company of Baltimore published W. W. Goldsborough's first edition of *The Maryland Line in the Confederate States Army*. This pioneer history of Confederate units from Maryland, without a table of contents, preface, or index, was dedicated by the author to "Maryland's gallant son, Major General Issac R. Trimble . . ." and contained sketches of the 1st Regiment and 2nd Battalion of Maryland Infantry, the 1st Battalion of Cavalry, and the 2nd or Baltimore Light Artillery. Also included was a presumably tall tale in the style of Mark Twain concerning "Atkin's Brigade" at second Manassas. Shortly after the book's appearance, Goldsborough accepted a position as editor of the *Philadelphia Record* and moved to that city. He edited this daily newspaper until 1896 when, having survived two vicious war wounds and a less than tender imprisonment, he was run down by a bicycle, suffering a crushed thigh. Left crippled and dependent upon crutches, he retired from active journalism shortly thereafter. Goldsborough died at the age of 70 on Christmas Day, 1901 and is buried on Confederate Hill at Loudoun Park Cemetery in Baltimore.

Having perhaps realized the inadequacies of organization as well as the omissions from his previous edition, in the mid-1890's Goldsborough, aided by an old comrade from the 1st Maryland, Captain George W. Booth, began to revise and enlarge it. Published in 1900, this new edition, besides revisions and corrections, included sketches of the other Maryland units, particularly the 2nd Cavalry Battalion and 1st, 3rd, and 4th Batteries. Gone was the story of "Atkin's Brigade". Gone also were the half-dozen or so woodcuts in the earlier edition, replaced by numerous photographs utilizing a printing process not possible thirty-one years earlier. Appended was a description of the Maryland Line Confederate Soldiers Home for whose benefit the book was published. This home, established in 1888 at the former United States Arsenal in Pikesville, Maryland, would continue well into the twentieth century as a Confederate old soldiers' home. The buildings, which still stand, are today used as barracks by the Maryland State Police.

Butternut Press takes great pride in presenting this new edition of W. W. Goldsborough's *The Maryland Line in the Confederate States Army*. In addition to this new introduction, included are a previously unpublished photograph of Captain William F. Dement of the 1st Maryland Battery and an index originally prepared in 1944 by Mrs. Charles Lee Lewis, then Historian of the Maryland Division, United

Daughters of the Confederacy. This index, published at the time by the State of Maryland as Hall of Records Publication number 3, is used with their kind permission.

My sincere thanks are extended to those who have assisted in this project. Among them are Robert K. Krick, Chief Historian of the Fredericksburg and Spotsylvania National Military Park who shared both his experience and his vast research on Confederate soldiers. Also, thanks are due Father John Brady of St. Josephs Parish in Pomfret, Maryland and Father Robert Keesler of St. Mary of the Mills Parish in Laurel, Maryland for providing various information. To Ann Hudak, Head of the Maryland Room, McKeldin Library, University of Maryland and her student assistant Eric Short, as well as Timothy Lee Nearhoof of Montgomery College, Rockville, Maryland, my special thanks are also offered. Steven Hanecker, who acted as photographic consultant, and Dr. George Callcott, Professor of History at the University of Maryland who proofread this work and extended his ideas, both placed me in their debt. Finally, thanks are due to Jim Moody of the Butternut Press for allowing me to participate in the deserved republication of Major Goldsborough's fine work.

E. Philip Schreier III

Kensington, Maryland
October, 1983

INTRODUCTION.

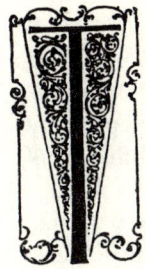THIS is not a war history. It does not propose to take the reader to every well-fought field during a four-year's conflict, from Manassas to Appomattox and tell him how battles were lost and won. Of histories of that character we have had many. Some of them have been made into text-books and used in the public schools of the country, serving no purpose save that of filling the minds of the young with prejudices and distorted facts; while others, written by the actors in the great events which they record, have their value alike to the North and the South, and will always be bright and luminous. Nor does this book aim to show the character of the events that led up to a great contest in which a peaceful people suddenly found themselves involved; or to point out the vast social, political and constitutional changes brought about by the war — that is the task of the philosopher, the statesman, and the thinker.

This is a round, unvarnished tale of a few hundred heroes from a border State, who stepped bravely to the front when their rights of manhood, of freedom and of citizenship, under what should be one protecting flag, enfolding all in its embrace, were threatened. Their identity was lost in the great gathering; no herald ever blew his trumpet in the market-place or on the housetops and told the story of their deeds to an assembled people, their statues do not stand in any national Walhalla, crowned with the laurel — they were born, they lived, they fought, they died — that was all. And so this book seeks to rescue them from the oblivion into which in coming years they might fall, to tell of their self-sacrifice and their heroism; in short, to be a simple story of four years in the lives of true and brave-hearted men.

And yet, to make the story rounded and complete, and to give a reason for the position which they took and the sacrifices which they made, it is necessary to go back a little way and speak briefly of the causes which led up to the great struggle, and how, when the blast of war sounded in their ears, these men never hesitated, but stood on the side of justice and liberty.

On the 6th of November, 1860, Abraham Lincoln was elected President of the United States, and it was felt that a great crisis had come at last, that slavery agitation had reached its climax, that the South, politically, was overwhelmed, and that it stood practically alone. And yet with all this, the people of the Cotton States were far from being agreed as to the wisdom and expediency of secession, and the ordinances of secession were not, as a general rule, submitted to the people for ratification.

In the Border Slave States there was also a marked difference of opinion and feeling on the question. As late as April 11, 1861, three resolutions which were presented in the Virginia Convention containing declarations in favor of the withdrawal of that State from the Union under certain conditions were rejected by decisive and significant majorities.

Prior to April 15, 1861, the people of Kentucky and Missouri were, if possible, more decided in their opposition to secession than were the people of Virginia, and in Maryland, before the date mentioned, practically the whole population was opposed to the action of the Cotton States, and desired a peaceful solution of the public difficulties, and the maintenance of the Union.

To carry out any plan of pacification, and to endeavor to adjust the practical questions connected with the institution of slavery in its relations to the Federal Government, the Border Slave States were ready to give that Government their support, and from the election of Mr. Lincoln, the people of these States never ceased to urge upon the Federal authorities the policy of peace.

While affairs were in this critical state, there came the bombardment of Fort Sumter, and before the smoke had rolled away from Charleston harbor there came, on April 15, 1861, the proclamation of President Lincoln, declaring that the laws were being opposed, and that their execution was obstructed in the Cotton States, and calling forth the militia of the several States of the Union to the aggregate number of 75,000 men to cause the laws to be duly executed.

What was the effect of this proclamation upon the people of the Border States? They had been offering their support to the Federal Government on all constitutional measures for the preservation of peace, and now they were commanded to submit to the exercise, by the President of the United States, of powers unwarranted by the Constitution and the laws, and their resolution was quickly taken. Arkansas, North Carolina, Tennessee and Virginia each passed an ordinance of secession, and, although the free expression of change in the feeling of the people of Kentucky, Missouri and Maryland, which was very decided, was prevented by force, the action of the Federal Government was strongly resented.

The position of Maryland was a most critical one; and while, after the President's proclamation, a large number of her people sympathized with the South, there was a feeling underneath that, on account of her geographical position, her fortunes were linked with those of the North. In the call of the President for troops, four Maryland regiments were included, and after that call a marked division manifested itself among the people of Baltimore. Business was almost suspended, a spirit of unrest and strife seemed to be in the air, and it was difficult for the police to preserve the peace.

On the 18th of April notice was received from Harrisburg that two companies of United States artillery and four companies of militia would arrive in the city that afternoon. A large crowd assembled at the station, and followed the soldiers on their march through the streets to take the train for Washington, with abuse and threats. Outbreaks occurred in various parts of the city and a meeting was held, attended by men well known and respected in the community, at which strong ground was taken against the passage of any more troops through Baltimore, and armed resistance to it was threatened.

On the forenoon of the 19th of April the Sixth Massachusetts regiment arrived in Baltimore on its way to Washington. The cars were, according to daily custom, to be detached from the engine at the Philadelphia station and drawn by horses for the distance of a mile to the Washington station. Nine cars made the passage, although missiles were thrown and some of the windows were broken. But obstructions having been placed on the track, the other cars turned back, and four companies formed on the street, and began their march to the station. The crowd on the way was not large, and there was no concert in its action, but the attack on the troops was violent. Rioters rushed at the soldiers, and attempted to seize their muskets. Men fell dead or wounded on both sides. The police bravely protected the soldiers, and, although there was confusion when the station was reached, the soldiers were safely placed in the cars, the train moved out, and passed on to Washington.

After the news of the fight spread through the city, the excitement became more intense. The Governor of the State, the Mayor and prominent citizens were all agreed that if more troops should pass through the city there would be a bloody conflict ; and the Mayor sent a letter to Washington requesting that no more troops should be ordered by the Government to do so. Next morning, the 20th, the excitement and alarm had deepened. The City Council assembled and appropriated $500,000 to be used in putting the city in a complete state of defense against any danger that might arise, and the banks promptly advanced that sum.

Next came a letter from the President to the effect that troops would march around Baltimore, but not through it. Preparations for the defense of the city were nevertheless continued. Armed men marched through the streets, military companies moved about in every direction, and the various railroad bridges leading into the city were burned by order of the authorities. On the 21st it was rumored that 3,000 troops were near the city on their way from Pennsylvania, but they halted at Cockeysville, and were finally ordered to return to their own State. For days the city was in a feverish condition, but the authorities were determined to resist all open acts of hostility to the Federal Government, and they accomplished their purpose.

On April 22 Governor Hicks convened the General Assembly of the State to meet in Annapolis on the 26th and take measures to maintain peace and order within the limits of the State, but two days afterward, " on account of the extraordinary condition of affairs," he changed the place of meeting to Frederick. The men who composed the Assembly were men of great weight and force of character, and they maintained the constitutional rights of the State with much ability. They refused to negotiate a treaty of alliance, offensive and defensive, with Virginia. On the 27th of April the Senate, by a unanimous vote, issued an address to the people, declaring that it had no authority to take any action leading to secession, the House of Delegates following with a similar declaration. Then both House and Senate passed a series of resolutions protesting against the war as unjust and unconstitutional, and declaring that Maryland would take no part in its prosecution.

On the 5th of May General Benjamin F. Butler, with two regiments and a battery of artillery, took possession of the Relay House, some seven miles from Baltimore, and fortified his position. On the night of the 13th of May, and while a violent thunder-storm was raging, he entered Baltimore and took possession of Federal Hill, which overlooks the harbor and commands the city. He met with no opposition, and yet for this exploit he was made a Major-General, thus showing, as Shakespeare says, that " while some men are born great and some achieve greatness, others have greatness thrust upon them."

A memorable event next followed. The President had suspended the writ of *habeas corpus* without the sanction of an Act of Congress, and on May 25th Mr. John Merryman was arrested by General Keim, of Pennsylvania, and lodged in Fort McHenry. A petition was presented for the writ of *habeas corpus* to Chief Justice Roger B. Taney, of the Supreme Court of the United States, who at once issued the writ to General Cadwallader, then in command in Maryland, ordering him to produce the body of Mr. Merryman in Court on May 27. On that day an aid-de-camp appeared with a letter from the General, stating that Mr. Merryman had been arrested on charges of high treason, and that he had been authorized by the President of the United States in such cases to suspend the writ of *habeas corpus*. The Chief Justice ordered an attachment to issue against General Cadwallader for disobedience to the writ, returnable at noon of next day.

At that hour the case was called, and the Marshal stated that he had gone to Fort McHenry to serve the writ ; that he sent in his name at the outer gate ; that the messenger returned and said that there was no reply, and that, therefore, he could not serve the writ. The Chief Justice then said that he had the power to summon the *posse comitatus* to bring the defendant into Court, but that he (the Marshal) would in such an event be resisted in the discharge of his duty by a force much superior to his own. He would therefore not require him to perform that duty, although if the defendant were before him he would punish him by fine and imprisonment, but would reduce to writing the reasons under which he had acted, and forward them, with the proceedings, to the President, so that the latter might discharge his constitutional duty to "take care that the laws are faithfully executed."

That opinion will always be remembered, and, in the words of the biographer of the Chief Justice, "will command the admiration and gratitude of every lover of constitutional liberty so long as our institutions shall endure." The action of that venerable man was as brave as was that of England's steel-gloved barons when they wrested Magna Charta from King John under the branching oaks of Runnymede.

There were still stirring events to follow in Maryland, but they do not directly belong to this history, and so the reader must now follow the fortunes of the Maryland Line.

MAJ. GEN'L ARNOLD ELZEY.
FIRST COLONEL FIRST MARYLAND INFANTRY.

FIRST MARYLAND INFANTRY.

CHAPTER I.

DURING all these days of dread, excitement and anxiety, men went about their daily occupations half-heartedly, and with their thoughts always bent on the possible disasters of the near future. The first act of a drama that had a continent for its stage had opened. The pageant of military array was unfolding itself all over the country; "the trumpet to the cannon spoke, the cannon to the heavens, the heavens to earth," and while the hosts of the North were being marshaled, those of the South, too, were gathering, and her people were being roused to a sublime enthusiasm of self-devotion. Hundreds of young men, firm in a spirit of resistance to what they conceived to be the exercise of arbitrary power, and with an unconquerable faith in the future, left the State to cast in their fortunes with their brethren in the South. Every day it became more difficult and hazardous to pass through the cordon of troops that had been drawn around the City of Baltimore; but this did not daunt them, and by the middle of May the greater part of those who were afterward to compose the First Maryland infantry and the other organizations early in the field, stood safely upon Virginia soil. During the ravages of the four years' struggle thousands of others also made their way through the Union lines, and either filled up the gaps which war had left in the ranks of the earlier organizations, or helped in the formation of other commands.

The late gallant old Confederate, General Isaac R. Trimble, for years before his death endeavored by every means possible to ascertain the number of Marylanders in organized commands and those scattered throughout the various regiments in all the armies of the Confederacy. He even went so far as to employ a clerk to search the Confederate archives in the War and Navy Departments at Washington, and to his surprise he discovered that there were twenty-two thousand of them in the army, besides those in the Confederate navy.

At the time referred to (April 19, 1861) there was only a comparatively small body of uniformed militia in Baltimore, but it was composed of excellent and soldierly material. The Maryland Guards and the Baltimore City Guards were the two largest organizations, and then came the Independent Grays and the Law Grays. From each of these bodies the First Maryland drew largely.

Three companies were formed in Richmond principally of this material— those of Captains J. Lyle Clark, E. R. Dorsey and William H. Murray. These companies were mustered into the service of the State of Virginia for one year, and subsequently transferred to the Confederate Government with the other

Virginia troops. The companies of Murray and Dorsey became afterward a part of the First Maryland, but that of Captain Clark was attached to the Twenty-first Virginia.

Captain Clark has been unjustly blamed for not attaching his company to the First Maryland. It was no fault of his, for he had organized his company for that purpose.

Some misconception existed in the War Department at Richmond relative to the terms of enlistment of the Maryland companies. It was thought the Harper's Ferry companies were all enlisted for the "war," when, in fact, two of them were mustered only for twelve months. The erroneous impression also prevailed that Dorsey's and Murray's companies were war companies.

In the effort to organize the so-called war companies into one regiment Dorsey and Murray were ordered to Winchester, and Clark was assigned to the Twenty-first Virginia Regiment. These errors caused Captain Clark, as well as the men of his fine company, much regret, but nevertheless, although separated from their fellow-Marylanders, they proved themselves worthy of the name they bore, the "Maryland Guards," on many a battle-field.

A few days prior to the formation of the companies in Richmond, Captain Bradley T. Johnson had marched his company from Frederick City to the Point of Rocks. This company had been organized on the 19th of April and joined the military of Baltimore to prevent the passage of troops through the city.

It was the first to be mustered into the service of the Confederate States at the Point of Rocks, and consequently afterward became the senior company of the First Maryland. Company B, commanded by Captain C. C. Edelin, was also mustered in at the Point of Rocks on the same day — May 21, 1862.

Several hundred other Marylanders had also assembled at Harper's Ferry, and at that place there were organized Companies C, Captain Frank S. Price; Company D, Captain James R. Herbert; Company E, Captain Harry McCoy; Company F. Captain Thomas Holbrook; Company G, Captain Wilson C. Nicholas, and Company H, Captain Wellmore, when for good and sufficient reasons skeletons of companies were merged into others, and Captains Price, Wellmore and Holbrook were relieved of their commands.

The six companies were mustered into the service of the Confederate States by Lieutenant-Colonel George Deas, P. A. C. S., on May 22, 1862, at Harper's Ferry. The two companies at the Point of Rocks were ordered with them, and the battalion of eight companies placed by Colonel T. J. Jackson under the command of Captain Bradley T. Johnson, of Company A.

By June 1, Captain George H. Steuart, of the Second United States Cavalry, reported to General Joseph E. Johnston, who had relieved Colonel Jackson in command at Harper's Ferry, and he assigned Captain Steuart to command the Maryland Battalion.

As soon as Captain Steuart took charge he found that several companies were only skeletons, with no prospect of filling up to the legal complement, and by authority of General Johnston he consolidated the companies of Price and Holbrook, thus making six companies of the battalion, which thus consisted of : Company A, Captain Bradley T. Johnson ; Company B, Captain C. C. Edelin ; Company D, Captain James R. Herbert ; Company E, Captain Harry McCoy ; Company F, Captain Louis Smith; Company G, Captain Wilson C. Nicholas. Three companies from Richmond were subsequently ordered to it, consisting of Company C, Captain E. R. Dorsey ; Company H, Captain William H. Murray ; Company I, Captain Michael Stone Robertson. And these nine companies constituted the First Maryland Regiment.

It was organized June 16, 1862, by commissioning Arnold Elzey, late Captain of Artillery, United States Army, as Colonel ; George H. Steuart, late Captain of Cavalry, United States Army, as Lieutenant-Colonel, and Bradley T. Johnson as Major.

After General Joseph E. Johnston had evacuated Harper's Ferry and fallen back to Winchester, that General learned that much property still remained at Harper's Ferry which had escaped the torch of Lieutenant Jones when he evacuated the place. Among this property were 17,000 gun stocks, which at that time were of inestimable value to the Confederate Government. Lieutenant-Colonel Steuart, with his Maryland command, was ordered by General Johnston to Harper's Ferry to complete the work of destruction that had been left undone by Lieutenant Jones, and remove the property above mentioned. How well and fully this duty had been performed is shown by the following official order of General Johnston :

HEADQUARTERS, WINCHESTER, June 22, 1861.

Special Order.

The commanding General thanks Lieutenant-Colonel Steuart and the Maryland regiment for the faithful and exact manner in which they carried out his orders on the 19th instant at Harper's Ferry. He is glad to learn that owing to their discipline no private property was injured and no unoffending citizen disturbed. The soldierly qualities of the Maryland regiment will not be forgotten in the day of action.

BY ORDER OF GENERAL JOSEPH E. JOHNSTON.

W. H. WHITING, *Inspector-General.*

When the middle of May had passed, it was rumored in the camp of the companies in Richmond that the men from Maryland were to be organized and placed under the command of Colonel F. J. Thomas, a former officer of the United States Army and a Marylander. The report proved to be correct, for, on May 17, he assumed command of the Maryland troops and issued the following notification, which bore the indorsement of Colonel T. J. Jackson :

HEADQUARTERS MARYLAND VOLUNTEERS SERVING IN VIRGINIA, May 17, 1861.

Colonel R. S. Garnett, Adjutant-General.

Colonel—Pursuant to instructions from Colonel Jackson, based upon a letter to me from Colonel French, aide-de-camp to His Excellency Governor Letcher, I have this day assumed command of the Maryland volunteers in this State. Numbers of the men, and especially a large number of the most valuable of the officers, have gone to Richmond and other points in Virginia. As it is very desirable that all the Maryland men should be together, I respectfully request an order to be issued for them to report here, or at such other point as the General-in-Chief may designate. I can control about three thousand two hundred of active and generally well-drilled men from Baltimore and vicinity. Until better arms can be procured, I shall proceed to arm them with the flint-lock muskets issued to Mr. T. Parkin Scott, of Baltimore, by Governor Letcher.

Very respectfully, your obedient servant.

F. J. THOMAS, *Colonel Commanding.*

[*INDORSEMENT.*]

There are some of the Maryland volunteers who object to serving under Colonel Thomas, and, in order to secure their services, I would suggest that they be mustered into the service of the Southern Confederacy, and that none except those who muster into the service of Virginia be placed under the command of Colonel Thomas.

T. J. JACKSON,
Colonel Virginia Volunteers, Commanding at Harper's Ferry.

Immediately after he had assumed command, Colonel Thomas went to Suffolk with the companies of Captains Clark and Dorsey, that were then in Richmond, and from Suffolk they marched to Chuckatuck, where they remained a short time as the guests of the hospitable people of that place. Their experience was undoubtedly the most delightful of any that a body of Maryland soldiers had during the war, and the recollections of it must still dwell in the hearts of the survivors. They saw no enemy on the way to Chuckatuck, but they had a little scare. The march was made by night, and some two or three of Colonel Thomas' volunteer aids were riding in advance. At one part of the road they imagined the fireflies in a distant field to be a company of the enemy firing at long range, and in their excitement they discharged their pistols. The troops were naturally thrown into confusion, so unexpected was the apparent collision. The command was halted and guns were loaded, but the cause of the alarm was soon discovered, and the march was resumed. After the return of the companies to Richmond the following modified official order was promulgated:

HEADQUARTERS VIRGINIA FORCES, RICHMOND, VIRGINIA, May 27. 1861.

The volunteers from the State of Maryland accepted into the *service of Virginia* will assemble at Charlestown, Virginia, and be there organized into regiments by Colonel Francis J. Thomas and instructed in their duties. This command will be under the orders of the commanding officer at Harper's Ferry for service on that frontier.

BY ORDER OF MAJOR-GENERAL LEE.

R. S. GARNETT, *Adjutant-General.*

The opposition to Colonel Thomas — for reasons that are not apparent — of which Colonel Jackson spoke officially, soon became stronger and more marked; and after the proclamation of Governor Letcher, on June 8, transferring the land and naval forces of the State of Virginia to the Confederate Government, Colonel Thomas was relieved of his command, and Arnold Elzey was appointed in his stead. Colonel Thomas was soon afterward attached to the staff of General Joseph E. Johnston, and was killed at Manassas on July 21. In his official report of the battle General Johnston thus refers to a gallant soldier:

Many of the broken troops, fragments of companies and individual stragglers were re-formed and brought into action with the aid of my staff. . . The largest body of these, equal to about four companies, having no competent field officer, I placed under the command of one of my staff, Colonel F. J. Thomas, who fell while gallantly leading them against the enemy.

The objection to Colonel Thomas on the part of the Harper's Ferry companies was not personal, but because the officers there aspired to command themselves the companies they had raised and brought from Maryland. They sent an officer to Richmond with a petition to the President to appoint Captain Charles Sidney Winder Colonel, Bradley T. Johnson Lieutenant-Colonel, and E. R. Dorsey Major.

It was considered best by the authorities to organize the regiment as above stated, and the command, officers and men, submitted with loyal gallantry and served under them faithfully until they were promoted and the regiment came to be commanded by Colonel Bradley T. Johnson.

On June 25 the companies of Dorsey and Murray reached Winchester and united with those under command of Lieutenant-Colonel Steuart, when the regiment was fully organized with the following field and company officers:

OFFICERS.

Colonel, ... Arnold Elzey.
Lieutenant-Colonel, ... George H. Steuart.
Major, ... Bradley T. Johnson.
Acting Adjutant, ... Frank X. Ward.

COMPANY A.

*W. W. Goldsborough, *Captain.* Charles W. Blair, *Second Lieutenant.*
George K. Shellman, *First Lieutenant.* George M. E. Shearer, *Third Lieutenant.*

COMPANY B.

C. C. Edelin, *Captain.* Joseph Griffin, *Second Lieutenant.*
James Mullen, *First Lieutenant.* Thomas Costello, *Third Lieutenant.*

COMPANY C.

E. R. Dorsey, *Captain.* Septimus H. Stewart, *Second Lieutenant.*
Robert C. Smith, *First Lieutenant.* William P. Thomas, *Third Lieutenant.*

COMPANY D.

James R. Herbert, *Captain.* William Key Howard, *Second Lieutenant.*
George W. Booth, *First Lieutenant.* Nicholas Snowden, *Third Lieutenant.*

COMPANY E.

Harry McCoy, *Captain.* John Lutts, *Second Lieutenant.*
Edmund O'Brien, *First Lieutenant.* John Cushing, Jr., *Third Lieutenant.*

---

* Elected from Company C upon the promotion of Captain B. T. Johnson to the rank of Major.

COMPANY F.

J. Louis Smith, *Captain*.
William D. Hough, *First Lieutenant*.
William J. Broadfoot, *Second Lieutenant*.
Joseph H. Stewart, *Third Lieutenant*.

COMPANY G.

Wilson C. Nicholas, *Captain*.
Alexander Cross, *First Lieutenant*.
Edward Deppish, *Second Lieutenant*.

COMPANY H.

William H. Murray, *Captain*.
George Thomas, *First Lieutenant*.
Frank X. Ward, *Second Lieutenant*.
Richard T. Gilmor, *Third Lieutenant*.

BRIG. GEN'L GEORGE H. STEUART,
LIEUTENANT COLONEL AND COLONEL FIRST MARYLAND INFANTRY.

CHAPTER II.

These companies constituted the regiment that was to cover itself with so much glory on that hot and fateful July afternoon at Manassas, but it was subsequently increased by two other companies, I and C (Second), of which mention will be made hereafter.

The regiment numbered some seven hundred men, but only two of the companies were uniformed — those of Murray and Dorsey, from Richmond. The rest were clad in the garb in which they had left home, but it was sadly changed. Sleeping out in the mud and rain had despoiled the citizens' dress, and worn it threadbare, and in many cases it was in tatters. Looking at these men, Sir John Falstaff might have said : "I'll not march through with them, that's flat," but there all resemblance ends between them and the fat knight's motley company. They were yeomen's sons, brave and warm-hearted ; many of them were men of education and refinement ; they never murmured or complained, and they cheerfully responded to the call to their various camp duties.

Lieutenant-Colonel George H. Steuart took virtual command of the camp, and through his unceasing and tireless energy they soon became proficient in company movements.

But at this time a good angel appeared in the camp in the person of a woman — Mrs. Bradley T. Johnson.

Seeing the condition of affairs, this noble and unselfish woman set out for North Carolina, her native State, escorted by Captain Nicholas and Lieutenant George M. E. Shearer, and reached Raleigh in safety after overcoming many difficulties. The morning after her arrival she made her appearance before Governor Ellis and the Council of State, stated the necessities of the Maryland troops, and in a feeling manner appealed to them for assistance. The Governor and Council immediately presented her with five hundred Mississippi rifles and ten thousand rounds of cartridges.

Before Mrs. Johnson left Raleigh a public meeting was called under the auspices of the Honorable W. E. Edwards, Chief Justice Thomas Ruffin, and other distinguished men. In addressing the meeting the Honorable Kennith Raynor said :

" If great events produce great men, so, in the scene before us, we have proof that great events produce great women. It was one that partook more of the romance than of the realities of life. One of our own daughters, raised in the lap of luxury, blessed with the enjoyment of all the elements of elegance and ease, had quit her peaceful home, followed her husband to the camp, and, leaving him in that camp, had come to the home of her childhood to seek aid for him and his comrades, not because he is her husband, but because he is fighting the battles of his country against a tyrant."

On May 29 Mrs. Johnson took her departure from Raleigh with her prize, stopped at Richmond for a day, and procured from Governor Letcher a number of tents, blankets and camp equipage, all of which she delivered to her husband, after an absence of ten days from camp.

The following interesting paper, still in the possession of Mrs. Johnson, is perhaps without a parallel:

Received, Ordnance Department, Harper's Ferry, June 3, 1861, of Mrs. B. T. Johnson, five hundred Mississippi rifles (calibre 54), ten thousand cartridges, and thirty-five hundred caps.

G. M. COCHRAN, *Master of Ordnance.*

Then the question arose as to how to secure uniforms and necessary clothing for the men. Once more this noble woman was equal to the emergency, and very soon, and that entirely through her own exertions, the men were clad in neatly fitting gray uniforms. And what a change was there! The boys no longer blushed through the bronze on their cheeks if any of the fair ladies of Winchester chanced to be in camp, and behind them when the commanders of companies gave the order, " Parade rest ! " they stood erect, a cubit was added to their stature, and they looked boldly into dark and soft eyes that beamed on boys in gray. Verily, Carlyle is right; there is a philosophy in clothes.

All the officers worked faithfully to bring the command up to a state of proficiency, and they were aided and encouraged by the men themselves, who entered upon their hard and, to nearly all of them, unaccustomed duties with the greatest alacrity. The result was that the regiment soon became the pride of General Johnston's army, and was regarded with marked favor by the commanding General himself.

It was on July 1 that orders were received to cook two days' rations and prepare to move. The cause for this unexpected order was at first mere conjecture, but it soon became known that the Federal General Patterson had again crossed the Potomac with an overwhelming force, and was driving Jackson before him at Falling Waters.

At 4 o'clock on the afternoon of that same day General Johnston's little army of eleven thousand men marched out of Winchester toward Martinsburg. The men were in good spirits and eager for an opportunity to try conclusions with the enemy, despite the fact that they were but poorly armed, and that many of them did not have half of a dozen cartridges in their pockets, for cartridge boxes were at that time a scarce article in the equipment of a Confederate. That night the army went into bivouac at Bunker Hill. At early morning of the 2nd the march was resumed, and at noon of the same day the Confederate line of battle was formed at the village of Darksville, six miles from Martinsburg, which place Patterson had reached. As an evidence of the confidence which General Johnston had in the First Maryland, it was thrown on the extreme right of the line of battle, and had it been called upon, it would, doubtless, have shown itself worthy of the trust that he reposed in it.

For four days the troops lay upon their arms hourly expecting an attack, and several times being called into readiness through what in each instance proved to be a false report of the enemy's advance. But Patterson did not advance, and the brave men were spared the humiliation of possible defeat; for how could a command of poorly equipped men hope to combat successfully a force more than twice their number and clothed in all the panoply of war? Probably of all in that little army the most relieved man was Johnston himself, when, at the end of four days of weary and anxious waiting, he found that the enemy would not take up the gage of battle that had been so defiantly thrown down to him.

Still it was necessary to keep Patterson away from McDowell, and from the battle that was believed to be imminent at Manassas; and so, although General Johnston fell back to Winchester on the 8th of July, the cavalry, under Colonel J. E. B. Stuart, was left in Patterson's front.

Once more the First Maryland occupied its old quarters near hospitable Winchester, and the dull routine of camp life was kept up until July 18. At early morning of that day a telegram came to General Johnston from Richmond informing him that McDowell was advancing upon Manassas, then held by General Beauregard, and directing him, *if practicable*, to go to that commander's assistance. In the exercise of the discretion, thus given to him, by the terms of the order, General Johnston quickly decided to move to the support of General Beauregard. In order to accomplish this he must either meet and defeat Patterson, who was then in camp at Bunker Hill, or elude him. He chose the latter course. "Ah! then and there was hurrying to and fro." Camp was soon broken, the troops were eager for the advance, the march began, and while the western sky was aflame with glory, the last of the command filed steadily through the streets of old Winchester town, the people sorrowing over their departure, and feeling that now there would be no protection against the dreaded invaders who were then but a few miles distant, while here and there a gray-coated soldier boy, as he marched along the dusty road, thought with a sigh of the maiden he had left behind him.

All through the long night the steady march was kept up, and at early dawn the last of the column had reached the banks of the Shenandoah, where a halt was made to enable the wearied men to refresh themselves with breakfast. Fording the river at Berry's Ferry, the march was resumed at 8 o'clock, and all through that hot midsummer day the troops pressed eagerly forward. The sun beat down pitilessly, the crickets chirped in the grass, the katydid made her monotonous confession, birds sang in the trees, cattle were lowing in the fields, from the doors of cabins wondering children looked out on the long line of gray and butternut that seemed to dwindle to a thread in the distance ; hills were climbed, song and jest were passed around, and still the steady rhythm of tramping thousands beat the air. On and on they marched, through Ashby's Gap, through Upperville, the shadows lengthening and evening spreading her mantle on the mountains, until long after dark, and pelted by a pouring rain, footsore and weary they came to Piedmont, on the Manassas Gap Railroad, where they looked for transportation to the scene of conflict.

Previous to the departure of the army from Winchester the different regiments had been formed into brigades, although brigadier-generals had not been assigned to all of them. The First Maryland, Thirteenth Virginia, Tenth Virginia and Third Tennessee were formed into a brigade, known as the Fourth, to be attached to another brigade to form a division, and to be commanded by General E. Kirby Smith. In the absence of a brigadier-general, Colonel Arnold Elzey, of the First Maryland, and the senior Colonel, assumed command, and it was known as Elzey's Brigade.

The sun rose brightly on the morning of the 20th, and soon everything was bustle and confusion. Cars were filled with troops as rapidly as possible, and by noon General Johnston, with Jackson's Brigade (afterward the immortal " Stonewall ") and some Georgia, North Carolina, South Carolina and Alabama troops had reached Manassas. General Johnston had felt certain that he would have his whole command at Manassas by nightfall of that day, but the means of transportation was inadequate, and this condition of things was made worse by a collision between two trains, in which, although no person was hurt, an engine and several cars were wrecked.

All day long and during the night following, the troops that had been left behind at Piedmont chafed and fretted under the delay, but it was not until the morning of the 21st that Elzey's Brigade, one of the very last to leave, boarded the train for Manassas. Their progress was slow, and still further delay was occasioned by the breaking down of an engine, and it seemed almost an age before they reached Manassas. The battle had then been raging for hours, and the rapid discharge of artillery could be distinctly heard five or six miles away.

General E. Kirby Smith was awaiting the arrival of Elzey's Brigade, which he was entitled to command. Knapsacks were quickly thrown aside, and, under the broiling sun, the troops eagerly started at a double-quick in the direction of the sound of battle. They were almost hidden in a cloud of dust, and the heat grew more intense. Now they would slacken their swift pace to a walk, and again halt for a moment to cool their parched tongues and throats at a mud puddle ; and all the time, while the sky was blue, the far-off roll of thunder seemed to be in the air. But it was the boom of cannon answering cannon ; their defiant tones sounded more deeply at every step, and soon the rattle of musketry made a sharp staccato to the diapason from brazen throats. Then came the sight of wounded men moving slowly and painfully to the rear, first by twos and then in larger numbers, while the hurried and fragmentary story that they tried to tell as the troops passed on was not always one to brighten the eye or cause the pulse to beat proudly and joyfully.

From high overhead of the command there came a screaming sound. None of the troops had ever before heard such a strange sound, but, as if by intuition, all knew that it was a shell, and for the first time felt what was really meant. "Bang !" "Bang !" went two more, and then they came literally in showers. It seemed as if that little brigade was the target for all the artillery of the Union Army. Then it began to dawn upon the wondering men that the clouds of dust which they were raising on their march had told the Federals that Confederate reinforcements were moving to the front. And still General Smith rode grimly and sternly forward.

Now rifle balls begin to "zip" on every hand, and many a man who had sworn never to bow his head at the sound of a bullet found himself doing so involuntarily ; and there were some who, when they raised their faces in shame, expecting to meet the jibes and laughter of their comrades, found them all making a like obeisance.

And now came a critical moment. The First Maryland was on the right of the advancing column, with General Smith riding silently at its head, when suddenly, as it entered a strip of wood, a fierce volley of musketry was poured into it at short range. General Smith fell from his horse desperately wounded, and several of the men in the First Maryland were also injured. Sergeant John B. Berryman, of Company C, being shot in the groin and rendered a cripple for life.

This was the First Maryland's baptism of fire, but it never faltered. Instinctively, and as it seemed without an order, with steady precision, it calmly swung into line. At once Colonel Elzey assumed command, and quickly placed in position Colonel Gibbon's Tenth Virginia and Colonel Vaughn's Third Tennessee, A. P. Hill's Thirteenth Virginia, having been detached to Blackburn's Ford.

And now there happened something that helped to turn the tide of battle.

With the quick and keen instinct of a soldier, Elzey, finding himself too far to the right, moved obliquely to the left through the strip of woods until he approached its edge. Then a strange sight greeted the eyes of his men. On a ridge across the wheat field in their front, and as far down to their right as the eye could reach, was an unbroken line of blue, from which came volumes of smoke, except in the brigade's immediate front. Colonel Elzey had reached a position by which he had outflanked the enemy and made its standpoint untenable, unless it could prolong its line. All this General Elzey saw at a glance, and felt, too, that not a moment must be lost. He knew that his presence had not yet been discovered, but he determined to make it known. Swiftly moving his column forward to the very edge of the woods, he opened fire. That long, sinuous line of blue showed its surprise, but it quickly returned the fire, and from the woods and the ridge the bullets flew thick and fast. The fire from the Confederate side was effective, and here and there breaks could be seen in the blue line, but as Elzey's column had the advantage of the position in the woods, the casualties on its side were comparatively few, the only man killed in the First Maryland being Private John Swisher, of Company A, who was shot in the head, and died instantly.

For some time the fierce duel continued, but with no evidence of weakness on either side. Then Elzey determined to make the attack. Riding along the line he stirred the hearts of his men by words of praise and encouragement, and then, when every man was quivering and throbbing under the tension to which he had been subjected, and felt like a swift horse under the bridle, or a fleet greyhound held back by the leash, the command "Forward!" came from the gallant soldier's lips like a clarion blast. The men answered with a will. Leaping over the fence that separated the woods from the wheat field, they dashed forward with a yell. The fate of the Confederate Army was in their hands that day, for all along the line the gallant boys in gray had been driven back or mowed down. Would the charge succeed? There was no hope that it would, for the enemy held a strong position and Elzey's men had three hundred yards to cross over an open field. But the gray line swept on. One hundred yards were passed, and still their ringing cheers were heard, while the echoes floated back and died away in the sombre woods. Two hundred yards, and the pace began to tell. Would they ever reach the goal? The fire of the enemy grew fiercer; that blue line with the baleful and vengeful light that flashed from its steady front seemed to mock the peaceful cerulean of the summer sky. Three hundred yards, and the ridge was reached. Panting and gasping, they pull themselves upward; their vision expanded. That blue line was made up of men, stern and fierce men, each with a gun in his hands. They could tell the color of his eyes; they could count the buttons on his coat. Was this what they had seen from the woods?

Was this what they had crossed the wheat field to meet? It was man to man now, it was strength against strength. And lo! as they gasped and wondered, that long blue line grew dim. Were their eyes failing them; was the angel of death smiling on them? Fainter grew the blue; it seemed to dissolve; it melted away like the baseless fabric of a vision; it blended with the blue sky; it disappeared in the woods behind the hill.

Halting the column upon the position just held by the now vanished enemy, Elzey re-formed his troops, and then pressed forward in pursuit. Through the thick pines he went, until he reached the open country. What a sight met the gaze of his victorious command! Thousands of men struggling frantically with each other in their wild flight to reach the rear, and others less fortunate surrendering themselves prisoners at every step. The victors were exhausted, and their commander had to halt them for a rest.

It was during this pursuit that President Davis and Generals Johnston and Beauregard rode up to Colonel Elzey, the former with much emotion, and with extended hand exclaiming: "*General* Elzey, you are the Blucher of the day!"

General Joseph E. Johnston, in his official report of the battle of Manassas, says:

"About 3 o'clock, while the enemy seemed to be striving to outflank and drive back our left, and thus separate us from Manassas, General E. K. Smith arrived with three regiments of Elzey's Brigade. He was instructed to attack the right flank of the enemy now exposed to us. Before the movement was completed he fell, severely wounded. Colonel Elzey, at once taking command, executed it with great promptitude and vigor. General Beauregard rapidly seized the opportunity thus afforded him and threw forward his whole line. The enemy was driven back from the long-contested hill, and victory was no longer doubtful."

General Irvin McDowell, in his official report of this battle, says:

"It was at this time that the enemy's reinforcements came to his aid from the railroad trains (understood to have just arrived from the valley with the residue of Johnston's army). They threw themselves in the woods on our right, and opened a fire of musketry on our men, which caused them to break and retire down the hillside. This soon degenerated into disorder, for which there was no remedy. Every effort was made to rally them, even beyond the reach of the enemy's fire, but in vain. . . . The plain was covered with retreating groups, and they seemed to infect those with whom they came in contact. The retreat soon became a rout, and this soon degenerated still further into a panic. . . . . In the panic the horses hauling the caisons and ammunition were cut from their places by persons to escape with, and in this way much confusion was caused, the panic aggravated, and the road encumbered. Not only were pieces of artillery lost, but also many of the ambulances carrying the wounded."

Inclining to the right, Colonel Elzey halted his command near the Henry house. The ground around there was thickly strewn with dead and wounded men of both armies. Conspicuous amongst them were those of the Sixty-ninth (Irish) and Seventy-ninth (Scotch) New York Regiments. At that point the struggle had been a terrible one, and the loss of life very great.

The wounded who were lying around uncared for were pleading piteously for water, and the soldiers of the First Maryland were soon tenderly caring for them. A Union officer, who wore the uniform of the Seventy-ninth New York, lay dying on the field, having been shot through the head. Captain James R. Herbert, of the First Maryland, raised the unconscious man's head, poured some water into his mouth, and unloosened his coat and waistcoat. As he did so a large pocketbook dropped to the ground, which the Captain opened, finding in it a package of letters from the dying man's wife, with the name of Brown on the envelopes. There were also seventy dollars in gold. Captain Herbert took possession of the letters and the money. Two years later, and when he was Lieutenant-Colonel of the Second Maryland Infantry, he was desperately wounded at Gettysburg and made prisoner. During those two years and through all the changes and hardships of war he had kept both letters and gold as a sacred trust, and he now caused a personal to be inserted in the *New York Herald* asking for information as to the widow of the dead officer. In a short time the lady arrived at Gettysburg, saw Lieutenant-Colonel Herbert, and heard from his lips the story of the last moments of her husband. It renewed her grief, and yet it consoled her, and she left happy in the possession of the letters. The gold she took with reluctance.

The men rested for some time at the Henry House, and soon felt refreshed. All of them had food, too, although it came from the haversacks of Union enemies now lying stiff and cold in death. They felt confident that a march was now to be made upon Washington, and the thought of entering the Capital as conquerors reconciled them to discomfort and privation. They were, therefore, bright and cheerful when Colonel Elzey moved his brigade over the Stone Bridge in the direction of Centreville. After marching some three miles along the turnpike, the troops were moved to the right into a large field and ordered to rest.

Hour after hour passed away, and still no order came to move, and when near nightfall the troops retraced their steps and took the road to Manassas murmurs of dissatisfaction were heard on every hand. Soldiers are sometimes grumblers when not allowed to have their own way; every officer and man occasionally considers himself a general, and no doubt there are times in which the advice of the rank and file would bring victory, but that this was one of them seems ridiculous. At least General Joseph E. Johnston did not think the time had arrived to make a successful advance in the direction of Washington, and his opinion in the matter should be paramount to any other. Upon this subject General Beauregard says in his official report:

"An army which had fought as ours did on that day, against uncommon odds, under a July sun, most of the time without water and without food except a hastily snatched, scanty meal at dawn, was not in condition for an eager, effective pursuit of an enemy immediately after the battle."

President Davis said:

"It could not be expected that any success obtainable on the battle-field would enable our forces to carry the fortifications on the Potomac, garrisoned and within supporting distance of fresh troops; nor after the actual battle and victory did the Generals on the field propose an advance on the Capital, nor does it appear that they have since believed themselves in a condition to attempt such a movement."

All of this has been particularly dwelt upon here for the reason that the idea has always prevailed in the South that there was a diversity of opinion between President Davis and Generals Johnston and Beauregard as to the propriety of advancing upon Washington after the battle of Manassas. There was no such diversity. The impossibility of a successful advance upon the Capital was apparent, and the idea was never entertained for a moment.

CHAPTER III.

The brigade of General Elzey (for his promotion dates from July 21, 1861) reached the neighborhood of Manassas in the early part of the night and in the midst of a heavy rain, which dampened the spirits of the men and heightened the disappointment felt by them. A great battle had been won — of that there was no doubt — but, like little Peterkin in the ballad, they were wondering what good had come of it, when they were not to be permitted to see the dome of the Northern Capitol.

The men, however, were wet and weary, and while the rain fell they wrapped themselves in their blankets and slept soundly, until aroused by the reveille at early dawn. All that day the rain fell, everything was dull and dreary, and the men fretted and fumed under their inactivity and the depressing surroundings. And when darkness fell upon them, when they lay down shivering and weary, and no orders had been given them to move, those of the First Maryland gave vent to their disappointment in low-spoken but unmistakable language.

But at midnight the long roll sounded through the camp, and at once every man was on his feet. What could this mean ? Was the enemy advancing, or was this the signal for their own forward movement ? The explanation soon came. Colonel J. E. B. Stuart had been ordered to advance to Fairfax Court House, and the First Maryland and the Third Tennessee were to report to him.

The movement was soon begun, and all through the long night the troops marched slowly, wading through mud, pelted by the pitiless storm of rain, and stumbling in the darkness, until daylight came, and the turnpike leading to Alexandria was reached. The rain had ceased, the clouds took on a brighter hue, and rolled away in light and fleecy folds. Then a light breeze sprung up and they were driven faster across the sky, melting away in the distant blue. No shipwrecked mariner in mid-ocean, tossing on a frail raft, ever welcomed the sight of a sail more gladly than did these worn and haggard men the rising sun. It seemed to smile on them, it warmed and gladdened them ; they forgot all the suffering of the past thirty-six hours ; they were themselves again.

As they marched along the road evidences of the wild flight of two days before were to be seen on every hand. It was a sight that baffled description. Artillery was there just in the position in which it had been when the horses were cut loose, and joined in the mad stampede. There were ordnance wagons, their lumbering wheels wedged in deep ruts ; there commissary and quartermasters' wagons, their varied contents jumbled in a general wreck ; and again carriages which had been abandoned by those invincible sons of Mars — Northern members of Congress who had started with the army to go on to Richmond. And there, too, strewing the road for miles were muskets, cartridge boxes, belts, swords, pistols and camp utensils, flung away in mad fear, and to aid the flight of an army, while the fields on either side were filled with abandoned camps and their immense quantities of stores. It was a picture of rout and confusion worthy the brush of a painter of battles.

Fairfax Court House was reached at noon, amid the glad welcomes of its people, and passing proudly through the village, the First Maryland went into camp in a strip of woods half a mile away.

The original organization of this command had been somewhat altered by the promotion of Colonel Elzey to the rank of Brigadier-General. By his promotion Lieutenant-Colonel George H. Steuart became Colonel, Major Bradley T. Johnson Lieutenant-Colonel, and Captain E. R. Dorsey, of Company C, Major. By the promotion of Captain Dorsey, Robert C. Smith, of Company C, became Captain; Septimus H. Stewart, First Lieutenant; William P. Thomas, Second Lieutenant, and William Smythe, Orderly Sergeant, was made Third Lieutenant.

As day after day passed by in camp and there was nothing to indicate a forward movement, Colonel Steuart determined to take advantage of the inaction and instruct the officers and men in company and battalion drill, so long neglected and so much needed. He was a capable instructor, and the men were willing to learn of him.

There was nothing else to vary the monotony of camp life, save the picket duty performed by the First Maryland at Padgett's Tavern, and then at Mason's Hill, from which latter point the streets of Alexandria and the Capitol at Washington could be plainly seen.

One morning, whilst picketing at Padgett's Tavern, Companies A and H, under command of Captain W. W. Goldsborough, were sent forward to feel the enemy in front. At Demming's Crossroads the Federals were discovered in considerable force, and a sharp exchange of musket shots followed. The two companies had performed their task, and they were withdrawn, the only "casualty" being the piercing of Private Frank Markoe's cap by a bullet.

CHAPTER IV.

After a stay of several weeks at Fairfax Court House, the First Maryland and the Third Tennessee were ordered to rejoin the other two regiments of Elzey's Brigade, then at Fairfax Station, some three miles distant. The change was gladly welcomed for several reasons, the principal one being the knowledge that the grounds were larger, and, therefore, better adapted not only for camp purposes, but for company and regimental drill. The First Maryland was encamped for many weeks at Fairfax Station, and it was there, above all other places that it was brought to the state of efficiency, both in drill and discipline, that caused it to be envied by every other regiment in the brigade.

Colonel Steuart's rigid system of discipline quietly and quickly conduced to the health and morale of this splendid command. His officers had to report to him daily to be examined in their various duties, and there were soon but few of them who could not have commanded the regiment had occasion required it. He was exacting with them, although just and impartial, and so he was with his men. It was only natural that such strict discipline should at first have been distasteful to all, but when they began to see its fruits they heartily seconded him in his efforts to make the First Maryland the peer of any regiment in the Confederate service. Strict and faithfully carried out sanitary regulations helped to make the health of the men almost perfect, and when either the companies or the regiment were out on drill the men from other commands surrounded them and witnessed their evolutions with great interest.

Colonel Steuart possessed an admirable quality, and one that is seldom found amongst old army officers. He was opposed to court-martials except for serious offenses. On all minor charges he sat in judgment himself, and some of his modes of punishment were unique. Possessing, as has been said, the implicit confidence of his men, they followed him fearlessly into the thick of the fight, knowing that when he called, they must be there, and that their lives would not be rashly or needlessly sacrificed. Whilst he admired the fighting qualities of the Third Tennessee, his spirit was shocked at their utter lack of discipline, and he thought he could inflict no greater humiliation, either on his officers or his men, than to call them Tennesseeans.

In the latter part of August, 1861, the ranks of the First Maryland were added to by the arrival of Company I, which had been raised in Richmond, and mustered into the service of the Confederate Government on June 15. It would have joined the regiment before, and shared in the glory of Manassas, but for the fact that the men did not procure their uniforms and equipments until the first of

August. After Manassas they were detailed to guard the prisoners in Richmond who had been captured in that battle, until they were ordered to join the First Maryland at Fairfax Station. The company was composed of young men principally from Charles County, Maryland, and it was officered as follows :

Captain, Michael S. Robertson ; First Lieutenant, Hugh Mitchell ; Second Lieutenant, Hezekiah H. Bean ; Third Lieutenant, Eugene Diggs.

During its stay at Fairfax Station, the regiment was frequently called upon to perform duties of an important and a hazardous character. General J. E. B. Stuart had formed an attachment for it, and when he needed the support of infantry he usually asked for the services of the First Maryland. It thus came about that it took part in the capture of Mason's Hill, and that after that fight Companies G and I, respectively commanded by Captains Wilson C. Nicholas and Michael S. Robertson, were detailed to aid in the capture of Upton's and Munson's Hills. In the fight at Upton's Hill Private Fountain, of Company I, was killed, and Lieutenant Hugh Mitchell, of the same company, was wounded.

Near the close of the fall of 1861 the enemy became restive. The small force of cavalry and infantry which held Munson's and Mason's Hills was withdrawn, and it and all outlying bodies were ordered to Centreville, which place was being strongly fortified by Generals Jonhston and Beauregard in anticipation of the enemy's advance in force at an early day.

It was Juliet who said to Romeo : "Parting is such sweet sorrow that I could say 'Good night' until tomorrow," but it was not thus that the boys of the First Maryland felt when they broke camp at Fairfax Station to march to Centreville. There were pleasant associations connected with their stay at the former place. Life-long friendships had been formed, kindnesses had been showered upon them, and so the last reveille seemed to have a note of discord in its music, and the summons to "Fall in !" was not responded to with that alacrity which always characterized men "so dauntless in war" as the sons of Maryland. It was on this camp, too, which they were leaving, that Mrs. Bradley T. Johnson and those lovely maidens, Constance, Jennie and Hettie Carey, used to throw the sunlight of their smiles. They cheered and ministered to the sick ; they looked after the comforts of those who were hale and hearty, and the charm of their sweet and gracious presence turned gloom into sunshine, and shone like an oasis on the dreariness of camp life. Many of the men whom they were wont to cheer have passed away ; some died on the battle-field, others in the quiet of home ; but they could never have forgotten those gentle women. And as for the survivors of that camp, men who are now growing old, there is not one who does not still remember those autumn evenings when the stirring music of "The Bonnie Blue Flag," "Maryland, My Maryland," and "Away Down South in Dixie," floated through the camp, upborne by the rich voices of these noble women and the stronger harmony from the regiment's glee club. There was not a man who did not feel the spirit of the hour while all could say :

> "The night shall be filled with music,
> And the cares that infest the day
> Shall fold their tents like the Arabs,
> And as silently steal away."

The site that was selected at Centreville for the camp of the First Maryland was on a plateau from whence could be seen the greater portion of the goodly sized army that Johnston and Beauregard were marshaling. Centreville was being strongly fortified, so far at least as earthworks were concerned, but had McClellan known the real character of what looked to be such formidable ordnance frowning so fiercely and threateningly upon all the approaches, he might not have hesitated to push forward the vast army he had gathered before Washington. There were few siege guns in position, but huge blackened logs answered the purpose fully as well.

The regiment arrived at Centreville on October 16, and from that time until it went into winter quarters Colonel Steuart devoted his energies to keeping it up to and even exceeding the standard of efficiency which it had attained, and in this he succeeded. Outside of camp duties the regiment was picketing along the Little River turnpike, in the neighborhood of Chantilly, but never came into collision with the enemy.

While in camp the election for President of the Confederacy took place. The exiles from Maryland were ineligible to vote, but they consoled themselves by holding an election of their own, and the scenes around a Baltimore polling-place were enacted, no feature being missing down to the "awl." When their vote was counted it was found that they had unanimously elected Colonel George H. Steuart President of the Southern Confederacy.

On December 18 Elzey's Brigade was ordered into winter quarters two miles from Manassas. It was in a dense pine thicket, which served as a shelter from the cold blasts of winter. A large space was cleared on which rude huts were erected, and the troops fared comfortably.

The army under General J. E. Johnston was at that time in such a weak condition that it would have been poorly able to defend itself against the enemy. Many of the companies in the various regiments had been enlisted for one year only, and it was feared, and with good reason, that when that time had expired a large number of men would return to their homes. The Government, therefore, issued an order in February granting furloughs to the one-year term men, if they would re-enlist for the war. Companies A, B, C, H and I of the First Maryland came under this order, and with but few exceptions the men of A and

B re-enlisted. Those of C, H and I elected to wait until their term had expired before doing anything in the matter, many of them preferring other branches of the service to that of the infantry.

The companies which remained with the regiment (A and B being off on furlough) performed picket duty near Sangster's Station, on the line of the railroad. On March 9, 1862, a picket post and a portion of its reserves, belonging to Company F, all under command of First Lieutenant Richard D. Hough, were charged by a detachment of the First New York (Lincoln) Cavalry, and in the fight that followed Lieutenant Joseph H. Stewart and fourteen men of Company F were captured, one of them, Sergeant Edward Sheehan, being slightly wounded. Lieutenant Hidden, who commanded the attacking cavalry, was killed.

Prior to this affair it had become evident to General Johnston and the Confederate Government that the large and splendidly equipped army under McClellan, which had been drilling for months near Washington, was about to assume the offensive. In view of the weak condition of Johnston's army, it was decided to dismantle the works around Centreville and Manassas, send all ordnance and commissary stores to a place of safety, and then abandon Manassas. On the night of March 8, 1862, all being ready, the order to march next morning was issued. What little had to be left behind was destroyed, and when McClellan reached Manassas all was loneliness and ruin. There was no foe to fight, no victory to strive for, nothing to compensate for the time and treasure spent in marshaling and equipping the great army which was to destroy the Confederacy. Johnston marched his troops along the Orange and Alexandria railroad until they reached the Rappahannock. They crossed that river to the south side, which was held by General R. S. Ewell with his division, whilst Johnston marched the remainder of his army to Richmond. To Ewell's division Elzey's Brigade was attached.

An advance of the enemy from Manassas was now expected daily, and the piers of the railroad bridge were mined and filled with explosives to be fired whenever McClellan's vanguard appeared. The First Maryland and the Baltimore Light Artillery were assigned to duty on the river front, and one day in the early part of April keen-eyed watches saw emerging from the distant woods on the opposite side of the river, first a long line of cavalry, next infantry and then artillery. A shot or two from the Baltimore Lights sent the cavalry galloping in every direction, and then the infantry skirmishers were thrown forward, advancing steadily toward the river. Company A, First Maryland, under command of Captain W. W. Goldsborough, was now deployed and thrown forward to meet this skirmish line. Thanks to Colonel George H. Steuart's training, the movement was beautifully executed. General Elzey declaring that it could not have been surpassed by a company of regular soldiers.

The two skirmish lines were soon engaged, as was also the Baltimore Light Artillery. One of the enemy's shells passed under General Elzey's horse, but exploded harmlessly. Hotter grew the fire ; shells shrieked overhead ; there were sharp rattles of musketry, and amid the din and roar, the piers of the railroad bridge were blown up, falling in a pile of ruins into the calmly flowing river. Although there had been a great deal of firing on both sides, and some of the men of Company A had been struck, no one was seriously hurt. What losses the enemy sustained was not known, and he soon withdrew, having evidently learned all he wished to know. Until the 19th of April several of these visits were made by the avant couriers of McClellan, the bulk of whose army still lay between Manassas and Centreville, each recurring scene being simply a repetition of the first.

A movement was now decided upon, and on the 17th of April tents were struck and shipped to some point of which the troops were ignorant. All that night and until the morning of the 19th the men were dispirited and wretched. With the tents had gone nearly all of the commissary stores, and the command was not only without shelter, but weak and hungry. On the 19th it flashed upon Lieutenant-Colonel Bradley T. Johnson (and doubtless also upon some of his command) that the day was the first anniversary of the troubles in Baltimore, and also the day upon which, on hearing of the disturbance, he marshaled a company of about seventy men in Frederick City, and hurried them to Baltimore to take part in the defense of that city. It was quickly decided to fitly observe the day, and the Colonel, being absent in Richmond on leave, the Lieutenant-Colonel relaxed his discipline and joined heartily with officers and men in the celebration. The affair was necessarily an informal one. There was neither banquet hall nor tables loaded with good cheer, but numerous small kegs and boxes suddenly made their appearance, and when they were opened and their contents were known the bare camp became the scene of good fellowship. Song, jest and story passed around, and mirth and jollity prevailed ; but there was a skeleton at the feast, for just when the glad spirit of the hour swayed each man, an order was received to move at once.

The order came like a clap of thunder, and never before had the First Maryland presented so ragged a front in its formation as it did that April evening. But the march over the railroad ties, through the darkness and rain soon began to show its beneficial effects, and when the regiment reached Culpeper, before daybreak, no one would have believed that the men of the command had been staggered but a few hours before by an enemy they had sought in vain to exterminate, and the rigid discipline, momentarily relaxed, was again resumed.

On the morning of April 20, after a heartily partaken breakfast, the troops of General Ewell's division continued their march, and passing through Culpeper the First Maryland Regiment took the road leading in the direction of Madison Court House, but the order to countermarch was received after the troops had gone some miles, and that night the regiment bivouacked on the railroad three miles below Culpeper. At length, hungry and wornout, after three days' marching and countermarching, Ewell's division reached Gordonsville.

A halt of here of three or four days greatly refreshed the troops, and as a move in some direction was momentarily expected their spirits revived, and when at last it became known they were to join the army of the immortal Stonewall Jackson in the valley of Virginia their enthusiasm knew no bounds. Jackson was then at Swift Run, on the other side of the Blue Ridge, having fallen back from Winchester after his fierce battle at Kernstown with the combined forces of Banks and Shields.

The march was made by easy stages, and on the night of the 30th of April, as the troops of Ewell's division came down the mountain side, and caught sight of Jackson's camp-fires, they made the welkin ring with their cheers.

But next morning when the men went forth to welcome old comrades they discovered to their surprise that Jackson with his command had quietly disappeared, and perhaps in Ewell's division no one knew whither he had gone, not even General Ewell himself.

BRIG. GEN'L BRADLEY T. JOHNSON,
MAJOR, LIEUTENANT COLONEL AND COLONEL FIRST MARYLAND INFANTRY,

CHAPTER V.

Ewell's division remained at Swift Run Gap for more than two weeks, when it was learned that Jackson had marched over the steep ranges of mountains that lay between Swift Run Gap and Milroy at McDowell, and, after administering a crushing defeat to that General, was then returning to the valley of Virginia, and Ewell was ordered to unite with him in the vicinity of Luray.

It was on this march, in the vicinity of Columbia Bridge, on May 16, 1862, that the term of enlistment of the officers and men of Company C, First Maryland, expired, and they were discharged from the service.

It was near Luray, on the 21st day of May, 1862, that the men of the First Maryland were gratified with a sight of the glorious Jackson. Away off in their rear, as they trudged along the turnpike, went up a mighty shout. Louder and louder it swelled in volume as it grew nearer. The Maryland boys had never heard that shouting before, and did not know its meaning until an old Virginia soldier who had heard it before called out : " Thar comes old Jack or an old har'." And presently an officer was seen riding furiously up the road bareheaded and bowing right and left. It was Stonewall Jackson, under whose leadership, through the long marches and hard battles that summer, the First Maryland was to win a reputation that will live for all time.

The evening of their arrival at Luray the following order was read, detaching the First Maryland from Elzey's Brigade and placing it under command of Brigadier-General George H. Steuart :

SOLON, May 17, 1862.

Major-General R. S. Ewell :

For the purpose of carrying out the order for organizing the Maryland Line, I have detached the First Maryland Regiment from Elzey's Brigade and assigned it to Brigadier-General George H. Steuart. Should you need the regiment, I have directed General Steuart to remain with you, but so soon as he can be spared I wish you would direct him to return to the Valley District, as it might facilitate the organization by being in the Valley.

T. J. JACKSON, *Major-General.*

The parting between the regiment and General Elzey was affecting in the extreme, and there were but few dry eyes present after their good old General had delivered his parting speech.

General Ewell did need the regiment, and took good care not to part from it during the Valley campaign, nor until after the battles before Richmond.

On the evening of May 22 Jackson's army, about 12,000 men, went into camp within an easy day's march of Front Royal, where it was expected the Federals would be first encountered, but in what force was mere conjecture.

Near noon on the 23d a halt was made some three miles from Front Royal, and whilst the men were resting themselves an aide rode up to Colonel Johnson, whose command was well in the rear, and handed him the following order:

Colonel Johnson will move the First Maryland to the front with all dispatch, and in conjunction with Wheat's battalion develop the enemy's position at Front Royal.

JACKSON.

Colonel Johnson read the order from General Jackson to the men, and proud of the distinction conferred upon them, the First Maryland moved to the front with an elasticity of step that elicited the admiration of the whole army.

Pushing rapidly forward, the commands of Johnson and Wheat, preceded by a small squad of cavalry, soon came in sight of Front Royal, within a mile of which a picket post was captured.

The surprise was complete, and in a few minutes the Confederates had full possession of the town, several of the enemy being captured in the streets. It was then learned that the infantry force in front of Johnson and Wheat was composed of the First Maryland Federal, two companies of the Twenty-ninth Pennsylvania, besides a detachment of the Fifth New York cavalry and two pieces of artillery, making, all told, 1,100 men, under command of Colonel John R. Kenly, of the First Maryland, a soldier of the Mexican War and known to be a gallant man. Johnson's force consisted of 275 men, Wheat's of 150; total, 425.

Drawing his forces up on a commanding ridge a short distance outside of the town, Kenly calmly awaited the attack.

Colonel Johnson quickly threw forward in skirmish line the companies of Captains Herbert, Nicholas and Goldsborough, all under command of Lieutenant-Colonel E. R. Dorsey, with Wheat on their left. These troops moved with admirable precision over the intervening bottom land under a heavy fire of musketry and artillery, until they reached a position that afforded them some shelter, from which their fire did much execution.

In the meantime the Confederate infantry were moving in considerable force to Kenly's left, whilst a large body of cavalry was crossing the river some distance to his right. Finding himself likely to be surrounded, Kenly was at last compelled to withdraw across the river and endeavor to effect his escape to Winchester. He had made a gallant fight, and had delayed Jackson's advance some hours, and this was precious time to Banks.

STONEWALL JACKSON'S RIVAL.

At the first evidence of Kenly's withdrawing his forces, Colonel Johnson ordered the whole of the First Maryland to advance (but three companies having been engaged), when many prisoners were captured on the river's bank, although the greater number succeeded in escaping over the two bridges, but in a disorganized condition.

At this point Colonel Johnson halted his command. It had fulfilled its mission, and the pursuit was to be conducted by cavalry. These overtook the fleeing Federals after they had gone some three miles, when after a desperate fight the entire body was captured, though not without severe loss to the attacking cavalry, for Kenly fought his troops like the brave man he was.

Thus ended the battle of Front Royal, in which First Maryland met First Maryland, and the scenes that were enacted that night when the prisoners were brought in are indescribable, for in the ranks of each were found dear friends, and in some cases near relatives, and the attention shown the vanquished by the victors did much to cheer them in their hour of captivity. Colonel Kenly and Adjutant Tarr were severely wounded, and to these Colonel Johnson and his officers paid particular attention. Colonel Kenly in his official report thus speaks of the treatment he and his command received at the hands of their captors:

"I desire also to state that since we fell into the hands of the Confederate troops our treatment has been kind and considerate, except that but a scanty allowance of food has been given to us, which I ascribe rather to its scarcity among them than to any disposition on their part to deprive us of it."

But this statement of "kind and considerate treatment of which Colonel Kenly speaks is at variance with the following extract from an official report signed by five officers of his command, who were evidently badly scared, and deserted their companions and their colors in their hour of need, and who never stopped running until they had reached Hagerstown, from which safe point of observation the report is dated:

The rebel infantry forded the North Branch stream and flanked us on the left. We were again ordered to move, left in front, up the road toward Winchester. We had marched about two miles when a wild shout was heard, and rebel cavalry came dashing into our lines, cutting right and left, showing no quarter, displaying a black flag. A portion of their cavalry captured our train, except one wagon and eight horses, which were cut loose by the teamsters (?) to escape on. A severe fight was kept up until our whole force was cut to pieces.

THOMAS SAVILLE, *First Lieutenant Commanding Company B.*
JOHN McF. LYETH, *First Lieutenant and R. Q. M., Company H.*
GEORGE W. THOMPSON, *Lieutenant, Company D.*
CHARLES CAMPER, *Lieutenant, Company K.*
GEORGE SMITH, *Captain, Company C.*

The reports spread by these men and others who had run away from the fight created a feeling of intense excitement in Baltimore, of which the rowdy element took advantage, and hundreds of the best citizens who were known to be in sympathy with the cause of the South were brutally assaulted upon the streets.

The comparatively small loss inflicted upon the command of Colonel Kenly is sufficient evidence that the Confederates were not fighting under a black flag. The black flag that these frightened officers saw was nothing more than the battle-flag which had been adopted owing to the fact that the similarity between the Confederate flag and the Stars and Stripes had upon several occasions brought Southern regiments into conflict, resulting in serious loss of life.

The following extract is taken from the columns of the *Baltimore Sun* of June 6, 1862:

Colonel John R. Kenly, of the First Maryland Regiment, in company with Surgeon Mitchell, who were captured at Front Royal, arrived in this city yesterday morning from Frederick. . . . . Colonel Kenly said it was needless to recount anything in regard to the fight, save and except to peremptorily deny that any brutality was shown by the Confederates toward himself or his wounded men. He speaks in the highest terms of the manner in which he was cared for after being taken prisoner. The story of his having been shot in an ambulance and his wounded men butchered upon the field, and other like horrible stories, are base fabrications. Colonel Kenly says many officers of the First Maryland Confederate Regiment visited him. The actions and treatment of these officers were particularly kind.

On the morning of May 24 the army moved forward, the greater portion under Jackson going in the direction of Middletown to intercept Banks, who it was believed would fall back from Strasburg to Winchester. General Ewell, with Trimble's Brigade, the First Maryland and Brockenbrough's Baltimore Light, had instructions to move toward Winchester. Brigadier-General George H. Steuart, who had been detached from the Maryland Line and placed in temporary command of the Second and Sixth Virginia Cavalry, was dispatched to Newtown. General Steuart was quite successful in this expedition, capturing many prisoners and wagons, and advising General Jackson of movements which indicated that Banks was preparing to leave Strasburg. But Jackson reached Middletown too late, for the main body had passed that point.

In the meantime General Ewell, with his command, augmented by the arrival of the two regiments under General G. H. Steuart, was advancing to Winchester by the turnpike from Front Royal, and had occupied a position about three miles from the town as early as 10 o'clock at night. Heavy firing on Ewell's left during the afternoon and until late in the night indicated that Jackson was steadily advancing upon Winchester from Middletown.

Before daylight in the morning of May 25 the First Maryland was ordered forward by General Ewell to open the battle in his front. Colonel Johnson deployed a portion of his regiment as skirmishers, and steadily they moved through the darkness toward Winchester. But as the day dawned a fog arose so dense that objects could be seen only a few feet away. Not knowing where he was, and fearing that he might run into a superior force of the enemy, Colonel Johnson wisely assembled his men and ordered them to lie down in an orchard. And it was well he did, for when the fog lifted in a measure right in front of him, not over two hundred yards away, lay a large body of the enemy behind a stone fence. It would have been folly for Colonel Johnson to have attacked them with his little command, for it would have meant their destruction.

But the spattering fire of musketry was heard on the left, and it was evident that Jackson was moving forward to the attack. Suddenly the fog disappeared entirely, and the sight that met the gaze of the Maryland boys was, indeed, inspiring, although for the moment they were compelled to hug the ground closely for fear of being seen by the enemy, for they were completely isolated from the remainder of Ewell's command. In front of them, and off to their left was a long line of Federal troops drawn up on the outskirts of Winchester. Their skirmishers were falling back before those of Jackson. Suddenly there emerged from the woods a long line of Confederates. They moved with the most beautiful precision, although their trail was marked by dead and wounded men at every step. It was General Dick Taylor's glorious Louisiana brigade and the Tenth and Twenty-third Virginia.

Beautifully the line advanced upon the doomed Federals, and as the right of Taylor's Brigade brushed by the First Maryland, Colonel Johnson could remain a passive spectator no longer, and he led his Marylanders in the headlong charge along with the men from Louisiana and Virginia. The enemy could not withstand the attack, but broke and fled through the streets of Winchester in dire confusion, closely pursued by the victorious Confederates.

But on the right Ewell was too slow, and had he pushed forward at the moment that Colonel Johnson left him, but a small number of Banks' army would have recrossed the Potomac.

In his official report of this battle General Jackson said:

"With the First Maryland on his left and Trimble's Brigade on his right, General Ewell now moved toward the eastern outskirts of the town. That advance was made about the time that Taylor's Brigade was so gallantly crossing the hill and charging toward the western side of the town."

But in this General Jackson is in error, as far as the First Maryland is concerned. That command entered Winchester on the western side and reached the eastern side almost before Ewell had put his troops in motion.

Even then the army of Banks should have been destroyed or captured had there been any cavalry to pursue the panic-stricken enemy. Where was Jackson's cavalry? Ashby's troopers were in the vicinity of Middletown and all the cavalry was disorganized by the victory or were out of place. It was left, then, for the infantry to pursue the fleeing Federals, which they did for some miles on the Martinsburg turnpike, when they were halted from sheer exhaustion. About an hour after the infantry had been halted General Steuart with his cavalry came up and renewed the pursuit in a highly creditable manner, but the main body of Banks' army was now beyond the reach of successful pursuit and effected its escape across the Potomac. General Jackson in his official report said: "There is good reason for believing that had the cavalry played its part in this pursuit, but a small portion of Banks' army would have made its escape to the Potomac."

Four miles beyond Winchester Colonel Johnson halted the First Maryland to await further orders. In the pursuit they had captured many prisoners, commissary stores, etc., but the most remarkable of their captures was a wagon partially filled with *breastplates*, one of which, taken from the person of an officer of the First New York Cavalry by Colonel Johnson himself, can be seen in the relic room at the Confederate Soldiers' Home at Pikesville. Federal officers wearing breastplates! Had these doughty soldiers on this occasion reversed the use for which they were intended and worn them on their backs many of them would have escaped what soldiers consider to be mortifying wounds. But, then, these breastplates served to amuse the Maryland boys exceedingly, and many of them were tied to trees and made targets of.

In this Winchester affair Lieutenant-Colonel E. R. Dorsey of the First Maryland was wounded, and never returned to the command. Two days after the battle of Winchester the First Maryland entered Martinsburg, and on May 29 the First Maryland, with Company A, Maryland Cavalry, and Cutshaw's Battery marched from Martinsburg to beyond Charlestown. On the 30th the enemy was found at Bolivar Heights, and an artillery duel ensued between Cutshaw's Battery and a battery on the Heights, but although of some hours' duration no damage was inflicted upon Steuart's command, and it is questionable whether the enemy suffered any loss, save the killing of a horse. After a time the fire from the Federal battery ceased, but it was not known that he had withdrawn. However, that question was soon settled by Private Richard Knox, of D Company, First Maryland Infantry, who, rifle in hand, boldly traversed the intervening space, ascended the steep, and stood in proud possession of the enemy's camp.

By order of General Steuart, Colonel Johnson then occupied Bolivar Heights with the First Maryland and Company A of the Maryland Cavalry. The enemy was seen in great numbers at some distance, gazing upon the invaders in mute astonishment. But this did not endure long, for soon a puff of smoke from a heavy piece of ordnance, followed by the explosion of a shell overhead, warned the invaders that they were not to be left in undisturbed possession of Bolivar Heights. Shell after shell came from two or three Federal batteries in rapid succession, and the reconnoisance (for that was all it was), having fulfilled its mission of conveying to the enemy the impression that Jackson intended to cross into Maryland at that point, General Steuart ordered Colonel Johnson to withdraw.

This expedition under command of General Steuart evidently frightened the Federals in Harper's Ferry out of their wits, and carried consternation to the authorities in Washington. It is amusing to read some of the many dispatches forwarded to Stanton by one General R. Saxton, then in command at Harper's Ferry, one or two of which we will quote :

HARPER'S FERRY, June 1, 1862.

The Honorable E. M. Stanton :

The enemy moved up in force last evening about 7 o'clock, in a shower of rain, to attack. I opened on them from the position which the troops occupy above the town and from the Dahlgren battery on the mountains. The enemy then retired. Their pickets attacked ours twice last night. A volley from General Hough's breastworks drove them back. We lost one man killed. My men are overworked. Stood by their guns all night in the rain. What has become of Generals Fremont and McDowell ?

R. SAXTON, *Brigadier-General.*

HARPER'S FERRY, May 31, 1862.

The Honorable E. M. Stanton :

Telegraph General McDowell to press on with all possible haste. All my pickets driven in last night. Enemy in force in my front, and, I believe, on both flanks. My position is strong. Shall try to hold it.

R. SAXTON, *Brigadier-General.*

Stanton telegraphs Saxton :

WASHINGTON, May 31, 1862.

Brigadier-General Saxton :

Report immediately by telegraph the particulars of the disgraceful conduct of Maulsby's Regiment in abandoning their post last night.

EDWIN M. STANTON, *Secretary of War.*

HARPER'S FERRY, June 1, 1862.

The Honorable E. M. Stanton :

I have reliable information that on Thursday Jackson had ordered his army to storm this place, but the shells from our batteries were so destructive that he drew back out of their range and endeavored to draw us out to attack him.

R. SAXTON, *Brigadier-General.*

And all this fright and commotion was caused by Dick Knox, supported by Bradley T. Johnson at the head of the First Maryland Infantry, and Frank A. Bond, with Company A, First Maryland Cavalry. To think that a visit of these gentlemen to Bolivar Heights should have stampeded Maulsby's Maryland heroes and caused poor, unhappy Falstaff Saxton to call upon Stanton to not only hurry up McDowell's army, but to send him that of Fremont's also! It is too amusing!

That night the First Maryland Infantry went into camp about three miles east of Charlestown. On the 31st the regiment was rear guard of the army, and marched seven miles beyond Winchester. At daylight on the morning of June 1 Colonel Johnson aroused his tired men, and the weary march was resumed. Why the occasion for this rapid retrograde movement? There was much discontent manifested among the troops, for all had thought they had come into the valley of Virginia to remain. But then they consoled themselves with the knowledge that they were with Jackson, and what Jackson did must be in their interest.

Little did these brave men know of the powerful combination that was being concentrated to insure their destruction, and nothing but the master hand of their great leader and their legs and indomitable courage averted it.

Fremont was coming from Franklin with 25,000 men to intercept Jackson somewhere near Strasburg, and this rapid marching meant that the Confederate Army, with its long line of wagons filled with valuable stores captured from the enemy, and the four thousand prisoners, should pass that point before Fremont should reach it. Fremont was held in check by a force thrown in his front near Strasburg, and Jackson's little army was safe for the time being.

But then Shields was marching a large force from McDowell's command to intercept him near Port Republic, and Jackson was still in imminent danger from an army in his rear of double his strength following him closely and one in front nearly his equal in numbers.

The enemy's cavalry vigorously pursued, and encounters with the rear guard under the glorious Ashby were of daily occurrence. At Ashby's request Colonel Johnson, with the First Maryland, was detailed to support him, and was consequently during the march from Strasburg well in the rear of the infantry column.

On the afternoon of the 5th of June, 1862, the rear guard of Jackson's command passed through the streets of Harrisonburg, and filing to the left a short distance below that town, took the road to Port Republic, Fremont's advance at the time being close up with Ashby's rear guard of cavalry. On the night of the 5th the troops went into camp about two miles from Harrisonburg. At reveille on the morning of the 6th the men were astir, and after partaking of a hasty breakfast the weary march was resumed. To many it was their last meal, for before the sun had disappeared in the western horizon the First Maryland had to mourn the loss of some of its best and bravest, who lay cold in the embrace of death, and the spirit of the chivalrous Ashby, the Bayard of the Confederate Army, had also winged its flight from earth. It was his error of judgment that brought about the disaster, and he paid the penalty with his life.

After laboriously advancing on their journey some four miles over a most wretched road, during which the wagons of the long train and the artillery were being constantly stuck in the mud, which greatly retarded the march of the infantry, a halt was ordered. Ashby and his cavalry were resting in a strip of wood, and a short distance beyond in a field was the First Maryland. Suddenly there was borne to the ears of the latter a yell, followed by the rattle of small arms. The enemy was upon Ashby, and that, too, most unexpectedly, for many of his troopers had unsaddled their horses.

For some minutes this firing and yelling continued. Colonel Johnson grasped the situation at once. Ashby had been attacked, but by what force? Hastily calling the First Maryland to "Attention!" Colonel Johnson led it in the direction of the wood from which these sounds of conflict emanated, but as the command advanced, the yelling and firing seemed to recede, until they were far away.

A dismounted prisoner was next seen coming to the rear under guard. He was a dashing-looking fellow, in a handsome, well-fitting uniform. He was nervously swinging one of his gauntlets in his hand, and seemed cast down and mortified at his ill fortune. At that moment the glorious, whole-souled Colonel Bob Wheat rode up. Springing from his horse he rushed up to the discomfited trooper. Their hands were extended simultaneously, for the recognition was mutual. "Why, Percy!" exclaimed Wheat; "why, Bob!" stammered the other, and then they sat down in a fence corner and talked of the good old times they had had together in Italy under Garibaldi. The Federal officer was Colonel Percy Wyndham, an Englishman, in command of the First New Jersey Cavalry. He had persistently followed Ashby for days, and Ashby had expressed his admiration for the daring cavalryman who had given him so much annoyance. But poor Wyndham had ventured too far and had met his Waterloo, for not only himself but sixty-three of his men were captured and many killed and wounded, and the remainder were driven in great confusion more than two miles back upon their infantry. But, alas! it was a dearly bought victory, as will be seen.

Whilst in pursuit of the fleeing enemy Ashby observed off to the right, isolated from any support, what appeared to be a regiment of infantry. He conceived the idea of capturing or destroying this force, and upon his return from the pursuit of the cavalrymen he reported what he had seen to General Ewell, and urged that General to give him infantry enough to accomplish that object. After much hesitation General Ewell reluctantly granted General Ashby's request, and placed the Second Virginia Brigade at his disposal. It was a very small brigade, under command of General George H. Steuart, and to this brigade the First Maryland had been temporarily attached.

Placing himself at their head, General Ashby moved up the road some distance in the direction of Harrisonburg and then struck off through the woods on his right. At this point, feeling that he should soon be in the presence of the enemy, General Ashby called upon Colonel Johnson for two companies of the First Maryland, which he wished to thrown out as skirmishers. Companies D and G, under the command respectively of Captains James R. Herbert and Wilson C. Nicholas, were given him, and with these he continued his advance, closely followed by the Fifty-eighth Virginia. It was not long before the enemy was encountered. The Fifty-eighth was then ordered to the support of the two Maryland companies, so desperately battling with overwhelming odds, and for a few minutes the fighting was very severe, and the little Fifty-eighth was evidently getting the worst of it. In those few minutes the noble Ashby had rendered up his life, after having had his horse killed under him. In the meantime the reserve companies of the First Maryland, under Colonel Johnson, had changed its position from the right to the left, and the men were lying on the ground with the right flank of the regiment toward the enemy. At this critical moment General Ewell rode up to Colonel Johnson and exclaimed: "Charge with the First Maryland, Colonel Johnson, and end this miserable affair!"

Calling his command to "Attention!" Colonel Johnson filed it to the right and faced it to the left, so as to bring it directly opposite the enemy, and then charged through the woods. Gallantly the Maryland boys dashed forward with a shout, and as they reached a slight elevation in the ground they received a galling fire from the enemy, who were posted behind a fence that separated the woods from a large open field. Some of the best and bravest of them fell at this fire, and Colonel Johnson was down, struggling to free himself from his horse, which had been killed, shot through the head. He was up in a minute in front of his line, and under a heavy fire this handful of brave men never faltered for a moment, and the next instant the crack of their deadly Mississippi rifles told that they were face to face with the enemy. The battle was of short duration, and

THE FIRST MARYLAND INFANTRY, HARRISONBURG, VA., JUNE 6, 1862.
(THE BUCKTAIL FIGHT.)

what remained of these brave men sought safety in flight from the pitiless fire of the First Maryland. It was then learned that the gallant command which had made such a stubborn fight and wrought such havoc in the ranks of the Fifty-eighth Virginia and First Maryland was the Battalion of Pennsylvania Bucktail Sharpshooters attached to Fremont's army, a body of picked riflemen, under command of Lieutenant-Colonel T. L. Kane, who was wounded and taken prisoner.

In this short, sharp encounter the First Maryland lost six killed and eleven wounded, six mortally. Colonel Bradley T. Johnson in his official report of this fight says :

"I lost Captain M. S. Robertson, Company I, a gallant officer, who fell at the head of his men in a charge, shouting : 'Go on, my men ; don't mind me !' Here also fell Second Lieutenant Nicholas Snowden, a true and brave soldier, who died as became his life, in the arms of victory, with his face to the foe. Near him fell the chivalrous Ashby. Here also died Privates William E. Harris and L. R. Schley, Company H ; Murphy, Company G, and E. W. Beatty, Company D. Beatty was advanced in years, and has steadily refused promotion at my hand, preferring to carry his rifle. My colors fell twice, but were caught before they touched the ground. Color Sergeant Joseph Doyle was severely wounded and left in a house in the neighborhood ; Color Corporal Taylor was badly shot, and Color Corporal Daniel Shanks carried them the rest of the time."

The First Maryland was highly complimented for its gallantry at the battle of Harrisonburg by both Generals Jackson and Ewell in their official reports, and the latter directed that one of the bucktails be appended to the color staff in the following order :

HEADQUARTERS THIRD DIVISION.

General Order No. 30.

In commemoration of the gallant conduct of the First Maryland Regiment on the 6th of June, when led by Colonel Bradley T. Johnson they drove back with loss the "Pennsylvania Bucktail Rifles," in the engagement near Harrisonburg, Rockingham County, Virginia, authority is given to have one of the captured "Bucktails" (the ensignia of the Federal regiment) appended to the color-staff of the First Maryland Regiment.

BY ORDER OF MAJOR-GENERAL EWELL.   JAMES BARBOUR, *A. A. G.*

General Jackson in his official report said :

. . . . . "In a short time the Fifty-eighth Virginia Regiment became engaged with a Pennsylvania regiment called the Bucktails, when Colonel Johnson, of the First Maryland Regiment, coming up in the hottest period of the fire, charged gallantly into its flank and drove the enemy with heavy loss from the field, capturing Lieutenant-Colonel Kane, commanding."

The night of the 6th the First Maryland retired to Union Church, on the road to Port Republic, carrying their dead and most of their wounded comrades with them. Next morning the dead were sadly and silently laid to rest in the little graveyard of that church.*

The sad services over, the line of march was taken up, and early in the day Ewell's division took position at Cross Keys, Jackson moving to the river, so as to take possession of the only bridge across the Shenandoah, which at that time was a rushing torrent, and across which it would have been impossible to lay pontoons, even had Jackson had them. It was an old-fashioned covered bridge, but it was the salvation of that little army, and across it the vast train and the long line of prisoners were safely marched, during which operation Ewell, with his division, except Taylor's Brigade, which had been sent to Port Republic, were called upon to keep Fremont in check.

There had been a race between Jackson and Shields for the possession of this bridge, and Shields had won, for early in the morning of June 8th General Carroll, in command of Shields' advance, had taken possession of Port Republic, had recaptured the prisoners taken at Harrisonburg, along with a guard from the First Maryland, and Jackson himself, who chanced to be in Port Republic, narrowly escaped capture. But General Carroll's stay was of short duration, for the Confederates coming up in force drove Carroll out in such haste that he left the recaptured prisoners and their guard behind him. Had Shields moved with the celerity which characterized the movements of Jackson, and thrown his fine army across the bridge and attacked Jackson in front whilst Fremont, only three miles away, attacked him in the rear, Jackson would have been destroyed.

Sunday, the 8th of June, was a bright, beautiful day. On that day a portion of Ewell's division was to measure strength with a mighty army. It was as a David against a Goliah, but every man in that command knew he had been called upon to do his best, and he meant to do it. Three Maryland general officers were to command most of the troops engaged in the battle — Generals Trimble, Elzey and Steuart, and upon the former fell the burden of the fight, and of that grand old hero's many battles, this was perhaps his best.

The position which the troops were to occupy was selected by General Arnold Elzey at the request of General Ewell, and met with that General's unqualified approval, and during the greater part of the day General Ewell kept General Elzey by his side as his adviser.

The line of battle was formed about 9 o'clock in the morning, Steuart's Maryland Line, which consisted of the First Maryland Infantry and Brocken-

---

*Their bodies have since been brought to Baltimore and reinterred in Loudon Park Cemetery.

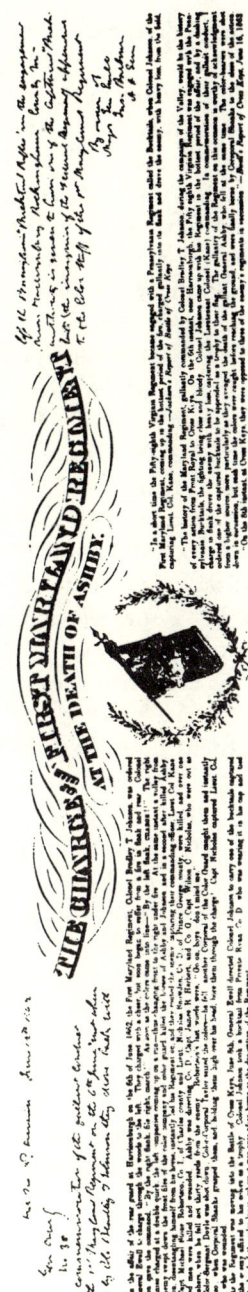

THE CHARGES OF THE FIRST MARYLAND REGIMENT AT THE DEATH OF ASHBY.

brough's Baltimore Light Artillery, on the extreme left, and Trimble's Brigade on the right, whilst Elzey's Brigade was in the rear of the centre, and in position to strengthen either wing, both wings being in the wood.

About 10 o'clock the enemy threw out his skirmishers and shortly after posted his artillery opposite Ewell's batteries. For some hours the artillery fire was kept up with great animation on both sides, when an attack was simultaneously made upon Trimble on the right and Steuart on the left. Both attacks were repulsed — that made upon Trimble with heavy loss to the enemy. The little First Maryland, not numbering over two hundred men, were fortunately posted in a wood, and in front of them was an open over which the enemy had to pass in making his attack. Had it not been for the shelter of this wood, they could not have survived five minutes, so terrific was the storm of shot and shell that was rained upon them. Never before had the Maryland boys been called upon to undergo such an ordeal. Three different times they drove back with heavy loss the overwhelming odds sent to dislodge them. Hour after hour this unequal contest continued. When a man would fall an officer would seize his gun and continue the firing, and the Mississippi rifle told with deadly effect. At 2 o'clock Colonel Johnson discovered that his ammunition was fast being exhausted. Sergeant William H. Pope, of Company A, volunteered to bring some, although it seemed almost certain death to venture for a moment from the shelter of the wood. The gallant fellow, however, succeeded in his mission and the firing continued, until, at 5 o'clock, when the battle was virtually over, the First Maryland was relieved, their guns having become totally unserviceable. Seven hours had this little command been under fire, and during that time, although sheltered in a measure, they had lost twenty-nine men and one officer (Lieutenant H. H. Bean) wounded. General George H. Steuart had been borne from the field with a ghastly wound in the shoulder made by a grape shot, and General Elzey had also been carried off with a serious wound. Some of the wounds received by the men of the First Maryland were very severe, having been made by explosive bullets, which the enemy fired in great numbers upon this occasion at least, although it has been denied.

The following highly complimentary extract is taken from the official report made by General Ewell :

> The history of the Maryland regiment, gallantly commanded by Colonel Bradley T. Johnson, during the campaign of the Valley, would be the history of every action, from Front Royal to Cross Keys.
>
> On the 6th instant, near Harrisonburg, the Fifty-eighth Virginia Regiment was engaged with the Pennsylvania Bucktails, the fighting being close and bloody. Colonel Johnson came up with his regiment in the hottest period of the affair, and by a dashing

charge in flank drove the enemy off with heavy loss, capturing the Lieutenant-Colonel (Kane) commanding. In commemoration of their gallant conduct I ordered one of the captured bucktails to be appended as a trophy to their flag.

The gallantry of the regiment on this occasion is worthy of acknowledgment from a higher source, more particularly as they avenged the death of the gallant General Ashby, who fell at the same time. Two color-bearers were shot down in succession, but each time the colors were caught before reaching the ground, and were finally borne by Corporal Shanks to the close of the action.

On the 8th instant, at Cross Keys, they were opposed to three of the enemy's regiments in succession.

Early on the morning of the 9th of June the First Maryland crossed the bridge at Port Republic, being among the last to do so, and shortly after it was set on fire and totally destroyed.

The fierce battle of Port Republic began soon after, and was, perhaps, the most bloody of any during the war, for the number of men engaged, the Federal troops under General Tyler, many being from the Western States, fighting with the most desperate courage. They were, however, signally routed, with great loss of men and artillery.

The First Maryland was spared from this battle, having well and truly done its duty the day before, although Private Joshua Simpson, of Company D, who was fighting with the Fifty-second Virginia, was severely wounded.

That afternoon, whilst engaged in burying the enemy's dead and ministering to their wounded, Fremont's batteries on the opposite side of the river opened upon the First Maryland and compelled the men to desist from their humane work.

On the evening of the 9th Jackson's force moved into the mountains by way of Brown's Gap, and on the 12th the army recrossed South River and went into camp at Weyer's Cave.

The battle of Port Republic closed Jackson's wonderful Valley campaign, and never in his remarkable career did his genius show to greater advantage. In less than six weeks he had beaten the army of Milroy, routed that of Banks, whipped that of Fremont and annihilated that of Shields, and all this with but twelve thousand men.

Arrived at Weyer's Cave, General Jackson resolved to carry out the order allowing all Marylanders in the Confederate Army who desired it to be transferred to the Maryland Line, whereby it was hoped at least a brigade could be formed. The Maryland Line had existed only in name, and the First Maryland Regiment had been so depleted by the hard campaign in the Valley that it became absolutely necessary that its ranks should be recruited. Moreover, the terms of service of two companies, H and I, were about to expire, which would leave but a handful of men to represent the regiment.

Therefore, for this purpose, on the 13th of June Colonel Johnson was ordered to take his regiment to Staunton, where upon its arrival Companies H and I were mustered out of the service. The void, however, occasioned by the departure of these companies was in a measure filled by the addition to its ranks of a company, just arrived from Richmond, commanded by Captain Edmund Barry. Captain Barry was an old Mexican soldier, and the men of which his company was composed were fine young fellows from the lower counties of Maryland. The company was given the title of C, as the first Company C had been mustered out some weeks before.

At this time reinforcements for Jackson were rapidly arriving, and it was confidently believed that another visit was to be paid to the vicinity of Winchester, upon which place Fremont had fallen back after Port Republic. The Washington authorities evidently thought so, too, for they were not long in learning of their arrival, and McClellan's importunities to be reinforced by McDowell, then at Manassas, availed nothing. And still the sending of these reinforcements to Jackson was but a blind as to General Lee's real movements, and the Federal authorities were easily misled.

Great, then, was the surprise of his troops when on the 17th of June Jackson put his army in motion and marched them aboard the many trains that had so mysteriously arrived at Staunton, and it soon became apparent to all that they were destined for Richmond.

CHAPTER VI.

Again the order to consolidate the Marylanders had to be postponed, for General Ewell could not spare their service, and they were the first to be sent off, and, as will be seen, were assigned the duty of opening the fight in Jackson's front a few days later at Gaines' Mill, or Cold Harbor.

At Fredericks Hall the troops were disembarked, and moved in the direction of Ashland, and on the afternoon of the 26th Jackson was fast nearing the position assigned him in the great army about to attack the enemy in his fortifications and raise the siege of Richmond.

It was late in the afternoon of the 26th that Jackson's troops heard the guns open at Mechanicsville, away down on the right, and in an instant their whole manner and bearing underwent a change, and they moved forward with an elasticity of step that could hardly have been expected of men who had marched so many weary miles.

Feeling that the enemy must be near, General Ewell ordered Colonel Johnson to throw forward a portion of his regiment as skirmishers, and it had hardly been done when the small body of cavalry in advance came in and reported the enemy in force but a short distance ahead.

The skirmishers from the First Maryland soon became hotly engaged, but they drove the enemy back steadily upon their heavy column of infantry, when the Baltimore Light Artillery was brought up and the enemy was pushed out of the way.

The march was resumed next morning, but had not continued many miles before a heavy column of infantry was observed a mile off to the right, moving parallel to that of Jackson. Jackson had not expected to see any Confederate troops in that quarter; but still he was fearful they might be friends. He, however, ordered a shot or two from a battery to be fired in their direction, when in an instant their skirmishers were thrown out, line of battle was formed, and the whole moved upon Jackson in perfect order.

A fearful tragedy now seemed inevitable, but was averted by the coolness and daring of Captain F. A. Bond and Lieutenant G. W. Booth, acting Adjutant. These officers, at the imminent peril of their lives, boldly rode forth in the direction of the advancing lines, and followed by watchful and anxious eyes were soon seen to enter their skirmish line and confer with the officer in command. They returned, and, to the relief of all, reported the advancing troops to be friends who had taken a wrong road and were thus out of position. A moment more and the head of Jackson's column would have been engaged with Mahone's

Brigade. As it was, no harm had been done other than the disquietude growing from the few shells our battery had landed in their midst.

The march was then resumed, and it was not long before heavy firing off on the right and front told Jackson that a great battle was in progress, and that he for the first time was late in getting into the position assigned him. But that was the fault of the ignorant guides he was compelled to depend upon, and many miles were needlessly marched through the dense pines which surrounded him.

But finally the enemy under Fitz John Porter was encountered in force north of the Chickahominy, when Jackson attacked him with great fury. For hours the fearful struggle continued, and still Jackson had made no impression upon the strong position held by the enemy. Some of his finest brigades had been sent forward only to be hurled back shattered and beaten.

During this time the little First Maryland, being attached to no brigade, had been kept in the rear and ordered to support the batteries. But this kind of work did not suit Colonel Johnson or his men, who had been chafing for two hours to move forward.

In the meanwhile the gallant George Kyle, of Baltimore, joined the regiment in citizen's dress, having ridden from Richmond to participate in the battle. He had with him a large batch of letters for members of the regiment from loved ones at home. Bidding his men to read their letters as hastily as possible, Colonel Johnson prepared to move forward.

Inclining to the left the regiment marched in line of battle with beautiful precision. It was, indeed, an inspiring sight to see this little line move all alone over that storm-swept field. Presently Lawton's fine brigade of Georgians were overtaken, moving in the same direction. The fire became too hot, and they were ordered to lie down, and as Colonel Johnson marched his regiment over the prostrate Georgians they broke into hearty cheers. On they pressed in the most perfect order. Coming to a ridge that gave his men shelter, Colonel Johnson halted them in order to rest them for the final struggle, which was to be for the possession of a battery in his front. It was a most desperate undertaking, and would have resulted in disaster had not matters turned out differently, for, as after events proved, Colonel Johnson had mistaken the strength of the enemy.

"Forward!" was the command, and the column resumed its steady advance. But a short distance had been traversed before fragments of regiments were encountered going to the rear in great confusion. The men of the First Maryland became unsteady for the first time as these fugitives crowded upon them and almost swept them off their feet. They began to tread upon each other's heels and the alignment was broken. Then was witnessed one of the most remarkable sights ever seen upon a battle-field, and proved the value of discipline.

"Halt!" cried out the gallant Johnson. "On the colors, dress!" The

THE FIRST MARYLAND INFANTRY AT GAINES' MILLS, JUNE 27, 1862.

men obeyed as readily as they had ever done. "Order arms! Shoulder arms! Present arms! Shoulder arms! Forward! March!"

The effect was magical. The men recovered themselves and the formation of the regiment was restored. But all this had its effect in another direction, for the brave men coming to the rear had observed it, and rallied on the regiment's flanks. The gallant color-bearer of Hampton's Legion planted his colors on the left of the Marylanders and swore it should go no farther to the rear. The men of the Legion rallied around it. They had no officers; they had been killed or wounded. Then came fragments of the Twelfth Alabama, Fifty-second Virginia and Thirty-eighth Georgia, and in the time it takes to narrate it Colonel Johnson had a small brigade around him that otherwise would have been lost.

But he was to be still further reinforced, for the gallant General Charles S. Winder had just come upon the field and had witnessed with admiration the conduct of his fellow-Marylanders. Divining Johnson's object, he sent Captain McHenry Howard of his staff to him with orders to wait until he could bring up his First Virginia Brigade.

Thus formed, they moved forward under the lead of that gallant officer. The enemy met this advance with great firmness. His heavy musketry and artillery fire was very destructive upon the advancing Confederate lines. Nothing daunted by the fall of officers and men the column pressed on. driving the enemy before them, until night prevented further pursuit.

Five guns, numerous small arms and many prisoners were among the fruits of this rapid and resistless advance.

General Charles S. Winder, in his official report of the battle of Gaines' Mill, says: "I cannot speak too highly of that soldier and gentleman, Colonel Bradley T. Johnson, with his small band of veterans, ever ready to advance on the enemy and aid our cause."

That night the First Maryland rested among the dead and dying of Sykes' regulars that lay around the McGehee house, and the next morning Ewell's division, with General J. E. B. Stuart's Cavalry, were ordered to destroy the York River Railroad at Dispatch Station.

On the 29th of June General Ewell moved his division to the vicinity of Bottom's Bridge to prevent the enemy crossing at that point, but on the following day was ordered to return to co-operate with the movements of Jackson's command, and on the morning of the 30th he crossed the Chickahominy.

On the afternoon of the 1st of July the First Maryland reached Malvern Hill. The battle had just begun, and the little regiment was held in reserve until its close, though during all that time under one of the most terrible artillery fires it had ever encountered, and nothing is so demoralizing to a soldier as to have to take an enemy's fire without being able to return it. During one period of this great battle one of Hays' Louisiana regiments, having lost all its officers but a Lieutenant, and suffered dreadfully in men, broke and went in great confusion to the rear. Colonel Johnson called the First Maryland to "Attention!" The brave fellows sprang to their feet, for they had been hugging the ground closely, and the gallant Louisianians quickly rallied on their left. Colonel Johnson then moved the whole through the darkness to the front, but the battle was over, and except an occasional shell from the gunboats there was nothing to disturb the stillness of the night but the cries and groans of the thousands of wounded men who covered that ghastly field.

Here again the First Maryland became temporarily attached to General Winder's command. In his official report that General says:

> Hearing of troops near by not engaged, I immediately sent for them, and was soon reinforced by a portion of General Lawton's Brigade, General J. R. Jones' Brigade, under Lieutenant-Colonel Cunningham, and a part of the Louisiana Brigade, and that gallant band of Marylanders under the brave Colonel B. T. Johnson. Colonel Johnson, hearing I needed assistance, came forward to tender his regiment, which I gladly accepted, and gave him the advance, directing him to extend our line some half a mile to the right, placing my picket on and near the flank of the enemy. This duty he executed rapidly and with good judgment, holding this position until after the enemy had retired the following day.

Long before daybreak on the morning of the 2d of July the Confederate Army was in line of battle ready to renew the conflict that had resulted so disastrously the day before, but McClellan had withdrawn during the night. Colonel Johnson ordered Companies A and D to move through a piece of woods and see if any of the enemy remained in that direction. The two companies, deployed as skirmishers, advanced in beautiful order, and upon emerging from the woods into the open country they encountered a body of cavalry, which hastily retired upon being fired upon. Thus it will be seen that the First Maryland opened the Seven Days' Battles on the 26th of June near Gaines' Mill and fired the last shot at Malvern Hill.

McClellan had withdrawn his shattered and demoralized army to Harrison's Landing and entrenched, where, under cover of his gunboats, he was safe.

The 4th of July found the First Maryland at Westover Church, where it remained for several days skirmishing with the enemy.

From Westover Church the First Maryland was ordered to Richmond, and encamped on the Central railroad, about three miles from the city.

The regiment, which had entered the field in the spring numbering seven hundred and twenty men, had from various causes been reduced to about one hundred and fifty. No regiment in the service had received more hard knocks, none had been the recipients of more flattering recognition from the Generals in command, and none were prouder of their record. But it had at last become absolutely necessary that the ranks of the regiment should be filled up. An order had long before been issued to recruit and thoroughly organize the Maryland Line, and the First Maryland was to be the nucleus upon which it was to be formed, but until now the regiment could not be spared. Therefore, about the middle of July it was ordered to proceed to Charlottesville for the purpose of carrying out the order of the War Department. But there were few Maryland recruits to be had, and but few Marylanders who cared to be transferred fom the regiments from other States in which they had so long served, and in which they had formed associations not to be parted from.

After remaining at Charlottesville until the 4th of August the regiment was ordered to Gordonsville.

General Jackson had in the meantime been detached from the army watching McClellan at Harrison's Landing, and was known to be in the vicinity of Culpeper watching Pope. Therefore, when the order was given to move to Gordonsville it was confidently expected the regiment would soon rejoin its old commander, Jackson. But these hopes were never to be realized. The First Maryland had participated in its last battle, and was within a few days to cease to exist.

On August 9, 1862, Jackson fought Banks at Cedar Run, or Slaughter's Mountain, as it is sometimes called, and again administered to that General a crushing defeat. Here that splendid young Maryland soldier, General Charles S. Winder, fell, but there was no First Maryland there to avenge his death, as there had been that of Ashby. The First Maryland had, however, from Gordonsville, heard Jackson's guns, and chafed under the restraint to which they were subjected. Little did this handful of battle-scarred veterans then dream of the humiliation in store for them. It was better that they did not know it.

On August 12 the prisoners captured at Cedar Run were brought to Gordonsville, and Colonel Johnson detailed Company A, under command of Captain W. W. Goldsborough, to convey them to the prisons in Richmond. Company A, under Captain Bradley T. Johnson, had been the first company formed in the regiment, and had done the first service at Point of Rocks, and it was destined to perform the last, for the very day the company with its prisoners arrived in Richmond, George W. Randolph, then Secretary of War, issued his order for the disbanding of the regiment, and upon receipt of this order, on the 17th day of August, Colonel Johnson mustered the men out of the service amid a scene of lamentation that perhaps had never before been witnessed under the circumstances, and strong men, veterans who had stood up and faced death on many a bloody field, wept like children. The little Maryland flag, which had been carried as the regimental colors in all its battles, was that day folded forever, but not before it had been fondly embraced by the brave men who had so often followed it to victory.

And this same little flag fell into befitting hands. By a unanimous vote of the battalion the color-bearer, Edwin Selvage, with a committee, was appointed to take it Charlottesville and present it to the noble woman who had so faithfully stood by them in their hour of need — Mrs. Bradley T. Johnson. The following letter is her acknowledgment of the honor shown her :

CHARLOTTESVILLE, VIRGINIA, August 18, 1862.

To Edwin Selvage, Color-Bearer and the First Maryland Regiment :

Gentlemen :—This emblem of your courage and State pride I have received. The trust you have reposed in me shall be sacredly guarded, and only to the same organization, with officers and men, will I ever yield it.

I take this means of assuring you all that, as I have been with you in all the trials you have undergone in the South, so will I ever be ; and no member of the First Maryland Regiment will ever want a friend while I live.

MRS. BRADLEY T. JOHNSON.

In disbanding the First Maryland Regiment, the Secretary of War meant to cast no reflection upon it. He was influenced to do so by men from Maryland who were ambitious to lead a Maryland command in the field, and who represented to the Secretary that around the material from it another regiment could be rallied, for at that time many Marylanders were arriving in Richmond. Another fine battalion was formed, it is true, of which the men of the old command formed a part, but when it came to an election for officers they preferred to choose men to lead them who had seen service.

Of the disbanded regiment, Colonel Bradley T. Johnson, Captain W. W. Goldsborough, Lieutenant George W. Booth and Surgeon Richard P. Johnson joined the command of General Jackson, then near Culpeper, and offered their services as volunteers in any capacity. On the 21st of August, 1862, General Jackson assigned Colonel Johnson to the command of the Second Virginia Brigade, in the absence of General J. R. Jones, who was absent on sick leave.

The important part this brigade took in the three days' battles at Manassas won the admiration of General Jackson, for it was only through the determined courage displayed by the Second Brigade, stimulated by the daring of their new commander, that the heavy columns of the enemy were foiled in their efforts to get possession of the railroad cut on the afternoon of the 30th of August :

There was no more desperate fighting during the war than that at this point, and when ammunition was expended the Confederates fought with stones. The following is an extract from Colonel Johnson's official report of the part his brigade took in the action on the 30th of August :

I could see that some movements were being made in that skirt of woods as early as 8 A. M., and during the day had frequent reports made to me to that effect. I, therefore, placed the Forty-second, Captain Penn, in the railroad cut, and having assigned Captain W. W. Goldsborough, of the late First Maryland (my old command), who was serving with me as a volunteer, to the Forty-eighth, as Adjutant, put it in a copse which ran at right angles from the railroad and the right of the Forty-second, and fronted the woods in which the enemy were obviously making some movement. These positions overlooked the enemy everywhere, and being very strong, were the ones I had determined to take and hold, if attacked. The Twenty-first and Irish Battalion I held in reserve, concealed in the woods on the hill, carefully instructing the officers at the order to charge without firing a shot.

About 4 P. M. the movements of the enemy were suddenly developed in a decided manner. They stormed my position, deploying in the woods in brigade front and then charging in a run, line after line, brigade after brigade, up the hill on the thicket held by the Forty-eighth and the railroad cut occupied by the Forty-second ; but as they uncovered from the wood in which they had been massing during the whole day I ordered the Twenty-first and Irish Battalion to charge, which they did with empty guns. I halted them under the shelter of the cut, where, with the Forty-second, they held back the enormous force pressing up the hill on them. Lieutenant Dabney had unfortunately been wounded early in the day, and Captain Goldsborough, whom I had ordered to take command, had fallen by my side in the charge, leaving the Forty-eighth without a superior officer with them, and they consequently were soon driven out by the tremendous odds against them ; but for a short time the three regiments above named, viz.: The Forty-second, Twenty-first, and Irish Battalion, by themselves breasted the storm, driving back certainly twenty times their number. As soon as their position was known the rest of the division came to their support, except the Third Brigade, which, under Colonel Taliaferro, was employed in whipping a division by itself. Before the railroad cut the fight was most obstinate. I saw a Federal flag hold its position for half an hour within ten yards of a flag of one of the regiments in the cut and go down six or eight times, and after the fight one hundred dead were lying twenty yards from the cut, some of them within two feet of it.

The men fought until their ammunition was exhausted and then threw stones. Lieutenant Lewis Randolph, of the battalion, killed one with a stone, and I saw him after the fight with his skull fractured. Dr. Richard P. Johnson, on my volunteer staff, having no arms of any kind, was obliged to have recourse to this means of offense from the beginning. As line after line surged up the hill time after time, led up by their officers, they were dashed back on one another until the whole field was covered with a confused mass of struggling, running, routed Yankees. They failed to take the cut. The battle of the left wing of the army was over, and the whole of Jackson's Corps advanced about a mile, its right on the Warrenton road toward the stone bridge, facing Bull Run. I was not further engaged that day.

Captain Goldsborough and Lieutenant G. W. Booth (First Maryland), my volunteer aides, were both wounded; and Doctor R. P. Johnson, also volunteer aide, had his horse twice shot on two different days.

On the 6th day of September, 1862, as the army was crossing into Maryland, General Jackson recommended Colonel Johnson for appointment to the rank of Brigadier-General in the following letter :

NEAR LEESBURG, September 4, 1862.

General S. Cooper, A. and I. Gen., C. S. A.:

General :—I respectfully recommend that Colonel Bradley T. Johnson, late Colonel of the First Maryland Regiment, be appointed Brigadier-General. While I was in command at Harper's Ferry, in the early part of the war, Colonel Johnson left his home in Maryland and entered our service, where he continued until his regiment was recently disbanded. I regarded him as a promising officer when he first entered the army, and so fully did he come up to my expectations, that when his regiment was disbanded I put him in command of a brigade ; and so ably did he discharge his duties in the recent battles near Bull Run as to make it my duty, as well as pleasure, to recommend him for a Brigadier-Generalcy. The brilliant service of his brigade in the engagement on Saturday last proved that it was under a superior leader, whose spirit was partaken of by his command. When it is so difficult to procure good general officers, I deem it due to the service not to permit an opportunity for securing the services of one of rare merit to pass unimproved.

I am, General, your obedient servant,

T. J. JACKSON, *Major-General.*

And again, in a letter to General R. E. Lee recommending the promotion of various officers, Colonel J. B. Gordon, Colonel Alfred Iverson, Colonel S. D. Ramseur and E. F. Paxton, to be Brigadiers, and Brigadier Jubal A. Early to be Major-General, General Jackson urges Colonel Johnson's promotion thus:

HEADQUARTERS VIRGINIA DISTRICT, October 25, 1862.

General R. E. Lee :

. . . . . In this number (of Brigadiers to be appointed) I would include Bradley T. Johnson, late Colonel of the First Maryland Regiment. He commanded a brigade in the engagements about Manassas, and won merited distinction. The First Virginia Bat-

CROSSING THE POTOMAC INTO MARYLAND, WHITE'S FORD, SEPTEMBER 6, 1862.

talion, P. A. C. S., which had been doing so badly before that I was disposed to take away its colors, behaved gallantly under Colonel Johnson. He is an officer of tried courage, industrious, enterprising, possesses an unusually good mind and constitution.

I am, General, your obedient servant,

T. J. JACKSON, *Major-General.*

After the occupation of Frederick City General Jones reported for duty, and Colonel Johnson was relieved of the command of the Second Brigade. Colonel Johnson was then ordered to Richmond, and appointed Colonel of Cavalry, and assigned for duty on the military court stationed in Richmond, here to await promotion.

ROSTER OF THE FIRST MARYLAND INFANTRY.

FIELD AND STAFF.

Colonels.

Arnold Elzey . . . . June 17, 1861.
    Promoted Brigadier-General July 21, 1861.
    Promoted Major-General December 4, 1862.
George H. Steuart . . . . July 21, 1861.
    Promoted Brigadier-General March 18, 1862.
Bradley T. Johnson . . . . March 18, 1862.
    Promoted Brigadier-General June 28, 1864.

Lieutenant-Colonels.

George H. Steuart . . . . June 17, 1861.
Bradley T. Johnson . . . . July 21, 1861.
E. R. Dorsey . . . . March 18, 1862.

Majors.

Bradley T. Johnson . . . . June 17, 1861.
E. R. Dorsey . . . . July 21, 1861.

Acting Adjutants.

Lieutenant Frank X. Ward . . . . Company H.
Lieutenant George W. Booth, ... Company D.

Surgeons.

E. S. Gallaird.   R. P. Johnson.

Assistant Surgeons.

Styles Kennedy.   Thomas S. Latimer.

Captain and A. Q. M.

Grafton D. Spurrier.   Septimus H. Stewart.
Charles W. Harding.   John E. Howard, *Captain and A. C. S.*

Chaplain, Stephen J. Cameron.

Sergeant-Majors.

George W. Bishop.   Philip L. Moore.

Q. M. Sergeant, Charles J. Wegner.

Chief Musician, Alexander Hubbard.

Drum Major, Hosea Pitt.

COMPANY A.

Bradley T. Johnson, *Captain.*
W. W. Goldsborough, *Captain.*
George K. Shellman, *First Lieutenant.*
Charles W. Blair, *Second Lieutenant.*
George M. E. Shearer, *Second Lieutenant.*
W. H. B. Dorsey, *Second Lieutenant.*
John F. Groshon, *Second Lieutenant.*
John F. Groshon, *First Sergeant.*

John T. Smith, *Sergeant.*
George Tyler, *Sergeant.*
D. Windsor Keesler, *Sergeant.*
W. H. Pope, *Sergeant.*
Francis T. Bender, *Corporal.*
William Ritter, *Corporal.*
Perry McDowell, *Corporal.*
James Abbott, *Corporal.*

Privates.

Ackhurst, Charles.
Agen, Peter.
Andre, John A.
Bowers, Cornelius.
Brown, John W.
Bush, George W.
Bride Samuel.
Butler, Cyrus S.
Bryan, Samuel.
Bobeth, Charles.
Bond, B. F.
Cook, William.
Chambers, Robert M.
Carrick, John.
Conrad, George.
Callan, John.
Carey, Timothy.
Daniel, ———.
Foreman, Valentine.
Gephart, Sol. A.
Geasey, James W.
Goldsborough, N. Lee.
Grove, Louis.
Goldsborough, Eugene Y.
Hahn, Reuben H.
Hecht, Robert H.
Hastings, Hugh.

Heck, Jacob.
Hewes James.
Hoppell, George W.
Hammell, Edward.
Hill, John A.
Hazell, Patrick.
Hamilton, Edward.
Harding, Charles W.
Hildt, John.
Hubbard, Alexander.
Kretzer, Hiram.
Kennedy, Arthur T.
Lechlider, Thomas G.
Lechlider, George.
Loveley, John E.
Lanahan, Daniel.
Lurtz, Nicholas.
Lawson, James A.
Mayberry, James P.
Maguire, George W.
Mallen, Henry.
McMahon, Francis.
McMullin, Charles.
McLanahan, William H.
McLaughlin, Thomas G.
Minnahan, John.
Mewberne, N. J.

Miles, George T.
Moore, Philip L.
Myers, Christeso P.
Owens, Samuel A.
Oates, Charles T.
O'Connell, Patrick.
Porter, Hugh.
Peters, Andrew.
Rider, Martin L.
Ritter, William.
Ryan, W. H.
Rosensteel, James.
Steele, John H.
Street, John H.
Strickland, Jesse.
Swisher, John.
Stewart, Edward B.
Snovell, D. M.
Schessler, Henry.
Tyler, John E.
Taylor, John B.
Williams, Edward.
Wheeler, Charles W.
Wever, Hiram.
Wentz, Louis.

COMPANY B.

CHARLES E. EDELIN, *Captain.*
JAMES MULLEN, *First Lieutenant.*
THOMAS COSTELLO, *Second Lieutenant.*
JOSEPH GRIFFIN, *Second Lieutenant.*
PETER BOYLE, *First Sergeant.*
GEORGE MOOG, *Sergeant.*
DANIEL DOUGHERTY, *Sergeant.*
JAMES LAMATES, *Sergeant.*
GEORGE BATES, *Corporal.*
WILLIAM HAFFEY, *Corporal.*
DENNIS O'BRIAN, *Corporal.*
GEORGE PROBEST, *Corporal.*
JOSEPH SMITH, *Musician.*

Privates.

ABEL, CHARLES.
AMEY, CHARLES.
BROMLEY, ORAM J.
BRUNER, HAMILTON.
BREMER, JOHN L.
CHANEY, WILLIAM.
CHENOWETH, JOSEPH.
CUSICK, FREDERICK.
CAIN, JOHN.
CAREY, MICHAEL.
CRENSHAW, WILLIAM.
DROPMAN, CHARLES.
DURKIN, JOHN.
DAMMEN, JOSEPH.
DISNEY, WILLIAM.
ECKHART, AUGUST.
FLANNIGAN, JEFFERSON.
GILLAND, STEPHEN.
GAVIN, WILLIAM.
GLENON, JOHN.
HUMMER, JOSEPH.
HEIMILLER, HERMAN.
HAFFEY, JOHN.
HISSEY, JOHN.
HIRCHT, ALBERT.

JONES, WILLIAM.
KLISER, AUGUST.
KAVLADGE, JOHN.
KRIES, GEORGE.
KENNEY, BERNARD.
KELLEY, STEWART.
KOHLHEPP, JOHN.
LUTZ, CONRAD.
LOWE, DANIEL W.
MOOG, JAMES R.
MILLER, WILLIAM H.
McCALL, ALEXANDER.
McGEE, DANIEL.
McGEE, JOHN.
MANNEN, BARTLEY.
MURRAY, JOHN.
MURRAY, THOMAS.
McLAUGHLIN, MARTIN.
MITCHELL, JAMES.
MICHAELS, JOHN.
MICHAELS, JOSEPH.,
MOORE, ROBERT.
MICOU, THOMAS.
NOONAN, MICHAEL.
OPEL, JOHN.

O'NEAL, PATRICK.
O"NEAL, ANDREW.
PATTON, WILLIAM.
PLATT, AUGUSTUS.
REYNOLDS, PATRICK.
RYAN, PATRICK.
RHODES, GEORGE.
RUSH, PETER.
SHULTZ, WILLIAM.
SIMS, JOSEPH.
SMITH, FREDERICK.
SCHAEFFER, WILLIAM.
SHOCKNEY, SAMUEL.
SHERMAN, ROBERT T.
SOUTH, HOWARD.
STITELER, CHARLES B.
STEPHENS, JOHN.
SMITH, JOSEPH.
TYLER, WILLIAM.
WENTWORTH, GEORGE.
WOLF, JOSEPH.
WIEL, GEORGE.
WALSH, JAMES.
WEAVER, GEORGE.
WILSON, ———.

COMPANY C.

E. R. DORSEY, *Captain*.
ROBERT C. SMITH, *Captain*.
SEPTIMUS H. STEWART, *First Lieutenant*.
WILLIAM P. THOMAS, *Second Lieutenant*.
WILLIAM SMYTH, *Second Lieutenant*.
WILLIAM SMYTH, *First Sergeant*.
STIRLING MURRAY, *Sergeant*.

JOHN B. BERRYMAN, *Sergeant*.
JOHN H. UHLHORN, *Sergeant*.
CHARLES A. ARNOLD, *Corporal*.
JOHN O'LOUGHLIN, *Corporal*.
FRANK S. PRICE, *Corporal*.
HENRY C. SCOTT, *Corporal*.
HOSEA PITT, *Musician*.

Privates.

ANDERSON, JAMES.
ARNOLD, FRANK A.
ARNOLD, SAMUEL.
BARRY, DANIEL R.
BERRY, JOHN P.
BUSSEY, THOMAS J.
CONRADT, CHRISTIAN J.
CULBRETH, JOHN.
CODD, W. H.
DELEVIE, JACOB.
DUCK, HENRY R. S.
FEAST, LOUDON.
FITZGERALD, WILLIAM B.
FALCONER, EDWARD W.
FLACK, THOMAS J. A.
GUISE, ANDREW.
GASSAWAY, SAMUEL.
GOLDER, HAMILTON.
GROGAN, KENNEDY.
GLAUDEL, JOHN.
GOLDSBOROUGH, W. W.
HAYDEN, RICHARD A.
HOWARD, EDWARD L.
HOWARD, JAMES MCHENRY.

HYLAND, JOHN G.
HOPKINS, HENRY H.
HARTMIER, RICHARD J.
INLOES, ALFRED I.
JOHNSON, PHILIP P.
JOHNSON, JOHN W.
JOHANNES, MARTIN J.
JOHNSON, RICHARD P.
KANE, JAMES C.
LATIMER, THOMAS S.
LATIMER, GEORGE S.
LEPPER, CHARLES V.
MURRAY, WILLIAM H.
MORGAN, BENJAMIN H.
MCCABE, GEORGE W. E.
MCCLERNAND, JAMES.
MONTGOMERY, WILLIAM T.
MAGUIRE, JAMES W.
NORFOLK, W. H.
OSBOURN, JAMES E.
POSTLEY, CHARLES T.
PERREGOY, JOHN T.
PUE, WILLIAM H.
PITT, HOSEA.

ROGERS, JOHN C.
RINEHART, WILLIAM C.
RINEHART, ———.
ROGERS, WILLIAM H.
SLATER, GEORGE.
SISSON, OSCAR B.
SLOAN, CHARLES H.
SCOTT, CHARLES A.
SMITH, THOMAS J.
THOMAS, DANIEL L.
THORNTON, FRANK A.
TONGUE, RICARD H.
TIPPETT, GEORGE W.
VOSS, FRANKLIN.
WILSON, CHARLES G.
WHITE, FISHER A.
WHITE, DAVID D.
WEST, GEORGE F.
WATKINS, JOHN R.
WELCH, JOHN L.
WALSH, THOMAS K.
WARHEN, DANIEL.

COMPANY D.

James R. Herbert, *Captain.*
George W. Booth, *First Lieutenant.*
William Key Howard, *Second Lieutenant.*
Nicholas Snowden, *Second Lieutenant.*
George F. Ruff, *First Sergeant.*
Charles J. Wegner, *Sergeant.*
William H. Slingluff, *Sergeant.*
Edward S. King, *Sergeant.*

Mason E. McKnew, *Sergeant.*
Edwin Selvage, *Corporal.*
John Wranck, *Corporal.*
Washington Hands, *Corporal.*
William Weber, *Corporal.*
Charles Tuttle, *Musician.*
James M. Ruley, *Musician.*

Privates.

Annen, Henry.
Ackler, William.
Ashton, J. J.
Bull, John E.
Baker, Henry.
Boyd, Hamilton.
Berry, Thomas S.
Beatty, Edward W.
Brown, William.
Briddle, James.
Bird, Charles E.
Creamer, Jacob I.
Collins, John W.
Conn, William D.
Coyle, Patrick.
Connelly, Edward T.
Devitt, Edward I.
Dashield, George H.
Duvall, Ridgely.
Edell, Henry.
Edwards, William H.
Eno, Charles E.
Ferrell, J. Thomas.
Gray, William R.
Green, Hugh T.
Green, Matthew.
Howard, John E.

Hill, William.
Hendorf, Frederick.
Hitzelberger, Charles T.
Holbrook, John F.
Heimiller, William.
Howard, Charles.
Jennings, Benjamin R.
Jenkins, William.
Jones, John T.
Jones, John.
Key, John R.
Key, D. Murray.
Knox, James.
Knox, Richard.
Kelton, John.
Kneller, Jacob S.
Kelly, James S.
King, Walter.
Larabee, George S.
League, John S.
Lowndes, James A.
McCann, William V.
McKenna, Peter.
Murphy, Edward.
McIntyre, Joseph.
McIntyre, Robert.
McNulty, James.

Muth, Alfred.
Norton, John J.
O'Loughlin, Michael.
O'Neil, John.
O'Brien, Edwin.
Perry, Oliver.
Rogers, Henry C.
Robinson, William H.
Ryan, Robert S.
Ray, Alexander.
Ruley, James M.
Spurrier, Jay.
Small, C. W.
Soiskey, Isadore.
Simpson, Joshua.
Simon, August.
Simms, John.
Taliaferro, John R.
Travers, John M.
Tuttle, Charles.
Wells, Herschel.
Wilson, William A.
Wilson, John A.
Weeks, Henry.
Wegner, Henry F.
Whitely, Robert M.

COMPANY E.

Harry McCoy, *Captain*.
Edmund O'Brien, *First Lieutenant*.
John J. Lutts, *First Lieutenant*.
John Cushing, Jr., *Second Lieutenant*.
Joseph G. W. Marriott, *Second Lieutenant*.
George G. Raborg, *First Sergeant*.
Napoleon Camper, *Sergeant*.
Green H. Barton, *Sergeant*.
William T. Wallis, *Sergeant*.
Robert H. Cushing, *Sergeant*.
Patrick H. Williams, *Sergeant*.
Thomas H. Davidson, *Corporal*.
Joseph T. Doyle, *Corporal*.
Alfred Pearce, *Corporal*.
William Gannon, *Musician*.
Michael A. Quinn, *Musician*.

Privates.

Adams, Henry.
Archer, John R.
Bennett, Edmund.
Blake, Francis T.
Bourner, John.
Brandt, Alexander.
Bressner, John.
Brown, Charles A.
Clifton, Lewis R.
Connolly, Edward.
Davis, Howard I.
Dennis, James.
Donohue, Thomas.
Durham, James.
Edelin, Alex. W.
Elliott, Joseph W.
Ennis, Thomas.
Essender, William.
Fiege, Charles.
Fillis, Edward.
Ford, Clement.
Goodman, Julius D.
Griffith, Edward.
Hanna, George.
Harper, Lloyd.
Herster, Frederick.
Hogan, Thomas.
Holland, Thomas R.
Johnston, John J.
Johnston, John R.
Law, Edward.
Leddard, Bernard.
Leonard, Charles H.
Lockington, James A.
McCabe, Luke.
McGinnis, James.
McNamee James.
Melvin, George.
Miller, William.
Motter, John.
Mulhane, Bernard.
Merritt, Samuel.
Pearce, John.
Parsons, James.
Quinn, Michael A.
Rhodes, George.
Riley, John.
Roberts, Edward L.
Ruark, Michael.
Sandler, William.
Schaeffer, Henry.
Schaeffer, Benjamin.
Shannon, Michael.
Sherrington, Henry W.
Simonds, Albert.
Stanton, William.
Tourney, Sylvester.
Valiant, George E. W.
Webber, Edward.
Wellmore, Edward.
Welch, Martin.
Welsh, Edward.
Woods, Charles.
Wrea, John.

COMPANY F.

J. Louis SMITH, *Captain.*
WILLIAM D. HOUGH, *First Lieutenant.*
WILLIAM J. BROADFOOT, *Second Lieutenant.*
JOSEPH H' STEWART, *Second Lieutenant.*
GEORGE W. FOOS, *Sergeant.*
JOHN MARNEY, *Sergeant.*
JOHN MORRIS, *Sergeant.*

SAMUEL A. KENNEDY, *Sergeant.*
JOHN RYAN, *Corporal.*
MICHAEL McCOURT, *Corporal.*
EDWARD SHEEHAN, *Corporal.*
OWEN CALLEN, *Corporal.*
FRANCIS FARR, *Musician.*

Privates.

ANGELL, THOMAS.
ALLEN, JAMES.
BRANDT, WILLIAM.
BEHRENS, BARNEY.
BECKNELL, FREDERICK.
BEYER, ADAM.
BLAKE, JOHN.
CARR, THOMAS.
CHAPIN, CHARLES.
CONDELL, SAMUEL.
CONNOLLY, WILLIAM.
CUNNINGHAM, R.
CUMMINS, DANIEL.
DOUGHERTY, CORNELIUS.
DURST, JOHN.
EISENBERGER, GEORGE.
EVELINE, JOHN.
FARR, FRANCIS.
GAVIN, THOMAS.
GOLDEN, JOHN.
GIRVIN, JOHN.
GLOSSNER, HANAS.
GRAHAM, JESSE.
GRAHAM, GEORGE H.

HAGAN, JOHN.
HAMILTON, JACOB.
HANNA, JOHN.
HOFFMAN, GEORGE.
HUNTER, JOHN.
HUTCHINSON, THOMAS.
HARTZ, DAVID.
INGLEHART, EDWARD.
KENNEY, PATRICK.
KNAPP, HENRY.
LUSBY, JAMES.
LOUGE, JOHN.
LOUGE, MICHAEL.
MACCUBBIN, R. W., JR.
MARCUS, JAMES T.
MILLS, WILLIAM P.
MIHON, MARTIN.
McCARTHY, DANIEL.
McCEVITT, ARTHUR.
McCORMICK, JOHN.
McCLUTCHY, JOHN.
McDERMOTT, JAMES.
McDONALD, PATRICK.
McMANUS, JAMES.

McMAHON, JAMES.
MAGNESS, WILLIAM.
McNALLY, FELIX.
NOLAN, JAMES.
QUIN, MICHAEL.
QUIN, WILLIAM.
RYAN, JOSEPH.
RUSH, PETER.
RUDDEN, THOMAS.
SHEEDY, DANIEL.
SMITH, WILLIAM A.
SMITH, THOMAS.
SWAN, JAMES.
SWAN, GEORGE W.
SWEETING, BENJAMIN F.
THOMAS, HOLBROOK.
VOGHT, F. E.
WARDEN, WILLIAM.
WEITZELL, WILLIAM.
WILSON, JOHN.
WOODWARD, COLUMBUS.
WEDDINGER, FERDINAND.

COMPANY G.

Wilson C. Nicholas, *Captain.*
Alexander Cross, *First Lieutenant.*
Edward Deppish, *Second Lieutenant.*
John J. Platt, *First Sergeant.*
James Farrell, *Sergeant.*
Louis Needhamer, *Sergeant.*
James Shields, *Sergeant.*
George Ross, *Corporal.*
Eli Fishpan, *Corporal.*
Samuel Kirk, *Corporal.*
Charles Fercoit, *Corporal.*
Andrew Myers, *Musician.*

Privates.

Blunt, Robert.
Brashaers, Benton T.
Brady, Michael.
Byers, William.
Cantwell, Michael.
Coombs, Charles.
Dawson, John.
Deppish, Frank.
Doyle John.
Dyser, Luke.
Eckhart, Charles.
Eagger, Henry.
Farrell, William.
Forrest, Zachariah.
Fink, Henry.
Goodwin, John.
Gordon, John H.
Gesdon, Walter.
Griffith, John James.
Griffith, Greenberry.
Green, Charles.
Greenfield, William.

Hanley, Thomas.
Halpin, Thomas.
Hartley, William B.
Henderson, George.
Hempston, Alexander T.
Hughes, Patrick.
Hutchinson, Joseph.
Hood, George.
Isaacs, William.
Keyser, Herman.
King, John.
Leonard, Michael.
Logsden, John.
Lowrey, James.
Martin, William P.
Maloney, William.
Morris, George.
Morris, Harry.
Malden, Elias.
Murphy, John.
Murphy, Dennis.
Myers, Andrew.

Patrick, James Thos.
Phillips, James C.
Pigione, Joseph.
Pilker, Michael.
Quinn, John.
Raday, Patrick.
Rhodes, William Lee.
Ryan, James.
Ryan, Joseph.
Reed, Samuel.
Sahm, Joseph.
Scholl, Charles.
Simpson, H. A.
Simpson, Edward.
Stewart, Henry.
Strible, George.
Sheehan, William.
Sanders, James H.
Suit, Michael.
Wagner, John G.

COMPANY H.

William H. Murray, *Captain.*
George Thomas, *First Lieutenant.*
Francis X. Ward, *Second Lieutenant.*
Richard T. Gilmor, *Second Lieutenant.*
William P. Zollinger, *Second Lieutenant.*
John H. Sullivan, *Sergeant.*
McHenry Howard, *Sergeant.*
James Lyon, *Sergeant.*
Chapman B. Briscoe, *Sergeant.*
Edward Johnson, *Corporal.*
Richard C. Mackall, *Corporal.*
Clapham Murray, *Corporal.*
William S. Lemmon, *Corporal.*

Privates.

Blackistone, George W.
Bolling, John W.
Bond, John J.
Briscoe, David S.
Briscoe, Henry.
Brogden, Sellman.
Burke, John M.
Blackistone, William T.
Carr, Wilson C. N.
Coakeley, Philip A.
Colston, William E.
Coode, Demetrius.
Cook, George R.
Costigan, Dorsey T.
Davies, William H.
Davis, James A.
Denton, George.
Dorsey, Richard B.
Dorsey, Ezekiel S.
Douglass, Jackson.
Farr, Joseph R.
Gardiner, William F.
Gill, John.
Gist, Washington I.
Grayson, James B.
Greenwell, Thos. W. H.
Grogan, Charles E.
Goldsmith, John W.
Gwynn, James J.
Hance, James J.
Hebb, Henry J.
Hebb, Thomas A.
Harris, William E.
Hoblitzell, Fetter S.
Hollyday, William H.
Hough, Gresham.
Inloes, Charles E.
Laird, James W.
Laird, William H.
Law, J. G. D.
Lemmon, George.
Lemmon, John S.
Levering, Thomas H.
Mackall, Thomas B.
Markoe, Frank.
Marriott, Henry.
McKim, W. Duncan.
McKim, Randolph H.
Monmonier, John N. K.
Perry, William T.
Peters, Winfield.
Phillips, John J.
Pinkney, William S.
Pitts, Frererick L.
Post, John E. H.
Purnell, William.
Pinkney, Campbell W.
Price, ———.
Redmond, George.
Rives, Francis S.
Russell, Elisha T.
Rogers, Samuel B.
Russell, Thomas A.
Ryan, James A.
Ryce, Francis W.
Schley, Lake R.
Schliephake, Henry T.
Shanks, Daniel.
Sindall, Samuel W.
Smith, William F.
Sollers, Summerville.
Sothron, Webster H.
Thomas, Edwin.
Thomas, John H.
Thomas, James W.
Tippett, James B.
Tongue, James.
Turner, Duncan M.
Valiant, Thomas R.
Watkins, Nich. I.
West, Edward L.
White, James McK.
Williams, Aug. A.
Williams, John P.
Williamson, George.
Wise, Charles B.
Wright, Daniel G.
West, Charles.
Yellott, Washington.
Zollinger, William P.

COMPANY I.

MICHAEL S. ROBERTSON, *Captain*.
HUGH MITCHELL, *First Lieutenant*.
HEZEKIAH H. BEAN, *Second Lieutenant*.
EUGENE DIGGS, *Second Lieutenant*.
JOHN J. BRAWNER, *First Sergeant*.
JOHN H. STONE, *Sergeant*.
F. L. HIGDON, *Sergeant*.
WILLIAM H. RISON, *Sergeant*.
WARREN W. WARD, *Sergeant*.
Z. FRANCIS FREEMAN, *Corporal*.
FRANCIS L. HIGDON, *Corporal*.
THOMAS I. GREEN, *Corporal*.
THOMAS L. HANNON, *Corporal*.

Privates.

ADAMS, FRANKLIN.
ADAMS, JOHN S.
BAILEY, HENRY M.
BEALL, WILLIAM B.
BIVIN, ZACHARIAH.
BIVIN, WILLIAM F.
BRUCE, WILLIAM.
BURTTES, CHARLES H.
BURTTES, THOMAS W.
BRISCOE, MARSHALL.
BRISCOE, GIRARD.
BARBER, JOHN G.
BALL, DIONYSIUS.
CISSELL, JAMES T.
CLARK, JOHN E.
CLEMENTS, FRANCIS.
CHAPALIN, GEORGE.
CORRY, HENRY.
DEMENT, BENJAMIN F.
DEMENT, JOHN H.
DOWNING, JOHN L.
DORSETT, JAMES A.
DAVIS, WILLIAM F.
DENT, GEORGE H.
DOOLEY, ROBERT.
FERRALL, JOHN A.
FERGUSON, JOHN.
FREEMAN, PHILIP.
FREEMAN, THOMAS S.
GROVES, THOMAS F.
HAMMETT, JOHN M.
HERBERT, JOHN P.
HERBERT, WILLIAM.
HOWARD, ROBERTS.
HAYDEN, CHARLES G.
HANSON, JOHN D.
JENKINS, JOHN B.
JAMISON, FRANCIS.
KLENKIVITZ, BENJAMIN.
LACY, JAMES A.
LACY, ROBERT.
LEIGH, WILLIAM G.
LANCASTER, SAMUEL.
MARCERON, ALBERT.
MUDD, EDWIN C.
NICHOLSON, FRANKLIN T.
PAGE, CHARLES C.
RANDLE, WALTER I.
RANSLE, ANDREW.
RICHARDS, GEORGE.
SELBY, JOHN.
SHIERBORN, WILLIAM.
SHORTER, THOMAS O.
SIMMES, HENRY M.
SWAN, JOHN.
SANDERS, JOSEPH.
SOLLERS, JAMES H.
SOTHRON, MARSHALL.
TAYLOR, GEORGE.
THOMPSON, THOMAS M.
WARD, WILLIAM.
WEBSTER, GEORGE.
WEBSTER, WILLIAM.
WILSON, ALGERNON.
WOOD, HENRY W.
WHEATLEY, WILLIAM F.

LIEUT. COL. JAMES R. HERBERT,
SECOND MARYLAND INFANTRY.

SECOND MARYLAND INFANTRY.

CHAPTER I.

AFTER the disbanding of the First Maryland Infantry, the men who had composed it took various directions. Some of them had become tired of the infantry arm of the service, and not many days after their discharge they had entered the ranks either of some Maryland cavalry or artillery command. The majority of them, however, made their way to Richmond to enjoy a well-earned vacation.

But these true sons of Maryland, who had exiled themselves from their homes and State to battle for the South, soon tired of the tinsel and glamour of the Southern Capital. Its gaily-dressed officers, strutting the streets day after day, had no attractions for them. Among this gay throng of officers and civilians they were mortified to see many from their own State who had been in Virginia as long as themselves, and who were willing to accept any position under the Confederate Government that did not compel them to go to the front. It was no wonder, then, that these veterans soon began to long once more to hear the sound of battle. They had gone to Virginia to offer up their lives in a cause they held most dear, and they felt that every day passed away from their comrades in the field only the more betrayed the sacred trust reposed in them by fathers, mothers, kinsmen and sweethearts at home.

Among the veteran officers of the old First who had gone to Richmond were Captains William H. Murray and James R. Herbert, and Lieutenants George Thomas, Clapham Murray and William P. Zollinger, and it was to these officers that the men of the old regiment looked forward to for the formation of companies, and who would once more lead them against the enemy.

At this time many young men were arriving in Richmond from Maryland, especially from Anne Arundel and the lower counties, although every county in the State was represented among them. These young men had come to Richmond to espouse the cause of the South, as had the members of the disbanded First Maryland, and they were eager for the formation of companies.

The first company to be formed was that of Captain William H. Murray, of Baltimore City, and the next that of Captain J. Parran Crane, of St. Mary's County, and they were mustered in the same day, an unfortunate circumstance, as it gave rise subsequently to considerable discussion, and no little feeling, as to the seniority of the companies. At the instance of Captain Crane the matter was brought to the attention of the Secretary of War, who issued an order to Captain

Archer to examine into the matter and settle the dispute. This Captain Archer did, and decided in favor of Captain Murray. But, notwithstanding this decision, when the two companies reached Winchester, Crane appealed to Steuart, and he also decided in favor of Captain Murray. Still Crane was not satisfied, and he appealed to General William E. Jones some weeks later, and that General suggested that they draw lots, and thus definitely settle the dispute. Again Captain Murray won, and the matter there ended.

Captain James R. Herbert's company was mustered in on the 11th of September, and that of Captain John W. Torsch, about the 14th of September. Captain Torsch had up to a short time before served in the company commanded by Captain Richard Thomas. Captain McAleer's company quickly followed that of Captain Torsch, making five companies in all.

The companies of Murray and Crane had already reported to General George H. Steuart, commandant at Winchester, and the companies of Herbert, Torsch and McAleer joined them on September 28, 1862. Upon reaching Winchester a fifth company was formed. The men composing it had come on from Richmond with Companies C, D and E, with the understanding that they should be allowed to form their own company upon reaching Winchester. This company was commanded by Captain Andrew J. Gwynn, of Prince George's.

The following is a list of the officers of the different companies:

OFFICERS.

COMPANY A.

Captain, ... WILLIAM H. MURRAY.

Lieutenants.

GEORGE THOMAS.   CLAPHAM MURRAY.   WILLIAM P. ZOLLINGER.

COMPANY B.

Captain, ... J. PARRAN CRANE.

Lieutenants.

JOHN H. STONE.   CHARLES B. WISE.   JAMES H. WILSON.

COMPANY C.

Captain, ... JAMES R. HERBERT.

Lieutenants.

F. C. DUVALL.   CHARLES W. HODGES.   JOSEPH W. BARBER.

COMPANY D.

Captain, ... JOSEPH L. MCALEER.

Lieutenants.

JAMES S. FRANKLIN.   J. T. BUSSEY.   S. T. MCCULLOUGH.

COMPANY E.

Captain, ... JOHN W. TORSCH.

Lieutenants.

WILLIAM J. BROADFOOT.   W. R. BYUS.   JOSEPH P. QUINN.

COMPANY F.

Captain, ... A. J. GWYNN.

Lieutenants.

JOHN W. POLK.   DAVID C. FORREST.   JOHN G. HYLAND.

Before the formation of Gwynn's company General Steuart was anxious to have the battalion fully organized by the election of a Major, but not being entirely satisfied as to the course he should pursue in the matter, he addressed the following communication to the Secretary of War:

HEADQUARTERS, WINCHESTER, VIRGINIA, October 13, 1862.

General George W. Randolph, Secretary of War:

General:—I have the honor to state there are now here five fine companies of the Maryland Line, over five hundred men. Another is rapidly forming, and I hope there will soon be a full regiment. In accordance with your instructions, I had an election for Major, and Captain James R. Herbert, of Company C, was elected. This leaves a vacancy, and I would like to know whether it is to be filled by election or promotion, as Paragraph 5, Special Orders, No. 186, Adjutant and Inspector-General's Office, which disbanded the old First Maryland Regiment, states:

"The members thereof, with all other native and adopted citizens of Maryland, desirous of enlisting into the service of the Confederate States, are invited to enroll thmselves into companies, etc., the officers of which are to be elected."

In the present case none of the company officers have sufficient experience to fill the post of Captain, and it would be better to get some eligible person. Will you be kind enough to tell me what staff and non-commissioned staff officers are allowed to a battalion of six companies or less?

I have received the greatest assistance from the officers under my command, and the quiet and good order now prevailing in the town is due to the Provost-Marshal, John B. Brooke, and to that excellent soldier, Captain J. Louis Smith, commanding the provost-guard.

I hope you received my letter relative to them; also one requesting the appointment of Mr. McHenry Howard as ordnance officer on my staff, he being an officer of merit and aide-de camp to the late Brigadier-General C. S. Winder. Some three weeks since General Lee sent me over three hundred paroled prisoners (Confederate), to be kept in camp until exchanged, and as it required an officer of experience to keep them from wandering off, I detailed First Lieutenant Wilson C. Nicholas for that purpose, thinking he had a commission. He has taken remarkably good care of them, but the other day I received Special Orders No. 232, stating his resignation as drill master had been accepted. I earnestly recommend he may be again appointed to that or some other position in the Provisional Army — First Lieutenant or Captain.

I am, with great respect, your obedient servant,

GEORGE H. STEUART, *Commanding Post.*

[*INDORSEMENT.*]

OCTOBER 21, 1862.

Inform him that after the first election in the Maryland troops, like others, the promotion will be by seniority, unless a board pronounces the next officer incompetent. A battalion of six companies has a Lieutenant-Colonel and Major; a battalion of five or less has a Major only. A Quartermaster is allowed, who acts also as commissary. The Adjutant is detailed from the subaltern officers.

G. W. R.

Upon receipt of the above indorsement General Steuart ordered an election, and Captain James R. Herbert was chosen Major, and First Lieutenant F. C. Duvall was elected Captain, Charles W. Hodges was promoted to First Lieutenant, Thomas C. Tolson to Senior Second, and Joseph W. Barber was elected to fill the vacancy thus created.

In November General George H. Steuart was ordered to withdraw from Winchester, and the Maryland battalion was temporarily assigned to the command of General William E. Jones, who had just been appointed to Munford's Brigade of cavalry. General Jones received the Second Maryland in the vicinity of Strasburg, and until January 2, 1863, it was moved from point to point in the valley, as circumstances required.

In the meantime Captain W. W. Goldsborough, of the old First, having recovered from wounds received in the second battle of Manassas, had made his way to Richmond to accept a First Lieutenancy in the provisional army, and had received orders to report to Colonel Shields at Camp Lee. The duties to which he was assigned there did not prove congenial, and after two weeks he resigned his commission and repaired to Richmond in hopes of organizing another company, with which to join the Second Maryland in the Valley of Virginia. In this he was eminently successful, and with the assistance of Thomas R. Stewart, of Dorchester County, a fine company of over eighty young Marylanders, mostly from the lower counties, was formed, and the following officers elected : Captain, W. W. Goldsborough ; First Lieutenant, Thomas R. Stewart ; Second Lieutenant, James A. Davis ; Third Lieutenant, William H. Wrightson.*

On the 30th day of December, 1862, Captain Goldsborough had the proud satisfaction of marching his company through the streets of Richmond to the depot, with Volandt's (Baltimore) Band at its head, followed by a large concourse of people, and on the evening of the 31st it arrived at Staunton, over the Virginia Central Railroad. From Staunton the company made a rapid march to Newmarket, where the Second Maryland was in camp, arriving there at daylight on the morning of January 2, 1863, just in time to see General Jones' whole command file through the streets on its way to Moorefield, to which point an expedition had been planned, and it was a week before the Second Maryland returned, the men completely broken down by the hardships they had been compelled to undergo, the expedition having accomplished nothing commensurate with their sufferings.

With the addition of Company G, the Second Maryland Infantry† now numbered nearly six hundred men, and a finer body of troops never marched to the tap of the drum. They were, indeed, worthy successors of the men of the First, many of whom were in their ranks, and as proudly bore the little flag of their native State from Winchester, in 1863, to Appomattox, in 1865, as had the gallant First, from the first Manassas in 1861 to Malvern Hill in 1862.

Shortly after the return of the battalion from the Moorefield expedition, by order of General Jones, an election was held for Lieutenant-Colonel, when Bradley T. Johnson was elected, but in justice to the officers who had been instrumental in forming the battalion, Colonel Johnson magnanimously declined to accept the command, whereupon Major James R. Herbert was elected, and soon after Captain W. W. Goldsborough, of Company G, was appointed Major by the Secretary of War.

---
* After Captain Goldsborough was promoted to the Majority, First Sergeant G. G. Guillette was made Lieutenant.
† It was originally called the First Maryland Battalion, but to distinguish it from the First Maryland Infantry it was soon designated the Second Maryland Infantry.

CHAPTER II.

The Second Maryland passed the winter of 1862-63 at various points in the Valley, notably at Lacey's Springs, Edenburg, Newmarket, Woodstock and Harrisonburg. It was a severe winter, and the men were much exposed, not having any tents, and their only shelter consisted of rude sheds made of brush and leaves, which were designated " shebangs." Notwithstanding this fact, there was comparatively little sickness — not near so much as there had been in the First Maryland the year before, when tents were plentiful. Very many of the men did not even avail themselves of this protection, but simply built a fire and, rolling themselves in their blankets, lay down before it and slept soundly until the reveille awoke them in the morning. Indeed, it was no unusual thing to see several hundred men arise from a covering of a foot of snow that had fallen during the night.

Whilst they were not engaged with the enemy at any time during this period, still their duties were very arduous, as often the command was compelled to make long marches, and some of them through blinding snowstorms. A large quantity of pig iron was stored in the furnaces near Edenburg, and as it was of great value to the Confederate Government General Jones organized expeditions for its removal.

On March 26, 1863, there was an alarm in the camp of the Second Maryland, then encamped near Edenburg, which went to prove the efficiency and discipline of the command. Early in the morning of that day Captain F. A. Bond, entirely upon his own responsibility, attacked and captured a Federal picket near Kernstown. The alarm being given, Captain Bond's little party was quickly pursued by a large body of the enemy's cavalry. A courier was sent back by Major Ridgely Brown, in command of the First Maryland Cavalry, to notify General Jones of their approach. This courier had first to pass the camp of the Second Infantry, where he gave the alarm, and although the men were about camp performing their various duties, in five minutes after the long roll began to beat every man was in his place in line, and the command was on the move to meet the enemy. Of this affair General Jones, in his official report says :

" The courier, passing the camp of the Maryland Infantry, gave information, and Lieutenant-Colonel James R. Herbert and his noble men, without waiting for orders, seized their arms and flew to the protection of our trains in quest of forage about Woodstock. Their conduct on this occasion is worthy of the highest praise."*

On April 21, 1863, General Jones broke camp at Lacey's Springs, with all his available force, to make an expedition to West Virginia. The object of the

---
* For full account of the fight, see cavalry.

expedition was to co-operate with General Imboden in the destruction of as much of the Baltimore and Ohio Railroad as possible, the collection of supplies and to capture and disperse the enemy wherever found.

The morning the command left Lacey's Springs the weather was everything that could have been desired, but before night a hard, cold rain had set in. The mountain streams, then almost dry, soon became raging torrents, and the men of the Second Maryland (it comprised the only infantry connected with the expedition) were compelled to ford many streams waist deep. For three days the rain continued, and when, at the end of that time, Moorefield was reached, the infantry was much broken down, nor was the cavalry and artillery in a better plight. To add to their suffering, the brigade quartermaster failed to have supplies near Moorefield, as he had been ordered. Men who had marched for three days under such circumstances were not, then, likely to bestow any very complimentary criticisms upon the commanding general, who, of course, is blamed for everything.

But this was all forgotten when the next morning the good people of Moorefield turned out *en masse* and contributed unsparingly to their wants, and the trip to Moorefield was ever after a pleasant remembrance to the members of the Second.

The enemy having failed to make his appearance in the vicinity of Moorefield, and the subsequent movements of the cavalry, to be successful, required a celerity not attainable by infantry and artillery, it was deemed best to send these, under Lieutenant-Colonel Herbert, back to the Valley as convoy to the wagon train. After remaining at Moorefield two or three days the return trip of the infantry and artillery was made by way of Franklin, the whole reaching Harrisonburg on the evening of April 30, after an uneventful trip, and reported to Lieutenant-Colonel Funsten, who had been left behind by General Jones to watch the enemy in the Valley.

During the absence of the Second Maryland, Captain Joseph L. McAleer, of that command, who had been left behind by reason of his not having been at that time physically able to make so long and arduous a march, had been placed in command of one hundred and fifty dismounted cavalry and ordered to report to Major S. B. Myers at Fisher's Hill. On April 28 two regiments of Federal cavalry, four regiments of infantry and some artillery made their appearance at Fisher's Hill. The cavalry (Twelfth and Thirteenth Pennsylvania) were easily drawn into an ambuscade, and seventy of them killed, wounded or captured. Colonel Funsten, in his official report, says:

"Much credit is due to Major Myers and Captain McAleer for the skill and bravery which they displayed in this affair."

Again he says, after the return of the Second Maryland to Harrisonburg:

"On the morning of the 8th of May the enemy had advanced above Newmarket, and I moved up the Maryland infantry and all of the dismounted cavalry who had guns, with the artillery, below Harrisonburg, and prepared to give them battle. We remained in this position until about 8 o'clock the next morning, when the enemy fell back toward Winchester."

And it was a blessing to Colonel Funsten and his little band that the enemy, in overwhelming force, did fall back, or the Second Maryland might have ceased to exist right there.

A short time after the above event the Second Maryland, under command of Major W. W. Goldsborough (Lieutenant-Colonel Herbert being on court-martial duty) was ordered to Fisher's Hill to relieve Major S. B. Myers. The infantry was accompanied by the First Maryland Cavalry, Captain F. A. Bond; Baltimore Light Artillery, Captain W. H. Griffin, and Chew's Virginia battery.

It will thus be seen that the Maryland Line was represented by every branch of the service, and efforts to concentrate and recruit the three arms were again to be made. The Government had offered inducements for Marylanders to transfer their services from the various regiments to which they were attached, but few availed themselves of it, and never during the war were the different commands together for any great length of time. This was unfortunately mainly due to the fact that a brigade, instead of a regiment, of infantry could not be raised.

General George H. Steuart had for some time ceased to be identified with the Maryland Line, having been appointed to the command of the brigade formerly commanded by General Colston.

A commander at this time was, therefore, absolutely necessary, for it was believed the spring campaign would soon be inaugurated, and no time was to be lost. Application was made to the War Department for the privilege of electing a head, and upon its being granted Colonel Bradley T. Johnson was unanimously chosen. Colonel Johnson was at this time a member of a military court sitting in Richmond, and Lieutenant J. Thomas Bussey was at once dispatched to Richmond to notify him of his election. Accordingly, on June 22 a commission was issued him as Colonel of the Maryland Line, and also giving him the following authority:

CONFEDERATE STATES OF AMERICA, WAR DEPARTMENT,
ADJUTANT AND INSPECTOR-GENERAL'S OFFICE,
RICHMOND, VIRGINIA, June 22, 1863.

Colonel Bradley T. Johnson:

Sir:—You are authorized to recruit from Marylanders and muster into service companies, battalions and regiments of infantry, cavalry and artillery, to serve for the war, and to be attached to and form part of the Maryland Line.

BY COMMAND OF JAMES A. SEDDEN, *Secretary of War.*

SAMUEL W. MELTON, *Major and A. A. G.*

Although Colonel Johnson started off at once, in company with Lieutenant-Colonel Ridgely Brown and Captain George W. Booth, both of whom had just recovered from wounds received in General Jones' raid into Western Virginia, he did not reach the command until after the disastrous charge at Culp's Hill, Gettysburg, which had reduced the splendid battalion to a skeleton. The fact that the army was compelled to so soon return to Virginia made it impossible to recruit and organize a brigade in Maryland, and as he had but a handful of infantry left, Colonel Johnson's services could be better employed, and he was again placed in command of Jones' Infantry Brigade, the Second Brigade of Jackson's Division, with which he had won so much distinction at the second Manassas.

Shortly after the arrival of the Maryland command and Chew's battery at Fisher's Hill it was joined by General A. G. Jenkins' splendid brigade of Virginia cavalry, and General Jenkins assumed command of the whole. Before the arrival of General Jenkins the enemy's cavalry paid frequent visits to Strasburg, two miles away, and after taking a look at the rebels on the hill returned to their camp at Winchester. A trap was set by Major Goldsborough to catch them one morning, and the companies of Captains Torsch and Stewart were marched during the night into Strasburg and placed in position to intercept the enemy, should he make his appearance. He did come next morning, but, unfortunately, at that moment the gallant Torsch had stolen off to whisper for a brief period sweet nonsense into the ears of a rustic beauty, and the damage inflicted was trifling, compared to what it would have been had he been present.

On the 10th of June, 1863, orders were received to move from Fisher's Hill and encamp at Cedar Creek. It was evident that the campaign was about to open, but the destination of the handful of Marylanders, who were assembled at this point, could not, of course, be even conjectured. The infantry, cavalry and artillery had been together longer than ever before, and it was hoped the Maryland Line would for some time longer, at least, remain intact, and all anxiously awaited the arrival of Colonel Johnson, in whom the Maryland troops placed great confidence.

On the afternoon of the 12th a dispatch was received by General Jenkins from General Ewell that immediately changed the whole aspect of affairs. To everyone's surprise, General Ewell, with his command, was near Front Royal, when he was supposed to be on the Rappahannock with General Lee. General Jenkins was ordered to report at once to General Ewell, and late that night Lieutenant-Colonel Herbert received orders to move the Maryland Line next morning to the vicinity of Newtown and await the arrival of General J. A. Early. The command consisted of the Second Maryland Infantry, the Baltimore Light Artillery and Company A, First Maryland Cavalry. The men were in high spirits and eager to encounter the enemy, who were believed to be in their immediate front. Beyond Newtown a body of Federal cavalry was observed at some distance on the turnpike. Lieutenant-Colonel Herbert ordered Captain Griffin to bring up a piece of his artillery, and, masked by a half dozen horsemen, it was deliberately sighted and fired. The shot was a good one, whether it did any execution or not, and had a magical effect, for the cavalry disappeared like the mist. The enemy was evidently taken by surprise, for the Maryland troops were then not more than five miles from Winchester, and still had met with no opposition. How long it would be, though, before a large force would present itself to confront this handful of men was becoming a serious problem, when, much to their relief, a cloud of dust in the distance heralded the approach of General Early with his division. But the enemy by this time had become thoroughly alarmed, and before General Early could come up Carlin's Federal battery, posted on Pritchard's Hill, was raining shell upon the little Maryland command. But the gallant Griffin, of the Baltimore Lights, soon got to work, and then occurred one of the prettiest artillery duels of the war.

Upon the arrival of General Early, he immediately ordered Lieutenant-Colonel Herbert to throw forward three companies of the Second Maryland, under Major W. W. Goldsborough, as skirmishers and develop the enemy's infantry. This movement was beautifully executed, and on the outskirts of Kernstown the skirmish line of the Second encountered that of the enemy, who were quickly driven back. But Carlin's battery still paid attention to them, and for half an hour they were compelled to remain under a heavy fire of artillery. In the midst of this pandemonium the glorious Early put in an appearance, when Major Goldsborough pointed out the fact that he had accomplished what he had been sent out to do, and as the enemy had an accurate range, he asked permission to withdraw his men a short distance to the rear, as he did not wish to sacrifice them needlessly. General Early said:

"You have done your work thoroughly. You have a splendid body of men in your Maryland command, and I wish there were more of them. I have just placed Gordon in position, and he will drive the enemy into Winchester. When you hear them 'yell' you will be relieved, but remain where you are until then."

The "yell" soon came, and the Maryland skirmishers were relieved from their perilous position.

That evening the skirmishers were moved forward to Hollingsworth's Mill, on the outskirts of Winchester. The rain had begun to fall in torrents, and the darkness was impenetrable. To shelter his men from the pitiless elements Major Goldsborough called them in and placed them under shelter of a deserted barn. Before morning the rain ceased, and at daylight the men were in position, and pushed forward until they had penetrated into the streets of Winchester. Here the fighting was spirited, until the troops were ordered out of the town by General Early. But they went no farther than the outskirts, and during the day kept in check the Fifth Maryland Federal Regiment with its supports.

On this day Major Goldsborough's orders were to keep the enemy engaged, but not to press forward. The object was to amuse him and distract his attention from the real points of attack.

After a reconnoissance of the enemy's position by Generals Ewell and Early, it was determined to move Hays', Hoke's and Smith's Brigades and the rest of Jones' and Brown's battalions of artillery to the left, across the Romney road, about three miles from Winchester. After crossing the Romney road General Early soon reached a good position for posting his artillery within easy range of the enemy's works on the hill overlooking his main fort. Colonel Jones, in command of the artillery, placed his guns in position as quietly and quickly as possible. The artillery was divided so as to put twelve pieces in an orchard and eight pieces on the edge of a cornfield north of a woods. Hays' splendid Louisiana Brigade had been selected to make the assault upon the fort.

About an hour before sundown Jones brought his artillery by hand over the crest into position, and opened with the whole of his twenty pieces before the enemy was aware of his proximity, so much was he absorbed in the skirmishing so vigorously pressed by the Second Maryland Infantry on the opposite side of the town.

So rapid and destructive was the fire from Jones' batteries that in half an hour the enemy's guns in his fortifications were silenced, when General Harry Hays was ordered to make the assault. With a yell, the gallant Louisianians dashed forward, over abatis of brushwood, over every obstacle, and swarmed into the fort, taking six pieces of artillery, and at once turned them upon the columns of the enemy that were being formed to recapture the fort.

In the meantime the skirmishers of the Second Maryland Infantry had not been idle, and their vigorous and persistent attack upon the enemy posted in the cemetery had not only diverted his attention from the real point of attack, but had kept a large force from co-operating with the main body. When night set in they held the position they had been ordered to in the morning by General Early, and had successfully repulsed two assaults of the enemy, in one of which Lieutenant Joseph P. Quinn, of Company E, was captured through his own indiscretion.

Late in the evening of the 14th Major Harry Gilmor brought an order from General Ewell to Major Goldsborough to press on into Winchester at the break of day, and if possible ascertain at intervals during the night what the enemy was doing. From reports made by several of his most reliable men who were sent into the town, Major Goldsborough became convinced that the forts were being evacuated, and so reported to General Ewell.

At daybreak of the 15th Major Goldsborough put his skirmishers in motion and proceeded cautiously through the streets of Winchester without encountering the enemy. At the Taylor Hotel Captain William I. Raisin, of the First Maryland Cavalry, was found. He had been severely wounded and captured three or four days before in an ambuscade near Newtown. At this moment the roar of artillery was heard some three miles out on the Martinsburg road. It proved to proceed from an encounter of General Edward Johnson's Division with the retreating enemy. This division had been thrown around from the right during the night for the purpose of intercepting Milroy's retreat. The battle was fierce and bloody, but the enemy lost heavily in killed, wounded and prisoners. The Second Maryland skirmishers, with the exception of that portion of Company A under command of Lieutenant George Thomas, immediately took possession of the Star Fort, capturing some two hundred prisoners. Lieutenant Thomas, proceeding alone, pretending not to have heard the command to halt, ran into a large body of the enemy's cavalry, dismounted them and mounted his own command, and marched his prisoners in triumph into town. It was so comical a sight that Major Goldsborough administered but a mild reprimand to the gallant young officer for his disobedience of orders.

The Star Fort for the day was made a receptacle for prisoners and garrisoned by Company G, under command of Captain Thomas R. Stewart, whilst the remainder of the Second Maryland were detailed for provost duty. In the evening the battalion was relieved by the Thirteenth Virginia, under Colonel Terrill, and was temporarily attached to Steuart's Brigade, Edward Johnson's Division, Ewell's Corps, composed of the First and Third North Carolina, Tenth, Twenty-third and Thirty-seventh Virginia Regiments.

The Confederate victory at Winchester had been complete. Milroy lost the greater part of his army, and his artillery, wagon train and a vast amount of stores fell into the hands of the victors.

Of the part the Second Maryland Infantry took in the engagement, General Early, in his official report, makes the following complimentary mention:

. . . . Having received the instructions of the Lieutenant-General commanding, the wagons, excepting the ambulances and regimental ordnance and medical wagons, were left at Cedarville, and I diverged from the Winchester and Front Royal turnpike at Ninevah and reached the Valley turnpike at Newtown, and thence advancing toward Winchester I found Lieutenant-Colonel Herbert, of the Maryland Line, with his battalion of infantry, Baltimore Light Artillery, and a portion of the First Maryland Cavalry, occupying the ridge between Bartonsville and Kernstown, and engaged in occasional skirmishing with a portion of the enemy which had taken position near Kernstown. . . . Herbert was ordered to take position with his battalion of infantry on the right of Gordon. . . . . When Hays' and Gordon's skirmishers had advanced to Bowers' Hill, Major W. W. Goldsborough, of the Maryland battalion, with the skirmishers from that battalion, had advanced into the outskirts of the town of Winchester, but fearing that the enemy would shell the town from their main fort, I ordered him back . . . All the arrangements of Colonel Jones and the conduct of himself and his artillery were admirable. I must also commend the gallantry of Lieutenant-Colonel Herbert and Major Goldsborough, of the Maryland Line, and their troops.

The casualties in the Second Maryland were as follows :

COMPANY A.—Captain William H. Murray.

WOUNDED—Sergeant E. S. Dorsey, severely ; Privates Sommerville Sollers, slightly ; John Wilson, slightly.

COMPANY B.—Captain J. P. Crane.

WOUNDED—Privates J. E. Joy, mortally ; H. Corry, slightly ; William Herbert, slightly.

COMPANY C.—Captain Ferdinand Duvall.

WOUNDED—Captain Ferdinand Duvall, severely.

COMPANY D.—Captain Joseph L. McAleer.

WOUNDED—Private John Devries, mortally.

COMPANY E.—Captain John W. Torsch.

WOUNDED—Lieutenant W. R. Byus, slightly. CAPTURED—Lieutenant Joseph P. Quinn.

TOTAL—Nine wounded and one captured.

CHAPTER II.

On the morning of the 16th, Steuart's Brigade took up its line of march in the direction of Smithfield, where it arrived about dusk, and went into camp for the night.

The next morning the march was resumed and led in the direction of the Potomac, much to the joy of the exiled sons of Maryland, who at last began to entertain the belief that they would soon once more tread the soil of their native State. Nor were they deceived or disappointed. The column crossed the Baltimore and Ohio Railroad at Kerneysville, and in the afternoon went into camp within three miles of Shepherdstown, pretty well used up from the effects of the heat.

The camp of the Second Maryland was not far from the beautiful residence of the Honorable Alexander H. Boteler, and during their first evening several of the command visited this estimable family, and spent a few delightful hours. Mr. Boteler was from home in the service of his country, and Mrs. Boteler and her family had been subjected to many indignities at the hands of the Federal vandals who had infested the neighborhood for some time prior to the arrival of the Confederates, as had also the family of Honorable Edmund J. Lee, a near neighbor, and a relative of the great chieftain who was now about to invade the enemy's country. Alas! it was not many weeks after that both these beautiful homes were burned to the ground with all their contents by General Hunter. In retaliation for these deeds of vandalism, and some others equally as atrocious, General Early destroyed the town of Chambersburg, Pennsylvania, during the following summer.

On the afternoon of June 18 the troops were once more put in motion, and took the road leading to Shepherdstown, through which beautiful town they passed amid the joyous shouts of its inhabitants. About two miles below Shepherdstown Boteler's ford of the Potomac was reached, and the men plunged into the water, nearly waist deep, and made for the Maryland shore. It was an indescribable scene, as thousands struggled through the water, singing and shouting in the excess of their joy. Poor fellows, very many of them were never to return. When the men of the Second Maryland once more stood upon their native soil they could not restrain their feelings, and many were moved to tears, whilst others acted as though they had lost their reason. As for General Steuart, Quartermaster John E. Howard afterward declared he turned seventeen double somersaults before he ceased, and then stood on his head for five minutes, all the while whistling "Maryland, My Maryland."

That night the troops encamped on the river bank, and the next morning the division passed through Sharpsburg and camped upon that bloody field of the year before. Three days were consumed here, when the division once more got in motion and passed through Hagerstown, where the Maryland boys were most hospitably received by those friendly to the cause, and the delightful family of Doctor McGill were particularly cordial in their attentions to them.

Greencastle, Pennsylvania, was reached next day. At last the enemy's country was invaded, and if its inhabitants expected no mercy at the hands of the invading army, never were a people more agreeably surprised.

On June 21 General Lee issued the following order:

HEADQUARTERS ARMY NORTHERN VIRGINIA, June 21, 1863.

General Orders No. 72.

While in the enemy's country, the following regulations for procuring supplies will be strictly observed, and any violation promptly and vigorously punished.

No. 1. No private property shall be injured or destroyed by any person belonging to or connected with the army, or taken, except by the officers hereinafter designated.

No. 2. The chiefs of the commissary, quartermaster, ordnance and medical departments of the army will make requisitions upon the local authorities or inhabitants for the necessary supplies for their respective departments, designating the places and times of delivery. All persons complying with such requisitions shall be paid the market price for the articles furnished, if they so desire, and the officer making such payments shall take duplicate receipts for the same, specifying the name of the person paid, and the quantity, kind and price of the property, one of which receipts shall be at once forwarded to the chief of the department to which such officer is attached.

No. 3. Should the authorities or inhabitants neglect or refuse to comply to such requisitions, the supplies required will be taken from the nearest inhabitant so refusing, by the order and under the directions of the respective chiefs of the department named.

No. 4. When any command is detached from the main body, the chiefs of the several departments of such command will procure supplies for the same, and such other stores as they may be ordered to provide, in the manner and subject to the provisions herein prescribed, reporting their action to the heads of their respective departments, to which they will forward duplicates of all vouchers given or received.

No. 5. All persons who shall decline to receive payment for property furnished on requisitions, and all from whom it shall be necessary to take stores and supplies, shall be furnished by the officer receiving or taking the same with a receipt specifying the kind and quantity of the property received or taken, as the case may be, the name of the person from whom it was received or taken, the command for the use of which it was intended, and the market price. A duplicate of said receipt shall be at once forwarded to the chief of the department to which the officer by whom it is executed is attached.

No. 6. If any person shall remove or conceal property necessary for the use of the army, or attempt to do so, the officers hereinbefore mentioned will cause such property, and all other property belonging to such person that may be required by the army, to be seized, and the officer seizing the same will forthwith report to the chief of this department the kind, quantity and market price of the property so seized, and the name of the owner.

By Command of General R. E. Lee.

R. H. Chilton, *A. A. and I. G.*

Lieutenant-General R. S. Ewell, Commanding Second Army Corps.

On June 27 General Lee issued his second order, and it is certainly in great contrast with anything that had ever emanated from a Federal General in Virginia or any other one of the invaded Southern States:

Headquarters Army of Northern Virginia,
Chambersburg, Pennsylvania, June 27, 1863.

General Orders No. 73.

The commanding General has observed with satisfaction the conduct of the troops on the march, and confidently anticipated results commensurate with the high spirit they have manifested. No troops could have displayed greater fortitude, or better performed the arduous marches of the past ten days. Their conduct in other respects has, with few exceptions, been in keeping with their character as soldiers, and entitles them to approbation and praise.

There have, however, been instances of forgetfulness on the part of some that they have in keeping the yet unsullied reputation of the army, and that the duties exacted of us by civilization and Christianity are not less obligatory in the country of the enemy than in our own. The commanding General considers that no greater disgrace could befall the army, and through it our whole people, than the perpetration of the barbarous outrages, upon the innocent and defenceless, and the wanton destruction of private property, that have marked the course of the enemy in our own country. Such proceedings not only disgrace the perpetrators and all connected with them, but are subversive of the discipline and efficiency of the army and destructive of the ends of our present movement. It must be remembered that we make war only upon armed men, and that we cannot take vengeance for the wrongs our people have suffered without lowering ourselves in the eyes of all whose abhorrence has been excited by the atrocities of our enemy, and offending against Him to Whom vengeance belongeth, without Whose favor and support our efforts must all prove in vain.

The commanding General, therefore, earnestly exhorts the troops to abstain with most scrupulous care from unnecessary or wanton injury to private property; and he enjoins upon all officers to arrest and bring to summary punishment all who shall in any way offend against the orders on this subject.
R. E. Lee, *General.*

At Greencastle Steuart's Brigade was detached from the division and ordered to proceed to Chambersburg by way of Mercersburg and McConnelsburg. The object was to collect through that region necessary supplies of every description for the use of the army. At Mercersburg a goodly quantity of shoes were obtained for the barefoot soldiers, which were paid for in Confederate money, agreeably to General Lee's order.

In passing over the mountain from Mercersburg to McConnelsburg various barriers across the road were encountered, which had been erected by the State militia, and two or three times the troops were fired upon, but no serious opposition was met with, and an occasional shell from one of Steuart's batteries cleared the way.

After a stay of a day at McConnelsburg, Steuart's Brigade united with the division at Chambersburg, and on the 27th the command passed through that thriving town, not many months after to be consigned to the flames, and took the turnpike leading to Carlisle, and on the afternoon of June 28 the wearied troops went into camp about three miles from that place.

It now became evident that the objective point of a portion of the great army of invasion was Harrisburg, the Capital of the State of Pennsylvania, and there were few who did not believe that Philadelphia would soon be in possession of the invaders. The idea of defeat never occurred to Lee's veterans, for they were fully aware of the fact that such an army had never before been marshaled under the flag of the Confederacy, and believed themselves to be invincible.

Late in the afternoon of the following day orders were received to move, and great was the surprise of the officers and men of the division when they found themselves countermarching over the road they had traveled the day before.

Trifling as this may seem, here occurred the second great mistake of the campaing. Stuart's Cavalry raid around Washington, in which the eyes of the army were lost, by reason of his being cut off from the army during its march into Pennsylvania, was the first. Johnson's Division was now but thirty miles from Gettysburg, yet by order of General Ewell it was marched by circuitous roads fifty miles or more to reach that point, whilst the remainder of the corps took the direct road.

Some two or three years after the war the author met General Ewell at Capon Springs, in Virginia, and in the course of conversation asked him why Johnson's Division had not been taken the direct road to Gettysburg. General Ewell answered :

"At the time, of course, I did not know of the proximity of the Federal Army, and did not wish to crowd the one road to Gettysburg. I had no reason to believe that there was any occasion to make haste. It was unfortunate. Had Johnson's fine division been with me on the 1st of July there would have been no second day's battle at Gettysburg ; that would have been fought somewhere else, possibly upon ground of our own choosing, and certainly with a better prospect of success."

The second evening after the division left the vicinity of Carlisle the troops went into camp near Fayetteville, more than twenty miles from Gettysburg, and on the morning of July 1 the march was resumed in the direction of that place.

A short distance beyond Fayetteville the men of Longstreet's Corps were passed in camp, and the heart of every man in the Second Maryland was made to beat with pride, as five hundred strong and drums beating, the battalion marched by these veterans of many battles and heard their unsparing praise of the fine appearance and soldierly bearing of the boys from Maryland.

The weary miles were slowly unreeled that hot July day, for the road was blocked by a long train of wagons ; but finally that obstruction was passed, and the marching became easier.

And now more than one-half the distance between Fayetteville and Gettysburg had been traversed when a sound ahead as of distant thunder was wafted to the ears of the tired infantrymen. The veteran knew too well what that meant ; the novice scarcely noticed it, or was uncertain as to its meaning. A commotion was soon observed ahead, and presently staff officers were dashing furiously along the column. Louder, more distinct, the thunder became, and it was apparent to all that a furious battle was in progress. The command, " Close up, men ; close up ! " was heard on every hand, and faster grew the pace, and thus, sometimes at a double-quick, eight miles were gone over, and Johnson's Division was fast nearing the field of strife, and as it did so a shocking sight met the gaze of the men, for hundreds of mutilated and dying soldiers filled the roadside. Thousands were indifferent to the sight, for they had witnessed it many times before, but most of the men of the Second Maryland had never seen it, and while it made many a face pale, the compressed lips showed the firm determination to willingly undergo the same suffering, the same death, for the cause of their beloved South as had the heroes around them.

But as still nearer the division approached the field the sound of artillery almost ceased, until only an occasional gun was heard. The battle was over — for that day at least.

Passing on, over heaps of dead and dying of both armies, the division entered the streets of Gettysburg, and halted to rest. The battle of that day had, indeed, been long and bloody, but the enemy had been driven to the heights on the other side of the town, shattered and demoralized, thousands of their number having been captured in the streets. Even then it was not too late to administer a crushing defeat, for Early with his splendid division was there, and had not been heavily engaged, and Johnson was there, his men eager to be led on, notwithstanding their long and rapid march, but the enemy was allowed to remain unmolested in his strong position, and before morning he had been reinforced by many thousands. The first opportunity was lost. Now for the second.

On the evening of the 1st of July, after dark, Johnson's division moved on a line parallel with the York turnpike, crossing which about a mile below Gettysburg it took its place in line of battle along the road leading to Hanover. That night the troops slept upon their arms, ready to renew the conflict in the morning.

The line of battle was formed with Longstreet on the right, Hill in the centre and Ewell on the left. Longstreet had orders to attack at 9 o'clock in the morning, but unfortunately he did not agree with General Lee in his plan of attack, and, in hopes of inducing or compelling him to conform to his views, he allowed the day to pass by until near 5 o'clock, when, because of still more peremptory orders to begin his attack, he reluctantly obeyed. His troops attacked with great vigor, and had they done so even an hour earlier Little Round Top, the key to the whole Federal position, would have fallen into their possession. As it was, it was only averted by the opportune arrival of large reinforcements of the enemy at the very moment when success seemed assured. Had the attack been made in the morning at 9 o'clock, as Longstreet had been ordered to make it, he would have found the position comparatively unoccupied, and the enemy, this position once in the hands of the Confederates, would have been compelled to make a precipitate retreat, which would have degenerated into a rout. Thus was lost the second opportunity.

In the meantime Ewell, who was to attack at the first sounds of Longstreet's guns, was in anxious expectancy, and when at length, after this irritating delay, the welcome signal to move forward was heard Ewell immediately put his troops in motion, preceded by a cloud of skirmishers.

The ground over which Johnson's Division moved was rough enough at first, but became much rougher after it had crossed Rock Creek and struck the wooded hill, known as Culp's Hill. Here immense rocks and bowlders were encountered, which greatly retarded the progress of the troops, and darkness came on, and no enemy save a few skirmishers had been encountered.

The regiments comprising Steuart's Brigade were assigned the following positions in line: Third North Carolina on the right; Second Maryland, Thirty-seventh Virginia, Twenty-third Virginia and Tenth Virginia, the First North Carolina being held in reserve. Finding that he was inclining too far to the left, General Steuart moved obliquely to the right, which movement brought the Third North Carolina and Second Maryland face to face with the enemy behind a line of log breastworks, and these two regiments received their full fire at very short range, for, owing to the darkness, the breastworks could not be seen ; at the same moment the Third North Carolina and Second Maryland received an enfilading fire from Green's New York Brigade, which was posted in an angle of the works, about three hundred yards to the right. The balance of Steuart's Brigade was on the other side of the ridge, and was not exposed to the fire at all. To make matters still worse, the First North Carolina, which was marching in reserve, believing they were being fired upon by the enemy, opened fire, by which a number of men in the two right regiments were killed and wounded.

The Second Maryland and Third North Carolina were staggered for a moment by the enemy's fire, but, quickly recovering, pressed forward and drove the enemy out of the works.

By this terrific fire in front and flank Lieutenant-Colonel James R. Herbert fell wounded in three places, and the Third North Carolina and Company A, on the right of the Second Maryland and commanded by Captain William H. Murray, suffered severely.

In describing the part taken by the Second Maryland Infantry in the battle of Gettysburg after the fall of Lieutenant-Colonel Herbert and the capture of the breastworks, the author will present it more in the form of a personal narrative, as he believes thereby it can be better understood and made more interesting to the reader :

After the fall of Colonel Herbert, finding myself in command of the regiment, I immediately threw the three left companies, commanded by Captains Torsch, Stewart and Crane, over the breastworks, at right angles with it, and, sheltered by the immense rocks, I was thereby enabled in a measure to open an enfilading fire upon the enemy in the angle, although we had but the flashes of their guns to guide our fire. That there were no troops in our immediate front I was convinced. Therefore, having acquired some knowledge of the country in my youth, and knowing the Baltimore turnpike was but some four or five hundred yards distant, I ordered Captain John W. Torsch to take one of his most reliable men and feel his way through the darkness until he reached the turnpike, unless he encountered the enemy in the meantime. This Captain Torsch did, and reported to me that he had been so close to the turnpike that he was able to see the wagons in motion. This satified me that we were not only on their flank, but in the rear of the enemy's right. This information I imparted to General Edward Johnson in person a very short time after.

In the meantime the three left companies kept up a steady fire, and I knew from the frequent cries to " cease that firing ; you are shooting your friends ! " that it was doing some execution.

Meanwhile a heavy body of troops were assembling in my front, and several officers and men came into my lines by mistake, and I learned from them that the breastworks we occupied had been thrown up by Geary's Division the day before, but that Geary had been called over to the left to assist in repelling Longstreet's attack, leaving but the brigade of Green in the works.

Upon the angle above spoken of Johnson made a direct assault and was repulsed with heavy loss. He could easily have flanked it, leaving a regiment or two to keep Green in the angle, and, moving down the enemy's flank, could have taken his line in reverse before the return of Geary. But, then, General Johnson was not a Stonewall Jackson, and the opportunity was allowed to pass unimproved.

Fearing a sudden attack, I returned the three left companies to the breastworks, where the men of the Third North Carolina and Company A were falling every minute from the deadly fire of the enemy in the angle. Had the brigade been moved a hundred yards to the left over the ridge, all could have been sheltered, and many a life saved. But these brave men were kept in their exposed position and needlessly slaughtered.

Until 11 o'clock in the night the firing continued steadily, and after that time it broke out fitfully until daylight, when it was renewed with redoubled fury, for during the night reinforcements to Green numbering many thousand men had assembled in front of Johnson's Division.

To add to the horrors of the situation a battery or two opened upon the division at short range, and most of their shells fell among the men of Steuart's Brigade, who were compelled to closely hug the ground behind the breastworks for protection. A more terrible fire men were never subjected to, and it was a miracle that any escaped.

In describing this fierce struggle for the possession of Culp's Hill the historian Bates says :

What a field was this ! For three hours of the previous evening, and seven of the morning, had the most terrible elements of destruction known to modern warfare been wielded with a might and dexterity rarely ever paralleled. The woods in which the battle had been fought was torn and rent with shells and solid shot and pierced with innumerable minnie balls. Trees were broken off and splintered, and that entire forest, where the battle raged most furiously, was, on the following year, leafless, the stately but mute occupants having yielded up their lives with those whom they overshadowed.

And speaking of the state of the hill on the 4th :

We came upon numberless forms clad in gray, either stark and stiff, or else still weltering in their blood. . . . Turning whichever way we chose, the eye rested upon human forms lying in all imaginable positions. . . . We were surprised at the accuracy as well as the bloody results of our fire. It was, indeed, dreadful to witness.

About 8 o'clock on the morning of the 3d I made my way to the right of the battalion to see how it was faring. Company A had suffered dreadfully, and I found Captain Murray much distressed over the slaughter of his men. The Third North Carolina, being still more exposed than Company A, was almost annihilated, and Colonel Parsely informed me he had but nineteen men left, and, as he spoke, one of them fell dead in Captain Murray's lap. " And now," said the gallant Parsley, " I have but eighteen."

To add to our difficulties, the men were almost out of ammunition, but a noble spirit promptly responded to their call, and Lieutenant R. H. McKim, aide to General Steuart, started off through the dreadful fire, and safely returned with the much-needed supply.

At the request of Captain Murray, I took the responsibility of allowing him to withdraw his men a short distance, and shelter them behind some rocks, for a few minutes' rest. He had not been gone over ten minutes when the gallant Captain George Williamson, acting Adjutant-General of the brigade, came up and ordered me to move my battalion by the left flank, file to the right, and unite with the right of the Virginians, formed in a strip of wood. I saw in an instant the object of the movement, and told Captain Williamson " it was nothing less than murder to send men into that slaughter-pen." Captain Williamson agreed with me, and, moreover, said that General Steuart strongly disapproved of it, but that the order from General Edward Johnson was imperative.

Sending for Captain Murray, I imparted the order to him, and directed him to take his place in line. Having great confidence in Captain Murray, and knowing the veteran material of which his company was largely composed, and he being the Senior Captain, I assigned him to the command of the right of the battalion, believing I could better control the comparatively raw companies on the left in our desperate undertaking ; but, as subsequent events proved, the new men fought as gallantly as the veterans.

Filing to the left, and then to the right, all the companies of the battalion but two crossed a stone fence running parallel with the log breastworks, and about one hundred yards distant. The companies on the left of the stone fence formed on the edge of the woods, but on emerging from its cover had a field to cross without any shelter whatever, whilst the two companies on the right of the stone fence were sheltered by the woods throughout the whole charge. On our left were the three Virginia regiments and the First North Carolina.

The line being formed, I passed along the front of the battalion and observed the expression on many faces to see if the men realized the gravity of the situation. If they did they betrayed no weakness, but to the contrary seemed eager to be led forward. It was a dreadful moment, the moment before the order was to be given that would usher so many souls into eternity.

CHARGE OF MARYLAND INFANTRY (C. S.), GETTYSBURG, JULY 3D, 1863.

Presently there was heard from the right a voice, clear and distinct, and a command many of us had heard and obeyed before. It was that of the gallant Steuart. "Attention! Forward, double-quick! March!" At a right-shoulder shift the little battalion started forward to meet death and defeat. But ten feet of woods intervened before the left companies of the Second Maryland and the Virginia regiments and First North Carolina came into the field and were exposed to the view of the enemy strongly posted in the woods less than two hundred yards off. The woods uncovered the men of the regiments on the left of the Second Maryland and they threw themselves upon the ground, and despite the pleadings and curses of their officers refused to go forward. Never shall I forget the expressions of contempt upon the faces of the men of the left companies of the Second Maryland as they cast a side glance upon their comrades who had proved recreant in this supreme moment. But the little battalion of Marylanders, now reduced to about three hundred men, never wavered nor hesitated, but kept on, closing up its ranks as great gaps were torn through them by the merciless fire of the enemy in front and flank, and many of the brave fellows never stopped until they had passed through the enemy's first line or had fallen dead or wounded as they reached it. Three hundred Marylanders and eighteen North Carolinians charging a strong position defended by three brigades!

But flesh and blood could not withstand that circle of fire, and the survivors fell back to the line of log breastworks, where they remained several hours, repulsing repeated assaults of the enemy, until ordered by General Johnson to fall back to Rock Creek.

General Steuart was heartbroken at the disaster, and wringing his hands, great tears stealing down his bronzed and weather-beaten cheeks, he was heard repeatedly to exclaim: "My poor boys! My poor boys!"

In this disastrous charge the noble Murray was killed, and being wounded myself the command devolved upon the next ranking officer present, the veteran Torsch.*

Ah! it was a sad, sad day that brought sorrow to many a poor Maryland mother's heart.

Some years after the battle of Gettysburg the author was going over the field in company with Colonel Batchelder, the Government historian. Arriving at the point where the foremost of the men of the Second Maryland had fallen, Colonel Batchelder said he would tell me an incident related to him by a Federal officer who had assisted in repulsing

---

* In the "Maryland Line" published in 1869, by an oversight the author said Captain Crane the ranking officer, after the fall of Murray, took command of the battalion when it fell back to the breastworks on the morning of the 3d. Captain Crane became separated from his command in some manner during the charge, and did not immediately rejoin it.

the charge. He said that officer told him one of the members of the Second Maryland Infantry fell wounded within a few feet of his men. After his comrades were driven back he was seen to raise himself in a sitting position and deliberately proceed to load his gun. Perceiving this, the Federal officer directed some of his men to shoot the wounded Confederate should he attempt to fire upon them. After having reloaded his gun the brave fellow exclaimed: "I will die before you shall make me a prisoner!" and placing the muzzle of his gun to his head he pressed the trigger with the ramrod and blew his brains out. Whose mother's brave son was this?

The casualties in the Second Maryland were frightful during the two days, and many of the wounded were left behind when the army fell back.

The following is a list of killed and wounded, as near as can be ascertained:

FIELD AND STAFF.

WOUNDED.

Lieutenant-Colonel James R. Herbert, seriously.
Major W. W. Goldsborough, seriously.

COMPANY A.—Captain William H. Murray.

KILLED.

Captain William H. Murray.

Privates.

Bruce, William.
Hardesty, John W.
Iglehart, James, Jr.
Kennedy, Arthur.
Lloyd, C. T.
McIntyre, George W.
Morrison, Wilbur.
McCormick, Henry A.
Nicholai, Herman.
Starlings, George C.
Windolph, John H.

WOUNDED.

First Lieutenant George Thomas, severely.
First Sergeant William J. Blackistone, severely.
Sergeant James W. Thomas, severely.
Corporal Charles E. Maguire, severely.

Privates.

Bond, John, slightly.
Bowley, Willam H., mortally.
Barry, Philip, slightly.
Braddock, Charles S., slightly.
Bolling, Wallace, severely.
Bolling, Thomas B., severely.
Carey, James E., slightly.
Chandler, William S. J., mortally.
Clayville, Moses, severely.
Davis, Jacob N., severely.
Edelin, William J., slightly.
Freeman, Bernard, severely.
Fulton, Alexander, slightly.
Gardiner, William F., severely.
Glenn, Samuel T., slightly.
Hanson, Notley, slightly.
Hopkins, Samuel J., severely.
Howard, D. Ridgely, severely.
Hollyday, Lamar, dangerously.
Ives, Leonard W., mortally.
Klemkiewiez, T. A., severely.
Loane, W. T. V., slightly.
Lowe, W. E., severely.
Laird, William H., slightly.
Lake, Craig, severely.
Marney, John, dangerously.
Pindell, Philip, mortally.
Sanderson, Frank H., mortally.
Sollers, A. J., slightly.
Steele, Charles H., severely.
Thelin, William T., severely.
Trail, Charles M., severely.
Trippe, Andrew C., severely.
Williams, John P., dangerously.
Zollinger, Jacob E., severely.

CAPTURED.

Emory, Albert.
Hubball, Bernard.
Luchesi, David H.
Peregoy, James A.
Smith, H. Tillard.

⚜

COMPANY B.—Captain J. Parran Crane.

KILLED.

Sergeant Thomas S. Freeman.   Private Warren F. Moore.

WOUNDED.

Second Lieutenant James H. Wilson, severely.
Sergeant Francis Z. Freeman, slightly.
Corporal George Hayden, mortally.
Corporal Thomas Simms, severely.
Corporal William F. Wheatley, slightly.

Privates.

ALVEY, JAMES P., severely.
CHUNN, JOHN H., slightly.
COMBS, EDGAR, slightly.
DELOZIER, THOMAS J., seriously.
FENWICK, ALBERT, slightly.
FORD, HENRY, slightly.
HAYDEN, JOHN A., severely.
KEECH, JAMES H., severely.
MAGILL, THOMAS F., slightly.
MILSTEAD, JOSEPH H., slightly.
SIMMS, WILLIAM H., severely.
TURNER, HENRY, severely.
TURNER, WILLIAM L., slightly.
WEBSTER, JAMES R., dangerously.
WILLS, JOHN W., severely.
WILLS, JAMES A., severely.

COMPANY C.—CHARLES W. HODGES COMMANDING.

KILLED.

FIRST SERGEANT ROBERT H. CUSHING.

Privates.

DUVALL, DANIEL.
DAVIS, MICHAEL.
DULANEY, JEREMIAH.
KENNEY, BERNARD.
O'BYRN, JOHN T.
PAYNE, BENJAMIN.
LANHAM, BENJAMIN L.
McWILLIAMS, JAMES.

WOUNDED.

SECOND LIEUTENANT JOSEPH W. BARBER, mortally.
SECOND LIEUTENANT THOMAS H. TOLSON, slightly.
SERGEANT GEORGE PROBEST, severely.
CORPORAL BEALE D. HAMILTON, mortally.
CORPORAL JAMES A. LAWSON, mortally.

Privates.

ANDERSON, SAMUEL, mortally.
CLOUGH, ROBERT H., slightly.
DUVALL, TOBIAS, seriously.
EDGAR, THOMAS, mortally.
HAMILTON, SAMUEL H., slightly.
HAMMOND, EDGAR, mortally.
HAMMOND, CHARLES, slightly.
McGENA, JOHN, severely.
McCANN, WILLIAM V., seriously.
NASH, JAMES, mortally.
NICHOLS, WILLIAM L., mortally.
STEELE, FRANK K., severely.
SKINNER, WILLIAM H., slightly.
SHIPLEY, WILLIAM A., severely.
WHITE, JOHN G., slightly.

CAPTURED.

Corporal Edward A. Welch.

Privates.

Dawson, Robert M.
Mulliken, Walter.

Storm, Francis E.
Schultz, Justus.

COMPANY D.—Captain Joseph L. McAleer.

KILLED.
Privates.

Brown, James A.
Kerns, Cornelius.

WOUNDED.

Sergeant William Jenkins, slightly.   Corporal Joshua Owings, mortally.
Corporal Emmett M. Webb, mortally.

Privates.

Green, Lewis, severely.
Hays, John, slightly.
Hines, Thomas J., seriously.
Killman, Richard G., slightly.

Lipscomb, Philip, slightly.
O'Brien, James H., severely.
Septer, John H., severely.
Watts, William, slightly.

CAPTURED.
Privates.

William Hogarthy.   John Lamb.

COMPANY E.—Captain John W. Torsch.

WOUNDED.

First Lieutenant William J. Broadfoot, mortally.
Sergeant P. M. Moore, mortally.
Corporal John Cain, slightly.
Corporal James Reddie, severely.

Privates.

Barry, Michael, severely.
Byus, Charles E., severely.
Brown, John, severely.
Brandt, Alexander, slightly.
Fallon, James, slightly.
Fallis, Edward, severely.
Halbig, J. S., severely.
Lemates, James, severely.
Martin, John N., slightly.
Moran, William P., severely.
McGee, Daniel, slightly.
Roberts, Frank, severely.
Radecke, Herman H., severely.
Sullivan, John, severely.
Wilkinson, William A., slightly.

CAPTURED.

Michael Burke

COMPANY F.—Captain Andrew J. Gwynn.

KILLED.

Henry G. Taylor.

WOUNDED.

Captain Andrew J. Gwynn, slightly.
Second Lieutenant John G. Hyland, slightly.
First Sergeant Nicholas J. Mills, severely.
Sergeant Joseph S. Wagner, severely.

Privates.

Anderson, Leroy, slightly.
Clagett, George H., slightly.
Clagett, J. W., slightly.
Doyle, Philip, severely.
Dunnington, Lemuel, slightly.
Dement, Benjamin F., severely.
Hodges, Benjamin, slightly.
Holden, Robert, severely.
Knott, Minion F., severely.
Keepers, Alexis V., slightly.
Polk, Samuel, severely.
Thompson, John W., slightly.
Wagner, R., severely.

COMPANY G.—Captain Thomas R. Stewart.

KILLED.

Second Lieutenant William C. Wrightson.

Privates.

J. S. Littleford.   J. H. Gossom.   W. B. Cator.

WOUNDED.

Captain Thomas R. Stewart, severely.
First Lieutenant James A. Davis, slightly.
Corporal J. Edward Briddell, severely.

Privates.

Abbott, James, severely.
Adkins, S. E., slightly.
Breslin, E. W., mortally.
Boyles, Daniel, slightly.
Clarke, Charles A., severely.
Fentswait, J. R., mortally.

Fountain, W. B., mortally.
Robbins, William, slightly.
Twilly, Benjamin F., severely.
Tingle, D. B. P., severely.
Vickers, W. A., severely.
Woolford, J. L., slightly.

CAPTURED.

Privates.

L. H. Weaver.   Ross Messick.

General Thomas P. Kane, of the Second Pennsylvania Brigade, says in his official report of the engagement :

"At 10.30 o'clock the enemy made their last determined effort by charging in column of regiments. Their advance was Steuart's Brigade of Johnson's Division. The First Maryland Battalion (Confederate States) left most of their dead in line with our own. It cannot be denied that they behaved courageously."

General Kane little knew — and would have been ashamed of the fact — when he penned that report that instead of a charge in "column of regiments" upon him and the masses of troops supporting him, that there were no Confederates to receive their fire but three hundred Marylanders, who alone constituted the "charge in column of regiments." Yes, "they behaved courageously."

General John W. Geary, who commanded the division attacked, says:

"At 10.25 o'clock two brigades of Johnson's Division, having formed in column of regiments, charged upon our line on the right. They met the determined men of Kane's Brigade, which poured into them so continuous a fire that when within seventy paces their columns wavered and soon broke to the rear. The First Maryland Battalion (rebel) was in the advance, and their dead lay mingled with our own."

No greater tribute could be paid the little Second Maryland Infantry. Three hundred brave men, magnified into two brigades closed in "columns by regiments," charging into a division! And yet "their dead lay mingled with our own." Truly, to mingle the dead of the Second Maryland with the Federal dead is the best evidence that the noble fellows charged to the very muzzles of the guns of the enemy, where they died.

Surely, the present generation of Marylanders, and the countless generations to come, should be proud of the valor displayed by their forefathers in this, the fiercest battle of the great Civil War.

But it was not only at Gettysburg, but in many battles before, and many battles afterward, that the same sublime courage and devotion to the cause was made manifest by Maryland's sons.

CHAPTER III.

During the afternoon of the 3d, the Second Maryland was ordered back to the line of Rock Creek, followed by the enemy's skirmishers, but at a respectful distance, and the casualties were consequently few. The Northern historians, without exception, assert that Steuart was driven out of the works at the point of the bayonet, and so do the official reports of some of the Federal commanders. There never was anything farther from the truth, and it is very much like that story of the battalion " charging in column of regiments." The fact is, the brigade remained in the breastworks captured from the enemy on the evening of the 2d until ordered back by General Edward Johnson on the afternoon of the 3d, when it retired deliberately to Rock Creek, where some little skirmishing occurred at long range.

The brigade held its position on Rock Creek until about midnight, when it moved to the right, and by daylight it had formed line of battle in the rear of Seminary Hill.

This position was held all day of the 4th, and the skirmishers of the Second Maryland were on the outskirts of Gettysburg, where they remained until the retreat began.

About 2 o'clock on the morning of the 5th of July the command took the road leading to Monterey Springs, Johnson's and Rodes' Divisions bringing up the rear of the army.

But we had enough of the dreadful in the last chapter, and it is unnecessary to give a detailed account of the suffering and misery endured by the heroic survivors of the Army of Northern Virginia during their return march through the rain and mud and darkness until Hagerstown was reached. And still these men were cheerful to a degree that could hardly have been expected under the trying circumstances surrounding them, and they felt the loss of comrades left behind torn and bleeding on that bloody field at Gettysburg more than they did their own sufferings. Their sufferings were mental, more than physical. They had, it is true, fought a drawn battle when they should have won one, but that could be evened up by winning the next one, and they were made happy when at length, on July 11, the vicinity of Hagerstown was reached, and General Lee formed his line of battle, this time on ground of his own choosing, and threw down the gauntlet to General Meade. So far that General had only *followed* the Confederate Army. No *pursuit* had been attempted except by his cavalry, which contented itself with raids upon the wagon trains, and, although Lee marched leisurely, General Meade marched more leisurely. Between Hagerstown and

Sharpsburg, however, General Lee hoped to bring on an engagement. The position he chose was not really a strong one, nothing like so strong as that held by Meade at Gettysburg, but General Lee — and so did his army — felt confident of administering a crushing defeat to Meade could he be induced to attack.

General Lee here issued the following order, which set the army wild with enthusiasm:

HEADQUARTERS ARMY OF NORTHERN VIRGINIA, July 11, 1863.

General Orders No. 16.

After long and trying marches, endured with the fortitude that has ever characterized the soldiers of the Army of Northern Virginia, you have penetrated to the country of our enemies, and recalled to the defenses of their own soil those who were engaged in the invasion of ours. You have fought a fierce and sanguinary battle, which, if not attended with the success that has hitherto crowned your efforts, was marked by the same heroic spirit that has commanded the respect of your enemies, the gratitude of your country, and the admiration of mankind.

Once more you are called upon to meet the enemy from whom you have won, on so many fields, names that will never die. Once more the eyes of your countrymen are turned upon you, and again do wives and sisters, fathers and mothers, and helpless children, lean for defense on your strong arms and brave hearts. Let every soldier remember that on his courage and fidelity depend all that makes life worth having, the freedom of his country, the honor of his people, and the security of his home. Let each heart grow strong in the remembrance of our glorious past, and in the thought of the inestimable blessings for which we contend; and, invoking the assistance of that benign Power which has so signally blessed our former efforts, let us go forth in confidence to secure the peace and safety of our country. Soldiers, your old enemy is before you. Win from him honor worthy of your right cause, worthy of your comrades dead on so many illustrious fields.

R. E. LEE, *General Commanding.*

For three days General Lee held his army in line of battle, and during these three days he resorted to every means in his power to bring on a general engagement, but in vain. General Meade had had enough, and contented himself with watching and waiting for Lee to move on, when he, too, would resume the monotonous march to the Potomac and slowly follow the Confederate Army into Virginia.

At length, on the evening of the 13th, disgusted with Meade's timidity, General Lee left his position, and on the 14th recrossed the Potomac.

On the 18th of the previous month (June) the Second Maryland Infantry had crossed this same river under vastly different circumstances, and the fact was remarked more than once during the passage across. Then it was a battalion five hundred strong ; now it was a skeleton of its former self, three hundred of those composing it then having been left behind in an inhospitable country, dead, wounded and prisoners ; then it crossed amid joyous shouts and joyous songs, now not a word is spoken, for all are too busily thinking, and wondering whether the events of the past few days are not the imaginations of a disordered brain. But such are the fortunes of war.

On July 15th, the battalion, in conjunction with the rest of the brigade, proceeded in the direction of Martinsburg, and thence to Darksville, where it remained until the 20th, when it was ordered to tear up the Baltimore and Ohio Railroad tracks in the vicinity of Martinsburg, which work was pretty thoroughly accomplished for a considerable distance. Thence the brigade marched to Winchester on its way to Orange Court House, crossing the Blue Ridge Mountains through Thornton's Gap.

Reaching Orange Court House on the 1st of August Steuart's Brigade proceeded to take the rest they so much required after the hardships of the two months that had passed, and soon the Maryland boys had recovered their old spirits and longed to be avenged for the disappointment they had suffered in not having been permitted to spend the summer, at least, among their friends across the Potomac.

The camp near Orange Court House was pleasant enough. It is true, there were drills, guard mounts, and policing, but the Maryland boys did not shirk either. The members of the old First who were in the Second knew too well General Steuart's peculiar ideas about the latter duty, and the other members of the battalion who had not before had the opportunity to see "Big Injun" in his element were not long in discovering the fact that a slovenly man or a dirty street incurred his displeasure for all time. The result was that in the Second, as in the First, the men heartily seconded General Steuart's efforts in their behalf. It was not only his love for a clean camp, but a desire to promote the health and comfort of his men that made him unyielding in the enforcement of sanitary rules. You might influence him in some things, but never in this.

About August 23 an inspection was held preparatory to a grand review by Generals Lee and Ewell. The inspection was very rigid, and greatly were the members of the Second Maryland pleased when, after it was over, it was officially announced that they had carried off the first honors in the division.

The grand review by Generals Lee and Ewell took place a few days later, on which occasion General Edward Johnson remarked to General Lee, as the battalion passed, in beautiful line, division front, with Mike Quinn's drum corps at its head : "General, they were as steady as that at Gettysburg." General Lee also honored the battalion by taking off his hat as its right got within saluting distance, and remained uncovered until it had passed. He was proud of the little command, and he more than once expressed himself to that effect. He felt for them in their exile, for they were not citizens of a seceded State, and their self-sacrifice won his admiration and excited his sympathy.

The latter end of August, 1864, the strength of the battalion was augmented by the arrival of Company H, commanded by a Captain Callan. This company had been enlisted for the cavalry, but was for some reason assigned to the Second Maryland Infantry, because Callan and his men claimed to be Marylanders. This was not a fact. There were few of them who had ever been in the State, and with some exceptions they were a bad lot. But the battalion soon got rid of Captain Callan and his Lieutenants, and for awhile the company was commanded by Sergeant Thomas O'Brien, an old United States soldier, and a good man. By the time Hanover Junction was reached later in the season the undesirable element had taken their departure, and what remained did good service. In February of the following year Lieutenant J. Thomas Bussey, of Company D, was elected to the command of the company.

CHAPTER IV.

The weeks had now rolled around in this pleasant camp near Orange Court House, and the army was rested and in fine condition to take the field, and the men longed once more to measure strength with the enemy. The ranks of the different regiments had been recruited by the return of absentees and convalescent wounded and sick, and the army again bore a strong resemblance to that which had marched so proudly into the enemy's country earlier in the year. Their old foe, with whom they had parted at Williamsport, were not far off, and it seemed to be but a little while when the two armies would again be brought face to face.

On the 14th of September the troops were startled by hearing the long-roll beat. The enemy were reported to be advancing in force beyond Orange Court House, but after marching two or three miles in that direction it was discovered that the alarm was occasioned by the enemy making a cavalry reconnoissance in force, but they were easily driven back by the Confederate cavalry which they encountered.

After this incident, which had served to do a little "limbering up," Johnson took up a position on the Rapidan, and covered Merton's Ford: and here the brigade remained until October 8.

In the meantime Longstreet's Corps had been sent to Tennessee, leaving those of Ewell and Hill to confront Meade. General Lee had planned an attack upon that General somewhat similar to that brilliant movement against Pope at the second Manassas, but unfortunately he had not a Jackson to carry out his daring conception, and it failed.

To accomplish successfully this well-conceived plan to administer to the enemy a crushing blow, Ewell was to make a detour of some seventy miles so as to get in the enemy's rear, whilst Hill was to attack him in front, having but fifteen miles to march. Ewell moved slowly in the direction of Culpeper Court House, and leaving that place to the right he crossed Hazel River and struck the Warrenton turnpike at Jeffersontown, and thence moved to the Rappahannock, where a portion of his forces had a slight skirmish. The corps then moved along the Warrenton pike, through Warrenton, until it had reached within five miles of the old battle-field of Manassas. Thence Johnson's Division marched to Bristow Station, where a sharp fight ensued, but without material results. The enemy had taken the alarm and retreated within his strong fortifications at Centreville.

For the failure of this short campaign General A. P. Hill was much blamed, and narrowly escaped a court-martial. Upon this occasion, at least, General Hill moved too cautiously, and neither did General Ewell perform the task allotted to him with that vigor essential to insure success. Some severe fighting ensued, however, and about three thousand prisoners were taken, and much of the Manassas Gap Railroad destroyed, but otherwise little was accomplished where a great victory was within the grasp of the Army of Northern Virginia. General Lee was much disappointed at the result.

Johnson remained in the vicinity of Bristow Station for two days, busily engaged in destroying the railroad, when he fell back to Brandy Station and went into camp.

Here, on October 22d, the long-looked-for order was received detaching the Second Maryland from Steuart's Brigade, and transferring it to the command of Colonel Bradley T. Johnson, who had been ordered by General Lee to assemble the Maryland Line, and picket the line on his flank from the White House to Kent Court House, and protect his communications with Richmond, with his headquarters at Hanover Junction, where the bridges over the North and South Anna Rivers were of vital importance to him.

On the 2d of November the battalion took the cars at Brandy Station, and arrived at the Junction next day.

Although the men had suffered great privations in the long and arduous campaign of the summer, they left the front with many regrets; but they still earnestly hoped to see the Maryland Line assume respectable proportions, and they now believed the time had come when it would.

On arriving at Hanover Junction the battalion was at once set to work building winter quarters, and in a short time a well-arranged and beautifully-located camp for infantry, artillery and cavalry was completed, and for the first time since leaving the Valley of Virginia the different arms of the Maryland Line were united and camped together.

In addition, also, to the Second Maryland Infantry, First Maryland Cavalry and Baltimore Light Artillery, the strength of the Line was here augmented by the assignment of the First Maryland Artillery, Captain William F. Dement, and the Fourth Maryland (Chesapeake) Artillery, Captain W. Scott Chew.

The field and staff of the Maryland Line as now organized was as follows:

Colonel commanding, Bradley T. Johnson; Captain George W. Booth, A. A. G.; Captain Wilson C. Nicholas, Assistant Inspector-General; Major Charles R. Harding, A. Q. M.; Major George E. Kyle, A. C. S.; Surgeon Richard P. Johnson, Medical Director; Lieutenant A. C. Trippe, Ordnance Officer; the Reverend Mr. Duncan, Chaplain.

The strength of the different commands also began to increase by the return of convalescents and by reason of the order granting the privilege to Marylanders in other commands to be transferred to the Maryland Line. Of the latter, unfortunately, there were few, and in the effects of this order there was a disappointment, but there were nevertheless some transfers, and of very superior men, as a general thing.

Having located and thoroughly cleared and policed the site for their camp, the men of the Second Maryland next turned their attention to the building of their cabins, and by the 1st of December this work was completed.

But there was something else to be done. A chapel for religious worship was to be built, and in this work Mrs. Bradley T. Johnson and her sister, Miss Saunders, took the liveliest interest. And what would not the boys of the Second Maryland do for the ladies, and for Mrs. Johnson in particular, whom they all loved so well? They might have built a chapel, for they were God-fearing men, but it would have been a rude affair compared to the neat little structure built under the supervision of these ladies.

Episcopal services were held in the chapel for the first time on the 17th of January by the Chaplain, Reverend Mr. Duncan, and on the 31st Reverend Mr. Peterkin came up from Richmond and entertained the boys with an impressive sermon, taking for his text: "What Shall I Do to Be Saved?"

It was here at Hanover Junction, on the 20th of January, that it was determined to call the battalion the Second Maryland Infantry, as it had been known up to that time as the First Maryland Battalion, although the reader will observe that the author has persisted in speaking of it as the Second Maryland Infantry throughout this work.

The winter was delightfully passed at Hanover Junction. Various were the methods resorted to by the boys to pass the time. Several parties, balls and concerts were given, and one of the latter, for the purchase of a library, netted five hundred dollars.

As considerable snow fell during the winter, snowball battles frequently took place between the infantry and cavalry, in one of which a flanking party of the infantry carried off the colors of the cavalry — the first instance on record where infantry outflanked cavalry.

But spring was growing apace, and all knew that another active summer's campaign would soon be inaugurated. It, therefore, behooved them to recruit their ranks as much as possible. Captain John W. Torsch was sent to Charleston, South Carolina, in hopes of inducing many of the Marylanders there in South Carolina regiments to consent to a transfer, but every obstacle was thrown in his way to prevent it, though, indeed, but few of the men themselves seemed to desire to be transferred, as they were satisfied where they were. General Beauregard and his chief of staff, General Jordan, violently opposed these transfers, saying that the Marylanders in the service of the State of South Carolina were too valuable to part with. Under these discouraging circumstances, Captain Torsch returned to the command without having accomplished much.

Soon after the return of Captain Torsch from his unsuccessful mission to South Carolina it was proposed by Colonel Bradley T. Johnson to mount the Second Infantry, and Lieutenant Zollinger and William Smith ran the blockade and went to Baltimore to raise the necessary funds for that purpose. They soon secured $25,000 from the patriotic citizens of Baltimore, and they then started to return to their command by different routes. Lieutenant Zollinger returned in safety, but Smith, who had the money, was captured and came near being hanged as a spy. Thus this scheme came to naught.

On the 1st of May, 1864, what with recruiting, transfers and return of wounded and prisoners, the Second Maryland numbered 325 men present for duty. The command was in fine condition, and ready and anxious to take the field at a moment's notice.

The enemy was becoming restless, and the batteries of Dement and Chew were sent to the front, and never again seen with the other commands of the Maryland Line, after a sojourn with them of nearly a month. Indeed, it was but a few days when these, too, were widely separated, and never again brought together, from which time the Maryland Line existed only in name.

To all who followed the fortunes of the constituent parts of the old Line in the subsequent campaigns, and observed how magnificent a spirit of bravery, and dash, and fortitude they displayed in the battles which followed each other in such quick succession it will always be a matter of profound regret that their scattered rays of glory could not have been gathered to one focus. The war covered a wide area, and was waged by armies of such magnitude that the deeds of small bodies, however meritorious, could not affect the general result sufficiently to engross the public attention. The multiplicity of details in the formation of an army like the Army of Northern Virginia fatigues the mind, and one finally fixes his attention only upon the larger units — divisions or brigades, at least. The smaller bodies, regiments, battalions and companies, upon whose individual efforts the character of the whole depends, are sure to be neglected, and thus the smaller units are robbed of the credit due them. It was from a knowledge of this fact that the promoters of the Maryland Line urged the expediency of assembling all the Marylanders in the Confederate service in one body; but as this failed it became the duty of all who had the honor of their State at heart to make the best of the situation and endeavor to reflect all the credit possible upon the old and honored State of Maryland through the small commands sent across the border. The unprejudiced historian will say that in this Maryland's sons were successful to a degree certainly gratifying to those at home who followed them throughout the long and bloody struggle with the keenest interest.

On the 8th of May the Second Maryland broke camp at Hanover Junction, around which lingered so many pleasant memories, and took position to cover the bridges over the North and South Anna Rivers, and thus keep open General Lee's communication with the South, from which he received most of his supplies. Colonel Johnson had before gone off with the cavalry, and was closely watching that of the enemy.

A few days after, General John C. Breckinridge moved up with his division, when the Second Maryland was assigned to his command, but remained an independent command, being attached to no brigade. General Breckinridge established his line along the Virginia Central Railroad, his left at Hanover Junction and his right extending toward Hanover Court House.

General Breckinridge seemed much pleased at having the little battalion assigned to his command, and complimented them highly upon their neat and soldierly appearance, thanks again to the good offices of Mrs. Bradley T. Johnson.

About the 20th of May General Lee had fallen back on the line of the South Anna, and at the same time the enemy advanced a corps across the North Anna, occupying position on the plantation of Major Thomas Doswell.

Here they were attacked and driven back with heavy loss. During the time they remained there, however, a Federal Maryland regiment on picket called to some of Hays' Louisianians, who were in front of them, that they would like very much to meet the Second Maryland Confederate Regiment. This coming to the ears of the boys they sent a committee of officers to wait upon General Breckinridge with the request that they take the place of the Louisiana regiment and be allowed to give the Federal Maryland regiment a little brush. This request the General refused to grant.

Soon after General Breckinridge moved his command toward Hanover Court House, passing through and going into camp a few miles from that point on both sides of the railroad leading to Richmond.

And here the boys were for awhile, until their identity was discovered, subjected to a good deal of ridicule, for as the old Army of Northern Virginia came along the neat and cleanly uniforms they wore attracted the attention of the veterans: "Go home, you nice little soldiers; we're here now!" "Oh! don't he look purty!" "Nice little Richmond soldiers, wear good clothes, don't you!" "Go home, boys, and tell Mammy Mars Bob's boys are right down here, and they won't let you git hurt, son," etc.

But presently their jibes were turned to cheers of welcome. "Hold on, thar, boys; them ain't melish, them's the Murlanders; how are you, old Murland?" and another, "Hurra for old Murland;" "Have you j'ined us again? Sure 'nuf; come along; Mars Bob's waitin' for you." So from being unmercifully ridiculed the boys were wildly cheered by these heroes of the old Army of Northern Virginia, with whom they were soon once more to unite in the bloody battles of the campaign already opened.

As the Army of Northern Virginia gradually fell back in the direction of the old battle-field of Gaines' Mill, or Cold Harbor, the battalion was daily under fire, and a number of the men were wounded, but none seriously.

On the evening of the 2d of June General Lee had formed his line of battle upon the historic field of two years before. It was here the First Maryland won fame, and it was here that the Second was to prove itself a worthy successor of the First. The battle fought in June, 1862, was one of the most desperate of the war, and the one in June, 1864, was no less bloody, but in the latter the loss of the enemy was appalling, whilst that of the Confederates was insignificant. In the first the Confederates assumed the offensive, in the latter it was the Federals. As a distinguished Southern officer said soon after the battle: "Cold Harbor was not war; it was murder;" and was it a wonder, then, that Grant's troops, after repeated repulses, in which they saw their comrades slain by thousands, refused finally to renew the unequal contest? The indomitable Grant well said it was the only battle he ever fought that he regretted having made. In this, as in all the battles that he fought with Grant, General Lee's superior genius was apparent. From the time he crossed the Rapidan with an army so overwhelming in numbers that a speedy termination of the war seemed imminent, Grant had been foiled in his every attempt to march direct upon Richmond, and his repulses had been repeated and bloody.

In this engagement the Second Maryland was assigned a position in reserve some three hundred yards in rear of a salient held by Edgar's battalion of Echols' Virginia Brigade of Breckinridge's Division.

It was midnight of the 2d of June when, after much countermarching, the battalion halted and the men were ordered to lay upon their arms to await any emergency. They were tired, for they had marched many weary miles in the past few days, and the strain to which they had been subjected had been fearful. No wonder, then, they slept soundly, and their awakening was rude and rather unexpected. From where they lay wrapped in their blankets they were sheltered somewhat from the direct fire of the enemy owing to a rise in the ground in their front, but not so from a flank fire on their left, where a body of Federal troops held a position on higher ground. Between the Second Maryland and the salient held by Echols' troops was a dwelling and outhouses which somewhat obscured their view of the salient, where eight pieces of artillery were in position. In the rear of the Marylanders, some three or four hundred yards was Finnigan's Brigade of Floridians, which had been engaged in throwing up a reserve line of works, to be used in case any disaster should occur at the first.

It will thus be seen that the position assigned the Second Maryland was a most responsible one, and one well calculated to put them to their mettle should anything befall Echols. And that very same came to pass, and proved that

General Breckinridge was not in error when on placing them where he did he should observe : " This is a most important position, and I feel I can intrust it to that battalion." And how well he was justified in that confidence daylight of that morning proved.

Captain J. Parran Crane was at this time in command of the battalion and Captain John W. Torsch was next in command. Captain Crane gave his immediate attention to the right, while Captain Torsch looked after the left.

Before daylight on the morning of the 3d the enemy began a skirmish fire, but this did not arouse the sleeping men. A few arose and folded their blankets, but the majority of them slept on. But what did these few early risers see? Through the dim mist they saw what appeared to be a heavy skirmish line of Echols' command running back on their left front. Then a body of men came forward and halted and clustered around the dwelling and outhouses already referred to and then opened fire upon the Marylanders still in their blankets, and many of them were thus shot while they slept. Who were these men who had so suddenly aroused them from their slumbers ? Certainly they could not be of the enemy, for was not Echols in their front. By this time the men were in line, ready to obey any command ; but there was the dread uncertainty as to whether the early morning visitors were friend or foe, and no order was given. Private Charles H. Weems, of Company A, familiarly known as " Buck " Weems, and who was conspicuous for the big straw hat he wore that day, suddenly exclaimed : " I see the gridiron, boys ; let's charge 'em," and at the same moment Captain John W. Torsch, down on the left, called out : " It is the enemy — Charge ! " but even before he gave the command the men were in motion ; Weems on the right had started them, and without an instant's hesitation they dashed forward upon the enemy. The dwelling and outhouses between them and the salient were soon reached and here was found a swarm of Federals, who had broken through the salient by a sudden attack and advanced as far as the buildings. Although in overwhelming numbers, these were quickly driven back, with heavy loss, by the furious onset of the Marylanders. Onward the gallant battalion rushed until they reached the salient, there also to find a large force of the enemy who had manned the guns, double-shotted, and who were about to turn them upon their assailants. The conflict was brief, but terrible ; it was hand to hand ; the artillery was wrested from the Federals, and they were driven out of the salient at the point of the bayonet. Lieutenant Charles B. Wise, of Company B, called for volunteers to man two of the guns. In an instant men drilled in the artillery service during the winter at Hanover Junction had them in charge, and they were belching forth canister into the mass of fleeing men who but a few minutes before were exulting in their successful assault upon the Confederate lines. Then, and not until then, had Finnigan been able to get up, when the works were once more fully manned, and the disaster that had threatened Breckinridge was averted. The recapture of the works was solely due to the Second Maryland. Finnigan's Brigade contributed no more to the result than the moral support of its presence.

It was a splendid achievement, and one of which every man who participated might well feel proud.

General Breckinridge, after the charge, in a glow of enthusiasm, exclaimed: "I knew I could trust those men!" and General Lee, in his official report of the battle, complimented the battalion upon its behavior.

From other sources, also, the battalion was spoken of in terms of praise, as the following communication in the *Richmond Sentinel* fully proves:

NEAR RICHMOND, June 6, 1864.

Mr. Editor:

The public have already been informed, through the columns of the public journals, of the general results of the late engagements between the forces of General Lee and General Grant. But they have not yet learned the particulars, which are always most interesting, and in some instances, owing to the confusion which generally attends large battles, they have been misinformed on some points. It is now known by the public that the enemy were momentarily successful in one of their assaults on the lines held by Major-General Breckinridge's Division, which might have resulted in disaster to our cause.

It will be interesting to all to know what turned disaster into victory, and converted a triumphant column into a flying rabble. The successful assault of the enemy was made under cover of darkness, before the morning star had been hid by the light of the sun. They came gallantly forward in spite of a severe fire from General Echol's Brigade, and in spite of the loss of many of their men, who fell like autumn leaves, until the ground was almost blue and red with their uniforms and their blood. They rushed in heavy mass over our breastworks. Our men, confused by the suddenness of the charge, and borne down by the rush of the enemy, retreated, and all now seemed lost. At this juncture the Second Maryland Infantry were roused from their sleep. Springing to their arms, they formed in a moment, and, rushing gallantly forward, poured a deadly fire into the enemy and then charged bayonet. The enemy were, in turn, surprised at the suddenness and vim of this assault. They gave back — they became confused. General Finnegan's forces coming up, they took flight; but not until nearly a hundred men were stretched on the plain, from the fire of the Second Maryland Infantry, and many others captured. Lieutenant Charles B. Wise, of Company B, now took possession of the guns, which had been abandoned by our forces, and with the assistance of some of his own men and some of General Finnegan's command, poured a deadly fire into the retreating enemy.

Thus was the tide of battle turned, and this disaster converted into a success. I am informed that the whole force of the enemy which came within our lines would have been captured had it not been for the mistake of an officer who took the enemy for our own men, and thus checked for a few moments the charge of the Second Maryland Infantry. I take pleasure in narrating these deeds of our Maryland brethren, and doubt not you will join in the feeling.

A VIRGINIAN.

Considering the desperate fighting which took place within the fifteen minutes required to retake the salient, and the severe artillery and musketry fire to which the battalion was subjected during the remainder of the day, even though the men were sheltered behind the works they had recaptured, their loss was not so heavy as might have been expected out of about four hundred men. Appended is a list of casualties :

COMPANY A.—CAPTAIN GEORGE THOMAS COMMANDING.

KILLED — Privates William H. Hollyday, Henry C. Owens.
WOUNDED — Alexander Fulton, mortally; Thomas O'Brien, severely; Frederick Hoerster, slightly; William Hoffman, severely; John C. Henry, slightly; Thomas D. Harrison.

COMPANY B.—FIRST LIEUTENANT JOHN H. STONE COMMANDING.

WOUNDED — First Lieutenant John H. Stone, severely; Privates James R. Herbert, severely; Rinaldo J. Moran, slightly; A. W. Neale, slightly.

COMPANY C.—CAPTAIN FERD DUVALL COMMANDING.

WOUNDED — Second Lieutenant Thomas H. Tolson, severely; Privates William H. Clagett, severely; C. S. Ford, severely; Henry Loughran, slightly; R. B. Willis, severely.

COMPANY D.—FIRST LIEUTENANT JAMES S. FRANKLIN COMMANDING.

KILLED — Private James Hurley.
WOUNDED — Second Lieutenant S. Thomas McCullough, severely; First Sergeant Thomas C. Butler, severely; Abram Phillips, severely.

COMPANY E.—CAPTAIN JOHN W. TORSCH COMMANDING.

KILLED — Private Charles E. Byus.
WOUNDED — Captain John W. Torsch, severely; First Sergeant Samuel Kirk, severely; Privates Levi G. Dawson, slightly; William Wilkinson, mortally; Joseph Smith, slightly.

COMPANY F.—Captain A. J. Gwynne Commanding.

KILLED — Lemuel Dunnington.
WOUNDED — Captain H. A. Gwynne, slightly; Sergeant R. F. Muirhead, severely; Privates Andrew Cretin, slightly; Hillary Cretin, slightly; Bernard Dooley, slightly; Alexis V. Keepers, slightly.

COMPANY G.—First Lieutenant G. G. Guillette Commanding.

KILLED — William S. Reed.
WOUNDED — Private Michael Hines.

COMPANY H.—Captain J. Thomas Bussey Commanding.

WOUNDED — Maurice Ward, severely; William Hardy, slightly.

WAITING IN LINE OF BATTLE.

CHAPTER VI.

For several days after the battle of Cold Harbor the enemy was comparatively quiet, and contented himself with keeping up a heavy artillery fire. Grant had had enough of Cold Harbor, and was looking about him to find means to extricate his army from the unfortunate position into which he had led them.

On the 6th of June, much to the regret of the battalion, Breckinridge's Division was ordered to report to General Early in the Valley of Virginia. Gladly would the battalion have accompanied him, for it was believed that Early intended the invasion of Maryland. A communication was sent to General Lee asking that the battalion be not detached from General Breckinridge, or at least that they be sent to General Early's command at all events. To this General Lee made the following reply:

HEADQUARTERS, July 19, 1864.

Communication respectfully returned. General Early is now in the Valley of Virginia. The object of this application cannot now, therefore, be accomplished. Should an opportunity occur for gratifying the wishes of this brave battalion, it will be remembered.

R. E. LEE, *General.*

After the departure of General Breckinridge the battalion was assigned temporarily to Frye's Brigade, Heth's Division, A. P. Hill's Corps, and their position changed to some distance to the rear and right, where it was held in reserve.

On June 13th the battalion was marched to White Oak Swamp, where it was sent out to skirmish with the enemy, and soon became hotly engaged. In this encounter John G. Wagoner, of Company A; Lewis H. Viet, of Company C, and William H. Calhoun, of Company G, were killed.

Except marching and countermarching, picket duty, throwing up earthworks, etc., nothing of importance transpired until the 18th, when the battalion was marched to Drewry's Bluff, where it crossed the James River on a pontoon bridge, and halted below Port Walthall Station, in Chesterfield County, after a hot and dusty march of over twenty miles. Taking the train some distance below Port Walthall, the battalion rode four or five miles, when they were again compelled to march to within a mile of Petersburg, where on the north side of the Appomattox River they threw up breastworks for their protection.

The Second Maryland was now fairly in the trenches around Petersburg, where they were destined to spend so many weary months of privation and suffering. The battalion had been tried at Winchester, at Gettysburg and at Cold Harbor, but never before had it been called upon to undergo the terrible hardships that day and night duty in the trenches entailed. Without shelter from the weather, half-starved, they were subjected to a steady fire from the enemy every hour of the twenty-four, and were called upon from time to time to come forth from the partial protection their earthworks afforded from the shot and shell of the enemy and fight vast odds in the open field. And still under all these trying conditions there was but one desertion from the ranks of the battalion, whereas from others there were hundreds. This fact was well known to their division commander, and even to those higher in authority, and it was no wonder, then, that they were called upon to perform more than their share of outpost duty. If the men of the battalion felt proud of their achievements at Gettysburg and Cold Harbor, they had yet other laurels to win at Peebles Farm, the Weldon Railroad and Hatcher's Run, of which they were equally as proud.

During the time they occupied the trenches many of their number were stricken down. On August 9th John Parker, of Company H, was wounded; August 12th James Abbott, of Company G, who had served in the old First from the first Manassas, was severely wounded, it being the sixth time since his enlistment. Richard T. Anderson, of Company C, was wounded at the same time; and on the 15th George Langford, of Company G, was severely wounded.

By August 15, 1864, Grant had assembled 110,000 men around Petersburg, and this immense army was held in check by a force under General Lee of 36,000 men. After the failure of Burnside's mine, Grant abandoned the idea of further direct attack, and spent the autumn and part of the winter in attempting to extend his left around Petersburg, and in efforts to pierce the Confederate lines north of the James.

On August 16 a movement was made from the direction of Deep Bottom upon the works at Chafin's Bluff, which failed, and another movement, in which the Second Maryland became interested, was made on August 18 for the purpose of getting possession of the Weldon Railroad, over which supplies came for General Lee's army.

On the morning of the 18th the Fifth Corps reached a point about five miles southwest of Petersburg, and about one mile east of the Weldon Railroad. Warren, in command, upon reaching this point proceeded to throw out skirmishers, which soon came in contact with Deering's Brigade of Cavalry, which for some hours stubbornly disputed the Federal advance. Deering was finally forced back to within a mile or two of Petersburg, when A. P. Hill suddenly fell upon Warren and drove him back, with heavy loss. In the meanwhile General Griffin had been sent with a portion of the Fifth Corps to seize the railroad, which he did, and immediately proceeded to intrench himself.

On the afternoon of the 19th General Lee sent Heth's and Mahone's Divisions of Hill's Corps to drive Warren back. A vigorous attack was made upon Warren, and he retired from his advanced position, but was not dislodged from the railroad. After the close of the fight the Confederates withdrew to their main line, when Warren next day occupied the ground he had lost.

The above is by way of introduction to the following interesting account, by a member of the battalion, of the part taken by the Second Maryland in the first day's engagement:

Thursday, the eighteenth day of August, 1864, found the Second Maryland Infantry, then attached to Archer's Brigade, Heth's Division, A. P. Hill's Corps, bivouacked in a little valley about one hundred yards wide, the hills on either side crowned with a few stately pines, and a bold stream coursing through the centre. We had only a short time before been relieved from the trenches, and were congratulating ourselves on the prospect of rest. Near midday we heard the boom of artillery away around on our extreme right; then slowly and solemnly another boom, and then another. Soon the drum beat the "assembly." "Right face! Forward! March!" was the command, and off we went to the Weldon Railroad. The whole column marched southward on the track. A piece of artillery unlimbered in the road and fired down it, betokening danger ahead. We soon filed off to the left, Davis' Brigade to the right, and formed a line on either side and at right angles to the railroad. In a short time the two brigades received orders to advance. As we emerged from the woods the view that presented itself was an open space, nearly level, about half a mile wide, with a forest on the southern side. When half across the enemy commenced firing. Onward we moved, our line being bent like a bow, the Second Maryland well up in front. When scarcely two hundred yards from, and in the immediate front of the enemy's line of battle, we came to a lane with a fence on either side.

We climbed these fences in the face of the enemy's fire, and why they did not ruin us I have never been able to understand. Still we pushed on, firing all the time. As we entered the woods we came upon fifty or sixty killed and wounded in our battalion front. We drove the enemy back easily, and advanced several hundred yards into the woods. On the enemy threatening our flanks, we fell back to the line from whence we had first driven them. The enemy attempted to charge us, but a few well-directed volleys drove them back.

While this attack was being made a new brigade was brought up. and lay down in our rear. We felt proud as we heard their officers say to their men, as they pointed to us: "Look how these men are standing up to their work!" After this attack had been repulsed we moved to our left to the support of our skirmish line, which had been holding the enemy's line of battle in check. We remained there until 8 or 9 o'clock, when we left our skirmish line and fell back to Petersburg. We had but three brigades engaged, and the enemy a much larger force, as they overlapped our flanks.

The night was dark and damp. We kindled our fires, roasted our corn, and lay down on our wet wrappings for a night's rest.

But severe as was the first day's fight on the Weldon Railroad, the little battalion was to go through a still more trying ordeal the next day, when more of the heroic band, already reduced to a handful of brave men, were to disappear from its ranks, alas! many of them forever.

On that day (August 19) General Lee determined to make another attempt to regain possession of the Weldon Railroad. Again it was a portion of A. P. Hill's Corps that was ordered to the attack. The route taken on the 19th was the same as that of the day before, and through a drenching rain the troops moved steadily to meet the enemy. Line of battle was formed just as it had been on the 18th, and upon nearly the same ground. Breastworks more numerous now, even, and stronger than the day before, were to be stormed. The ground was unfavorable for attack, and it was apparent to all that the day was to see some hard fighting, with but little prospect that success would crown the Confederate arms.

Skirmishers were thrown out and the heavy line of battle moved forward to meet the enemy. It was not long before the irregular fire of the skirmishers in front gave warning that the work had been cut out. "Forward, double-quick!" was the command, and the line of battle swept on with beautiful precision, and the enemy in heavy masses were met on the edge of the wood. The spattering fire of the skirmish line had now changed to one continuous roar of musketry, and brave men on both sides fell by hundreds. The enemy was driven back, and the first line of works were soon in the hands of the Confederates. Archer's Brigade, to which was attached the Second Maryland, captured the second and afterward the main line of works, but the supports on the left were unable, or, through someone's blundering, did not get to the breastworks where the little brigade was battling with an overwhelming force. For an hour this unequal contest was waged, when Colonel Christian in command of the troops in possession of the fort ordered the Second Maryland to be thrown obliquely to the right and form line, which movement had hardly been performed when the enemy came on in heavy force, with bayonets fixed and not firing a shot. The battalion poured a heavy fire into them, which staggered them for an instant, but they still pressed on until they had reached the fort. Here a hand-to-hand conflict ensued, the Confederates on the inside trying to retain, and the Federals on the outside trying to regain possession of the fort. But this unequal contest could not long continue, for the Federals soon swarmed into the works, where for awhile the fight was continued, the survivors then trying to fight their way out. Some succeeded, but one-third of that gallant band of Marylanders lay dead and wounded or were prisoners in the hands of the enemy.

Many were the noble spirits who fell in those two days of desperate fighting, among them Adjutant J. Winder Laird. Thus a comrade speaks of him:

"On that day, too, J. Winder Laird, our heroic Adjutant, tall and handsome in figure, and not less perfect in character, fell, shot through the brain. We would not leave him to be insulted by the foe. Pearson, Gill, Ridge Howard and Grayson placed his body on their guns and hurried off to the Davis house on the railroad. Here they dug his grave, and each of us, taking a blanket from his scanty store, wrapped it about our dead comrade, and so buried him. Soon the guns of the enemy reopened, and we returned to the front."

Appended is a list of the killed, wounded and captured in the two days' battles:

BATTLE OF WELDON RAILROAD.

Captain J. Parran Crane Commanding.

FIELD AND STAFF.

KILLED — Adjutant J. Winder Laird.

WOUNDED — Captain J. Parran Crane, received a severe contusion.

COMPANY A.—First Lieutenant Clapham Murray Commanding.

KILLED — Private Jacob W. Davis.

WOUNDED — Lieutenant William P. Zollinger, slightly; Corporal Willis Brannock, slightly; Privates J. E. Fitzgerald, slightly; John C. Henry, severely; N. Heenan, severely; D. Ridgely Howard, severely; George W. Marden, slightly; Sommerville Sollers, slightly; Richard C. Tilghman, severely; Joseph I. Joy, severely.

CAPTURED — First Lieutenant Clapham Murray, First Sergeant James F. Pearson, Sergeant James W. Thomas, Privates William Adair, Charles S. Brannock, J. R. Phelps, Theophilus N. Deale, William J. Edelin, H. L. Gallagher, James S. Raley.

COMPANY B.—First Sergeant C. Craig Page Commanding.

KILLED — First Sergeant C. Craig Page.

WOUNDED — Sergeant P. T. Reeder, slightly; Corporal J. Z. Downing, severely; Privates Dyonisius Ball, severely; John H. Chum, slightly; J. J. Delozier, slightly; J. Marion Freeman, slightly; Washington Page, severely; Henry Turner, slightly.

CAPTURED—Sergeant F. Z. Freeman, Corporal W. F. Wheatley, Private James F. Keech.

COMPANY C.—First Lieutenant Charles W. Hodges Commanding.

KILLED — Sergeant Robert T. Hodges.

WOUNDED — Privates Daniel Duvall, severely; H. H. Crawford, slightly; John G. White, slightly.

CAPTURED — Corporal Edward A. Welch, Privates Theodore Cooksey, W. C. Gibson, John C. Miller, Robert H. Welch.

COMPANY D.—First Lieutenant James S. Franklin Commanding.

WOUNDED — Privates John Johnson, slightly ; Philip Lipscomb, slightly.

CAPTURED — First Lieutenant James S. Franklin, Sergeant William Jenkins, Privates John Lynch, William Killman.

COMPANY E.—First Lieutenant William R. Byus Commanding.

WOUNDED — First Lieutenant William R. Byus, severely ; Privates S. M. Byus, slightly ; Thomas McLaughlin, severely ; James Hanley, severely ; Elisha Butler, severely.

CAPTURED — Sergeant George L. Ross, Corporal John Cain, Privates James Lamates, John L. Stansbury, John Cantrell, John Grant, James Applegarth.

COMPANY F.—First Lieutenant John W. Polk Commanding.

WOUNDED — Private Josiah T. Boswell, severely.

CAPTURED — Sergeant Joseph L. Wagner, Corporal J. T. Brown, James H. Dixon.

COMPANY G.—Lieutenant G. G. Guillette Commanding.

KILLED — John D. Edelen.

WOUNDED — Private Martin L. Rider, slightly.

CAPTURED — Lieutenant G. G. Guillette, Sergeants Daniel A. Fenton, George W. Manning, Algernon Henry, Corporal Benjamin F. Twilly, Privates William L. Brannock, W. L. Etchison, Levi Wheatley.

COMPANY H.—Captain J. T. Bussey Commanding.

WOUNDED — Captain J. T. Bussey, severely ; Private William Hargy, slightly.

CHAPTER VII.

After the battles of the 18th and 19th of August on the Weldon Railroad the brigade, or what was left of it, returned to Battery No. 37, and for weeks were constantly engaged on the fortifications and in manning the trenches.

On September 2d the Second Maryland was withdrawn from the trenches and placed three miles west of Petersburg, between the Weldon and Southside Railroads, forming a part of the force designed to oppose movements of the enemy's left. The battalion remained here for several weeks employed in building a series of earthworks to cover the exposed left flank and rear of General Lee's army. Among this series of works thus constructed was a strong hexagonal fort upon the farm of Dr. Peebles, within a short distance of the Squirrel Level road. This fort it was hoped the brigades of Archer and Walker were destined to man, and the men felt confident of their ability to hold it against a much superior force. But such was not to be the case, for on the 30th of September Archer's Brigade was ordered to the Star Fort, situated about half a mile to the right of Petersburg, at which point Lee was concentrating troops in anticipation of an attack. And it was made that day in overwhelming force. It was simultaneous on both flanks — the expedition of Hancock north of the James, which resulted in the capture of Fort Harrison, was followed by that of Warren, who attacked with four divisions of infantry and one of cavalry, and they swept the handful of artillerists who had been left in charge of the strong defenses built by Archer and Walker, and they carried everything before them. The strong fort which had cost these brigades so much labor was wrested in a moment, and with little defense. Hancock, the splendid soldier that he was, continued his movement and made his success complete. He had gained a strong position, from which he felt confident of dealing sledge-hammer blows upon his antagonist, and in this he made no mistake. Hancock had made these achievements before. He overrun Johnson's Division at Spottsylvania, and achieved the only success that can be accredited to Grant's " On to Richmond," though he was unfortunate at Cold Harbor, as were all of the other subordinate commanders of General Grant.

When Warren's movements were made known to General Lee, Archer's Brigade was ordered back to the position they had occupied, and General Heth formed his command in the rear of the main line of Confederate works, with the view of assaulting and recapturing the position the enemy had carried.

It might be well to describe the positions held by the opposing forces prior to inaugurating a battle of unusual severity.

The two lines were almost parallel. Half way between the contending forces was a large open field, and on the left of this opening was Pegram's house, and as the battle was fought principally upon Pegram's farm it should properly be called the battle of Pegram's farm, as Peebles' farm was some hundreds of yards distant, but in this case, as in many other battles of the war, usage and not facts is conformed to. Beyond the open field mentioned was a long stretch of swampy woods, and at the farther side and extreme edge of the woods was a deep ravine, but beyond this the ground arose to a considerable elevation, and here was the line of works constructed by the enemy, and which was the objective point of General Heth's attack.

The Confederates advanced as follows: First, a thin line of sharpshooters; next, a brigade of Virginians; then the Second Maryland and Thirteenth Alabama, First, Seventh and Fourteenth Tennessee, in the order named; following came Davis' Mississippi Brigade, and upon the extreme right McGowan's South Carolina Brigade.

The South Carolinians were the first to encounter the enemy as they dashed across the open space in magnificent order, and lost heavily, but carried the point of works in their front.

The Second Maryland plunged into the woods and crossed the swampy ground. Emerging from the woods into the open they were greeted with a heavy fire from the enemy's skirmishers, but, supported by the Thirteenth Alabama, they brushed aside the skirmishers and attacked his line of battle posted deep in the woods, and soon had possession of the enemy's outer trenches, but unfortunately the left held back from some unaccountable reason, and these troops in advance were placed in a difficult and dangerous position, and were subjected to as terrible a fire of musketry and artillery as any they had ever experienced. But tenaciously did the Marylanders and Alabamians hold on to the position gained, with the enemy but a few feet above their heads. Many were killed and wounded by the artillery and musketry fire, among the latter Captain Ferd. Duvall, who was in command of the Second Maryland, when the command devolved upon Captain John W. Torsch. This desperate state of affairs existed from 5 o'clock in the evening until midnight, during all of which time the contending forces were but a few feet apart. At length, after seven hours in the enemy's trenches, Captain Torsch withdrew his command and sought the works which they had left in the morning.

In a measure General Heth's attack was not a success, although he inflicted heavy loss upon the enemy in killed and wounded, and brought off four hundred prisoners. But Heth determined to make one more effort to regain the lost position, and an attempt was to be made to gain Warren's right and rear, and thus compel him to retire.

After an hour's rest, the Second Maryland was marched across the country toward Petersburg. The point to be attacked was not over half a mile away, but to reach which it was necessary to make a detour of over five miles. It was a most tedious march, owing to the crowded condition of the road, and the fact that it was made in the night, and it was not until 6 o'clock in the morning (October 1) that Heth reached the point from which he intended to deliver his attack upon Warren's right and rear.

A rest of a couple of hours was first necessary, when the battalion formed line of battle in readiness to advance.

At length the command was given, and in beautiful order the battalion moved forward under a heavy fire, drove the skirmishers from the works in their front, crossed the felled timber and entered the woods. Continuing obliquely to the right, through the woods, after crossing the Squirrel Level road the battalion was run into by Stone's Mississippi Brigade, which was moving up obliquely at a brisk pace, and it was thrown into considerable confusion.

However, this was but momentary, as the battalion formed again speedily behind some buildings upon the right of the road, and opened fire upon the line of breastworks in their immediate front.

All day long did Heth wrestle with the enemy, but in vain. His position was a strong one, and he outnumbered Heth two to one.

At night the whole Confederate force withdrew, when the Second Maryland returned to the trenches they had occupied previously, having suffered in the two battles (Peebles' farm and Squirrel Level road) a loss of fifty-three men in killed and wounded, a terrible loss out of less than three hundred men, and it attests the desperation with which the battalion charged and fought during those trying two days.

Following are the lists of casualties at Peebles' farm and Squirrel Level road :

BATTLE OF PEEBLES' FARM.

CAPTAIN FERDINAND DUVALL COMMANDING.

WOUNDED — Captain Ferdinand Duvall, severely.

COMPANY A.—CAPTAIN GEORGE THOMAS COMMANDING.

KILLED — Corporal S. Pinckney Gill, George Deatore.
WOUNDED — Captain George Thomas, severely ; Second Lieutenant William P. Zollinger, slightly ; Privates John Goodwin, severely ; Frederick Huster, severely ; William A. Hance, slightly.
MISSING — Private William H. Hubbard, supposed to have been killed.

COMPANY B.—Second Lieutenant Charles B. Wise Commanding.

KILLED — Private John H. Junger.
WOUNDED — Sergeants John G. Barber, slightly; Whittingham Hammett, slightly; Privates Robert Beall, severely; Charles J. Foxwell, slightly.

COMPANY C.—Sergeant George Probest Commanding.

KILLED — Private Richard T. Onion.
WOUNDED — Sergeant George Probest, slightly; Privates William Grace, severely; Thomas L. Mitchell, severely.
CAPTURED — Private John T. White.

COMPANY D.—Sergeant Isaac Sherwood Commanding.

WOUNDED — Privates David Hammett, slightly; W. Beale Owings, severely; John Spence, severely.
MISSING — Philip Lipscomb.

COMPANY E.—Sergeant William Heaphy Commanding.

WOUNDED — Corporal Benjamin F. Amos, severely; Privates John Keppleman, severely; Michael Noonan, severely.
CAPTURED — Private Martin O'Hallon.

COMPANY F.—Captain A. J. Gwynne Commanding.

KILLED — Private Abel Hurley.
WOUNDED — Captain A. J. Gwynne, slightly; Privates John H. Claggett, severely; John W. Claggett, slightly; Thomas J. Webb, severely; Hillary Cretin, severely.

COMPANY G.—Second Lieutenant George Brighthaupt Commanding.

WOUNDED — Lieutenant George Brighthaupt, mortally; Corporal William Lord, severely; Private Robert Mumford, slightly.
CAPTURED — Sergeant Michael Hallohan, Privates Jesse Waters, Michael Elligett.

COMPANY H.—Corporal Patrick Heenan Commanding.

KILLED — Corporal Patrick Heenan.
WOUNDED — Private Edward Welch, severely.

BATTLE OF SQUIRREL LEVEL ROAD

❦

CAPTAIN JOHN W. TORSCH COMMANDING.

COMPANY A.—SERGEANT CHARLES E. MAGUIRE COMMANDING.

WOUNDED — Private William T. Bailey, severely.

COMPANY B.—SECOND LIEUTENANT CHARLES B. WISE COMMANDING.

WOUNDED — Private William Herbert, mortally.

COMPANY C.—CORPORAL C. M. CLAYTON COMMANDING.

WOUNDED — Privates John M. Blumenauer, severely; Charles Hammond, severely; Frank Wheatley, mortally.

COMPANY D.—SERGEANT ISAAC SHERWOOD COMMANDING.

WOUNDED — Sergeant Isaac Sherwood, severely.

COMPANY E.—SERGEANT SAMUEL KIRK COMMANDING.

WOUNDED — Privates John Brown, severely; William Gwynn, slightly.

COMPANY F.—SERGEANT JOHN W. POLK COMMANDING.

WOUNDED — Charles A. Hoge, mortally.

COMPANY H.

WOUNDED — Private James Powers, slightly.

While the events just narrated were transpiring on General Lee's right, others of no less importance were taking place on his left. Grant had evidently begun to appreciate the fact that Lee's army was numerically much inferior to his own, and stung to the quick at the many repulses he had met with since he crossed the Rapidan, he determined upon a more aggressive course. His successes at Peebles' farm and Squirrel Level road had convinced him that he should avail himself more frequently of his vast preponderance of numbers, and thus by attrition accomplish what he never could accomplish by strategy. In Lee's hands, with anything approaching the proportions of an army under his command, Grant was but a pigmy, and well he knew it. Attrition, therefore, was henceforth to be the policy of the Federal commander, and in this he showed his wisdom, but it was an unmilitary one, and cannot reflect creditably upon his reputation as a great military chieftain. Grant, therefore, began to pinch Lee harder wherever it was possible. He captured Fort Harrison, a work of much importance, and one which Lee in vain attempted to recapture.

Slowly, but surely, the Confederate Army was dwindling away. Hundreds of desertions were occurring every day, and the inevitable was not far off. Men were starving, and were naked in the trenches. The sufferings of the poor fellows were beyond endurance. Their families were appealing to them for relief; their wives and children were at home reduced to gaunt spectres, and these appeals caused many a brave man, who had faced the enemy upon a hundred bloody battle-fields, to leave his comrades and wend his way to his desolate home. Their excuse was that all was over, and now they had a sacred duty to perform in protecting their loved ones. To some this seemed akin to desertion, but there certainly was some justification for the act.

These numerous desertions entailed additional duties upon the Second Maryland. It had been reduced to little more than two hundred men, but these two hundred men were expected to do the duty of a regiment. So far but one desertion had occurred from its ranks, and that was the only one that ever did occur. They were, therefore, kept almost constantly upon picket duty, for the Marylanders could be trusted where others could not be.

Thus the weary, dismal winter passed slowly away. There had been during that time some welcome visitors to the camp of the Second Maryland, and among them Colonel George P. Kane, of Baltimore. He was shocked at the condition of the men, and he was moreover surprised at their cheerfulness under such trying circumstances. When he left the boys he promised them each a new uniform and a change of underclothing. He kept his promise, and on the 4th of March, 1865, they arrived. Many a "God bless you, Colonel Kane," went up from those poor boys as they threw aside the miserable rags in which they were clad and donned their comfortable suits.

But to go back a few weeks: February 5, 1865, was a memorable day in the annals of the Second Maryland. About 10 o'clock of that day the brigade, now under command of Colonel William McComb, was moved to the right near Hatcher's Run, where it joined heavy bodies of troops. At 3 o'clock P. M. the whole force crossed their breastworks, and passing over a broad open space between the two picket lines, and obliquely to the right, entered a swampy woods, where the enemy's skirmishers were encountered and driven into their works some distance beyond.

The Second Maryland held the centre of the attacking line and advanced to within twenty yards of the enemy's fortifications — nearer than any other troops in the column, but the brigades to the right and left fell back, leaving McComb's command in a precarious position. The order was given to lie down, though many of the men of the Second Maryland availed themselves of the numerous stumps to keep up the fire. It was here that Lieutenant Charles W. Hodges, of Company C, acting Adjutant, was shot through the head and instantly killed. In the death of Lieutenant Hodges the battalion lost one of the best officers it had ever had. A Christian gentleman, kind to all, and fearless in the discharge of his duty, he was universally beloved.

The first attacking column having failed to make any impression upon the enemy's works, Evans was ordered up with his division, but he, too, failed, as did Mahone, when at nightfall McComb fell back to the works from which he had started. Again were the Confederates unsuccessful in their offensive operations against the enemy's strong works.

Following is a list of casualties in the Second Maryland at the battle of Hatcher's Run:

COMPANY A.—LIEUTENANT W. P. ZOLLINGER COMMANDING.

WOUNDED — Private Benjamin R. Jennings.

COMPANY C.

KILLED — First Lieutenant Charles W. Hodges, Acting Adjutant.

COMPANY F.—FIRST SERGEANT THOMAS O. HODGES COMMANDING.

KILLED — Corporal Washington Martin.

COMPANY G.—CORPORAL HENRY A. MUMFORD COMMANDING.

KILLED — Frederick A. Wingate. *   WOUNDED — Private John G. Davis.
MISSING — Corporal Henry A. Mumford.

COMPANY H.—ATTACHED TO COMPANY G.

KILLED — Private James O'Brien.

---
* Frederick A. Wingate was a volunteer in the fight, his time having long expired, but he would not ask for his discharge, which he could have received, but he preferred to remain with his Company.

CHAPTER VIII.

It was the latter part of March, and General Lee determined to put into execution, if possible, a plan that he had long before resolved upon. That he could no longer remain at Petersburg was becoming every day more painfully evident. Grant with his overwhelming army, now further augmented by the arrival of Sheridan with ten thousand cavalrymen, was fast closing in upon Lee. Could the latter but unite with Johnston, then moving through North Carolina, something might be done. The war was becoming enormously expensive to the North, owing to the vast armies it was necessary to keep in the field, and the people were becoming clamorous for peace. Could the war be prolonged one year by uniting the armies of Lee and Johnston, and by skillful manœuvering a crushing defeat could be administered to Grant, a recognition of the Confederacy *might* be effected. It was, indeed, a forlorn hope, but General Lee was not satisfied to surrender his army without making one more effort in a cause for which he and the brave men around him had battled for almost four years.

We will not give here a detailed account of the operations around Petersburg preliminary to its evacuation by the Confederates, but will follow those movements with which the Second Maryland was associated.

On April 1st Captain John W. Torsch, in command of the battalion, received the following order :

HEADQUARTERS McCOMB'S BRIGADE, April 1, 1865.

Captain Torsch, Commanding Maryland Battalion :

Captain :—You will report with your battalion, under arms, at once, at the chapel of General Davis' Brigade.

BY COMMAND OF BRIGADIER-GENERAL WILLIAM McCOMB.

JOHN ALLEN, *A. A. G.*

At 2 o'clock A. M. Captain Torsch repaired to the point designated, where he found three other battalions, and all had been assembled to attempt the recapture of some rifle pits taken from Cook's Brigade several days before.

Before daylight the men were ordered to quietly steal over their own works, and as noiselessly as possible approach the enemy. This was done with suppressed breaths, when at a signal agreed upon the different battalions rushed forward to take the pits in their respective fronts.

The following graphic description of what followed is given the author by Sergeant Daniel A. Fenton of Company G:

In the charge we obliqued slightly to the left, and hit the enemy fairly on his left. They were taken by surprise, and some of them jumped out of the pits and escaped, whilst others were captured and sent to the rear. We at once began to change the front of the rifle pits, using our hands and bayonets to dig the earth and arrange the pits for our defense.

The firing soon ceased and an oppressive stillness prevailed, and we anxiously awaited the coming of daylight. We did not know then that we would still more anxiously await the coming of night.

Slowly daylight began to appear. It never came so slowly before, to our excited imaginations. Had the troops to our right and left been as successful as ourselves? God grant they had. Anxiously we peered to the right and left through the approaching light. Suddenly a voice from one of the boys with brighter vision than the rest of us was heard: "My God; there are the Yanks!" And, sure enough, we were flanked at both ends. The rest of our contingent had utterly failed to take the pits in their front, and we were in "a hole," or, rather a series of holes, sure enough.

As soon as we realized the situation, some of the boys jumped out of their pits and rushed at the enemy so uncomfortably near, and thus we extended our line five or six pits.

A hot fire was at once opened, and kept up at intervals for several hours. About 10 o'clock A. M. our cartridges began to give out, and those who had them to spare threw them from one pit to another.

On looking back at our works about this time we saw they were alive with men, and a good deal of excitement seemed to prevail. And then we could see the muzzles of brass cannon protruding. Surely something was being done for our relief. But we must have ammunition before that relief arrives. "Who will go back to the works and procure it?" is asked by Captain Torsch. "I will, Captain," said Lee Goldsborough, a veteran who never missed a battle in which either the First or Second Maryland were engaged from the first Manassas to Appomattox.

Like a deer, he started on his perilous errand with two haversacks, and rushed into a gully a short distance away. The enemy opened fire upon him the instant he emerged from his pit, but we soon put a stop to that. He was next seen crawling along the ground like an Indian, and then, as the ground was favorable, he would spring to his feet and go like the wind, until at last he reached the works and bounded safely over them.

"But will he get as safely back?" is the question on every lip. "If not we are gone, sure!" After a brief interval his familiar figure is seen to recross the works, dragging something with him. With breathless anxiety we watch him as he takes the same precautions as before for his safety. Sometimes crawling, and sometimes running, he at length sprang into his pit with two haversacks full of cartridges. You should have seen how these cartridges were thrown from pit to pit.

The first words the brave boy uttered were: "Oh! Pshaw! you are not going to be captured; the boys back there will not let them capture you. They can't come out of their fort, for General McComb has brought up all the artillery possible, and will open on them if they show themselves; but he says we must stay here until night!"

Well, we stayed there all day, and that day was four years long. But night came at last — it always does, and you should have seen how the boys crawled out of their holes. And when we got within our works you should have heard that rebel yell!

And what do you think they told us when we got back — and don't you think we should have felt complimented? Well, it seems that when General McComb learned that our little battalion alone had succeeded in carrying that part of the line assigned to them, and that the rest of the attack was a failure, he was much worried. When daylight showed him our dangerous position he at once sent for General Harry Heth (who, by the by, was in command at the time of A. P. Hill's Corps), and upon that General's arrival McComb pointed out the situation in which we were placed. General Heth at once expressed his determination to prevent the capture of the battalion, saying: "Those men are too gallant to allow of it," and he ordered up three batteries to be brought to cover that portion of the picket line we occupied, or, you might say, the rifle pits. These were the guns we had seen, for we had left no artillery in the works.

That we were sleepy, you can rest assured, after our experience, and our sleep was long and restful.

But this detention in the rifle pits all day brought about a disaster that the Second Maryland could ill afford in its then depleted condition. Lieutenant Thomas Tolson had been sent out on picket the day before with thirty-two men. Captain Torsch from his position in the rifle pits could not recall him, as was his intention, and by an attack by the enemy in force Tolson and his command were captured.

At daylight on the morning of April 2, 1865, the battalion was ordered to form. There was an indescribable something in everyone's presence that portended of evil. What could it be? It was true, the soldiers of Lee's army had revolved the situation in their minds more than once, but then as long as "Mar's Bob" was there all seemed right. But "Mar's Bob" could not build up armies without material, and, alas! that once glorious army was fast dwindling away through desertion and casualties.

It seemed to those devoted troops that second day of April morning that the whole Federal Army had been let loose. Everywhere was heard the roar of artillery and the rattle of musketry. That handful of men composing the Army of Northern Virginia was now but a pigmy battling with a giant; and still that pigmy had not been of much greater proportions for many months, and yet the giant had not before ventured an attack along the line. But the end was fast approaching, and the end was as glorious as the beginning.

In this whirl of excitement the Second Maryland seemed to be ubiquitous. It was first ordered here, and then there, and, although its physical strength was not great, the example it set and the moral effect of its prompt and immediate obedience to orders made an impression.

Finally General McComb ordered Captain Torsch to hold a certain line of works, " and I will try to form the brigade on you." It was the last order given the Second Maryland by General McComb. The battalion formed in line, and some of the men (assisted by a few men of the battery) ran two guns of Purcell into position and opened a fire of grape and cannister upon the approaching enemy, then not over three hundred yards distant.

But that avalanche of men pressed on with resistless energy and were soon swarming inside the Confederate works. McComb's Brigade seemed at sea, and the only command intact in it was the Second Maryland. Foot by foot they resisted the encroachment of the enemy ; but such an unequal contest could not long endure. Fiercely the contest waged, and muskets were clubbed and crashed into human skulls, but all in vain. Captain Ferd. Duvall, with Lieutenants Polk, Zollinger, Byus and Wise, with about thirty men, were unable to escape from the works, and were captured. The remainder escaped in two different squads, one under Captain Torsch, and the other under nobody, but the latter, meeting remnants of the Seventh and Fourteenth Tennessee Regiments (a portion of their old brigade)united with them, and made for the north bank of the Appomattox River, which all succeeded in attaining by means of two flat-bottomed boats found along the river.

This remnant of the brigade rested that night after a march of eight or ten miles, and a weary lot they were.

On the morning of the 3d this fragment of a once famous brigade assembled and determined upon some sort of organization. Upon looking over the brave little band of Maryland boys it was discovered that there were twenty-three muskets present, and not a commissioned officer. Who had escaped from that wretched fort was to them an uncertainty ! but it was hoped before the day had passed to ascertain fully the situation in which the battalion was placed. Daniel A. Fenton, of Company G, the ranking non-commissioned officer, but a gallant soldier, then took command. Captain Torsch, however, soon came up, and the weary march continued until that fatal 9th day of April 1865.

But we will not harrow the feelings of the reader by going into details of the sufferings and privations and uncomplainingly endured by those left of the once glorious Army of Northern Virginia. When Amelia Court House was reached and the rations that all had expected to meet there were not found, these famished and footsore men only expressed bitter disappointment, but the thought of giving up the struggle never entered their minds.

Thus from Petersburg to Appomattox they dragged their weary and emaciated bodies, fighting by day and by night the hosts that had enveloped them. But, alas! the end was at hand — the end came.

The scene that ensued when these heroes of so many battles were called upon to lay down their arms can never be described by human pen. Brave men wept like children, and tore their hair in the delirium of their grief, and tears coursed freely down the bronzed cheeks of the great chieftain as he witnessed the affection and devotion of his children.

"Go to your homes and be good citizens," he said to them; but where were those homes to be found? The torch of the incendiary had been there in their absence, and but little had been left. And where were the survivors of the Second Maryland to go? They were denied this poor privilege by the fanatical set in their native State, and wandered for months through Virginia, partaking of the little left her noble people, but that little was freely bestowed.

Following is General Lee's last order to his troops:

HEADQUARTERS ARMY NORTHERN VIRGINIA,
APPOMATTOX COURT HOUSE, April 10, 1865.

General Orders No. 9.

After four years of arduous service, marked by unsurpassed courage and fortitude, the Army of Northern Virginia has been compelled to yield to overwhelming numbers and resources. I need not tell the brave survivors of so many hard-fought battles, who have remained steadfast to the last, that I have consented to this result from no distrust of them, but feeling that valor and devotion could accomplish nothing that would compensate for the loss that must have attended a continuance of the contest, I determined to avoid the useless sacrifice of those whose past services have endeared them to their countrymen.

By the terms of the agreement, officers and men can return to their homes and remain until exchanged. You will take with you the satisfaction that proceeds from the consciousness of duty faithfully performed, and I earnestly pray that a merciful God will extend to you His blessing and protection.

With an unceasing admiration of your constancy and devotion to your country, and a grateful remembrance of your kind and generous consideration for myself, I bid you all an affectionate farewell.

[SIGNED.] R. E. LEE, *General.*

Official:

[SIGNED.] O. LATROBE, *Lt.-Col. & A. A. G.*
[SIGNED.] R. H. FINNEY, *A. A. G.*
[SIGNED.] P. G. JOHNSON, *A. A. A. G.*

To Captain John W. Torsch, Commanding Second Maryland Infantry.

The following extract from General Lee's final report to President Davis announcing the surrender is interesting :

His Excellency Jefferson Davis :
Mr. President :—It is with pain that I announce to Your Excellency the surrender of the Army of Northern Virginia. . . . Upon arriving at Amelia Court House on the morning of the 4th with the advance of the army . . . and not finding the supplies ordered to be placed there, nearly twenty-four hours were lost in endeavoring to collect in the country subsistence for men and horses. This delay was fatal and could not be retrieved. . . . On the morning of the 9th . . . there were 7,892 organized infantry with arms, with an average of seventy-five rounds of ammunition per man. . . . I have no accurate report of the cavalry, but believe it did not exceed twenty-one hundred effective men. The enemy was more than five times our numbers. If we could have forced our way one day longer, it would have been at a great sacrifice of life, and at its end I do not see how a surrender could have been avoided. The supplies ordered to Pamplin's Station from Lynchburg could not reach us, and the men, deprived of food and sleep for many days, were worn out and exhausted.

With great respect, your obedient servant,

R. E. LEE, *General*.

List of officers and men of the Second Maryland Infantry surrendered at Appomattox Court House, April 9, 1865 :

John W. Torsch, Captain Commanding ; William R. McCullough, Adjutant; DeWilton Snowden, Assistant Surgeon ; Edwin James, Quartermaster's Sergeant ; Frank Dement, Sergeant-Major ; F. L. Higdon, Ordnance Sergeant ; M. A. Quinn, Chief Musician ; Charles F. Drewry, Joseph E. Smith, Musicians.

COMPANY A.—Corporal H. Tillard Smith, Privates William J. Edelin, Bernard Freeman, Henry Holliday, John J. Hunter, William H. Laird, William E. Lowe, N. L. Love, John W. McDaniel, Alex. Murray, Edward O'Donovan, Jas. A. Peregoy, Andrew T. Miller.

COMPANY B.—Sergeant Philip T. Reeder, Privates Henry Ford, Thomas Magill, William G. Matthews, John C. Mills, A. W. Neale, F. X. Semmes, James A. Wills. Walter Wood.

COMPANY C.—Corporal B. D. Mulliken, Privates Evans Duvall, Franklin Duvall, J. N. Blumenauer, William H. Clagett, William Grace, Thomas Mitchell, James R. Moog, Peter Orr, Joshua Watts.

COMPANY D.—Sergeants Thomas C. Butler, Isaac N. Sherwood, Privates Samuel B. Dove, R. H. Shepherd.

COMPANY E.—Sergeant Wilbur Rutter, Privates William Gavin, Edward Lawn, Joseph Ridgel, William Unkel, William F. Brawner, James Gardner, Elisha Rutter.

COMPANY F.—Privates G. W. Clagett, G. N. Guy, John O. Hill, A. V. Keepers.

COMPANY G.—Sergeant Daniel A. Fenton, Privates John Callahan, William Pickel, Joseph Manly, William R. Mumford.

COMPANY H.—John Parker.

ROSTER OF THE SECOND MARYLAND INFANTRY.

FIELD AND STAFF.

Lieutenant-Colonel, ... JAMES R. HERBERT.
Major, ... W. W. GOLDSBOROUGH.
Surgeon, ... RICHARD P. JOHNSON.
Assistant Surgeon, ... DEWILTON SNOWDEN.
Assistant Quatermaster, ... JOHN E. HOWARD.
Adjutant, ... J. WINDER LAIRD.
Sergeant-Major, ... WILLIAM R. MCCULLOUGH.
Quartermaster-Sergeant, ... EDWIN JAMES.
Ordnance Sergeant, ... FRANCIS L. HIGDON.
Chief Musician, ... MICHAEL A. QUINN.

COMPANY A.

WILLIAM H. MURRAY, *Captain.*
GEORGE THOMAS, *Captain.*
CLAPHAM MURRAY, *First Lieutenant.*
WILLIAM P. ZOLLINGER, *Second Lieutenant.*
WILLIAM J. BLACKISTON, *First Sergeant.*
JAMES F. PEARSON, *Sergeant.*
JAMES W. THOMAS, *Sergeant.*

EZEKIEL S. DORSEY, *Sergeant.*
WILLIAM H. SMITH, *Sergeant.*
WILLIS BRANCOCK, *Corporal.*
CHARLES E. MAGUIRE, *Corporal.*
GEORGE DENTON, *Corporal.*
LAWRENCE K. THOMAS, *Corporal.*
WILLIAM GANNON, *Musician.*

Privates.

ADAIR, WILLIAM R.
BAILEY, WILLIAM T.
BARRY, PHILIP.
BOND, BENJAMIN F.
BOND, JOHN.
BOWDOIN, LLOYD.
BOWLING, CHARLES F.
BOWLING, THOMAS B.
BOWLING, WALLACE.
BRADDOCK, CHARLES S.
BRYAN, EDMUND.
BAXLEY, WILLIAM G. D.

BRUCE, WILLIAM.
BOWLY, W. H.
BURCH, JOHN H.
CLAYVILLE, MOSES.
CAREY, JAMES E.
CHANDLER, W. S. J.
DAVIS, GEORGE W.
DAVIS, JACOB N.
DEALE, THEOPHILUS N.
DURNER, JOHN F.
EDELIN, WILLIAM J.
EMORY, ALBERT T.

FEIGE, CHARLES L.
FITZGERALD, JOHN E.
FREEMAN, BERNARD.
FULTON, ALEXANDER.
GALLAGHER, HOWARD L.
GARDNER, WILLIAM F.
GILL, SOMMERVILLE P.
GLENN, SAMUEL T.
GOODWIN, JOHN.
GRAMMER, FREDERICK L.
GRAYSON, SPENCE M.
GROGAN, JAMES J.

GANNON WILLIAM.
HAMMETT, JOHN T.
HANCE, WILLIAM H.
HANSON, NOTLEY.
HARRISON, THOMAS D.
HARRISON, WILLIAM H.
HENRY, JOHN C.
HOERSTER, FREDERICK.
HOFFMAN, WILLIAM H.
HOLLYDAY, HENRY.
HOLLYDAY, LAMAR.
HOLLYDAY, WILLIAM H.
HOPKINS, SAMUEL J.
HOWARD, DAVID R.
HUBBALL, BERNARD.
HUNTER, JOHN I.
HUGHES, ALEXANDER.
HUBBARD, WILLIAM L.
HEENAN, N.
HARDESTY, JOHN W.
IGLEHART, I. JAMES.
IVES, LEONARD W.
JENNINGS, BENJAMIN R.
JOY, JOSEPH I.
JAMES, EDWIN.
KLEMKIEWIEZ, THAD. A.
KENNEDY, ARTHUR.
LAIRD, W. H.

LOANE, WILLIAM T. J.
LOWE, WILLIAM E.
LOWE, WRIGHTSON L.
LUCHESI, DAVID H.
LAKE, CRAIG.
LLOYD, T. CHARLES.
LAKE, JOHN C.
MARDEN, GEORGE M.
MARNEY, JOHN.
McCEVITT, ARTHUR.
McCORMICK, LEWIS D.
McCOURT, MICHAEL.
McINTYRE, G. W.
McCORMICK, H. A.
MORRISON, WILBUR.
McDANIEL, JOHN W.
McDONALD, PATRICK.
MILLER, ANDREW T.
MURRAY, ALEXANDER.
NICOLAI, HERMAN.
OWENS, HENRY C.
O'BRIEN, THOMAS.
O'DONOVAN, EDWARD.
PARE, DAVID P.
PHELPS, JAMES J.
PEREGOY, JAMES A.
PETERS, THOMAS.
PORTER, WILLIAM J.

PRENTISS, WILLIAM S.
PHYFER, HENRY.
PRATT, THOS. ST. GEORGE.
PINDELL, PHILIP.
QUINN, MICHAEL A.
RALEY, JAMES S.
SHANLEY, THOMAS E.
SMITH, H. TILLARD.
SOLLERS, ANDREW J.
SOLLERS, SOMMERVILLE.
STEELE, CHARLES H.
STARLINGS, GEORGE C.
SANDERSON, FRANK H.
TAYLOR, GEORGE L.
THELIN, WILLIAM T.
TILGHMAN, RICHARD C.
TREGO, JOHN L.
TOY, JOSEPH L.
TRAIL, CHARLES M.
TRIPPE, ANDREW C.
WAGNER, JOHN G.
WEEMS, CHARLES H.
WILLIAMS, JOHN P.
WINDOLPH, JOHN H.
WILSON, JOHN.
WHITE, JAMES McKENNY.
ZOLLINGER, JACOB E.

COMPANY B.

J. Parran Crane, *Captain.*
J. H. Stone, *First Lieutenant.*
Charles B. Wise, *Second Lieutenant.*
James H. Wilson, *Second Lieutenant.*
Philip T. Reeder, *First Sergeant.*
John G. Barber, *Sergeant.*
Francis Z. Freeman, *Sergeant.*

Wittingham Hammett, *Sergeant.*
Thomas Simms, *Sergeant.*
William F. Wheatley, *Corporal.*
John Z. Downing, *Corporal.*
Albert Fenwick, *Corporal.*
Charles T. Drury, *Musician.*

Privates.

Alvey, James P.
Artis, Jeremiah.
Ball, Dionysius.
Bailey, James T.
Beale, Robert.
Browne, Gustavus.
Bond, James O.
Ching, Garrett.
Chunn, John H.
Clark, John E.
Clark, William A.
Combs, Edgar.
Corry, James B.
Corry, Henry.
Dent, Clay H.
Delozier, George.
Delozier, Thomas J.
Delozier, John.
Duke, John F.
Drury, William C.
Drury, Charles T.
Evans, Dallas J.

Foxwell, Charles J.
Ford, Henry.
Freeman, Marion.
Freeman, Thomas S.
Grove, Thomas F.
Herbert, William.
Herbert, James R.
Hazell, Patrick.
Hayden, George.
Hayden, John A.
Jenkins, James E.
Junger, John H.
Joy, J. E.
Keech, James H.
Lambson, James B.
Long, Jeff. T.
Magill, Thomas F.
Matthews, William G.
Mills, John C.
Millstead, Joseph H.
Moran, Rinaldo J.
McLeod, Harry C.

Moore, Warren F.
Neal, Augustine.
Page, William.
Page, Washington.
Parsons, James T.
Penn, John T.
Paigo, C. Craig.
Robertson, G. H.
Semmes, Lewis S.
Semmes, H. F.
Smith, Peter P.
Simms, W. H.
Tennison, Bernard Z.
Turner, William L.
Turner, Henry.
Wills, John W.
Wills, James A.
Wise, Henry A.
Wood, Walter.
Wheatley, William F.
Webster, James R.

COMPANY C.

FERDINAND DUVALL, *Captain.*
CHARLES W. HODGES, *First Lieutenant.*
THOMAS H. TOLSON, *Second Lieutenant.*
JOSEPH W. BARBER, *Second Lieutenant.*
WILLIAM T. OUTTEN, *First Sergeant.*
ROBERT T. HODGES, *Sergeant.*
GEORGE PROBEST, *Sergeant.*

WILLIAM RITTER, *Sergeant.*
THOMAS D. BANNON, *Sergeant.*
EDWARD A. WELCH, *Corporal.*
BEALE D. MULLIKIN, *Corporal.*
JOHN W. COLLINS, *Corporal.*
CHARLES CLAYTON, *Corporal.*

Privates.

ANDERSON, RICHARD T.
ANDERSON, SAMUEL.
BLUMENAUER, JOHN M.
CLAGETT, WILLIAM H.
COOKSEY, THEODORE.
CLOUGH, ROBERT H.
CRAWFORD, HENRY H.
CUSHING, ROBERT H.
CASTLE, JAMES L.
DUVALL, DANIEL.
DUVALL, TOBIAS.
DUVALL, EVANS.
DUVALL, FRANKLIN.
DAWSON, ROBERT M.
DORSEY, JAMES E.
DUVALL, SAMUEL.
DAVIS, MICHAEL.
DULANEY, JEREMIAH.
ELLIS, THOMAS.
EDGAR, THOMAS.
FORD, CLEMENT S.
GRACE, WILLIAM.
GIBSON, WILLIAM C.
GARRISON, ROBERT D.

HAMILTON, SAMUEL H.
HOOD, JOHN M.
HERBERT, CHARLES F.
HARDCASTLE, WILLIAM R.
HAMMOND, CHARLES.
HALLER, JOHN E.
HAMILTON, BEALE D.
HAMMOND, EDGAR.
JUDGE, EDWARD S.
JONES, JOHN T.
LOUGHTON, HENRY.
LANE, WILLIAM B.
LANAHAN, BENJAMIN L.
LAWSON, JAMES A.
MILLER, JOHN C.
MACKABEE, W. S.
MACKABEE, RICHARD T.
MITCHELL, THOMAS L.
MULLIKEN, WALTER.
MICHAEL, JOHN.
MCGENA, JOHN.
MOOG, JAMES R.
MCCANN, WILLIAM V.
MCWILLIAMS, JAMES.

NASH, JAMES.
NICHOLS, W. L.
ONION, RICHARD T.
O'BYRN, JOHN T.
ORR, PETER.
PAYNE, BENJAMIN.
ROBERTS, GEORGE.
STEELE, FRANK K.
STORM, FRANCIS E.
SKINNER, WILLIAM A.
SHIPLEY, WILLIAM H.
SHUTZ, JUSTUS.
TWILLEY, GEORGE H.
TOLSON, FRANK A.
VALIANT, ED. S.
VEIT, LEWIS H.
WELCH, ROBERT H.
WHITE, JOHN G.
WENTWORTH, GEORGE W.
WHEATLEY, FRANK M.
WATTS, JOSHUA.
WATTS, JOHN.
WILLIS, ROBERT W.

COMPANY D.

James L. McAleer, *Captain.*
James S. Franklin, *First Lieutenant.*
Samuel T. McCullough, *Second Lieutenant.*
Thomas C. Butler, *First Sergeant.*
William Jenkins, *Sergeant.*
J. William Proudt, *Sergeant.*
Isaac Sherwood, *Sergeant.*
Edwin Gover, *Sergeant.*
George W. McAtee, *Corporal.*
Alfred Riddlemoser, *Corporal.*
John McCready, *Corporal.*

Privates.

Brown, James A.
Chilcot, Joshua.
Crummer, Armstrong.
Davis, George W.
Dode, Samuel.
Devries, John.
Goldsborough, N. Lee.
Green, Lewis.
Hammett, David.
Harney, Daniel.
Hogarthy, William.
Harley, Job.
Hays, John.
Hurley, Jobe.
Hines, Thomas J.
Johnson, John.
Jones, George W.
Kane, Bernard.
Killman, Richard G.
Kerns, Cornelius.
Lamb, John.
Leich, Christopher C.
Lipscomb, Philip.
Lynch, John.
Lamb, John.
McAtee, Henry.
McCready, Thomas D.
Owens, W. Beall.
Owings, Joshua.
Phillips, Abraham.
Riddlemoser, David.
Septor, John H.
Shephard, Richard H.
Spence, John.
Watts, William.
Webb, Emmett M.

COMPANY E.

John W. Torsch, *Captain.*
William J. Broadfoot, *First Lieutenant.*
William R. Byus, *Second Lieutenant.*
Joseph P. Quinn, *Second Lieutenant.*
Samuel Kirk, *First Sergeant.*
George L. Ross, *Sergeant.*
Wilbur Rutter, *Sergeant.*
William Heaphy, *Sergeant.*
John Cain, *Corporal.*
Lewis P. Staylor, *Corporal.*
James Reddie, *Corporal.*
Benjamin F. Amos, *Corporal.*
Joseph Smith, *Musician.*
James L. Aubrey, *Musician.*

Privates.

Applegarth, James B.
Aubrey, James L.
Barry, Michael.
Byus, Charles C.
Byus, Stanley M.
Brown, John.
Brandt, William.
Brandt, Alexander.
Burke, Michael.

BUTLER, ELISHA.
CARTWELL, JAMES.
CLARKE, JOSEPH.
DAWSON, ROBERT A.
DAWSON, LEVIN G.
FALLON, JAMES.
FALLIS, EDWARD.
GAVIN, WILLIAM.
GIBBONS, JOHN.
GRANT, JOHN.
HALBIG, J. STEPHEN.
HANLEY, JAMES.
HAGLEY, ALPHONSUS.
KOPPLEMAN, JOHN.
LYONS, WILLIAM H.

LEMATES, JAMES.
LAWN, EDWARD.
LEE, WILLIAM C.
MURRAY, JOHN.
MOORE, AUGUSTUS.
MILLER, JACOB.
McLAUGHLIN, THOMAS.
MARTIN, JOHN N.
MORAN, WILLIAM P.
McMAHON, FRANK.
MOORE, P. M.
McGEE, DANIEL.
MINCH, CHRISTOPHER.
NOONAN, MICHAEL.
O'HALLIN, MARTIN.

RUSH, PETER.
ROBERTS, FRANK.
RUTTER, ELISHA.
RIDGEL, JAMES.
RADECKE, H. H.
STANSBURY, JOHN L.
SHEEHAN, EDWARD.
SHIELDS, OWENS.
SHEEDY, DANIEL.
SULLIVAN, JOHN.
SMITH, JOSEPH.
UNKLES, WILLIAM F.
WILKINSON, WILLIAM A.

COMPANY F.

A. J. GWYNN, *Captain.*
JOHN W. POLK, *First Lieutenant.*
DAVID C. FORREST, *Second Lieutenant.*
JOHN G. HYLAND, *Second Lieutenant.*
NICHOLAS J. MILLS, *First Sergeant.*
WALTER J. RANDALL, *Sergeant.*

PHILIP T. MUIRHEAD, *Sergeant.*
THOMAS O. HODGES, *Sergeant.*
JOSEPH WAGNER, *Sergeant.*
JAMES H. DIXON, *Corporal.*
JAMES T. BROWN, *Corporal.*
WASHINGTON MARTIN, *Corporal.*

Privates.

ATZRODT, HENRY.
ANDERSON, LEROY.
BOSWELL, JOSIAH T.
BRISCOE, MARSHALL.
BRAWNER, WILLIAM F.
BROOK, JOHN P.
CLEMENT, FRANCIS.
CLAGETT, GEORGE H.
CLAGETT, EDWARD L.
CLAGETT, JOHN W.
CRETIN, ANDREW L.

CRETIN, HENRY.
CRETIN, HILLARY.
DEMENT, BENJAMIN F.
DEMENT, WILLIAM S.
DOOLEY, BERNARD.
DOYLE, PHILIP.
DUNNINGTON, LEMUEL.
GRAY, JOSEPH.
GARDNER, JAMES.
GUY, GEORGE W.
GREEN, JOHN T.

HODGES, BENJAMIN.
HEARNE, WILLIAM H.
HUFFINGTON, JOHN.
HUBBARD, JOHN L.
HURLEY, ABEL.
HOGE, CHARLES A.
HOLDEN, ROBERT.
KEEPERS, ALEXIS.
KNOTT, M. T.
KENNERLY, WILLIAM R.
MESHAW, EBENEZER.

MARTIN, JOSEPH.
OPPER, CONRAD.
OBENDOFFER, AUGUSTUS.
POLK, SAMUEL.
SOLLERS, JAMES H.
SMITH, WILLIAM S.

THOMPSON, JOHN E.
TAYLOR, HENRY G.
THOMPSON, JOHN W.
WADE, CHARLES E.
WADE, GEORGE A.
WEBB, THOMAS J.

WILCOMBE, CASPAR.
WRIGHT, JOEL D.
WOODFORD, ARTHUR.
WAGNER, R.

COMPANY G.

W. W. GOLDSBOROUGH, *Captain.*
THOMAS R. STEWART, *Captain.*
THOMAS R. STEWART, *First Lieutenant.*
JAMES A. DAVIS, *First Lieutenant.*
WILLIAM C. WRIGHTSON, *Second Lieutenant.*
GEORGE BRIGHTHAUPT, *Second Lieutenant.*
G. G. GUILLETTE, *Second Lieutenant.*
G. G. GUILLETTE, *First Sergeant.*
DANIEL A. FENTON, *First Sergeant.*
EUGENE SMITH, *Sergeant.*

GEORGE W. MANNING, *Sergeant.*
ALGERNON HENRY, *Sergeant.*
MICHAEL HOLOHAN, *Sergeant.*
PATRICK O'CONNELL, *Corporal.*
JAMES E. BRIDDELL, *Corporal.*
HENRY A. MUMFORD, *Corporal.*
WILLIAM LORD, *Corporal.*
BENJAMIN F. TWILLEY, *Corporal.*
DANIEL LANNAHAN, *Corporal.*

Privates.

ABBOTT, JAMES.
ATKINS, SAMUEL E.
ASHE, JAMES.
BRANNOCK, THOMAS S.
BOWEN, HENRY.
BRANNOCK, WILLIAM J.
BOYLES, DANIEL.
BRESLIN, EDWARD W.
BELL, SAMUEL.
BRYAN, HENRY B.
CALLAHAN, JOHN.
CLARKE, CHARLES A.
CATOR, WILLIAM B.
CALHOUN, WILLIAM H.
CORNWELL, CHARLES C.
DUVALL, JOHN H.

DAVIS, JOHN S.
EDELIN, FRANCIS D.
ETCHISON, WILLIAM L.
ELLIGETT, MICHAEL.
EAGAN, PETER.
EDELIN, JOHN D.
ETCHISON, JOHN.
FREELAND, THOMAS E.
FEUTHSWAIT, J. R.
FOUNTAIN, W. B.
GOSSON, JAMES H.
HUTCHINSON, JOHN T.
HOPKINS, HENRY H.
HENDERSON, WILLIAM W.
HENDERSON, PETER.
HUTCHINS, JOSEPH.

HINES, MICHAEL.
HECK, ROBERT.
HECK, JACOB F.
HARGY, WILLIAM.
LANGFORD, GEORGE W.
LANAHAN, DANIEL.
LITTLEFORD, J. T.
LYONS, WILLIAM.
MANLY, JOSEPH.
MUMFORD, WILLIAM R.
MAYBERRY, J. P.
MESSICK, ROSS.
PATTISON, ———.
PICKEL, WILLIAM.
PICKEL, JOHN.
PURNELL, JOHN J.

PAUL, WILLIAM J.
ROBEY, WILLIAM H.
RIDER, MARTIN L.
REED, WILLIAM T.
ROBBINS, WILLIAM.
RIDER, GEORGE J.
RAYFIELD, WILLIAM.

SCOGGINS, DANIEL.
TIMMONS, WILLIAM.
THOMPSON, JOHN W.
TINGLE, DAVID P. B.
VICKERS, WASHINGTON A.
WATERS, JOHN W.
WATERS, JESSE.

WINGATE, FREDERICK A.
WILLIAMSON, PHILIP B.
WEAVER, LEWIS H.
WHEATLEY, LEVIN.
WOOLFORD, JAMES L.
WARNER, GEORGE.
ZELLERS, JOHN.

✠✠✠

COMPANY H.

J. THOMAS BUSSEY, *Captain.*
THOMAS O'BRIEN, *First Sergeant.*
JOHN J. POWERS, *Sergeant.*

PATRICK KEENAN, *Corporal.*
JOHN J. WARD, *Corporal.*

Privates.

ADAMS, J. Q.
BROWN, JAMES.
BOOTH, JOHN.
BUSH, WILLIAM.
CAVANAUGH, FRANCIS C.
CARROLL, JAMES.
CARLIN, LAWRENCE.
COLLINS, CHARLES.
CARROLL, LAWRENCE.
COLLINS, RICHARD.
CLARK, JAMES.
CHRISTY, WILLIAM.
DEGREY, LEWIS F.
DONOHUE, JOHN.
DRISCOLL, JAMES.
DUNAHUE, JOSEPH.

EAGAN, THOMAS T.
FLANNIGAN, JOHN.
FLOOD, PETER.
GRAHAM, THOMAS.
GEVIN, PETER M.
GARDINER, BENJAMIN.
HARGEY, WILLIAM.
HOLLOWAY, MICHAEL.
HAYS, J. G.
KELLEY, JAMES.
KELLEY, JOHN L.
KELLEY, JOHN.
MORGAN, WILLIAM.
MURPHY, JOHN.
MARTIN, JOHN.
MURRAY, WILLIAM.

MCKEA, JOHN.
NICHOLS, JOHN.
NEADHAM, GEORGE.
O'BRIEN, JAMES.
PARKER, JOHN.
POWERS, JOHN.
RYAN, JOHN.
ROBINSON, JAMES.
SHETKINS, JOHN.
STEPHENS, JOHN.
WARD, MAURICE.
WELCH, EDWARD.
WALSH, EDWARD.
WAGNER, J. J.

COMPANY B, TWENTY-FIRST VIRGINIA.

ONE of the finest companies to enter the Confederate service from Maryland was Company B, Twenty-first Virginia Infantry. The company was formed by Captain J. Lyle Clarke, and was composed principally of members of the Maryland Guard, at that time a famous military organization in Baltimore.

This company was mustered into the service at Richmond on the 24th of May, 1861, and sent out to Camp Lee, or rather the Camp of Instruction.

Captain Clarke there found another Maryland company under command of Captain E. R. Dorsey, which had been mustered into the service a few days before, and still later a third company was formed by Captain William H. Murray. These three companies enlisted for one year, but in some unaccountable manner the War Department conceived the idea that the companies of Murray and Dorsey were war companies, and they were consequently sent to Winchester to help form the First Maryland Regiment.

Captain Clarke and the splendid men under his command were dreadfully chagrined at being thus separated from their comrades, and pleaded to be sent after them, but the Secretary of War was inexorable. They were told to remain in camp until other companies were formed, when they would be sent to join the First Maryland, though they were but a battalion.

But, unfortunately, in the meantime troops were badly needed to operate against McClellan in West Virginia, after General Garnet's defeat at Phillipi, and all of the available companies then at Camp Lee were hastily formed into regiments, and under General Robert E. Lee were sent out to Valley Mountain, Captain Clarke's Maryland company being attached to the Twenty-first Virginia, under Colonel William Gilham, of the Virginia Military Institute.

After the memorable campaign against Rosecranz, in the summer and fall of 1861, the Twenty-first was transferred to the command of Stonewall Jackson, then in the Valley of Virginia, and participated with him in his wonderful campaign in 1862 up to the expiration of their term of service, on May 24.

Captain Clarke had the proud satisfaction of seeing nearly all of the company that had been spared immediately enlist in different branches of the service and those that survived served until the surrender.

Company B was certainly one of the best drilled companies in the Army of Virginia, and General Lee upon two occasions stated that it was the best drilled infantry company he ever saw, not excepting the regulars.

Following is a correct roster of this fine company, commonly known in the army as the "Maryland Guards":

ROSTER OF COMPANY B, MARYLAND GUARD, 21st VIRGINIA INFANTRY.

Captain, ... J. LYLE CLARKE.
First Lieutenant, ... R. CURZON HOFFMAN.
Second Lieutenant, ... W. STUART SYMINGTON.
Third Lieutenant, ... JOSEPH SELBY.

GEORGE G. GIBSON, *First Sergeant.*
RICHARD M. BARNES, *Sergeant.*
JOHN W. SCOTT, *Sergeant.*
JOSEPH SELBY, *Sergeant.*
D. BOWLY THOMPSON, *Sergeant.*
CHARLES E. HAYWARD, *Sergeant.*

GEORGE D. MERCER, *Corporal.*
WILLIAM T. OUTTEN, *Corporal.*
ADRIAN D. PRICE, *Corporal.*
ROBERT LEMMON, *Corporal.*
JAMES SELBY, *Corporal.*

Privates.

BUCK, A. KIRKLAND.
BESTOR, ROLLIN JOHN.
BESTOR, JOHN ROLLIN.
BRADY, JOHN H.
BAYLY, JAMES P.
BOYD, DAVID.
BLANFORD, SAMUEL H.
CRISE, GEORGE W.
COOKE, WILLIAM.
CARROLL, M. PHILIP.
CROYEAU, EDWARD A.
CARUSI, SAMUEL P.
COLSTON, WILLIAM E.
CARTER, WILLIAM H.
CLOSE, JAMES.
CARR, W. C. N.
CAULFIELD, JAMES.

CARROLL, T. STAPLETON.
DORSEY, RICHARD B.
DUGAN, PIERRE C.
DOUGLAS, BERNHARD.
DUGAN, HAMMOND.
DUSENBERY, H. BOWIE.
DALL, H. MCPHERSON.
DUVALL, LEONIDAS.
ELDER, PHILIP L.
ERNULL, A. W.
FREEMAN, R. M.
FASSITT, WILLIAM P.
FREEMAN, LEWIS.
FOSTER, JAMES H.
FOSTER, ROBERT E.
FORSYTH, A. M.
GUYTHER, WILLIAM.

GOWDEY, JAMES.
GILMOR, C. J.
GREENWELL, JOSEPH A.
GROGAN, JAMES J.
GREEN, J. F.
GADD, W. F.
HEINER, CHARLES M.
HAYWARD, CHARLES E.
HARRISON, J. W.
HAASE, T. H. B.
HIGGINS, JOHN P.
HULL, JOHN.
HIGGINS, EUGENE.
HODSON, E. PAYTON.
IGLEHART, W. T.
JENKINS, E. COURTNEY.
JENKINS, THEODORE.

JENKINS, JOHN CARROLL.
KREBS, CHARLES.
KEECH, SHELTON A.
LEVERING, THOMAS.
LARABEE, H. CLAY.
LITTLESTON, T. P.
MARTIN, PATRICK.
MCGEE, GEORGE R.
MONTAGUE, POWHATTAN.
MAGUIRE, CHARLES E.
MCCALEB, JAMES.
MCARDLE, HENRY A.
NORRIS, W. EPA.
NEALE, E. C.
NORFOLK, GEORGE S.

O'BRIEN, EDWARD.
PEARSON, CHARLES.
PRESSTMAN, GEORGE R.
RATCLIFFE, GEORGE E.
RODGERS, JAMES P.
ROCHE, THOMAS F.
ROGERS, EDWARD G.
SULLIVAN, JOHN H.
SIMPSON, NATHAN.
SHAKELFORD, GEORGE.
SNOWDEN, J. H.
STRAHAN, CHARLES.
SELBY, JAMES.
SMITH, A. AUSTIN.
SCHULBAK, WILLIAM F.

SMITH, WILLIAM F.
SYMINGTON, WILLIAM H.
SULLIVAN, CLEMENT.
SPENCER, E. N.
THOMAS J. WILLIAM.
TENNANT, T. M.
TIFFANY, HENRY.
THOMPSON, B. BOWLY.
WEBB, GEORGE W., JR.
WILSON, JAMES.
WRIGHT, D. G.
WAMBERSIE, J. E.
WARD, FRANK X.
WILLIAMS, T. P.
WOOTTEN, WILLIAM T.

LIEUT. COL. RIDGELY BROWN
FIRST MARYLAND CAVALRY.

FIRST MARYLAND CAVALRY.

CHAPTER I.

ON the 15th of May, 1862, eighteen young Marylanders who had served one year in Company K, First Virginia Cavalry, but who had refused to re-enlist, believing a Maryland regiment could be formed, met in Richmond and proceeded to organize Company A, which served as the nucleus of what was destined to be one of the most distinguished cavalry commands in the Confederate service. Among these young men were Ridgely Brown, of Montgomery; Frank A. Bond, of Anne Arundel; Thomas Griffith, of Montgomery, and J. A. V. Pue, of Howard. Ridgely Brown was elected Captain and the rest Lieutenants as their names stand.

It had long been the desire of these Marylanders to have their State represented in the cavalry arm of the service. They were all dashing horsemen, and, as many kindred spirits had come and were coming to Virginia without any effort being made to organize a larger body than a company, which had been absorbed at once by some Virginia regiment, they built up this company with the express stipulation that it was one around which all future companies of Maryland cavalry were to rally.

Recruiting went on briskly, and in a short time the ranks of Company A were filled up with some of the finest young men who had left the State of Maryland. They were fortunate, too, in the selection of their officers, and under their leadership the company subsequently won a reputation second to that of no company in the Confederate cavalry.

After its organization the company was ordered to the Valley of Virginia and attached to Colonel Munford's Second Virginia, there to remain until other cavalry companies had been organized, with which to form a battalion or regiment. In the meantime Company A did good service, serving with Jackson in his memorable Valley campaign. It particularly distinguished itself with Ashby in the engagement near Harrisonburg with Percy Wyndham's First New Jersey Cavalry, and was complimented by General Ewell for its gallantry upon that occasion. It was with Jackson before Richmond, and subsequently in the Maryland campaign, where it distinguished itself in many encounters with the enemy.

Up to this time Company A was the only representative Maryland cavalry company, but upon its return from the Maryland campaign it found that three other fine companies had been formed, and were ready to effect a battalion organization.

This was done at Winchester on the 25th of November, 1862, and the companies composing the battalion and their officers were as follows:

OFFICERS:

Major, ... RIDGELY BROWN.
Adjutant, ... GEORGE W. BOOTH.
Quartermaster, ... IGNATIUS DORSEY.
Surgeon, ... WILBUR F. MCKNEW.

COMPANY A.

Captain, FRANK A. BOND.
First Lieutenant, THOMAS GRIFFITH.
Second Lieutenant, J. A. V. PUE.
Third Lieutenant, EDWARD BEATTY.

COMPANY B.

Captain, GEORGE W. EMACK.
First Lieutenant, M. E. MCKNEW.
Second Lieutenant, ADOLPHUS COOK.
Third Lieutenant, HENRY BLACKISTON.

COMPANY C.

Captain, ROBERT C. SMITH.
First Lieutenant, GEORGE HOWARD.
Second Lieutenant, T. JEFF SMITH.
Third Lieutenant, W. S. TURNBULL.

COMPANY D.

Captain, WARNER E. WELSH.
First Lieutenant, W. H. B. DORSEY.
Second Lieutenant, STEPHEN D. LAWRENCE.
Third Lieutenant, MILTON WELSH.

Soon after the battalion was joined by the following additional companies:

COMPANY E.

Captain, W. I. RASIN.
First Lieutenant, JOHN B. BURROUGHS.
Second Lieutenant, NATHANIEL CHAPMAN.
Third Lieutenant, JOSEPH K. ROBERTS.

COMPANY F.

Captain, AUGUSTUS F. SCHWARTZ.
First Lieutenant, C. IRVING DITTY.
Second Lieutenant, FIELDER C. SLINGLUFF.
Third Lieutenant, SAMUEL G. BONN.

In July, 1864, Company K, then under command of Captain Gustavus W. Dorsey, was transferred from the First Virginia to the First Maryland, after having made an enviable reputation during its long service in the Virginia regiment. In many of the official reports of Generals Steuart, Jones and Fitzhugh Lee they make special mention of the conspicuous gallantry displayed by Company K. In one of the many encounters the regiment had with the enemy Lieutenant Rudolphus Cecil was killed. This young officer's dash and daring is spoken of again and again by Fitzhugh Lee in his official reports, and his untimely death was deeply deplored.

After the organization of the battalion it was ordered to Newmarket to unite with the Second Maryland Infantry and Baltimore Light Artillery there encamped. These three commands constituted the Maryland Line.

The winter of 1862-63 was passed at various points in the Valley, with its usual routine of picket duty, and naught else to vary the monotony of camp life. On the 2d of January General William E. Jones made an expedition to Moorefield in hopes of encountering the enemy, but it was fruitless of results, though the old General consoled himself by procuring a portable bake-oven he brought back, the single trophy to commemorate the privations its capture had entailed upon the command. But as the winter disappeared, more stirring events were promised.

On the 23d of February Companies A and D, commanded respectively by Captain Frank A. Bond and Lieutenant William H. B. Dorsey, two daring young officers, were sent on picket near Strasburg. On the evening of the 25th, the men being anxious for some excitement, Captain Bond determined to gratify them. Having learned the exact location of the enemy's pickets, the two companies, comprising sixty men all told, started about 10 o'clock at night on their perilous expedition. At daybreak they arrived to within less than two miles of Winchester, on the Cedar Creek road, and finding the infantry picket, charged through it, receiving a few scattering shots. At the junction of the Cedar Creek and Staunton roads they were met by a volley of musketry from a house, but it did not check them, and turning up the Staunton road toward home they rode down a third infantry picket. At Kernstown they found a cavalry picket quietly warming themselves in a house. This they attacked and fourteen men and fifteen horses were captured, and several of the enemy left dead and wounded in the house. Captain Bond then returned to Strasburg with his prisoners and horses, having lost but one man missing.

The news of the daring raid had in the meantime been conveyed to Milroy at Winchester, and he at once dispatched the First New York and Thirteenth Pennsylvania Cavalry in pursuit. These came upon Bond so suddenly at Strasburg about 8 o'clock in the morning that he had only time to get off his prisoners and make a hasty retreat up the back road, losing one man wounded and one captured.

Major Brown had that morning sent Company B, Captain G. M. Emack, and Company C, Lieutenant T. J. Smith, to relieve the companies on picket. These companies fell in with the enemy's advance on the turnpike, killed one, captured seven men and six horses. A courier was immediately sent back to notify General Jones of the advance of the enemy in force.

General Jones at once placed himself at the head of the Eleventh Virginia Cavalry, commanded by Lieutenant-Colonel O. R. Funsten, and started to meet the enemy. Owing to the fact that many men of the Eleventh were absent on various duties, Lieutenant-Colonel Funston had but one hundred and twenty men under his command when he suddenly came upon the enemy five hundred strong at Maurertown. Nevertheless the brave old man charged into their midst, routed and pursued them with sabre and revolver with good effect until Cedar Creek was reached, a distance of twelve miles. By this time Funston had more prisoners than he had men, and Colonel R. H. Dulany, with the Seventh Virginia, coming up, Lieutenant-Colonel Funsten turned the pursuit over to him, and it was continued beyond Middletown, when Colonel Dulany was compelled to halt his regiment owing to the exhaustion of his horses, after a race of twenty-six miles.

In the meantime Major Ridgely Brown, hearing that Captain Bond was being pursued on the back road, went to his assistance with thirty men of the Maryland battalion, all he had in camp, and sent for Emack and Smith, who were on the turnpike, to join him. Major Brown followed the enemy rapidly on the back road, but upon reaching the turnpike, finding Funsten and Dulany ahead of him, he desisted from the pursuit, having captured in the meantime fourteen men, with their horses and equipments.

The indirect result of this daring raid upon the enemy's pickets by the two Maryland companies was the capture of over two hundred men and horses, and the killing and wounding of many more.

A little incident that is worth narrating transpired during the flight of the Federal cavalry. Charley Hutton, of Company A, First Maryland, was captured in the morning when Captain Bond was surprised, and, unarmed, was riding with his captors when Lieutenant-Colonel Funsten made his attack. In the rout which ensued Hutton determined to make his escape. Awaiting a favorable opportunity, he sprang from his horse and dashed into a thicket and ran for his life; but at every step he could plainly hear the sound of horse's hoofs behind him. But not a sound escaped the pursuing enemy. Faster and faster ran Hutton, but the relentless enemy still pursued. He was afraid to look behind him, and was in momentary expectation of hearing the crack of a pistol and feeling the shock of a bullet as it entered his body. But no command to "Halt!" was given, nor was there a sound of pistol shot. At last, exhausted and unable to go farther, he turned to surrender to his pursuer, when what was his surprise and joy to find that it was his own faithful horse that had followed him and given him such a scare.

CHAPTER II.

For some time prior to April 21, 1863, the camp was full of rumors of a move in some direction, and on that day General William E. Jones marshaled his forces and started from Lacey's Springs upon his celebrated raid into West Virginia. Leaving Lieutenant-Colonel Funsten in command of the cavalry whose horses were not deemed sufficiently strong to undergo the trip, General Jones moved in the direction of Moorefield, Hardy County, with quite a large force of cavalry, the Second Maryland Infantry, the Baltimore Light Artillery and Chew's battery.

The morning upon which the start was made was all that could have been desired, but before many hours the rain began to fall in torrents, and but fifteen miles were made that day. The weather continued bad during the whole march to Moorefield, which was reached on the third day.

Here General Jones determined to send his infantry and artillery back to the Valley, as he found that they would embarrass his movements.

Pressing on, then, with his cavalry the first obstacle he encountered was the south branch of the Potomac, the waters of which he found very high and rapid, which compelled him to make a detour by Petersburg to get over. Here the ford was found rough and dangerous from the swiftness of the stream, and in making the passage several men and horses of the Sixth Virginia Cavalry were drowned.

Contrary to his information, General Jones found the pass at Greenland occupied by the enemy. Finding a loss of time must be incurred by attempting to turn this post, and fearing his plans might in the meantime be discovered, General Jones determined to attempt a surprise, and, failing in this, to carry the place by storm. Colonel Dulany, with the Seventh Virginia Cavalry, charged it gallantly, but failed to prevent the garrison from occupying a church building which completely defended the pass. In this assault Colonel Dulany had his horse killed and was himself wounded through the arm. Upon the repulse of the Seventh, Major Brown, of the First Maryland, sent Lieutenant Adolphus Cook with Company B out upon the New Creek road to guard against a surprise, and Companies E, Captain W. I. Rasin, and D, Lieutenant W. H. B. Dorsey commanding, were dismounted to open fire with their long-range guns upon the church. This they did, but with little effect, and being deceived by the flag of truce, sent by the commanding General, in the hands of one of the prisoners captured on the picket, they rushed upon the house, thinking the enemy had surrendered, but were undeceived when a well-directed volley was poured into them at very short range. By this unfortunate mistake Private Swamley was killed and Private Charles Lambden was wounded, both of Company D, and Company E lost Private John C. Spencer, killed.

Finding the place could not be carried without great sacrifice of life, General Jones determined to wait until dark. Then Company C, Captain R. C. Smith, and Company A, Captain F. A. Bond, were dismounted to storm the house, Major Brown taking command of the whole. The necessary arrangements having been made, at 9 o'clock the advance was ordered. Plunging into the mountain stream that flowed between them and their prey, the Maryland boys dashed upon the house in the midst of a heavy fire from the enemy ; but a delay became necessary after they had reached the house, owing to the fact that the pioneers were not up, who were to set it on fire. Upon their arrival, however, the windows and doors were broken in, and the place set on fire by bundles of ignited straw being thrown in, and the enemy to a man were either killed, wounded or captured.

In this unfortunate assault, Color-Corporal Carvill, of Company B, was killed, as also was Private Samuel Dorsey, of Company C. Major Brown was badly wounded, as was Adjutant G. W. Booth and Captain R. C. Smith, severely ; also Lieutenants J. A. V. Pue and Edward Beatty. Thus of seven officers of the battalion five were wounded. Private K. Grogan, of White's Battalion, had left his command and went into the fight by the side of his brother, Robert Riddle Grogan, who belonged to Company C, First Maryland. He was killed and his brother was wounded.

The following additional description of this severe fight will be found highly interesting. It is an extract from a paper read before the Beneficial Association of the Maryland Line by Captain George W. Booth, who was severely wounded at the time :

The advance regiment was the Seventh Virginia, under Colonel Dulany. Then followed the First Maryland, and White' Battalion and the other commands, constituting a column which stretched out for a mile or more, through the narrow defiles and narrower roads of this mountainous region. After a march of some eighteen or twenty miles, the head of the column encountered a Federal Infantry picket, posted at a small bridge where the road crossed a mountain stream. It was the work of a moment to charge and capture the post and its guard, when it was learned the road was blocked by the main body of the enemy — some two companies of infantry, and about one hundred strong, who had taken post in a log church located immediately on the roadside. Colonel Dulany, without hesitation, put his regiment into rapid motion and charged ahead. On approaching the church, he was met by a heavy fire, under which he lost a number of men and horses, receiving himself a serious wound ; but some two hundred of his column ran the gauntlet and passed the church, taking post beyond, while the remainder of his column was driven back. This unlooked-for event necessitated a halt, and an examination of the situation. In a short while it would be dark, and it was imperative to take immediate measures to overcome this obstacle, which threatened to retard the progress of the march. The location was found to be a crossing of the mountain known as Greenland Gap. The road was through a wild, rocky range. On the right the ground rose almost perpendicular, and was entirely inaccessible to a mounted force ; on the left was a small clearing of something like an acre in extent ; in this opening was erected a substantial log church of considerable dimensions. The road passed almost alongside of this building, in which the Federal force had taken post and refuge. The portion of Dulany's regiment which had passed the church in his charge effectually blocked the way and prevented the retirement of the enemy. Nothing was left for them but a stern defense, or an unconditional surrender. One of the captured men was shown our column, that he might know it was no mere guerrilla force that was seeking passage, and then allowed to go to the church and report to his commander, who was at the same time summoned to surrender. Time was of great value, and General Jones sought to avoid unnecessary loss of life, and as well of precious hours. Already the success of his movement had been seriously endangered by the day consumed in effecting the crossing of the Potomac, and the enemy had doubtless received information of his purpose and was gathering troops to meet him. The Federal commander was found to be defiant, and he not only refused to surrender his command, but intimated in terms most emphatic that he would fire on anyone approaching his post. Now, but for one shot from our battery which the flood had compelled us to leave behind at Moorefield ; but as sad as were the fates which deprived us of this strong help in a need like this, regrets would not serve to clear the pass.

It was a case where a large body was held in helplessness until the obstruction could be removed ; and what was to be done must be done quickly. Numbers were of little avail, as only a limited number of men could be brought into action. Various plans were suggested and considered, only to be dropped and then considered again. It was now night, and we were still confronted with the fact that if we would go forward the church must be stormed and its occupants taken out by main force. By reason of the repulse of the Seventh Virginia, the First Maryland held the advance. The men of the leading squadrons were dismounted and formed into a storming column, taking only such as were armed with pistols and carbines, for at this period in our organization the liberality of the enemy had not been so severely tested in the way of contributing the necessary equipment of a cavalry command, as was the case not much later on. A detachment from White's Battalion was added to the column, and now with pistol in hand and with men bearing axes and trusses of straw and other inflammable matter, together with chunks of fire, the order was given to " Forward ! Double-quick ! " The moon shone out brightly and lit up the road so that it was almost as distinct and clear as under the noonday sun. With a wild rush and a loud yell, on went the devoted column, until it was soon under fire from the church, from the windows and doorways of which was poured the leaden hail. A winding stream crossed the road some several times in the distance of a hundred yards. Through this stream and under this deadly fire on rushed our brave boys. The weather was bitterly cold, and on emerging from the water their clothing soon stiffened in ice. But personal discomfort was not to be thought of in a time like this. One by one the men dropped, victims to the well-directed fire; but onward pressed the column, and soon ranged itself around the house, where for a moment was a respite of safety, as under its walls the fire from the windows could not be depressed so as to be effective. Then came the ringing blows of the axe as door and window were assailed and battered. Those carrying fire had soon kindled a blaze under the house, on which was thrown the straw and kindlings.

No shots were fired by the assaulting column, except by those immediately at the doors and windows, as no enemy was to be seen, and the stout logs which protected them could not be penetrated. Soon the fire from the house was renewed, and the falling of our men at once disclosed that the chinking between the logs was being pushed out, and from the ground floor of the church its defenders were dealing death and destruction. The writer was standing to the right of the door, with back as close to the walls as he could get, when he was literally pushed out of the way and half turned around by the projecting muzzle of a musket from between the logs. The force of the blow, perhaps, saved him from the effect of the discharge, which immediately followed, but in a moment he received a severe wound from another quarter. The blows on the door were now telling, and it slowly gave way. At its first opening, in sprang that gallant soldier, Sergeant-Major Johnson, who, finding himself shut up with the enemy in their citadel, and alone, did not hesitate, but loudly demanded them to surrender. The work of the fire was now beginning to show, and one corner of the building was lighted up in a blaze. Again and again fell the heavy blows from the axe on the door, until it gave way, and our men crowded in, when the cry of surrender rose up from all quarters of the house. My personal recollections cease at this point, and when consciousness again asserted itself, I found kind and loving friends were bearing me back, but the last sight that I recall was in the very height of the scene, when the cries of "Surrender!" were ringing in my ears, and the light of the blazing fire, together with the brilliancy of the moon, made clear the ground surrounding the church, which was white with the forms of our brave boys who had fallen.

This detention at Greenland Gap was unfortunate, as it prevented General Jones from capturing a train in which were most of the officers of General Mulligan's command.

Arriving at the Northwest Grade General Jones divided his command, and Colonel A. W. Harmon, of the Twelfth Virginia, was sent with his regiment, the First Maryland and McNeill's Partisan Rangers, to burn the bridge at Oakland, and to march thence by way of Kingwood on Morgantown. The remainder of the force moved on Rowelsburg.

Colonel Harmon's force reached Oakland next day, and the First Maryland Cavalry took part in the charge on the place, in which forty prisoners were captured. That night Colonel Harmon encamped on Cheat River, and next day advanced in the direction of Morgantown, the First Maryland some miles in advance, where several hundred citizens had assembled with arms, determined to dispute the Confederate entrance into their town. Feeling that an attack would cause much loss of life and destruction of property, Major Brown permitted Captain F. A. Bond to go forward with a flag of truce demanding the unconditional surrender of the town. After some little hesitation this demand was complied with, when Morgantown was entered and all arms found destroyed.

As soon as Colonel Harmon joined the advance two hours afterward, the entire force moved in the direction of Independence, and went into camp seven miles from that town. On the 28th, after meeting and uniting with the forces under General Jones, from which Harmon had separated soon after leaving Greenland Gap, the whole command retraced its steps to Morgantown. On this latter march, a portion of the Maryland battalion comprised the advance guard under Captain Bond. In passing through a mountainous section it was fired upon by bushwhackers, and Captain Rasin's horse was killed. After a lively chase three of the scoundrels were caught, and by order of Captain Bond were shot upon the spot.

On the 29th the command arrived at Fairmont, which was held by about three hundred infantry. Company E was dismounted and fought as infantry, whilst the remainder of the battalion charged the place under a heavy fire. Finding themselves cut off, the garrison surrendered. The battalion lost one man killed and two wounded in this affair.

The next day Major Brown charged into Bridgeport and captured one company of cavalry and one of infantry. Major Brown had one man killed.

From here General Jones proceeded by easy stages to Buckhannon, where the wound received by Major Brown at Greenland Gap became so much worse that he was peremptorily ordered home by Dr. Johnson. Throughout all these long and hard marches this brave man had refused to leave his command, although at times scarcely able to maintain his seat in the saddle.

At Weston the command rested for two days, and then moved on Oiltown, where it arrived on May 9. Here all the oil tanks and machinery were burned. From Oiltown, General Jones marched by way of Glenville and Sutton to Summerville, and thence homeward by easy stages to Harrisonburg, in the Valley of Virginia.

In thirty days Jones' command had marched seven hundred miles through a mountainous country, gathered subsistence for man and horse, killed thirty of the enemy and wounded three times as many, captured seven hundred prisoners and arms, with one piece of artillery, and two trains of cars, burned sixteen railroad bridges, one hundred and fifty thousand barrels of oil, many engines, and brought home one thousand cattle and twelve hundred horses, losing in the meantime ten killed and forty-two wounded.

In General Jones' official report he says :

"If any one officer or man deserves special mention, it is Major Ridgely Brown, of the First Maryland Battalion of Cavalry. He was shot in the leg at Greenland, and yet he continued on duty until he arrived at Buckhannon, a distance of 168 miles, and then started home at the earnest solicitation of Doctor R. P. Johnson."

In this expedition the First Maryland Battalion of Cavalry lost five killed and fourteen wounded, more than any regiment in the command.

Upon the return of General Jones to the Valley of Virginia men and horses were much broken down from the hard and rapid marching they had undergone, and as the summer campaign was about to be inaugurated absolute rest was necessary for both man and beast.

The Second Maryland Infantry and Baltimore Light Artillery had been sent to relieve Major Sam Myers at Fisher's Hill, and the First Cavalry was ordered to unite with them. Thus once more was the Maryland Line collected together.

Whilst at Fisher's Hill the First Maryland, now under command of Captain F. A. Bond (Major Ridgely Brown being absent on account of wound received at Greenland Gap), picketed the back road, the turnpike not requiring that service, owing to the fact that an enemy approaching from that direction could be seen for a distance of three miles.

Shortly after the arrival of the First Maryland Cavalry General A. G. Jenkins reached Fisher's Hill with a fine brigade of Virginia cavalry, and he assumed command of the whole.

On the 10th of June General Jenkins moved his whole force from Fisher's Hill to Cedar Creek. Everything indicated an early move in some direction, and that probably on Winchester. The turnpike was now heavily picketed some miles in advance of the main body and the men throughout the command were anxiously awaiting the order to march.

Whilst thus awaiting orders at Cedar Creek an unfortunate affair happened in the vicinity of Newtown, which caused the death of five brave Maryland boys and the wounding and capturing of some thirty others.

On Friday, June 12, General Milroy sent out a strong reconnoitering party on the Strasburg road. This party consisted of the Eighty-seventh Pennsylvania Infantry, Thirteenth Pennsylvania Cavalry, and one section of Battery L, United States Artillery. At this time Captain W. I. Rasin, in command of Company E, First Maryland Cavalry, with Harry Gilmor and eight of his men and a few men of the Fourteenth Virginia Cavalry — sixty men, all told — were scouting near Middletown, when their presence became known to Colonel Schall, who was in command of the Federal forces. The infantry and artillery were immediately concealed, the former in a dense grove to the right of the road, and within one hundred yards of it, and the latter behind a ridge. Major Kirwin commanded the cavalry, and he sent forward a portion of his regiment to draw Rasin into the trap. In this he succeeded, and the gallant fellow, charging only cavalry, as he supposed, suddenly found himself in the presence of an overwhelming force of infantry, cavalry and artillery. The shock was terrific, and it was a miracle a man or horse escaped the dreadful fire of musketry and cannister that was poured into their ranks. Rasin, singling out Kirwin himself, never faltered until their sabres were crossed. But Kirwin was the stronger of the two, and a savage cut over the head brought Rasin to the ground, and his horse was killed at the same instant.*

---

* The author has met Major Kirwin since in New York, where he resides. He is a noble-hearted, brave, stalwart Irishman, and he spoke freely of the affair. He said: "That brave fellow, Rasin, came at me like a bullet, but I was the stronger and quicker and got in the first blow."

CHAPTER III.

On the evening of the 12th of June, General A. G. Jenkins left Cedar Creek with all the cavalry except Company A, First Maryland, commanded by Captain Frank A. Bond, which company was ordered to remain with the Maryland infantry and Baltimore Light Artillery until Winchester was reached, where Captain Bond was to report with his company to General Ewell for special service.

As this company was for a long time separated from the rest of the battalion, to make the operations of the whole intelligible to the reader it will be necessary to treat of them separately.

At this time Company A was as fine a body of cavalry as there was in the service. There were one hundred men in its ranks for duty, well equipped, splendidly mounted and thoroughly drilled and disciplined. The average age of the men was twenty-one years, and there was an unusual amount of intelligence pervading the whole. The officers had all seen two years' service, and one-half the men had seen the same, and most of the remainder one year. General Ewell had selected this company to be attached to his headquarters, not as couriers or as a headquarters guard, but for special service on important occasions, and to accompany the corps upon its advance across Maryland and into Pennsylvania. On the 13th of June, when Early made his attack upon Winchester, Company A was with the Second Maryland Infantry, and advanced with the skirmishers, taking position on their right.

From Winchester to Carlisle, Pennsylvania, Company A was in the advance of Ewell's Corps, but whilst not under fire during this time, Jenkins having preceded them, they rendered valuable service in guarding the stores abandoned by the enemy, and turning them over to the commissaries of the various infantry brigades. On June 28 Ewell's Corps was encamped around Carlisle, and on the 30th it moved to Heidlersburg, twelve miles distant. Company A was to remain at Carlisle until two hours after the last of the troops had left, and then to release one thousand prisoners under guard. Captain Bond's situation became a critical one when the one thousand prisoners and citizens realized that the city was in the possession of but one hundred cavalrymen, and a collision seemed inevitable. But the firmness of Captain Bond prevailed, for he assured them that he would drench their streets with blood and destroy their city should they attack his command.

After reaching General Ewell's headquarters on the afternoon of the 30th, Captain Bond was ordered to proceed to Gettysburg, as a report had come that a body of the enemy's cavalry had been seen in that vicinity. Reaching the immediate vicinity of Gettysburg without encountering the enemy, Captain Bond left Sergeant Hammond Dorsey with six men as a picket, and then returned to General Ewell, and reported no enemy near.

During the night Sergeant Dorsey captured three members of a Pennsylvania battery, who, having been refused leave to go to their homes, had taken horses and slipped away, thinking they could return before daylight without being missed. These men gave General Ewell the first information he had of the whereabouts of Meade's army. The next morning, July 1, Ewell moved in the direction of Gettysburg.

Company A was not engaged at Gettysburg, but was in possession of the town, Captain Bond acting as provost marshal for three days.

On July 4 Captain Bond was ordered by General Ewell to stretch his company across the front of his entire corps, remain until daylight, make careful observation of the enemy's position, and then follow the corps. It was a dark, rainy, dismal night that this little band kept their weary vigils, and daylight was never more welcomed. But when day broke all was quiet along the company's front, and Captain Bond drew in his men and reported to General Ewell about noon of the 5th, when he was ordered to pass to the front and assist in protecting the wagon trains, which were expected to reach the Potomac at Williamsport during the afternoon of the 6th.

In the interval that we have been following Company A, it is necessary to state that the remaining companies of the First Maryland Cavalry had been temporarily placed under command of Major Harry Gilmor at Winchester. That officer was ordered by General Ewell to move forward to Boonsboro, and if possible reach the Monocacy bridge, across that stream near Frederick, and destroy it. Major Gilmor reached Frederick City with the First Maryland Cavalry, numbering about two hundred men, captured some prisoners, but found the bridge too strongly defended for cavalry to venture a successful attack. Major Gilmor then returned through Frederick City to the top of South Mountain, near Boonsboro. From South Mountain the First Maryland moved to Hagerstown, where Major Gilmor was ordered to join General George H. Steuart, whose brigade had been detached from Major-General Edward Johnson's Division and ordered to make a detour to the left as far as McConnellsburg. Gilmor took the advance, and on approaching McConnellsburg his command was fired upon from the mountain side. Hearing the place was occupied, Major Gilmor charged through the town, but found no enemy, they having made a hasty retreat upon his approach.

Steuart's command remained in McConnellsburg two days, and during that time the First Maryland Cavalry was engaged in collecting horses and cattle from the surrounding country, and in this they were very successful. Gilmor's orders, however, were in effect to leave a pair of plow horses and milk cows on each farm, and to respect all other property. These orders were strictly followed, much to the surprise of the inhabitants.

After leaving Chambersburg, which place is about twenty-five miles from McConnellsburg, Gilmor made a wide circuit westward, and rejoined Steuart's Brigade at Shippensburg, on its way to Carlisle. When within a few miles of that place Gilmor was ordered down the York road, his command passing through Papertown and Petersburg to Cashtown, and thence to Gettysburg, where Gilmor had orders to report to General Ewell.

Upon reaching Gettysburg on July 1 the command found the battle in progress, and it was at once ordered to the support of Pogue's and Carter's batteries. Major Gilmor posted his men in a ravine in rear of the batteries, and consequently suffered no loss from the severe artillery fire that was delivered by the Federal batteries.

Major Ridgely Brown reached Gettysburg on the 2d, and he at once assumed command of the battalion. This gallant officer had been absent since the fight at Greenland Gap, when he was severely wounded.

During the remainder of the fighting around Gettysburg the companies of the battalion were much scattered, having been detailed for various duties, and consequently did not participate in the great cavalry battle on the Confederate left, as some writers have asserted.

When the army fell back on the 4th the battalion was assigned to the duty of protecting Ewell's wagon trains, but on a different road to that taken by Captain Bond with Company A, and, owing to the length of the train, the companies were much drawn out.

In the meantime the enemy was not idle. On the morning of the 4th Kilpatrick moved from Gettysburg, and was ordered to attack the trains which were passing along the Fairfield road leading toward Waynesboro. Leaving Emmittsburg in the afternoon, Kilpatrick joined Huey's Brigade near that place, and moved on to Monterey Gap. Two roads leading westward from Fairfield cross the mountains, one on the north and the other south of Jack Mountain. Upon the northern road General Ewell's trains were passing. General Robertson was in the vicinity of Fairfield with five regiments of cavalry, having a picket at the intersection of the Emmittsburg road. When Kilpatrick attacked this picket it retired in the direction of Fairfield, leaving no force of Robertson's on the road to Monterey Gap.

By a fortuitous circumstance someone had placed Captain Emack with his company on this road, and farther back was Captain Warner G. Welsh with Company D, First Maryland. The enemy attacked Emack and his gallant little command with great fury, but were repulsed and held in check for some time by this handful of brave Marylanders.

The following extract from a letter written by Captain Emack descriptive of his night's experience will be found of thrilling interest. It is taken from McClellan's " Campaigns of Stuart's Cavalry " :

On the evening of the 4th of July, 1863, as Lee's army was on the retreat from Gettysburg, I was ordered to place a picket on the Emmittsburg road near Monterey. Selecting Sergeant Sam Spencer and six men for the post, the rest of my company, under Lieutenants Cook and Blackiston, were sent foraging. The advance picket had been on duty but a short time, when I was notified of the advance of a large body of Federal cavalry and artillery from the direction of Emmittsburg. I immediately returned to Ewell's wagon train, which was coming into the road in my rear, and going down the road half a mile, stopped the wagons from coming farther, and started those in advance at a trot, so that, should the enemy break through my picket, they would find no wagons in the road. In doing this I came across a Lieutenant of a North Carolina battery, who had but one gun and only two rounds of ammunition. With this he galloped up the road to my picket ; and, placing him in position, I directed him to put both charges in his gun and await orders. Sergeant Spencer was placed in rear with five men, while I advanced down the road, accompanied by Private Edward Thomas, until I met the head of the enemy's column. It was then dusk and raining ; and as we wore our gum coats the Federal cavalry failed to recognize us. Without making any demonstration, we turned and retreated before them at a walk, shielding the gun as much as possible as we neared it. As soon as we passed the gun the Lieutenant fired into the head of the column. Taking advantage of the halt and confusion which followed this fire, I charged with my little party, in all only eight mounted men, and succeeded in driving them back for more than a mile, until they reached their artillery.

From the shouting and firing among the retreating enemy we concluded that they had become panic-stricken and were fighting among themselves.

The firing brought up Lieutenant Blackiston with the rest of my company ; and dismounting the men, we formed line in some undergrowth on one side of the road.

After fully an hour we heard the enemy advancing, this time with more caution and with dismounted skirmishers thrown out on each side of the road. Lying on the ground, we reserved our fire until they were within ten or fifteen paces of us, when we gave them a volley which caused another precipitate retreat. I now withdrew my men to another position, and formed them dismounted on either side of the road. Sergeant Spencer had charge of one squad and Sergeant Wilson of the other. Lieutenant Blackiston had charge of the horses and prisoners in the rear. Kilpatrick now commanded a general advance with mounted and dismounted men and with artillery, firing at every step, which to us was rather amusing, as we were about a mile distant and lying snugly on the ground. About midnight he reached Monterey, and opened a tremendous fire on us with artillery and dismounted men, to which we made but little answer. In the meantime the wagons had commenced to run in on the road in my rear, and I again went back on the Gettysburg road and stopped them. They were soon started again, and on going back to ascertain the cause I was informed that they were moving by General W. E. Jones' orders. I found General Jones and told him that I had only a handful of men opposed to all of Kilpatrick's cavalry ; and I urged the importance of keeping the road clear, so that when the enemy broke through he would find nothing on it. The General said that the train must move on, and if I could hold out a little longer the Sixth Virginia Cavalry would come to my assistance. I returned to my men and urged them not to yield an inch nor to waste any ammunition (we had but little at the commencement). The enemy now increased their fire until it seemed as if nothing could stand before it. Still these men lay there under it coolly, awaiting an opportunity to strike another blow. The enemy's skirmishers at last walked into my line, and I was told that one of them actually trod on Private Key, who killed him on the spot. The enemy was again driven back. My ammunition was entirely exhausted and some of my men actually fought with rocks : nor did they give back an inch.

The Fourth North Carolina Cavalry now made its appearance at the junction of the two roads in my rear, and after General Jones and his staff had exhausted every means to get them to my assistance, I finally succeeded in getting a Lieutenant and about ten men to dismount and advance to my line. The Sixth Virginia Cavalry, that I knew so well to be good fighters, never made its appearance during the night. At about 3 o'clock A. M., finding that he had no force of consequence opposed to him, Kilpatrick advanced his cavalry to within twenty yards of my position and gave the order to charge. A running fight now ensued amid wagons and ambulances. As we passed out of the mountain we met Captain Welsh's company of the First Maryland Cavalry at the junction of another road. Here the enemy was held in check for a moment, but they soon swept us aside, and on they went until they had captured all the wagons found in the road. The two portions of the train that I had cut off were not reached by the enemy ; and I do not believe that we would have lost any of the train had it not been started on the road after I had stopped it.

In this fight about half the men I had engaged were captured, and I myself was wounded. According to the official report of General Kilpatrick, his loss was five killed, ten wounded and twenty-eight prisoners, in all forty-three men, or more than I had in the fight, including horse-holders.

General William E. Jones says in his official report :

With my staff, I hastened on to rally all the stragglers of the train to the support of whatever force might be guarding the road. Arriving, I found Captain George M. Emack's company of the Maryland cavalry, with one gun, opposed to a whole division of Federal cavalry with a full battery. He had already been driven back within a few hundred yards of the junction of the roads. Not half of the long train had passed. This brave little band of heroes was encouraged with the hope of speedy reinforcements, reminded of the importance of their trust, and exhorted to fight to the bitter end rather than yield. . . . . . The last charge of grape was expended and the piece sent to the rear. For more than two hours less than fifty men kept many thousands in check. . . . The enemy, driven to desperation, resorted to a charge of cavalry that swept everything before it. The led horses, wagons, straggling infantry and camp followers were hurled down the mountain in one confused mass. Ineffectual efforts were made for a rally and resistance, but without avail, until at the foot of the mountain a few joined Captain W. G. Welsh's company of the Maryland cavalry, stationed at this point, and drove back the advance of the enemy. But this mere handful of men had to yield to the increasing numbers of the enemy.

Captain Emack and Welsh lost heavily for the number engaged in this affair, the greater part of their men being killed, wounded or made prisoners, and among the wounded and captured was Lieutenant Adolphus Cooke, of Emack's company, a most dashing young officer, who lay insensible for several days before regaining consciousness. Lieutenant Cooke remained in prison until the close of the war, much to the regret of the men of his company, with whom he was very popular.

We left Company A, First Maryland, under Captain F. A. Bond, with orders to move to the front and protect Ewell's wagon trains moving on another road from that upon which Emack and Welsh had fought the enemy so heroically.

The following interesting description of the experience of Company A is from Captain Bond to the author:

On the night of the 5th we encamped upon the top of the mountain, possibly ten miles from Hagerstown. By sunrise next morning we were on the march, and about noon reached the head of the column. There were miles of wagons, which had halted on the outskirts of Hagerstown. I had no authority to give orders, and as there appeared to be no enemy near, and a considerable body of our cavalry was in the town, I determined to get some food for men and horses, and for this purpose directed my men to break ranks for an hour, and then assemble at the same place unless sooner recalled by the bugle. I rode off, and was in a fair way to get a meal when I was informed that the enemy in force was approaching the town upon the opposite side to that by which we had entered. As the information seemed reliable I abandoned my dinner and hastened back to the rendezvous, and the bugle call soon rallied forty-six of my one hundred and nine men. With this handful I rode through the town in column of fours, and halted immediately in the rear of the Tenth Virginia Cavalry, commanded by Colonel J. Lucius Davis. This was a strong regiment, numbering, I thought, some five hundred men. I shall here state that I was accompanied from Gettysburg by George W. Booth, at that time Adjutant of the First Maryland, but who was not sufficiently recovered from a wound received two months before at Greenland Gap to do duty, but who was by my side during the entire affair. R. G. Harper Carroll, a brother of Ex-Governor John Lee Carroll, happened in the town as a civilian, and, although he had only a pocket pistol, he gallantly joined us, and later on, when it appeared we were running away, he appealed earnestly to me not to retreat.

Leaving my small party, I passed the Virginia regiment and saw a long column of Federal cavalry approaching by the turnpike, and about half a mile away. I urged Colonel Davis to meet their charge by a counter-charge, and under no circumstances to attempt to check them by remaining in position. He did not give any orders at all, and as it was apparent the enemy were going to charge I took a look at his regiment and saw that indescribable tremor run through it, which convinced me they would not, under the circumstances, withstand the charge.

I hastened back to my little command and resolved to wheel about by fours, turn down the first side street, the length of my column, then wheel to the front again, and when the Virginians were driven by me to dash out between them and the Federals and endeavor to check them and save the wagons. The wheel-about by fours was made, but before we reached a side street Davis' command swarmed around us, fleeing in the wildest panic. Every soldier knows the contagion of such a rout, but to the honor of our glorious old State each and every one of these gallant forty-six men moved as a machine, and the column was as solid as a rock. The enemy was immediately on the heels of the fleeing Confederates, and as soon as our rear (soon to become the front) was uncovered the order was: "Fours Right-about! Charge!" It was a tremendous struggle for the sections of fours to force their way around, crowded and pressed as they were by largely superior numbers, and the sections farthest from the enemy were much longer making the wheel than those who were first released from the pressure, and as each man dashed at full speed at the enemy the moment that he could face them the charge was made nearly in single file. Immediately that the enemy perceived that they had a force in their front that meant to stay, for awhile at least, they checked their pursuit and halted in a confused mass in the street, except one or two whose horses carried them into our midst, and they were promptly shot down. Sergeant Hammond Dorsey was the first man who dashed into the enemy's lines, and began to hew right and left. George Lechlider followed him closely, and almost immediately the enemy broke and ran, and was hotly pursued to their main body by the entire company. Five men fell under Sergeant Dorsey's sabre, the last one of them being a bugler. As the fellow in full flight leaned over his horse's neck his brass bugle protected his head, and it required repeated blows to disable him. The enemy made no counter-charge, and the wagon train was saved. General Ewell was an eye-witness to the whole affair, and he afterward declared it to be the neatest thing of the kind he had ever seen, and had undoubtedly saved his wagon train.*

Flushed with victory, we retired to our side of the town, where we were soon joined by reinforcements, and two pieces of artillery were added to my command. The enemy dismounted his sharpshooters and skirmished on the left of the town, but, dismounting a few men, we drove them back. In doing this Soper Childs and his brother Buck displayed conspicuous courage.

---

* In this fight the Federal advance was commanded by Colonel Ulric Dahlgren, who lost a leg by a shot from the pistol of Captain Bond, and was killed the following year in a bold attempt to liberate the prisoners on Belle Isle, assassinate President Davis and his Cabinet, and burn Richmond.

Soon after this General J. E. B. Stuart made his appearance in the vicinity, and by his orders I took my company and joined him, when he led a charge with about three hundred men upon a Federal battery some distance off, but the battery limbered up and escaped.

It was now dark, and as one of our own batteries still continued to shell the ground just occupied by the Federal battery, and which we now held I rode back to stop the firing, when a shell exploded in front of me. One piece cut off the collar of my overcoat, which was rolled and strapped across the front of my saddle, and another piece passed between Lechlider and myself as we rode touching knees, slightly wounding him and severely wounding me. It being found necessary to leave me behind, owing to the severity of my wound, I became a prisoner, and remained so until May, 1864.

CHAPTER IV.

Except some slight skirmishing at Williamsport, the First Maryland was not engaged after passing Hagerstown, and upon reaching Virginia it was ordered to Winchester to recruit.

It was here Company F, under command of the gallant Schwartz, joined the battalion. This company was a great acquisition, and was finely officered.

The battalion remained at Winchester ten days, when it was ordered to join Fitzhugh Lee, whose cavalry brigade was then encamped near Leetown. On the promotion of General Lee to the command of a division, a short time after, the battalion was assigned to the brigade commanded by General Lomax.

From this time until the 11th of October, 1863, the battalion was engaged in picket duty, occasionally skirmishing with the enemy.

A few days prior to the 11th, General Robert E. Lee began his movement to gain the rear of Meade's army, then confronting along the line of the Rappahannock.

On the 9th General Fitzhugh Lee broke camp, and at 3 o'clock on the morning of the 11th of October his division moved toward the Rappahannock, Lomax's Brigade marching toward Morton's Ford, whilst Wickham's Brigade marched to Raccoon Ford.

General J. E. B. Stuart personally superintended the movement of the whole cavalry column higher up the river, advancing by way of Culpeper Court House. These dispositions were designed to cover General Lee's movements, by interposing the cavalry between his line of march and the enemy.

Before Lomax's Brigade reached Morton's Ford reports from pickets represented the enemy as advancing in force, and upon reaching the river a heavy column was found occupying both sides. The collision between the hostile forces was abrupt and sudden, for to both it was unexpected. In a very few minutes the First Maryland was formed and vigorously attacked the enemy. The check, however, was only momentary, but long enough to enable Lomax to make some disposition of his troops.

The battle soon became general, and continued for more than three hours. Lomax did not have a single piece of artillery, whilst the enemy was well supplied. At length, by a sweeping charge of the whole line, the enemy were compelled to retire toward the river, and the struggle was over at this point. About half way down to the river's bank their cavalry turned and covered the retreat of the main body by making a gallant charge that struck the First Maryland Battalion, which held the extreme left of the line, but it was handsomely repulsed, the brave officer who led it falling mortally wounded in their midst.

The main body retreated across the river, rapidly pursued by Lomax, who came up with them within a few miles, when a running fight ensued to Brandy Station, often before the scene of heavy cavalry fighting.

Before reaching Brandy Station the brigades of Lomax and Wickham united, as had also the two columns of the enemy, for Wickham had been heavily engaged at Raccoon Ford. Here the enemy's cavalry met the infantry sent to support them, when they turned upon their pursuers, and the fight was renewed with redoubled fury, and charges and counter charges were made, until both sides paused from sheer exhaustion. The left of the Confederate line then crossed the road leading from Culpeper Court House to Brandy Station, and the battle was resumed.

Whilst it was raging fiercely, a short time before dark, a heavy dust in the direction of Culpeper warned the Confederates that reinforcements of the enemy's cavalry were rapidly approaching from that town.

Fearing an attack in the rear from this new enemy, General Fitz Lee immediately drew back his left, which was then in danger, and re-formed parallel to the road by which they approached. The Federal column came forward in splendid style, the sabres flashing in the rays of the declining sun, and to an inexperienced observer it would have seemed as though everything would have been swept from before it. Not so the gallant men who stood in its way awaiting the attack. But the enemy was evidently not seeking a fight, for suddenly he moved to the left upon discovering the Confederates in his path, and sought to pass without a collision. But this did not suit General Lee, who immediately ordered a charge, and Federals and Confederates were soon dashing along in most admirable confusion until the infantry was reached, when General Lee was compelled to retire out of range. A short time after General J. E. B. Stuart, with Hampton's Division, came down the Culpeper road, and then was ascertained the reason why the enemy had wished to pass so rapidly. That General had defeated them at Culpeper, and was then in hot pursuit.

General Thomas L. Rosser, then Colonel of the Fifth Virginia Cavalry, says of this incident in McClellan's "Stuart's Cavalry":

My regiment, with the First Maryland and Fifteenth Virginia Cavalry, extended across the road upon which these troops were coming up in our rear. Not knowing who they were, I sent to Fitz Lee to learn something about them, but before hearing from him they came near enough for me to observe that they carried the Federal flag; and to prevent being crushed between these two commands I withdrew my regiment, and advised the other Colonels to fall back so as to avoid the heavy blow in our rear. We did so, and re-formed perpendicular to Buford and parallel to the direction of march of the advancing column from the rear, and we were in good order when the head of Kilpatrick's column got opposite us. These troops were moving at a full gallop; they were not charging upon us, for we stood in line off to one side, and for a moment I looked on in amazement at the performance. I soon concluded that they were being pursued, and we charged them in flank, and never before did I reap such a rich harvest in horses and prisoners.

This was the first cavalry fight in which the Spencer repeating carbine was used by the enemy ; but, notwithstanding this advantage over the old muzzle-loading gun, they were badly beaten, having been driven upon their infantry, and engaged from early dawn until night put an end to the conflict.

The loss of the First Maryland was severe, as they were engaged almost continually during the fight, both mounted and on foot.

CHAPTER V.

On October 12 the cavalry corps crossed the Rappahannock at Warrenton Springs and moved down the Warrenton and Alexandria pike, and breaking into several columns marched by different but nearly parallel roads in the direction of Centreville. Fitz Lee's Division moved toward Catlett's Station, on the Orange and Alexandria Railroad. At a small place on Cedar Creek, called Auburn, Lomax's Brigade, to which the First Maryland was still attached, made a dash at the enemy's wagon train, then passing, but finding it protected by a large body of his infantry Lomax withdrew.

This affair, though brief and unsatisfactory, gave occasion for a complimentary order from General Lomax to the First Maryland which was well deserved, for by their gallant bearing they materially assisted in extricating that General from a most perilous position.

By this time Meade had divined the object of General Lee's movement, and his whole army was in retreat toward Washington, in order to prevent Lee from gaining his rear.

During this retreat the cavalry made several attacks upon his flank, in all of which the First Maryland was actively engaged. But little was effected, however, owing to the careful and compact order in which the enemy retired.

Finding his prey had escaped him, General Lee fell back to the line of the Rapidan, leaving the cavalry to guard his rear, which also fell back slowly, Hampton by the Warrenton pike and Fitz Lee by the Orange and Alexandria Railroad, the two running parallel.

The enemy's cavalry under Kilpatrick, thinking retreat meant defeat, pressed after Hampton, and his advance and Hampton's rear soon became engaged. Hampton continued his retreat until he reached within two miles of Warrenton, when the trap he had prepared for Kilpatrick was sprung.

So eager was that officer to immortalize himself, and so confident was he of success, that he never stopped to think of the danger that might be lurking behind the range of hills on his left. Fitz Lee was there, and when Kilpatrick thought to crush Hampton at a blow and drive him into the Rappahannock, the sound of a few cannon on his rear and left suddenly put a new phase on affairs.

With the sound of these guns Hampton ceased his retreat, and turning charged the pursuing enemy, while at the same moment Fitz Lee struck him in flank at Buckland. The fight which ensued was short, bloody and decisive, and Kilpatrick's exultant pursuit was converted into a precipitate rout, and his troopers scattered over the country in all directions.

During this fight the First Maryland fought on foot, but when the rout commenced, they mounted and pursued to near Gainesville, where the enemy met his infantry.

It was now dark, and Lieutenant-Colonel Brown (he had been some time before promoted from Major) could not see what was in his front; but halting a moment to rectify his line he gave the command to charge, when both cavalry and infantry broke and fled in the utmost confusion. Many were killed, wounded and captured, and Brown, now aware that he was in the presence of Meade's army, withdrew to Buckland, where was assembled the commands of Hampton and Lee, and where they congratulated each other on the signal victory they had achieved.

From this time until the latter part of November, when it was ordered to report to Colonel Bradley T. Johnson at Hanover Junction, the First Maryland was engaged in picket duty on the Rappahannock.

About the middle of November General J. M. Jones, to the command of whose brigade Colonel Bradley T. Johnson had been assigned on July 4 at Gettysburg, returned to duty, and Colonel Johnson was relieved, after having commanded the brigade with marked ability in many bloody engagements. But in spite of this fact, and notwithstanding he had been urged for promotion by Generals Lee, Jackson and Ewell for more than a year, his advancement was withheld.

In November Colonel Johnson was ordered to assemble the Maryland Line at Hanover Junction. The duty devolving upon the command was that of protecting the bridges over the North and South Anna and Middle Rivers, to protect Lee's right flank down the Peninsula as far as New Kent Court House, and to watch the lower Pamunkey, and to keep General Lee advised of the movements of the Federals from these directions.

The camp established was named St. Mary's, and here from November to May the time was pleasantly passed in drill, pickets and scouts.

At this time the Maryland Line consisted of the Second Maryland Infantry, the First Maryland Cavalry and Baltimore Light Artillery, but on the 22d of March, 1864, a general order from the Adjutant and Inspector-General directed all the Maryland companies then in service, save Company K, First Virginia Cavalry, to report to Colonel Johnson at Hanover Junction. By this order the force at Hanover Junction was increased by the addition of the First Maryland Artillery, Captain William F. Dement, and Third Maryland Artillery (Chesapeake), Captain W. Scott Chew.

On the 1st of March, 1864, Colonel Johnson received a telegram from General Lee to the effect that a large body of cavalry had passed his flank and was moving in the direction of Hanover Junction. Colonel Johnson immediately sent out his scouts, and they soon discovered it was a heavy column, indeed, and moving southward. The column crossed the Virginia Central Railroad at Frederick's Hall on Johnson's left, and took the road which led direct to Richmond.

This proved to be a force of thirty-five hundred men, commanded by General Judson Kilpatrick and Colonel Ulric Dahlgren, two daring Federal officers, who had conceived the bold, and, in part devilish, exploit of marching on Richmond, releasing the thousands of Federal prisoners confined on Belle Isle, burning Richmond, and giving it up to sack, and murdering President Davis and his Cabinet. The expedition was divided into two columns, that of Dahlgren moving rapidly across the railroad at Frederick's Hall and thence to Dover Mills, where he attempted to cross the James, about twenty miles above Richmond, but a freshet in the river made it unfordable at this point. Being thus foiled, Dahlgren rode rapidly down the river road toward the Capital.

In the meantime Kilpatrick had pressed down the Fredericksburg road in the direction of Richmond, and his route lay by Hanover Junction, the key to Lee's position, for by the railroad's passing this point General Lee was dependent for his supplies from the South and from the Valley of Virginia, and should the six bridges over the North and South Anna and Middle Rivers be destroyed Lee's position would be rendered untenable.

Colonel Johnson immediately ordered his pickets to destroy the boats on the Pamunkey, to cut off Kilpatrick's retreat in that direction, and with sixty men of the First Maryland Cavalry and two guns from the Baltimore Light Artillery — the only disposable force he had left after sending out his scouts to watch the enemy's movements — he followed in pursuit. A short distance outside of Taylorsville the enemy's pickets were encountered, driven in and pursued to Ashland. Here a large force was met on its way to destroy the railroad and buildings there. Johnson attacked this force with great vigor and drove it off.

Thence moving rapidly Colonel Johnson fell upon the enemy's flank at Yellow Tavern, and, posting his men, commenced to capture small parties that came along, among them a Sergeant with five men, who proved to be a bearer of dispatches from Dahlgren to Kilpatrick. Kilpatrick's guns were then thundering away at the outer defenses of Richmond, and Dahlgren's dispatch informed him that he would attack at dusk that evening on his road, and he looked for Kilpatrick to attack with vigor on his (Kilpatrick's) side of the city.

Colonel Johnson saw at once that he had destroyed the communication between the co-operating forces, and he prepared immediately to attack and harrass Kilpatrick's rear. Taking care not to expose the number of his force, he attacked a picket in the rear of the centre of the line of battle drawn up in front of Richmond, and drove it in. This bold act conveyed the impression to Kilpatrick that he was cut off, and seriously in danger in his rear. Hastily mounting his troops, he moved at a trot down the Peninsula toward the Pamunkey, and crossed the Chickahominy at Meadow Bridge before dark, and went into camp. Colonel Johnson encamped on the other side.

At daylight next morning Colonel Johnson crossed his small force over the river, and came up with Kilpatrick's rear guard near Old Church, which was immediately attacked, and several prisoners taken. Still taking every precaution not to expose to the enemy the smallness of his force, Johnson continued to harrass him, and drove his rear guard through Old Church in confusion. Here, thinking himself seriously menaced, Kilpatrick formed line of battle. It was too ridiculous — three thousand men in battle array to fight sixty men ! Moving a regiment in his rear, he compelled Johnson to fall back half a mile, but as soon as this returned to the main body he again renewed his attacks upon the unhappy rear guard.

In this way they moved down the Peninsula some miles, when a scout informed Colonel Johnson that a column of the enemy was moving down the road immediately in his rear. He was thus between two forces. Dismounting his men, and deploying them in the woods on each side of the road, he awaited their approach. Upon perceiving him, they made a charge and went through his thin line, not, however, without losing forty-five men and horses.

This proved to be a remnant of Dahlgren's marauders, four hundred strong, laden with plunder, much of which was abandoned in their flight, and fell into Johnson's hands, and many articles of value were by him afterward returned to the rightful owners.

From their statement, it appeared that Dahlgren, not receiving an answer to the dispatch sent to Kilpatrick, and which was fortunately intercepted by Johnson, as already seen, started with a hundred men to find him, but failed to get across the Pamunkey at Dabney's Ferry, owing to the destruction of the boats, as has been stated, and in his endeavors to escape through King and Queen County had been intercepted by Lieutenant James Pollard, of Company H, Ninth Virginia Cavalry, who had gotten together eight or ten of his men, and a company of boys under Captain R. H. Bagby. In the fight that ensued Dahlgren was killed and most of his command captured.

Kilpatrick, finding the expedition a failure and believing himself pressed by a superior force, although but sixty sabres were at his heels, made for the lower ferries of the Pamunkey, but failed to cross for the same reason that Dahlgren had, and finally reached Tunstall's Station and joined the forces under Butler, having been followed the whole way by the Maryland cavalry.

Colonel J. Thomas Scharf, in his "History of Maryland," gives the following interesting description of this most brilliant achievement of Colonel Johnson and his handful of gallant Maryland boys :

The first information reached him just before midnight of February 29 that a body of cavalry had passed the right of the army, accompanied by orders to find it without delay, ascertain its force and the direction it was moving, and its intentions and object, fight it if possible, and to save the bridges at all hazards. He immediately sent orders to his pickets to destroy the boats on the Pamunkey, between Hanover Court House and the White House, in order to prevent the escape of the enemy in that direction, and at the same time sent out an expanding circle of scouting parties to the north and west to ascertain the movements of the enemy. It was soon ascertained that they were moving on Hanover Junction, and that there was a large force. The extended pickets and necessary scouts had only left about sixty men of the First Maryland Cavalry present for duty, and these, with the infantry and artillery, were prepared to receive the expected attack. Moving out with the cavalry and two pieces of the Baltimore Light Artillery, just before light, on March 1, Johnson struck a force of the enemy near Taylorsville, two miles from the junction, and drove them off. Pushing on, he found that the main body had moved rapidly on Richmond, and were at least an hour ahead of him. He followed quickly on their line of march, and at the Yellow Tavern, five miles from Richmond, found them, under Kilpatrick, in line of battle a mile beyond him, preparing to attack the city, upon whose outworks they had already opened with artillery. Just then a straggler was captured, and finding there were forces in the rear, Johnson drew his squadron off on the side of the road, and posted a picket in Federal uniform on the road itself. In a few minutes a squad of five men rode into the ambuscade, who proved to be the guard of a bearer of a dispatch from Dahlgren to Kilpatrick.

It was a verbal one, but the officer who bore it was forced to give it up. It was information that Dahlgren had failed in his attempt to cross the James, but would charge into the city by the river road at dark, and asking Kilpatrick's co-operation in a joint attack at that time. Immediately on getting this information, Colonel Johnson charged Kilpatrick's picket and rear guard, which he had left behind him on the Brook turnpike, and drove them in on the main body. Whereupon Kilpatrick at once desisted from this attack, took horse and drew off his troops in the direction of the Peninsula, evidently aiming to escape over the Pamunkey, or down toward Williamsburg. Colonel Johnson with his sixty men followed close on his heels, and that night Kilpatrick camped on the eastern side of the Chickahominy, only four miles from Richmond, with Johnson on the other side of that river, between him and Richmond. During the night Hampton came on Kilpatrick's camp and drove him from it with loss in prisoners and horses.

At daylight on the 2d the Confederates were again on his track, and for the whole day kept harrassing him, constantly driving in his rear guard, and never losing sight of him, until he eventually escaped by joining an infantry force which was sent from Williamsburg to Tunstall's Station, on the York River Railroad, to rescue him.

So persistent and vigorous was the pursuit, so sharp and incessant the charges of the Marylanders, that at Old Church, sixteen miles from Richmond, General Kilpatrick was forced to go into line of battle and offer to fight his adversary. He displayed three thousand picked cavalry and a battery of six guns, prepared to resist the onslaught of the sixty hornets who had been stinging, exasperating and alarming him for nearly twenty-four hours.

Such an invitation was, of course, declined, but a regiment of the Union troops charged them and drove the Marylanders back to Old Church, with loss of one man.

As soon as the Federal regiment retired, however, the Marylanders went at them again, and while thus engaged were themselves charged in rear by a force of four hundred men, part of Dahlgren's command, who were seeking to unite with Kilpatrick. With three thousand men in front and four hundred in rear, the Marylanders, undismayed, opened their ranks, let them through, and actually closed in on their flanks, and brought off many prisoners, besides inflicting severe loss in killed and wounded.

In these whole series of fights Colonel Johnson's loss was comparatively trifling. Captain George M. Emack, of Company B, was slightly wounded; Lieutenant C. Irving Ditty, of Company F, seriously through the thigh; Private George T. Parker, Company B, sabre cuts over the head; Private R. K. King, sabre cuts over head and shoulders, and Private Richard H. Key, Company B, sabre cuts, and a prisoner by his horse being killed.

Colonel Johnson captured more than twice as many of the enemy as he had men in his command, besides inflicting heavy loss upon them in killed and wounded.

The daring and skill displayed by Colonel Johnson in this affair was not excelled by any achievements during the war, and he was justly called the savior of the Confederate Capital. In commemoration of his services General Elzey, in command of the defenses of Richmond, issued a general order complimenting the command, and General Hampton, in his report to General Lee distinctly gave the credit of saving Richmond to the First Maryland and their gallant leader, and at the same time he presented Colonel Johnson with a sabre, which is now in the relic room at the Confederate Soldiers' Home at Pikesville.

EXTRACT FROM HAMPTON'S REPORT, MARCH 6, 1864.

War Records, General No. 60, page 199.

In the first place, my observation convinced me that the enemy could have taken Richmond, and in all probability would have done so but for the fact that Colonel Johnson intercepted a dispatch from Dahlgren to Kilpatrick, asking what hour the latter had fixed for an attack on the city, so that both attacks might be simultaneous.

War Records No. 60, page 202, March 8, 1864.

I cannot close my report without expressing my appreciation of the conduct of Colonel Bradley T. Johnson and his gallant command.

With a mere handful of men he met the enemy at Beaver Dam and he never lost sight of them until they had passed Tunstall's Station, hanging on their rear, striking them constantly, and displaying throughout the very highest qualities of a soldier. He is eminently fitted for the cavalry service, and I trust it will not be deemed an interference on my part to urge as emphatically as I can his promotion.

War Records No. 60, page 216.

HEADQUARTERS DEPARTMENT OF HENRICO, March 8. 1864.

General Orders No. 10.

The Major-General commanding congratulates the troops upon their completely successful defense of the City of Richmond and its rescue from the ravages of the invader. . . . To Colonel Bradley T. Johnson and the officers and soldiers under his command the thanks of the Major-General are especially due for the prompt and vigorous manner in which they pursued the enemy from Beaver Dam to Richmond, and thence to the Pamunkey and down the Peninsula, making repeated charges and thwarting any attempt of the enemy to charge them.

BY COMMAND OF MAJOR-GENERAL ELZEY.

T. O. CHESTNEY, *Assistant Adjutant-General.*

(The order thanks Colonel Stevens, Brigadier-General G. W. C. Lee and Major-General Hampton and their respective commands.)

Thus, by these few men, was prevented the consummation of one of the most diabolical crimes ever conceived by human mind, and the names of Ulric Dahlgren and Judson Kilpatrick will be infamous for all time, for upon the inanimate body of the former was found the following paper, which needs no interpretation :

HEADQUARTERS THIRD DIVISION CAVALRY CORPS.

Guides, Pioneers (With Oakum, Turpentine and Torpedoes), Signal Officer, Commissary, Scouts and Picked Men in Rebel Uniform :

Men will remain on the north bank and move down with the force on south bank, not getting ahead of them ; and if the communications can be kept up without giving an alarm it must be done. Everything depends upon a surprise, and *NO ONE* must be allowed to pass ahead of the column. Information must be gathered in regard to the crossings of the river, so that should we be repulsed on the south side we will know where to cross at the nearest point. All mills must be burned and the canal destroyed, and also everything which can be used by the rebels must be destroyed, including the boats on the river. Should a ferry-boat be seized and can be worked, have it moved down. Keep the force on the south side posted of any important movement of the enemy, and in case of danger some of the scouts must swim the river and bring us information. As we approach the city, the party must take great care that they do not get ahead of the other party on the south side, and must conceal themselves and watch our movements. We will try and secure the bridge to the city (one mile below Belle Island) and release the prisoners at the same time. If we do not succeed, they must then dash down, and we will try and carry the bridge from each side. When necessary, the men must be filed through the woods and along the river bank. The bridges once secured and the prisoners loose and over the river, the bridges will be secured and the city destroyed. The men must keep together and well in hand, and once in the city, it must be destroyed, and Jeff Davis and his Cabinet killed. Pioneers will go along with combustible material. The officer must use his discretion about the time of assisting us. Horses and cattle which we do not need immediately must be shot rather than left. Everything on the canal and elsewhere of service to the rebels must be destroyed. As General Custer may follow me, be careful not to give a false alarm.

CHAPTER VI.

On the 9th of May, 1864, Sheridan began his raid around Richmond. Colonel Johnson had gone on a scout toward Yorktown and left Lieutenant-Colonel Ridgely Brown in camp in command of parts of four companies. On the afternoon of that day Colonel Brown received information that a portion of the enemy's cavalry were raiding on the rear of Lee's army, and had cut the railroad and destroyed the cars and provisions accumulated at some point above Hanover Court House. He immediately assembled his little command of one hundred and fifty sabres and set out to ascertain the truth of the report. Shortly after passing Hanover Junction the gleam of camp fires in the distance (it was just after dark) along the line of railway in his front seemed to confirm the rumor. The battalion pushed on at a trot, taking the usual precaution to throw out an advance guard and flankers, and about 11 o'clock P. M. arrived at a point about a mile from Beaver Dam, when it became evident that they were in close proximity to a large force that was taking no pains to conceal their presence. The battalion was halted, and Colonel Brown himself dismounted and went ahead on foot to reconnoiter. He found the enemy in great glee, laughing and shouting at the top of their voices, whilst at the same time they were busily engaged in burning railroad ties, and generally seemed to feel the existence of an enemy to be an absurdity. So close did Colonel Brown get to them that he came near surprising a party in a cut. After having taken a good view, he quietly returned to his command, which had been silently awaiting him, and dismounting all the men that could be spared, amounting to some eighty or ninety, he advanced on the railroad. Silently the little band crept on, carbine advanced, and ready to begin the work of death at an instant's warning. Not a word was spoken, and the men held their breath in anxious expectation, until right upon the bank of the railroad, when a whispered exclamation announced that the enemy had gone. Not far, though, for they could be plainly heard a short distance up the road.

The skirmish party was then formed in column, and moved to the left toward the county road, not a hundred yards distant, with the intention to again deploy and advance until the enemy was found. Not half the column had crossed the fence which bounded the road when there was a challenge and shot almost simultaneous, followed by a volley from both sides. In the darkness, blinded by the fires the enemy had lighted, the head of the column had come suddenly upon a Federal picket at a point which Colonel Brown, not half an hour before, had found entirely unguarded; but during his absence they had finished their work and gone to bed, posting pickets in the meantime, from habit more than anything else, as the picket stumbled upon was only a few yards from the main body, which appeared to be resting in a continuous line along and on both sides of the road.

Colonel Brown deployed at once, and advanced rapidly, the whole line keeping up a vigorous fire, which was made more effectual because, while being in the shadow themselves, the confused enemy was distinctly visible by the light of the fires they had built. This could be plainly seen, as in driving the enemy back they passed over the ground which had been held by them, and found many dead and wounded men and horses.

Still pressing the enemy back, Colonel Brown came to a skirt of woods, about half a mile from the point where he first met them, when a cavalry charge was made upon his thin line, which, however, was handsomely repulsed, and the enemy driven back in confusion. Passing through this woods, he found them posted in great strength on both sides of the road, in open fields, awaiting his attack. Upon observing this Colonel Brown slowly withdrew his command unmolested.

He now ascertained, from evidence before him and from prisoners taken, that instead of fighting, as he supposed, a small raiding party, he had engaged the advance of Sheridan's army of thirteen thousand men. Mounting his men, he held his ground until daylight, when a dispatch was received from General J. E. B. Stuart directing Colonel Brown to harrass and delay the enemy as long as possible, as he was in pursuit.

Accordingly, he at once advanced upon the enemy's pickets and drove them back, when they were reinforced, but again driven back several times in succession, until Sheridan pushed forward heavy reinforcements, when Colonel Brown deemed it advisable to retire a short distance, the enemy manifesting no disposition to pursue. Thus for some time the opposing forces watched each other in silence, when Brown moved his men some distance to the rear to feed the horses, but leaving a force of twenty men, under command of Lieutenant C. Irving Ditty, to observe their movements.

But a few minutes elapsed before the enemy became restive, and could be seen forming a strong column in the road, with heavy masses on each side of it, and clouds of mounted and dismounted skirmishers taking position in front. The fact was at once communicated to Colonel Brown. A bugle sound next announced the enemy's approach, and the heavy columns moved forward in imposing array upon Ditty's little force of twenty men. At this instant Brown came up at a gallop, and a spirited fight ensued. A dozen times did the column of mounted men attack, but a dozen times they were driven back in confusion, until the dismounted men moved through the woods on Brown's flank and compelled him to retire; and at last, about midday, they forced him back beyond the woods into the clear country, where Sheridan could see the insignificant force that had so many precious hours kept him in check. Then, and not until then, could his cavalry be brought to a charge, which the First Maryland, from its better knowledge of the country, easily avoided, not, however, without a parting volley, which emptied several saddles, two riderless horses running into their ranks. Colonel Johnson here returned and assumed command. The battalion then hurried on to Hanover Junction, whither it was supposed Sheridan was moving, where they united with the Second Maryland Infantry and Baltimore Light Artillery, when all prepared to give a good account of themselves should the enemy make his appearance. It was but a little band of brave men opposing an overwhelming force, and their destruction seemed inevitable, for General Lee had dispatched to them to hold the point to the last, and that he had no reinforcements to give them. Quietly as they stood in line of battle they discussed the matter, and determined that the Maryland Line of '64 should reflect no disgrace upon their hereditary name. But they were saved the sacrifice, for Sheridan, passing six or eight miles in their rear, marched directly upon Richmond.

In this affair at Beaver Dam Captain A. F. Schwartz, of Company F, and Lieutenant J. A. V. Pue, of Company A, were painfully, but not dangerously wounded, almost at the first fire. During the lull of hostilities, and before daylight, they were removed to the house of Mr. Redd, a kind Virginia gentleman, living about five miles from the scene of conflict. Here they were kindly cared for and rapidly improved, when General Lee fell back in the direction of Richmond, and they fell into the enemy's lines, who immediately sent a force of cavalry to capture them. Upon an examination of their condition by the surgeon with the party he declared it his belief that they would die if removed; but the officer in command, who seemed really ashamed of his brutal mission, said those were his orders, and he must obey them. However, he at last yielded to the entreaties of the ladies of the family, and reported the facts to his superior officer, who at once made the order for their removal imperative. This was done, and the two poor, suffering men were placed in an ambulance and started off, the guard stealing the covering thrown over them by the ladies of Mr. Redd's family before they had gone five miles. Being taken across the country to Fredericksburg, they were there placed on board a transport and conveyed to a Washington hospital, where, soon after their arrival, the gallant, whole-souled Captain Schwartz died in great agony, and Lieutenant Pue suffered months of excruciating pain.

On the day after the fight at Beaver Dam General J. E. B. Stuart came up and ordered Colonel Johnson to watch General Lee's flank with the First Maryland Cavalry, whilst he, with twenty-five hundred horse, threw himself between Sheridan and Richmond.

Stuart met the enemy at Yellow Tavern, and, after one of the most sanguinary cavalry fights of the war, he saved Richmond, but lost his own valuable life.*

---

* For an account of Stuart's death, see Company K, First Maryland Cavalry.

In the latter part of May, Lee fell back before Grant, and made Hanover Junction a point of defense. Sending for Colonel Johnson, he directed him to take Brown's battalion and pass around Grant and see what he was doing, and especially his base of supplies. The little command crossed the North Anna below Lee's right and pursued its way to Penola Station, on the Fredericksburg Rail road, where Colonel Johnson discovered a heavy column moving down from Bowling Green, and at the same time ascertained that the enemy drew his supplies from Tappahannock. Turning to retrace his steps, he found the whole of Sheridan's cavalry moving up through King William, in his rear, and all the fords on the lower Anna in his possession. This compelled him to cross higher up, which was effected by throwing the horses into the stream from a high bank. Johnson finally reached the main body in safety, having captured several couriers, from whom it was ascertained that Sheridan was coming up and Burnside moving down from Bowling Green.

For the signal service rendered upon this occasion, Colonel Johnson and his command were highly complimented by General Lee.

On the 27th of May, Colonel Johnson was ordered to report with his cavalry to General Fitz Lee, who was then at Hanover Court House. A short time after his arrival the enemy crossed at Dabney's Ferry, when by order of General Lomax he was ordered to go down and drive them back. Upon his arrival he found Colonel Baker, of the Fifth North Carolina, in command of Gordon's old brigade, skirmishing with a force not far from the ferry. Believing it to be a small body, it was arranged that Baker should hold them where they were whilst Johnson passed around to their flank, by which movement it was hoped they would capture the whole of them. Taking a side road, he had not gone more than a mile before he encountered Baker's pickets retiring in good order, followed by the enemy. Before he could deploy his men on some open ground on the side of the road, a stand was made for some twenty minutes under a fierce fire, when the enemy moved upon him in overwhelming force, and Johnson was forced to retire. His horse was killed. The greater part of the battalion had unfortunately just passed through a gate in to a field when the enemy charged. A dreadful hand-to-hand fight ensued, and before the gate could be opened for them to retreat many were killed and wounded, among the latter the gallant Brown by several sabre cuts over the head. It was soon perceived that the enemy were wrapping around the little battalion, and threatening it with destruction, when the order was given to retreat. This was conducted for a time in an orderly manner, but the enemy pressed them so hard that command was given for every man to look out for himself.

The First Maryland lost in this unfortunate affair at Pollard's farm between fifty and sixty men in killed, wounded and prisoners, among the latter Captain

George Howard, of Company C. Colonel Johnson and Lieutenant-Colonel Brown made narrow escapes, the former having his horse killed under him and his sabre shot away, whilst the latter received several severe sabre cuts on the head while gallantly endeavoring to pass his men through the gate which obstructed their retreat. If unfortunate for the Maryland battalion, however, it was fortunate for Baker, whose brigade of North Carolinians would most assuredly have been cut to pieces had the enemy not been held in check for a full half hour, thereby enabling them to escape. The force encountered turned out to be Custer's Brigade of four thousand men, supported by the rest of Merritt's division of cavalry.

CHAPTER VII.

For the next few days the battalion was engaged in skirmishing about Hanover Court House, the enemy occupying them there whilst his columns were crossing at Dabney's Ferry, and pressing on toward Richmond.

On the 1st of June, 1864, the enemy moved on the South Anna bridges, Johnson's small command of one hundred and fifty sabres and Griffin's Baltimore Light Artillery contesting every foot of ground in a fight lasting from daylight until 2 o'clock in the afternoon, when they were driven back by a brigade of the enemy's cavalry.

In this encounter the First Maryland Cavalry suffered an irreparable loss in the death of the noble Lieutenant-Colonel Ridgely Brown, who was killed by a stray bullet when all was comparatively calm, and no fighting going on. In many respects Ridgely Brown reminded one of the heroic and lamented Turner Ashby. A Christian gentleman, quiet, unassuming, dashing, brave, and, like all brave men, generous to a fault, Colonel Brown was the idol of his command, and his men never hesitated to follow his lead, it made no difference how desperate the undertaking. Like Ashby, after having survived a hundred fierce fights, though wounded time and again, he lost his life in a comparatively insignificant skirmish. In the death of Colonel Brown, Colonel Johnson lost an officer who had been invaluable to him, for to his sound judgment and advice that officer attributed much of his success in thwarting Kilpatrick and Dahlgren in their designs against Richmond.

In a general order issued on the 6th of June Colonel Johnson thus speaks of his death:

HEADQUARTERS MARYLAND LINE, June 6, 1864.

General Order No. 26.

Lieutenant-Colonel Ridgely Brown, commanding First Maryland Cavalry, fell in battle on the 1st instant, near the South Anna. He died, as a soldier prefers to die, leading his men in a victorious charge. As an officer, kind and careful; as a soldier, brave and true; as a gentleman, chivalrous; as a Christian, gentle and modest; no one in the Confederate Army surpassed him in the hold he had on the hearts of his men, and the place in the esteem of his superiors. Of the rich blood that Maryland has lavished on every battle-field, none is more precious than his, and that of our other brave comrades in arms who fell during the four days previous on the hillsides of Hanover. His command has lost a friend most steadfast, but his commanding officer is deprived of an assistant invaluable. To the first he was ever as careful as a father; to the latter as true as a brother.

In token of respect to his memory, the colors of the different regiments of this command will be draped, and the officers wear the usual badge of military mourning for thirty days.

BY ORDER OF COLONEL BRADLEY T. JOHNSON.

GEORGE W. BOOTH, *A. A. G.*

A correspondent in the *Richmond Sentinel,* who signs himself "A VIRGINIAN," pays the following handsome tribute to his memory :

Of the many brave and noble men who have fought the invaders of Southern soil, and have died in defense of Southern homes and Southern rights, none deserve a higher tribute of praise, or a larger measure of thanks from the Southern people than Colonel Brown. A native of Montgomery County, Maryland, and a citizen of that State, at the commencement of the present war, it would have been but natural for him to have taken the passive attitude which was assumed by his State, where he would now in all probability be gladdening by his presence a large circle of relatives and friends, instead of throwing dark shadows around their hearts from his lowly grave in Virginia. But, like many other noble sons of Maryland, he left his quiet and secure home to give his services to the Southern Confederacy, threatened with subjugation, and even extermination. He labored day and night in its service, and has poured out his life's blood upon its altar.

He came to Virginia on the first day of June, 1861, and was mortally wounded on the first day of June, 1864, just three years after. He entered the army in the capacity of a private. In less than a year he was raised to the position of a Lieutenant ; he soon reached the rank of Captain, and was then promoted to a Lieutenant-Colonelcy. To each of those positions he was lifted by merit alone, and would probably have soon reached much higher rank, had not envious death closed his career.

Never was there an officer more beloved by his command, and never was there one who more deserved it. As brave as a lion in time of danger, he was as careful of his men as a mother of her children. His men say that when thrown upon his own responsibility he never led them into a position of peril without first examining it himself ; nor ordered them to go where he was not ready to lead ; and they felt perfectly secure under his leadership. After his promotion to the command of a regiment of cavalry, it was remarked that he was much more silent than before. A friend asked him the reason. He replied that so many lives committed to his charge involved a responsibility which pressed heavily upon him.

He was a Christian man, and death has been his gain. The loss is all to those who remain behind — to his parents, who have lost a devoted son ; to his acquaintances, who have lost one of friendship's greatest treasures ; to the Confederacy, which has lost one of its most valuable defenders. But more than this — morality has lost one of its best exemplars, and chivalry one of her noblest sons. His influence for good in his command who can supply.

Many soldiers and many citizens will mingle their tears on his grave, to water the flowers which friendship and affection will plant there ; and when flowers shall wither, his memory will continue to bloom in many hearts.

After the death of the lamented General J. E. B. Stuart, General Wade Hampton was assigned to the command of the cavalry. On the 12th of June Hampton, with four thousand five hundred sabres, met Sheridan at Trevillian Station with eight thousand. The First Maryland was posted on Hampton's extreme left to support General Rosser. The dashing Custer opened the fight with a charge of his brigade, and he went through Hampton's centre, creating terrible confusion among the led horses and ordnance wagons ; but the daring and intrepid Rosser was in his way, and charging him in turn with his brigade and Johnson with the First Maryland, he cut him in two, and pursued him to his very wagon train, capturing his headquarters' wagon, and breaking up his brigade. This charge of Rosser's is pronounced one of the most brilliant of the many made during the war.

The battle of Trevillian raged for two days, and during that time charge after charge was made, with varying success. For two days sabres flashed in a hand-to-hand conflict, and the carbine and pistol did their deadly work, strewing the plain with hundreds of dead and dying men. In those two dreadful days the little First Maryland was ever in the van, and their gallant bearing elicited the admiration of all. They fought as though to avenge the fall of their comrades at Pollard's farm, and their sabres drank deeply of the blood of the foemen. But Sheridan had met his match in Hampton, and suffered an unmistakable defeat.

CHAPTER VIII.

During the winter of 1863-4 Colonel Johnson originated a plan for capturing President Lincoln, which he suggested to General Hampton, who, after several conversations with Johnson upon the subject, gave it his approval, and entered heartily into the undertaking.

Confederate spies in Washington had kept General Lee thoroughly posted as to the disposition and force of every command of the enemy in and around his Capital. To carry out this daring enterprise, then, Colonel Johnson was to take the Maryland battalion, numbering two hundred and fifty sabres, and cross the Potomac above Georgetown, make a dash at a battalion of cavalry known to be stationed there, and push on to the Soldiers' Home, where it was well known President Lincoln lived, and after capturing him to send him across the river in charge of a body of picked men, whilst the main body was to cut the wires and roads between Washington and Baltimore, and then move back through Western Maryland to the Valley of Virginia ; or, if that means of retreat was cut off, Johnson was to go up into Pennsylvania, and on west to West Virginia beyond Grafton. It seemed, indeed, a most desperate undertaking, but everything promised its successful accomplishment. Indeed, so sanguine was Hampton that the plan of Johnson would succeed that he wanted to undertake it himself at the head of four thousand horse, and was only prevented by Sheridan's advance upon the Confederate Capital.

After the fight at Trevillians, then, he gave Johnson orders to prepare for his trip. The best horses in the cavalry command were selected, and the best men in the battalion picked out, but whilst shoeing his horses and recruiting his men he was prevented from carrying out his much-cherished plans by an order from General Early to join him at once with his battalion in the Valley of Virginia, and cover his rear whilst that General went after Hunter, who had marched upon Lynchburg.

In a week General Early returned to Staunton, and it was then that Colonel Johnson received his long-delayed commission as Brigadier-General of cavalry, and was at once assigned to the command of the brigade formerly commanded by General William E. Jones, who had been killed at the battle fought near New Hope.

Much to his gratification, he was given permission, on the third day of July, 1864, to attach the First Maryland to his brigade, and then ordered to take the advance of Early's army, moving on Martinsburg. At Leetown the brigade encountered Mulligan's advance, and after a severe engagement the enemy was driven back with loss. In this affair the First Maryland surprised their new allies by their dashing style of fighting.

On the 5th of July General Johnson crossed the Potomac near Sharpsburg, where he met a small force of the enemy's cavalry, which Lieutenant George M. E. Shearer, with a detachment of the First Maryland pursued into Hagerstown, when coming suddenly upon a superior force he was compelled to retreat upon the main body. In the pursuit which ensued Shearer was taken prisoner, along with several of his men.

On the night of the 8th General Johnson was directed to report to General Early in person, near Middletown, Maryland. General Early at that meeting directed General Johnson to move early on the morning of the 9th and take position north of Frederick City and watch his (Early's) left during the battle that was to ensue next day at the Monocacy River. Being assured of Early's success, Johnson was then to strike across the country, destroying railroads and telegraphs north of Baltimore, then to sweep rapidly around the city and cut the Baltimore and Ohio Railroad between Baltimore and Washington. This accomplished, Johnson was to push on for Point Lookout and reach that place if possible on the night of the 12th of July, so as to co-operate with Captain John Taylor Wood, who was to be there at that time with an armed Confederate steamer. The ten or twelve thousand prisoners there released, Johnson was to march them to Washington, where Early was to wait for him. Should Early be successful in his contemplated attack upon the Federal Capital, these prisoners were to be armed from the several arsenals of that city.

It seemed utterly impossible for General Johnson to reach Point Lookout by the time specified, and he so expressed himself, but was perfectly willing to lead the expedition. Accordingly, on the morning of the 9th, he started from the vicinity of Frederick, and moving through Liberty, New Windsor, Westminster and Reisterstown, reached Cockeysville on the morning of the 10th, and burned the railroad bridge there. Colonel Harry Gilmor was here detached with his own and part of the First Maryland battalion, and ordered to raid the Philadelphia, Wilmington and Baltimore Railroad near the Gunpowder River, and if possible burn the bridge. In this Gilmor was successful. He not only burned the bridge, but he captured two trains, on one of which Major-General Franklin was a passenger. Franklin was captured, but subsequently made his escape.

From Cockeysville General Johnson shaped his course across Green Spring Valley, in Baltimore County, and after burning the residence of Governor Bradford, in retaliation for the burning of the home of Governor Letcher, in Virginia, which had been destroyed by firebrand Hunter under circumstances of peculiar brutality, General Johnson went into camp for the night at the "Caves," the home of John Carroll, Esq. Here General Johnson learned from a trusty scout, now president of a great railroad, he had previously sent into Baltimore that all the available transportation of the Baltimore and Ohio Railroad was concentrated at Locust Point, and that the Nineteenth Corps and part of the Sixth Corps were on transports from Grant's army, and expected every hour on their way to Washington.

This information General Johnson immediately forwarded to General Early, and then moved in the direction of Washington on his way to fulfill his hazardous mission of releasing the prisoners at Point Lookout.

In the meantime, after defeating Wallace at the Monocacy River, General Early marched direct to Washington, and appeared before the outer defenses of that city on the morning of the 11th, but owing to the extreme heat and the broken-down condition of the men the column was not closed up and the troops in position before late in the evening of that day. It was then impossible to put the men in, and the attack was postponed until the next morning for that reason, and because General Early had seen as he rode forward large bodies of troops filing into the fortifications.

In his " Last Year of the War " General Early thus speaks of his appearance before Washington :

" Under these circumstances, to have rushed my men blindly against the fortifications, without understanding the state of things, would have been more than folly."

After a consultation with Generals Breckinridge, Rodes, Gordon and Ramseur, General Early determined to make the assault next morning, unless some unforeseen circumstance should arise. And the unexpected did arise. General Early says :

" During the night a dispatch was received from General Bradley T. Johnson, from near Baltimore, informing me that he had received information from a reliable source that two corps had arrived from General Grant's army, and that his whole army was probably in motion. This caused me to delay the attack until I could examine the works again, and, as soon as it was light enough to see, I rode to the front and found the parapets lined with troops. I had, therefore, reluctantly to give up all hopes of capturing Washington, after I had arrived in sight of the dome of the Capitol and given the Federal authorities a dreadful fright."

While these events were transpiring, General Johnson was moving rapidly through Howard and Montgomery Counties. After passing Triadelphia, Johnson struck the Washington Branch near Beltsville, and after halting a short time to feed he turned the head of his column toward Upper Marlboro, on his way to Point Lookout, but had not proceeded far before he was overtaken by a courier from General Early, with orders to report at once to him at Silver Spring, on the Seventh Street (Washington) road. After driving back toward Washington a strong force of Federal cavalry, Johnson moved in the direction of Silver Spring, where he found the whole army in retreat. He was directed by General Early to close up the rear, with Jackson's cavalry brigade behind him. The rear passed through Rockville that day, where Jackson was hard pressed by the Second Massachusetts Cavalry, who made it very warm and uncomfortable. Getting tired of this General Johnson ordered Captain Wilson C. Nicholas and Lieutenant Thomas Green to take a squad of the First Maryland and charge into Rockville. This they did, scattering the pursuers in all directions, but the dismounted men took refuge in the houses and poured in a galling fire. The horses of Nicholas and Green were killed, and their riders wounded and taken prisoners. As soon as Johnson discovered the condition of affairs he led another charge, and Lieutenant Green was recaptured, but Captain Nicholas had been put on a horse and run off the field.

During the rest of that day the pursuers kept at a respectful distance, and on the next day (the 14th) the command reached Poolsville. There General Johnson effectually held the enemy in check with his cavalry until everything had crossed the Potomac to the Virginia side, when he withdrew, closely pressed by cavalry and infantry.

Thus ended one of the most remarkable episodes of the war. It had failed in the main object of the expedition, which was to release the prisoners at Point Lookout. The audacity of this movement was its safety, and no higher military skill was displayed on either side during the war than that shown by General Early in his daring attempt to surprise the Capital of the enemy with so small a force, and which was only averted by the energy and foresight of one man — John W. Garrett, President of the Baltimore and Ohio Railroad. He had foreseen when Early crossed the Potomac that his objective point was Washington, and at once began to assemble all the means of transportation possible on his road at Locust Point, and had himself hurried to Washington on a special train to inform the authorities of his suspicions, and urged that reinforcements be sent for from Grant's army. They came, means of transportation were at hand, and the Capital was saved by, oh, how narrow a margin!

CHAPTER IX.

For some time prior to General Early's return from his invasion of Maryland the wanton destruction of private residences by General David Hunter in Virginia had aroused the indignation of the people of the South and the Confederate Government had been appealed to to resort to retaliatory measures to put a stop to it, but as yet no steps had been taken in that direction, and General Early determined to take the matter into his own hands, and have the responsibility rest upon his shoulders.

Accordingly, General Early, on the twenty-ninth day of July, started the cavalry brigades of Generals McCausland and Bradley T. Johnson across the Potomac above Williamsport with directions to proceed to Chambersburg, in Pennsylvania, and demand an indemnity of $100,000 in gold from its citizens, otherwise the town would be burned. The people of Chambersburg, as were the people of the towns passed through by General Lee's army of invasion the year before, had been treated with so much consideration that they not only refused to raise the money, but laughed at the threat to burn their town, whereupon General McCausland proceeded to execute General Early's orders, and the greater part of Chambersburg was laid in ashes.

But of this expedition let General Early speak for himself, as he does in his "Memoirs of the Last Year of the War for Independence":

On the 26th of July, we moved to Martinsburg, the cavalry going to the Potomac. The 27th and 28th were employed in destroying the railroad, it having been repaired since we passed over it at the beginning of the month. While at Martinsburg it was ascertained, beyond all doubt, that Hunter had been again indulging in his favorite mode of warfare, and that, after his return to the Valley, while we were near Washington, among other outrages, the private residences of Mr. Andrew Hunter, a member of the Virginia Senate, Mr. Alexander R. Boteler, an ex-member of the Confederate Congress, as well as of the United States Congress, and Edmund J. Lee, a distant relative of General Lee, all in Jefferson County, with their contents, had been burned by his orders, only time enough being given for the ladies to get out of the houses. A number of towns in the South, as well as private country houses, had been burned by the Federal troops, and the accounts had been heralded forth in some of the Northern papers in terms of exultation, and gloated over by their readers, while they were received with apathy by others.

I now came to the conclusion that we had stood this mode of warfare long enough, and that it was time to open the eyes of the people of the North to its enormity by an example in the way of retaliation. I did not select the cases mentioned as having more merit or greater claims for retaliation than others, but because they had occurred within the limits of the country covered by my command, and were brought more immediately to my attention.

The town of Chambersburg, in Pennsylvania, was selected as the one on which retaliation should be made, and McCausland was ordered to proceed with his brigade and that of Johnson, and a battery of artillery, to that place and demand of the municipal authorities the sum of $100,000 in gold, or $500,000 in United States currency, as a compensation for the destruction of the houses named and their contents, and, in default of payment, to lay the town in ashes, in retaliation for the burning of those houses and others in Virginia, as well as for the towns which had been burned in other Southern States. A written demand to that effect was sent to the municipal authorities, and they were informed what would be the result of a failure or refusal to comply with it.

I desired to give the people of Chambersburg an opportunity of saving their town by making compensation for part of the injury done, and hoped that the payment of such a sum would have the desired effect, and open the eyes of the people of other towns at the North to the necessity of urging upon their Government the adoption of a different policy.

McCausland was also directed to proceed from Chambersburg towards Cumberland, Maryland, and levy contributions in money upon that and other towns able to bear them, and if possible destroy the machinery at the coal pits near Cumberland, and the machine shops, depots and bridges on the Baltimore and Ohio Railroad, as far as practicable.

On the 29th McCausland crossed the Potomac, near Clear Spring, above Williamsport, and I moved with Rode's and Ramseur's divisions and Vaughn's cavalry to the latter place, while Imboden demonstrated with his and Jackson's cavalry towards Harper's Ferry, in order to withdraw attention from McCausland. Breckinridge remained at Martinsburg, and continued the destruction of the railroad. Vaughn drove a force of cavalry from Williamsport, and went into Hagerstown, where he captured and destroyed a train of cars loaded with supplies. One of Rode's brigades was crossed over at Williamsport, and subsequently withdrawn.

On the 30th McCausland being well under way, I moved back to Martinsburg; and on the 31st the whole infantry force was moved to Bunker Hill, where we remained on the 1st, 2d and 3d of August.

On the 4th, in order to enable McCausland to retire from Pennsylvania and Maryland, and to keep Hunter, who had been reinforced by the Sixth and Nineteenth Corps, and had been oscillating between Harper's Ferry and Monocacy Junction, in a state of uncertainty, I again moved to the Potomac, with the infantry and Vaughn's and Jackson's cavalry, while Imboden demonstrated towards Harper's Ferry.

On the 5th Rode's and Ramseur's division crossed at Williamsport, and took position near St. James' College, and Vaughn's cavalry went into Hagerstown. Breckinridge, with his command, and Jackson's cavalry crossed at Shepherdstown, and took position at Sharpsburg. This position is in full view from Maryland Heights, and a cavalry force was sent out by the enemy to reconnoitre, which, after skirmishing with Jackson's cavalry, was driven off by the sharpshooters of Gordon's division.

On the 6th the whole force recrossed the Potomac at Williamsport, and moved towards Martinsburg; and on the 7th we returned to Bunker Hill.

On the 30th of July McCausland reached Chambersburg, and made the demand as directed, reading to such of the authorities as presented themselves the paper sent by me. The demand was not complied with, the people stating that they were not afraid of having their town burned, and that a Federal force was approaching. The policy pursued by our army on former occasions had been so lenient that they did not suppose the threat was in earnest this time, and they hoped for speedy relief. McCausland, however, proceeded to carry out his orders, and the greater part of the town was laid in ashes.

For this act I alone am responsible, as the officers engaged in it were simply executing my orders, and had no discretion left them. Notwithstanding the lapse of time which has occurred and the result of the war, I am perfectly satisfied with my conduct on this occasion, and see no reason to regret it.

McCausland then moved in the direction of Cumberland, but on approaching that town he found it defended by a force under Kelly too strong for him to attack, and he withdrew towards Hampshire County, in Virginia, and crossed the Potomac near the mouth of the South Branch, capturing the garrison at that place, and partially destroying the railroad bridge. He then invested the post on the railroad at New Creek, but finding it too strongly fortified to take by assault he moved to Moorefield, in Hardy County, near which place he halted to rest and recruit his men and horses, as the command was now considered safe from pursuit. Averill, however, had been pursuing from Chambersburg with a body of cavalry, and Johnson's Brigade was surprised in camp, before day, on the morning of the 7th of August, and routed by Averill's force. This resulted also in the rout of McCausland's Brigade, and the loss of the artillery (four pieces) and about three hundred prisoners from the whole command. The balance of the command made its way to Mount Jackson in great disorder, and much weakened. This affair had a very damaging effect upon my cavalry for the rest of the campaign.

The First Maryland Cavalry in this expedition was united with the battalion of Lieutenant-Colonel Harry Gilmor, and was under that officer's command. They were the first to enter Chambersburg, but met with slight resistance.

The work of destruction accomplished, it behooved McCausland to move expeditiously, as he had many obstacles to overcome before getting back to Virginia. General Averill, with a large force, was rapidly approaching, and as McCausland had several bodies of troops in his front he could not afford to have Averill too close on his heels.

Accordingly, at noon of the same day of the burning, the return march was begun, and that night the command went into camp at McConnellsburg. Next morning the march was resumed and at noon Hancock, Maryland, was reached. Here General McCausland ordered a levy of $50,000 upon the people. For some time there had been considerable friction between Generals McCausland and Johnson, and when the former made this preposterous demand upon a people who had been notoriously loyal to the Southern cause, this friction became intensified, and General Johnson denounced McCausland's demand in no mild language. In this he was sustained by Colonel Harry Gilmor, and for a time there threatened a revolt. General McCausland insisted, however, that if the money was not forthcoming within a given time he would burn the town, upon which, upon consultation with Colonel Gilmor, General Johnson ordered that officer to move his two battalions into Hancock and protect the people at all hazards. Here was a direct issue between two general officers, and it might have ended in bloodshed had not Averill put in an appearance and vigorously attacked McCausland's outposts. To repel this attack, and hold the enemy in check while the main body of the troops moved off, Colonel Gilmor with the two Maryland battalions was assigned. This duty he performed in his usual gallant style, and his little command constituted the rear guard in the retreat toward Cumberland, the vicinity of which was reached, after a forced night march, in the forenoon of the following day.

At Cumberland General Kelly was found with a large force strongly entrenched. With Kelly in his front and Averill in his rear, McCausland very wisely decided to move on, which he did after making a slight demonstration upon the enemy's outposts.

After a night march McCausland's command reached Oldtown, Gilmor's two battalions in the advance, where a considerable body of the enemy was found occupying a strong position in a block house, and also having an iron-clad battery attached to an engine on the railroad. This block house commanded the ford by which McCausland was to reach the Virginia side of the river, and as no time was to be lost it was imperative that this place should be reduced. An attack was accordingly made, but it was repulsed with considerable loss. Things were growing desperate when under a galling fire Lieutenant McNulty, of the Baltimore Light Artillery, brought one of his pieces into play, with his best gunner, McElwee, to sight it. The first shell went through the boiler of the engine and the second entered the porthole of the iron-clad, which was filled with troops, and exploding created a panic, and the battery was deserted. But it was impossible to bring the artillery to bear upon the block house, and an attack was ordered, which was repulsed. In this desperate strait someone suggested that a flag of truce be sent to the block house, and a demand made for its surrender. Captain Booth, with McCaull and Kid, two of Johnson's scouts, carried the flag and this demand. Great was the surprise of all when this demand was complied with.

It is not necessary to follow the movements of McCausland any farther, as General Early describes that up to the disastrous surprise of Johnson's Brigade at Moorefield. Of course, McCausland endeavored to throw the responsibility upon

General Johnson, and that General demanded an investigation, which exonerated him from all blame. But someone was to blame for placing the brigade in so hazardous a position, and if it was not Johnson it must have been McCausland, who was Johnson's superior officer. It has been more than once asserted that McCausland's dislike for General Johnson had much to do with bringing about the disaster, and, indeed, it has been hinted, that he was purposely sacrificed. It was certainly McCausland's place to know whether he was " safe from pursuit " or not ; and, failing in this, he showed shameful negligence, to say the least.

In this disastrous surprise Gilmor's battalion lost fifty men in killed, wounded and prisoners, and the First Maryland lost still more heavily.

Soon after the Moorefield affair Early moved to Fisher's Hill, when Gilmor was ordered to scout in his front with the two Maryland battalions. Shortly after Sheridan retreated to Winchester, and beyond this place Early pursued him. A series of desperate encounters ensued with the enemy's cavalry in the vicinity of Winchester, Martinsburg, Bunker Hill, Leetown and Charlestown, in which the First Maryland took a prominent part, and lost heavily.

One of the severest of these fights, which was but a repetition of them all, and will serve as an illustration, took place near Bunker Hill on the 13th of August, 1864. On that morning a brigade of Lomax's command, to which the First Maryland was attached, had advanced and driven in the enemy's pickets, and pushed back his cavalry several miles below Bunker Hill, where they halted for awhile, and then turned to retrace their steps. The enemy in the meanwhile had been heavily reinforced, and pressed hard upon the retreating column, of which the First Maryland formed the rear. The enemy became more and more pressing as they advanced, until a charge was ordered by Colonel Gilmor, which had the effect of checking them, and his vastly superior force only saved him from rout.

These charges had to be repeated again and again, the First Maryland retiring in excellent order at a walk. When the stream which crosses the pike at Bunker Hill was reached Gilmor, who had been much delayed in making these charges, found himself entirely unsupported, all the other regiments of the brigade having retired to the shelter of the infantry, which was formed in line about a mile distant.

At this juncture the head of the enemy's column, immediately in the rear of the First Maryland, had entered the stream before the rear of the battalion had reached the opposite bank, two other of his columns meanwhile moving unopposed parallel to the pike, and were some distance in the rear of the little band battling with ten times their number. At this most critical moment, right in the midst of the stream, the battalion wheeled, and again charged, meeting the enemy midway, when a most desperate hand-to-hand fight ensued, the blood of both intermingling with its current.

For some minutes they held the enemy in check, expecting reinforcements, but none were available, and under the desperate nature of the circumstances General Lomax ordered a battery near the line of battle which the infantry was forming, to open on the struggling mass. The artillery officer remonstrated, as he was satisfied he would damage friend as well as foe ; but the order was repeated. The first few shots fell in the ranks of the enemy, and rendered material aid to the handful of brave men in such imminent peril, but unfortunately a shell at last struck right in their midst, when, of course, the battalion broke.

The fire of a foe in front and a friend in rear was more than human nature could withstand ; but even then they did not leave the field, but retired stubbornly contesting every foot of ground until they reached a house standing in a field near the pike, and midway between Bunker Hill and the infantry line, where some of the command formed on both sides, which they were obliged to do to confront the now rapidly advancing enemy. Here a stand was made, and the fight continued for some time. On the side of the house next the pike was the color-bearer of the First Maryland, Colonel Gilmor, Captain Ditty, Captain Rasin and some fifteen officers and men, and, it becoming evident that they could no longer hold the enemy at bay, Colonel Gilmor turned to this handful and exclaimed : " Well, go at them again ! " but had not gone five steps, the battalion, or rather what was left of it, at his heels, when Colonel Gilmor dropped his pistol and wheeled around, the blood streaming from his neck, and galloped off, saying as he did so, " I'm shot ! " Seeing the folly of remaining longer, the command retired upon the infantry, which easily repulsed the enemy's cavalry.

In this desperate fight the gallant Lieutenant Henry C. Blackiston, of Company B, was killed. Lieutenant Blackiston was much beloved by his comrades, with whom he had engaged the enemy in a hundred battles.

After this affair, the battalion being much reduced, General Early ordered that it be consolidated with Gilmor's battalion. Not wishing to lose its identity, and for other reasons as well, this met with great opposition, and an earnest protest was sent to the War Department at Richmond, and the order was revoked.

Some time during the month of August, 1864, in obedience to an order from the War Department, Company K, First Virginia Cavalry, was transferred to the First Maryland. This company had been raised by Captain George R. Gaither in May, 1861, and soon after attached to the First Virginia Cavalry, then commanded by Colonel J. E. B. Stuart. It was composed entirely of Marylanders, and at the time of its transfer to the First Maryland was commanded by Captain Gustavus W. Dorsey, a most gallant soldier.

After the order of General Early had been revoked, and the First Maryland returned to its original status, Captain G. W. Dorsey was assigned to the command, with the rank of Lieutenant-Colonel, to fill the vacancy occasioned by the death of the lamented Ridgely Brown. This vacancy had existed for some time, and was only filled when it had become apparent that Major R. C. Smith, who had been wounded at Greenland Gap, was permanently disabled.

After Colonel Dorsey's accession to the command, the campaign was constantly active, and the enemy being nearly as strong in cavalry alone as General Early was in troops of all arms, his cavalry was compelled to contend with great odds. Fights and skirmishes of a greater or less magnitude were of daily and almost hourly occurrence, and with the picket duty to be performed men and horses were employed to the utmost limit of endurance.

In most of these engagements the Confederates were successful, but in one of them, at Fisher's Hill, on the 22d of September, the enemy gained considerable advantage by suddenly throwing a heavy force, consisting of two or three divisions, which he had moved up under cover of North Mountains on Early's left, upon the line of dismounted cavalry, which was all that General could spare to cover that point. Here, after they had broken the Confederate line, Colonel Dorsey ordered the First Maryland to charge, with the view to check the enemy, if possible, and gain time to bring up reinforcements, but the charge only availed to release some prisoners and to get the horses of the dismounted men out of the way. In the face of such odds Dorsey was forced back with some loss, and, although severely wounded himself, extricated his command and made an orderly retreat.

CHAPTER X.

The campaign of 1864 in the Valley of Virginia was marked with acts of barbarism and savage cruelty on the part of the enemy such as history scarcely parallels. In years long past the American heart was wont to burn with righteous indignation at the recital of the wrongs of Poland and Hungary, but then Russia and Austria were but in their rudiments, and it was reserved for the American Government to reduce barbarity to a science, to substitute the torch for the sword, murder for honorable warfare, and to elevate the incendiary's crime to the dignity of national policy.

Having failed to subdue the men of the South in the field, the soldiers of the Federal Army, with such vast odds in their favor of numbers and resources, and the whole world open to them and contributing immensely both of men and means — the Federal soldier, with all these advantages, descended to make mean war upon women and children and dumb brutes, seeking in the sufferings of these helpless victims the victory elsewhere denied them.

General Grant ordered that the Valley should be so devastated "that a crow flying over it should be obliged to carry its rations." And faithful and vigorous were the efforts made to carry out that policy. Acting under these orders from official headquarters, Sheridan's army in the Valley of Virginia obscured the light of day and illuminated the darkness of night with the smoke and flames of the conflagration that devoured alike the dwelling and the stable, the barn and the mill, stored with hay and grain, and the yet ungathered crops standing on the ground. For two weeks and more did their fires fiercely burn while the brave officers commanding this corps of incendiaries made report of their noble achievements, and the nation applauded.

The beautiful residence of Edmund J. Lee, a near relative of the great Southern chieftain, was invaded before daylight one morning by a Captain Martindale, who ruthlessly turned the family, consisting of three or four females, out of the house and set fire to it. In vain Mr. Lee's young and beautiful daughter pleaded with Martindale to save her piano, and when, at the risk of her life, the house all in flames, she rushed into it to secure some necessary clothing, as she reached the door on her return the little she had saved was ruthlessly torn from her by Martindale's order and cast back into the burning building. And so was served the homes of the Honorable Alexander R. Boteler and Andrew Hunter and hundreds of others by Hunter's and Sheridan's orders, and still the Northern people held up their hands in horror when Chambersburg was burned in just retaliation.

General Hunter, whose chief monument was the smoke from the Virginia

Military Institute and the private dwellings burned by his order, had the honor to inaugurate this system of warfare in the Valley, which was afterward so fully adopted by his Government.

All these brutal wrongs the First Maryland Cavalry witnessed, and where powerless to prevent did not forget to avenge where opportunity offered.

Other wrongs they had to remember and avenge, such as their whole prior experience had never known — the cold-blooded murder of their comrades.

In October, 1864, Churchill Crittenden and John Hartigan, privates of Company C, were detailed to procure provisions for their company, which could only be obtained from the neighboring farm-houses. The battalion was lying then in Page County, and as the country between the two armies had not been foraged so closely of its supplies, because of its being a middle ground, those two young men, so detailed, sought the required rations between the two lines. Whilst getting their supplies at a farm-house a large scouting party of the enemy came suddenly upon them. They attempted to escape, and a running fight ensued, which resulted in the death of two or three of the enemy and the wounding of Crittenden severely, and the capture of both himself and Hartigan.

The prisoners were taken back two or three miles, and there, by order of General Powell, then commanding Averill's old brigade, shot in cold blood, denying them the poor privilege of writing to their friends, though Hartigan, particularly, who had a young wife, earnestly entreated with his last breath to be allowed to send her a message.

These facts were all carefully traced out, and verified by the statement of the citizen at whose house the two young men were first attacked, and near which they fought and were captured ; by the statement of the citizen, some two miles to the rear, near whose house they were buried, not by the men who killed them, but by the pitying farmer, and by the evidence rendered by the opened graves of the poor men.

Henceforward General Powell's name was familiar to the ears and memories of the men of the First Maryland Cavalry, and many were the vows there uttered over the dead bodies of their comrades to avenge their death — and they were avenged, though Powell escaped.

CHAPTER XI.

In November, 1864, the First Maryland, now in General Davidson's Brigade of Lomax's Division, crossed the mountain and encamped near Washington, in Rappahannock County, in order to obtain supplies, which were now exceedingly scarce. For days at a time the only food was apples and bread made of corn meal of such miserable quality as to be utterly inedible except under pressure of the direst necessity. Coffee and sugar had long before disappeared — so long that it was a real effort of memory to recall their flavor — and the taste of meat was now a matter of rare occurrence, and then often obtained by the capture of a bewildered squirrel or rabbit, or the accidental falling of a tree on some luckless hog, which happened oftener than people would suppose or believe who are unacquainted with the pertinacity with which that animal will haunt a cavalry camp to steal from the horses, and at which they have often been known to be killed by a kick. Apples were, however, in abundance and excellent, and assisted greatly in keeping up the commissariat. Supplies of all kinds, however, were exhausted in two or three weeks, and the battalion moved back to the neighborhood of Madison Court House. Here it remained until December, when General Davidson was relieved by General Jackson, the former General having been only temporarily in command during the absence, while wounded, of the latter, the proper commander of the brigade.

At this time the enemy made a simultaneous advance upon Madison Court House, Staunton and Charlottesville, at which latter place Custer's division of cavalry was fought by Breathed's battery of horse artillery, composed mainly of Marylanders, without support of any kind, and so bold and vigorous was their defense that Custer retired with loss, under the impression that a large force confronted him.

The column advancing upon Madison Court House, consisting of two divisions, was engaged and held in check nearly a day by Jackson's Brigade, the fight having begun in the morning and lasting until 9 P. M. The battle was closed by a charge of the First Maryland upon the left flank of the enemy, which flank was most advanced. The charge was made less effective by reason of the leading squadron's stumbling into a deep and wide ditch, which, owing to the darkness, could not be seen until too late to prevent the horses from falling. But, although not damaging the enemy to the extent hoped for, it had the effect to break and scatter his line in confusion, and keep him quiet for the balance of the night.

After waiting for some time for further demonstrations from the enemy, and there being none, General Jackson quietly withdrew his brigade a few miles, and the men lay down in the snow, which covered the ground to the depth of ten inches, to get a little rest. In the meantime General Lomax, who had been notified in the beginning of the enemy's advance, was assembling at Liberty Mills his different brigades, which had necessarily been scattered in order to subsist.

By daylight General Jackson was moving to that point, where, after partaking of some food, the troops were directed to throw up rude breastworks, which was done by piling fence-rails along the banks of the stream. This had scarcely been accomplished when the enemy made his appearance and deployed most beautifully on the opposite hills, when a brisk skirmish began, which continued all day and until night, when the exhausted troops were ordered to unsaddle and seek some rest, but they had barely dismounted when a courier dashed up and reported that the enemy had crossed the stream, and that they were to be charged at once.

In an instant the gallant troopers sprang to their horses, and Jackson's Brigade dashed at the enemy's advance. For some time the ground was stubbornly contested, when Jackson's column to the right and left of the First Maryland broke, which compelled the whole to fall back. They were quickly rallied, however, when a desperate charge was made, and the enemy in turn compelled to retire. Lomax then withdrew his division to Gordonsville, where it rested that night, and at daylight it was again drawn up in line of battle to meet the enemy, who had made his appearance. A sharp but brief conflict ensued, in which the enemy was repulsed, when he withdrew, and finally retired by the road he came to Winchester.

After this last encounter with the enemy, Jackson's Brigade retired to within twelve or fifteen miles of Orange Court House, where it remained until about the 1st of March, 1865, when Sheridan moved down the Valley in heavy force, and captured the little that remained of Early's command near Waynesboro'. The First Maryland was ordered to hang upon his flank, which it did with great tenacity, first striking him on James River, beyond Charlottesville, and following him to the White House, on York River. So small a force could accomplish nothing by a direct attack, and it therefore confined its operations to cutting off scouting and marauding parties, which amounted in the aggregate to more than their own number three times over.

The battalion rested for some days near Richmond after it had returned from following Sheridan, when it was ordered to join Lomax in West Virginia. It accordingly marched to join that officer, and when about two days advanced on the journey was ordered back with all speed to report to General Fitzhugh Lee at Stony Creek, twenty miles from Petersburg.

Reaching Richmond on the evening of April 2, 1865, it went into camp on its suburbs. Early next morning (Sunday) the battalion moved through the city, and had the pleasure of greeting many of their comrades, prisoners on parole, awaiting exchange. The day had nothing of Sabbath quiet; churches were unattended, and the streets filled with anxious crowds of soldiers and citizens eagerly seeking and discussing the army news. Already many painful rumors were rife betokening disaster, but resolutely refusing to doubt the success of the cause in which their very souls were embarked, the little band of Marylanders — now reduced to less than one hundred in the saddle — pushed on, followed by the regrets and blessings of their paroled brothers, whose obligations forbade them, as yet, to take part in the stirring events then occurring. As the lines at Petersburg were approached, it was inexpressibly cheering to see everything calm, and the army apparently as confident and defiant as ever.

It was well known that the odds against General Lee were immense, but all Confederate victories had been won against such advantages, and an abiding faith in the justice of their cause and genius of their great chief kept up the spirits of Colonel Dorsey's command, in spite of all drawbacks. When, therefore, bodies of troops of greater or less force were seen in motion on or near the Petersburg road, in perfect order, and advancing toward the sound of the firing, which had all day been heard in their front, the Maryland boys took these facts as perfect confirmation of their pre-entertained opinion that all the news which had given rise to such distressing rumors were, instead of a retreat of the Army of Northern Virginia, only a strategic device on the part of General Lee to bring Grant out from behind his breastworks in order to attack and destroy him. Nor was this idea weakened at all when, after reaching Petersburg about dark, they found everything prepared for motion, and heard that General Lee's lines had been broken. The heavy batteries in front were in full action, and it naturally seemed that so much firing must indicate stout resistance.

Failing to find any orders from General Fitz Lee at this point, who had before this left Stony Creek, for some point to him unknown, Colonel Dorsey availed himself of such shelter as the ground afforded to rest and feed man and horse, and to await information or orders.

Here there was abundance of food and forage, for which there was not transportation, and orders had been issued for its destruction. Colonel Dorsey was therefore permitted to take as much of both for his command as could be carried, which was not much, as the horses were too weak, on account of long marches and insufficient food, to bear any considerable increase of burden. Horses and men, however, had one full meal, and it being the soldier's philosophy to let each day take care of itself, all were soon stretched upon the ground to catch such repose as might be vouchsafed them.

The enemy's fire seemed to increase in violence, and shot and shell soon began to pass over the encampment, and far in its rear, but did no damage, as the intervening hill gave full protection. In this situation, heedless of all the noises, exhausted nature demanded rest, and the First Maryland slept.

A couple of hours passed, when the command was aroused, saddled up, and prepared to move, Colonel Dorsey having at last received orders to follow in the rear of Mahone's Division, which formed the rear of the Confederate Army. This division had not yet come up, and while awaiting its appearance the command looked on and grieved over the destruction of ordnance and quartermasters' stores, which were now being fired in every direction to prevent their falling into the hands of the enemy.

These fires had evidently aroused the enemy into increased action, and his batteries were now in a constant blaze, while the explosion of his shells and the Confederate ammunition wagons made the night hideous with war's most infernal din. Fortunately, the enemy directed his guns at the fires, and as everybody kept away from them, no damage was done.

The First Maryland was drawn up along the roadside waiting to march, and coaxing their horses to eat as much oats as possible. Near by was a train of cars loaded with ammunition, and word was passed to look out, as it was about to be set on fire. For awhile every man stood to horse, but the explosion not ensuing as soon as expected, attention was called off, and the caution forgotten. Bridles were let go, and some of the men walked toward the quartermaster's stores, near the ammunition train, to make further selections. Suddenly a tremendous shock was felt, which threw many to the ground, whilst the horses reared and plunged and broke from their riders, and for a time all was the wildest confusion. When matters had become a little calm, two men belonging to the quartermaster's department were found dead, and twenty horses of the First Maryland had run off at full speed toward Richmond, though fortunately none of the men were hurt beyond a few bruises. The runaway horses must have been terribly frightened, for in their poor condition they ran twenty miles without halting, and only thirteen of the twenty were recovered; and thus the battalion lost the services of seven men, who, being dismounted, had to remain with the wagons. The explosion took place two hundred yards distant, but the force was great enough to knock down those nearest to it, and greatly shock the others.

Soon after this occurrence Mahone's Division came up at the quickstep and in fine order and spirits, which cheered the hearts of the little cavalry band beyond expression. Day had dawned before the rear passed, and just at that time, in the very gray light of morning, was seen a brilliant flash, and for a few moments the earth trembled under foot, and a tremendous explosion plainly told that the fortifications at Drury's Bluff were no more. In ten minutes another flash, shock and explosion ensued, and the Confederate gunboats on the James had shared the fate of the batteries on shore. Other similar explosions followed as smaller magazines were destroyed, filling the whole atmosphere with sulphurous smoke, while the flames licked the sky from many a conflagration, and it was with sad hearts that the little battalion turned and followed in the footsteps of the infantry. Thus commenced the retreat that ended in the surrender of the Army of Northern Virginia. The roads were muddy and wretchedly cut up by the passage of the artillery and heavy wagons, and the army, though in constant motion, made slow progress. By the next afternoon (Monday, April 3,) Amelia Court House was reached, when the enemy made a slight demonstration, but did not seriously attack. Early on the morning of the 4th Colonel Dorsey, ascertaining the whereabouts of General Fitz Lee, joined his division, in pursuance of his original order, and was assigned to Payne's Brigade.

Before this the small supply of provisions and forage brought from Petersburg had been exhausted, and as none had been issued, men and horses were almost starving.

The enemy's cavalry now became exceedingly active, and Payne's Brigade was daily engaged from daylight to dark, and often the struggle lasted all night. Grant's immense cavalry force enabled him to make simultaneous attacks at several points, and thus he succeeded in destroying a large portion of General Lee's wagon train, as it was impossible for the small force of Confederate cavalry to guard all points. The only thing to be done was to attack the enemy wherever he struck the train, and most vigorously was this plan followed.

In all these affairs, without exception, the Confederate cavalry was successful; and in one, when General Robert E. Lee was personally present and observing, repulsed a sudden and determined charge of Gregg's Division with great loss, and captured General Gregg himself.

Fate seemed to have determined that the Confederate sun should set in halo worthy of its noonday splendor, and gave a series of unbroken successes to the cavalry, and crowned all by the magnificent charge of Gordon's corps of infantry on the very morning of the surrender, when that gallant General swept away the enemy's lines and captured his batteries in a style that showed that nothing of his old vigor was lost.

There was a serious embarrassment, however, attending the cavalry victories—the capture of so many prisoners, which toward the last became nearly as numerous as General Lee's whole army, and presented a difficult question both as to feeding and guarding. No rations having been issued, men and horses had been subsisting from the 4th of April on a scanty supply of hard corn, which the troops had not even time to parch, and ate raw from the cob as they marched. On one occasion someone of the battalion got hold of a raw ham, and generously divided it as far as it would go. Raw ham, and raw corn from the cob may not be very palatable to one unfasted, but to Colonel Dorsey and his men it seemed a luxury.

At Amelia Springs there was a severe cavalry fight, in which the enemy was defeated and pursued some miles. Here a small portion of flour was issued to each man, but which there was no time to cook, and the flour was tied up in bags, handkerchiefs, stockings, or anything else at hand that might serve the purpose ; and so it remained for two days before opportunity to cook it offered, the battalion being in the meantime constantly engaged.

At last it was impossible for human nature to hold out longer, and the second night after the fight at Amelia Springs it was determined to cook the flour. As soon, therefore, as night came on — which rendered the enemy's fire less accurate, and induced his cavalry to become less aggressive — the brigade, leaving a strong picket force still actively skirmishing, withdrew behind a neighboring hill and prepared to cook. There were no cooking utensils nor any convenience to bake, but soldiers who had gone through a four years' war had many devices at hand to meet exigencies. A detail with canteens was sent to the stream near by for water, and oil cloths were substituted for kneading trays. In this way the flour was hastily moistened into a paste, and as hastily parched in the embers of the very spare fires which proximity to the enemy reduced to the smallest possible dimensions that could be dignified with the name of fire. The skirmishers were then relieved by some who had eaten, to make similar provisions for their wants.

From this time until Lynchburg was reached, on the night of the ninth of April, when General Lee surrendered at Appomattox Court House, the First Maryland subsisted on corn and some rations taken from the captured enemy. It was hard to take food from prisoners, perhaps, but necessity knows no law, and between starving men the weakest must yield.

Every day's history was much the same, a constant night and day struggle with the enemy's cavalry, who would scarcely be repulsed at one point before they had to be met at another, perhaps five or ten miles distant.

When the army reached the vicinity of High Bridge it was ascertained that a force of the enemy was directly in front, having by a forced march, and being unencumbered, passed around General Lee's left and thrown themselves directly in his path. The brigade, which was now commanded by General Munford, General Payne having been disabled by wounds at Amelia Springs, was at once ordered to attack them, which it did with much gallantry, all being dismounted except the First Maryland, which was sent to the left to cut off the enemy's retreat. The enemy, which proved to be a brigade of infantry and about two hundred cavalry, behaved very gallantly, and at once met General Munford vigorously. His cavalry charged several times, but were repulsed with heavy loss, while their infantry and Munford's dismounted cavalry kept up a heavy fire, both sides suffering severely, without material advantage to either. At length Deering's Brigade came up and dismounted, and joining Munford, a general charge was made by the dismounted men in front and the First Maryland, mounted, in the rear and right flank of the enemy, which resulted in the defeat and capture of his entire force. Nearly all the field officers on both sides were killed or badly wounded.

It will be remembered, in this connection, that although the Confederates had two brigades engaged here against the one of the enemy's infantry and the force of two hundred cavalry, yet he had greatly the advantage in numbers as well as of a deliberately selected position. Confederate brigades at this period of the war frequently did not number five hundred men, and on this occasion General Munford took into action (including Deering's men) a considerably smaller force than was captured.

For a short time Munford rested his command, when, after turning over his prisoners, he again sought the enemy toward the rear of General Lee's army. He here found Fitz Lee closely pressed, and joined his forces to impede as much as possible their advance.

A narrow and deep stream crossed the road over which the retreat was being conducted, and at the crossing place the mud was much worked up by the passage of the army. As this stream was neared, the enemy, from the crest of the range of hills about a mile distant, had a close view of the retreating forces. He hurried up his batteries and opened furiously, while his cavalry pressed hard upon the rear. Crossing the stream, a portion of the division, including Munford's Brigade, was deployed along its banks to dispute the passage. A slight and hastily constructed breastwork of fence-rails, thrown up under the fire of the opposing artillery, was all that Munford had to aid him against the immense force advancing.

The whole face of the country beyond the stream now seemed a mass of troops. Artillery crowned every available point, while cavalry and infantry in column advanced rapidly upon the handful of men that stood in their path.

It was necessary that a stand should be made to give time for the wagon and ordnance trains to pass a small bridge near Farmville. The enemy's skirmishers soon lined the banks of the little stream and poured in a rapid fire upon Munford, which was vigorously returned. In a few minutes a heavy column of cavalry charged at the ford, when they were received with a murderous fire at a range of not over forty yards. The ford was narrow, deep and marshy; the dead and dying men and horses encumbered their advance, and the enemy were forced to fall back defeated, after many of them had actually crossed the stream.

Several batteries were then opened upon Munford, but the firing was too wild, and everything having been accomplished that was desired, and the train safely over the bridge, the Confederate cavalry retired rapidly, but in excellent order, toward Farmville, moving in several different columns in order to present smaller marks to the artillery, which was firing with much increased accuracy, owing to the clear view which the open fields afforded.

The enemy then crossed the stream where he had been repulsed, and also at several other points lower down, and followed in rapid pursuit, and were soon charging Mumford's rear furiously through Farmville. One column charged a piece of woods in which lay a force of infantry in ambush, and was literally cut to pieces.

The streams about Farmville were much swollen, and in order to save time General Fitz Lee's Division, still in several different columns, crossed at as many different points, in most cases swimming their horses. At nightfall the fighting ceased, but was resumed in the morning with increased fury.

All this time a large force of the enemy, both infantry and cavalry, had marched rapidly by parallel roads, and had gotten between General Lee and Lynchburg, then his only depot of supplies, had captured all the trains with provisions sent out from that city to meet his army, then on the verge of starvation, and on the morning of April 8th, near Appomattox Court House, suddenly attacked his ordnance train, which, in advance of the whole army, was pressing on toward Lynchburg, guarded only by one small brigade of cavalry. But notwithstanding the great disparity of forces a severe fight was kept up nearly an hour, the artillery particularly being well and effectually served, and drove back the enemy in front.

The infantry and dismounted cavalry, however, now completely surrounded and drove the men from their guns, and captured all the artillery and wagons, which left General Lee almost destitute of both. Some few artillerists escaped on their horses, and fled down the road toward the infantry, followed by a column of cavalry. But the infantry was prepared for their approach, and permitting the flying artillerists to pass, they poured in a most deadly volley, which scattered the pursuers in all directions.

For the balance of the night all remained quiet, and the two armies anxiously awaited the coming of the morrow, which must decide the fate of the Army of Northern Virginia. Further retreat was impossible, as the enemy held the roads on all sides, and without cannon or ammunition, or rations to supply even the wants of twelve thousand men now left of the once grand army, General Lee, on the morning of April 9th, confronted Grant's mighty hosts. All the difficulties of the position were well known and appreciated by the Confederate Army, but the men who formed that army then, who had followed their flag through all the gloom and trials of the retreat — a retreat which needs only the pen of a Xenophon to make as famous as that of the "Ten Thousand" — those men, though not of numbers, but of country, in the dawn of that April morning, advanced to meet their persistent foe with all the calm and lofty courage that would have made Appomattox Court House a Thermopylæ. Those men, had their leader so willed it, would have laid down their arms and lives together. They were men, indeed, and worthy to close the record of the Army of Northern Virginia.

As soon as the day gave sufficient light, the battle opened fiercely, and all thought an engagement had commenced which was to prove the most desperate and terrible of the war.

General Fitz Lee's Division of cavalry, now under command of Brigadier-General Munford (General Fitz Lee being at the headquarters of the army), moved through Appomattox Court House, and formed in line of battle on the right of the road about half a mile beyond that place. The halt was brief, and it moved in column obliquely to the right and entered a heavy wood, where it soon came in contact with the enemy.

Throwing out skirmishers to engage them, General Munford moved again to the right oblique until they were again struck, when more skirmishers were thrown out, the first having fallen to the rear, and these movements were continued until he found a weaker place in the enemy's line, and made good his passage to the Lynchburg road.

Nothing was known positively. The sounds of a severe fight were plainly heard, and those movements of the cavalry excited much surprise and comment among the men and officers composing the division.

At first it was thought that the intention was to get in the enemy's rear and charge him while engaged in front with the infantry, which opinion was much strengthened by a near approach to a battery of the enemy's in full action against General Lee's infantry, but another detour proved its fallacy, and all were lost in conjecture until the Lynchburg road was reached, when it became evident that the immediate object of the movement was to reach that road, as the division at once halted and formed on each side. From this point the masses of Grant's army were plainly visible, standing as if on dress parade.

The firing had now ceased, and surprise at what seemed unaccountable movements gave place to alarm. Surrender of the army was whispered, but was heard with indignation by many who would not acknowledge their own fears to themselves, and all comment was unheeded, and by general consent it was determined to await events in silence. We could see, indeed, on the bronzed countenances of those veterans an anxiety too deep for words.

The First Maryland happened to be nearest to the road and to the enemy, the men dismounted, but standing to horse — the usual precaution of skirmishers in front having been, of course, observed. Everything was still. Not a sound betrayed the presence of the hosts of armed men in the vicinity, and but for the long lines of blue in sight upon the hills in front all might have been taken for a hideous dream.

Suddenly a heavy column of cavalry, moving rapidly along Munford's front and parallel to his line, was seen, about half a mile distant, marching toward the road, which they presently reached, and a part of the force, still in column, advanced by the road, and the remainder in line through the fields to the right of the road, and drove back the skirmishers.

As soon as the design of the enemy was perceived, Colonel Dorsey mounted his men and moved in column to the road, which was separated from him by a fence, in which gaps had been made. Through one of these gaps the First Maryland was passing as rapidly as was consistent with good order, but the first section had hardly cleared the fence when the enemy, now in full charge, was seen coming at them, not over one hundred yards distant.

Captain Rasin, who rode with Colonel Dorsey at the head of the column, at this moment remarked: "Colonel Dorsey, we must charge those people! it is our only chance!" and scarcely had the words left his lips when Dorsey, who had already seen the necessity, gave the command: "Draw sabre! Gallop! Charge!" and the little band of Marylanders hurled themselves against the heavy columns of the enemy, and drove him back. Again he advanced, and again the First Maryland charged and forced him back.

In this last charge — the last blow struck by the Army of Northern Virginia — while still pushing the enemy vigorously, the battalion was met by an officer carrying a flag of truce, who suddenly made his appearance from the right of the road. The fight instantly ceased, and the officer was asked his business. He replied that General Lee was about to surrender; that articles of capitulation were being prepared; that hostilities had ceased, and ended by demanding that the cavalry in front should come in and lay down their arms, as being part of General Lee's army, and included in the terms.

General Munford called a council of war of all his officers, and after discussing matters and taking a vote, it was determined not to surrender, being clearly not subject to the treaty between Generals Lee and Grant, as the division had broken through the enemy's lines before a surrender had been discussed by the leaders of the two armies, and more especially because the enemy had attacked the division during the truce, and had only spoken of it after having been thrice repulsed.

In the last charge of the First Maryland Cavalry, immediately before the appearance of the white flag, William C. Price, of Company E, Captain Rasin, was killed, thus yielding up his young life in the very last blow struck by the Army of Northern Virginia.

In accordance with the unanimous opinion of the council of war, General Mumford threw out a heavy skirmish line, and retired toward Lynchburg unmolested by the enemy, who contented himself with looking on.

Arriving at Lynchburg at night, General Munford's first care was to obtain food and forage for his command, which was done without much difficulty, as large supplies had been gathered at this point with a view of meeting the necessities of General Lee's army, a portion of which supplies, as before said, having been sent out to meet the army, and captured by the enemy near Appomattox Court House on the 8th.

After feeding, another council was held, and the chances and best means of reaching Johnston's army discussed. Without coming to any definite conclusion, it was determined to move to the north side of the James River and seek supplies until some news from General Joseph E. Johnston's army could be obtained, and then unite with that army.

Colonel Dorsey marched to the neighborhood of Waynesboro', where the kindness of the people to the soldiers had been before experienced, and there awaited orders. In about ten days he received a dispatch from General Munford to move up the Valley, by way of Lexington, toward Salem, on which route all the cavalry were to march, and to make their way to General Joseph E. Johnston's army. The First Maryland was immediately on the march, and arrived at Cloverdale, in Botetourt County, on the twenty-eighth day of April, where Colonel Dorsey, learning that General Munford was confined to his bed by sickness, rode to the house at which the General was lying, and received from him the following letter, which he had prepared to be read to the First Maryland, and which speaks for itself, the General expressing his regret that his sickness prevented him from saying farewell to the battalion in person :

CLOVERDALE, BOTETOURT COUNTY, VIRGINIA, April 28, 1865.

Lieutenant-Colonel Dorsey, Commanding First Maryland Cavalry :

I have just learned from Captain Emack that your gallant band was moving up the Valley in response to my call. I am deeply pained to say that our army cannot be reached, as I have learned that it has capitulated. It is sad, indeed, to think that our country's future is all shrouded in gloom. But for you and your command there is the consolation of having faithfully done your duty.

Three years ago the chivalric Brown joined my old regiment with twenty-three Maryland volunteers with light hearts and full of fight. I soon learned to admire, respect and love them for all those qualities which endear soldiers to their officers. They recruited rapidly, and as they increased in numbers, so did their reputation and friends increase, and they were soon able to form a command and take a position of their own. Need I say when I see that position so high and almost alone among soldiers, that my heart swells with pride to think that a record so bright and glorious is in some part linked with mine ? Would that I could see the mothers and sisters of every member of your battalion that I might tell them how nobly you have represented your State and maintained our cause. But you will not be forgotten. The fame you have won will be guarded by Virginia with all the pride she feels in her own true sons, and the ties which have linked us together memory will preserve. You who struck the first blow in Baltimore, and the last in Virginia, have done all that could be asked of you, and had the rest of our officers and men adhered to our cause with the same devotion, today we would have been free from Yankee thraldom.

I have ordered the brigade to return to their homes, and it behooves us now to separate. With my warmest wishes for your welfare, and a hearty God bless you, I bid you farewell.

THOMAS T. MUNFORD, *Brigadier-General Commanding Division*.

The scene which followed this announcement and letter can only be conceived by those who have had every energy and sentiment of soul and heart wrapped up in the attainment of some end a thousand-fold dearer than life, only to find after years of the bitterest struggles and dearest sacrifices that all was in vain, and themselves bankrupt of all that would make life supportable.

This little band of Maryland soldiers, despairing and broken-hearted, were hundreds of miles from home, but separated still farther by a wanton exercise of power forbidding them to return to Maryland, which exercise of power was due to the petty malice of some of the civil authorities of Maryland's cowardly jackals, tearing at the dead body of the lion, which living they dared not face.

With this letter of General Munford announcing the surrender of General Johnston's army perished the last hope of the Southern Confederacy, and the few surviving members of the First Maryland Cavalry prepared to bid each other adieu. That was a sad and solemn parting, indeed, and stout hearts melted, and tears from eyes unused to weeping were profusely shed when, hand clasping hand, farewell was spoken.

The old flag which had so often been followed to victory was saluted for the last time, and reverently taken from its staff and folded away. The last weeping word was spoken, and with breaking hearts the old First Maryland disbanded forever, some riding slowly away, others at full speed as if to fly from grief.

In their wanderings the exiled soldiers depended entirely upon the kindness and hospitality of the Virginia people. They had no money or means to supply their wants — nothing but their destitution and soldier's life to plead. But the people of Virginia did not forget their services, and hastened eagerly to relieve their necessities. At the end, as in the beginning, and throughout the progress of the war, the warm-hearted kindness and genuine hospitality of the Virginians adorned them with a lustre equal to their valor in battle. The soldiers of the First Maryland Cavalry must cease to have hearts or memories when they forget the Virginia people and their devoted attentions.

The following extract from a letter written by General Thomas T. Munford some time after the war is certainly very complimentary to the First Maryland:

During Stonewall Jackson's memorable Valley campaign and his battles with Pope, and our fight at Leesburg, Company B, of my regiment (Second Virginia), was detailed with General Longstreet's Corps as his bodyguard, and Company A, First Maryland Cavalry, Captain Ridgely Brown commanding, served with my regiment in their absence, with great credit and distinction. A more chivalrous and gallant band of soldiers never flashed a blade or answered a bugle's call. It is with especial pride that I enroll them with my old regiment, since they add a lustre to its fame.

ROSTER OF THE FIRST MARYLAND CAVALRY.

FIELD AND STAFF.

Lieutenant-Colonels.
RIDGELY BROWN.   ROBERT CARTER SMITH.
GUSTAVUS W. DORSEY.

Majors.
RIDGELY BROWN.   ROBERT CARTER SMITH.

Adjutants.
GEORGE W. BOOTH.   JOHN E. H. POST.

Assistant Surgeon, WILBUR R. MCKNEW.

Assistant Quartermaster, IGNATIUS W. DORSEY.

Sergeant-Majors.
EDWARD JOHNSON.   JOHN E. H. POST.
ARTHUR BOND.

Quartermaster-Sergeant, EDWARD JOHNSON.

COMPANY A.

Captain, FRANK A. BOND.
First Lieutenant, THOMAS GRIFFITH.
Second Lieutenant, J. A. V. PUE.
Second Lieutenant, EDWARD BEATTY.
First Sergeant, JOHN H. SCHOLL.
Sergeant, FRANK GRIFFITH.
Sergeant, JOSHUA RIGGS.
Sergeant, CHARLES R. COCKEY.
Corporal, WILLIAM WILSON.
Corporal, BAZIL CLARK.
Corporal, ARTHUR BOND.
Corporal, JOHN HARDING.

Privates.

ARTIS, JEREMIAH.
ARMSTRONG, JOSHUA.
BRACCO, EDWARD.
BROWN, JOHN R.
BECKETT, JOHN M.
BENDER, FRANK.
BELL, HENRY.
BOYD, ANDREW.
BOND, SAMUEL G.
BOND, W. W.
BOND, H.
BROWN, C. C.
CLARKE, DAVID.
CLARKE, JOHN.
CLARKE, WILLIAM.
CARTER, R. W.
COCKEY, SPRIGG.
CANBY, BENJAMIN.
CHILDS, W. H.
CHILDS, SOPER.
COVINGTON, JESSE.
CRANE, BRENT.
CLAGETT, JOHN.
CRAWFORD, THOMAS.
CARY, JOHN B.
CANNON, J. G.
DORSEY, JOHN.
DORSEY, PULASKI.
DORSEY, ANDREW.

DORSEY, LLOYD.
DORSEY, UPTON.
DORSEY, GUSTAVUS.
DORSEY, C. W.
DICKERSON, L. T.
DUNLOP, JOSEPH L.
DURBURROW, J. C.
DITTY, C. IRVING.
DORSEY, HARRY.
DORSEY, J. PEMBROOK.
DORSEY, I. G.
EDELIN, WILLIAM.
FOSTER, MICHAEL.
FORSYTH, HENRY.
FERGUSON, JOHN.
GRIFFITH, DAVID.
GILL, JOHN.
GRIFFIN, GEORGE C.
GEPHART, SOLOMON.
GRAHAM, ———.
HALL, EDWARD.
HANNAWAY, WILLIAM.
HENDEN, THOMAS.
HOUGH, GRESHAM.
HUTTON, CHARLES.
HAYDEN, HORACE E.
HUNTER, THOMAS.
HARRY, JAMES.
HEIGHE, JOHN M.

HENDERSON, GAITHER.
HAMMOND, CHARLES.
HORNER, FRANK.
HOUGH, SAMUEL J.
HARRISON, C. H.
JOHNSON, OTIS.
JOHNSON, J. N.
JOHNSON, JOHN.
JACKSON, ANDREW J.
JOHNSON, EDWARD.
JONES JOHN.
KEENE, ROBERT G.
KENNEDY, MCPHERSON.
KETTLEWELL, E. R.
KENLEY, J. R.
LECHLIDER, GEORGE.
LANGLEY, THOMAS.
LINTHICUM, EDWIN.
LOCKER, EDWARD.
LOCKER, WILLIAM.
LEISHER, G. W.
LEITER, CHARLES.
LINCOLN, RUSK J.
LIPSCOMB, FRANK.
MURDOCH, AUGUSTUS.
MOONEY, JOHN.
MAGRUDER ZACH.
MAYNARD, THOMAS.
MCDOWELL, CHARLES.

Mason, R. R.	Ridgely, John.	Thompson, Dorsey.
Miller, William.	Rozier, Charles.	Tschiffely, Edgar L.
Nelson, R. W.	Richardson, Howard.	Webster, W. H.
Pue, Ferd C.	Riley, Thomas S.	Warring, Henry.
Price, M. A.	Sellman, John.	Webb, William.
Polk, Truston.	Shipley, Samuel.	Worthington, Joshua.
Pretzman, D. C.	Smith, Daniel.	Warfield, A. G.
Price, Kennedy.	Stone, Henry.	Wooten, Henry E.
Patrick, Charles R.	Schwartz, Augustus.	Watkins, Lewis J.
Polk, Samuel.	Slinfluff, F. C.	Whalen, John W.
Patrick, John.	Stone, C.	Wisner, John D.
Perdue, John.	Scott, George.	Worthington, Charles.
Peddicord, S.	Tolby, George.	Warfield, G.
Porter, J. J.	Treackle, Emmett.	Woolford, A.
Rice, George.	Thompson, Edward.	Zepp, Charles P.
Riggs Reuben.	Thompson, G. L.	

COMPANY B.

Captain, George M. Emack.
First Lieutenant, M. E. McKnew.
Second Lieutenant, Adolphus Cook.
Second Lieutenant, Henry C. Blackiston.
First Sergeant, S. B. Spencer.
Sergeant, W. A. Wilson.
Sergeant, W. H. W. Guyther.
Sergeant, D. M. Turner.
Sergeant, O. H. Perry.
Corporal, G. M. Serpell.
Corporal, J. J. Spear.
Corporal, Pembroke Jones.
Corporal, J. R. H. Deakins.
Corporal, Robert Carvell.

Privates.

Aisquith, Hobart.	Boarman, J. N.	Boman, Joseph.
Baden, J. M.	Blackiston S. H.	Burst, George T.
Barry, W. D.	Brent, George T.	Birch, J. A.
Beale, Alexander.	Bryan, W. L.	Burling, D.
Bean, Thomas L.	Burch, J. H.	Crawford, H. V. D.
Bean, W. M.	Bullen, R. B.	Cropper, Thomas E.
Bond, J. W.	Bradley, J.	Cooper, W. T.
Bowling, Alexander.	Briscoe, P. T.	Coburn, ———.
Bowling, Nicholas.	Bryan, C.	Carvell, Robert.

Davis, P. A.	Hume, Frank.	Strong, W.
Deakins, J. R. H.	Jeffers, W. H.	Stermis, Joseph.
Dix, William T.	Jones, John.	Tolson, A. C.
Dutton, S. S.	Key, Richard H.	Tolson, Charles E.
Dyer, A. M.	Keets, John F.	Tunis, Theopilus.
Dutton, J. W.	Lyons, Bunton.	Tunis, John.
Dent, M.	McCormick, B. H.	Tunis, O.
Earle, James T.	McLeod, W.	Thomas, John E.
Eareckson, F. G.	McCall, R.	Thomas, Edwin.
Embert, J. R. H.	McCabe, ———.	Tippett, M. A. K.
Ebert, Charles.	Murray, ———.	Thomas, J. H.
Eckhardt, Charles H.	Nailor, T. K.	Vallandingham, Irving S.
Elliott, G. M.	Noel, E.	Waring, James.
Elliott, J. T.	Naylor, J. M.	Waring, Edwin.
Ferrall, J. Thomas.	Perrie, Thomas H.	Wissman, L. O.
Gibson, John E.	Price, James H.	Wilks, Thomas M.
Gough, Charles E.	Parker, George T.	Williams, John W.
Green, W. O.	Perkins, L. O.	Wooley, George.
Gibson, J. E.	Perry, O. H.	Wright, R. B.
Gibson, E.	Perrie, I.	Willis, Thomas.
Gibson, S.	Reed, Mingel.	Watkins, N. W.
Hambleton, J. P.	Smith, James.	Wilson, J. K.
Hill, J. P.	Scaggs, Edward O.	Willson, J. H.
Hickey, J. F.	Spear, D. W. C.	Waring, H. W.
Hickey, E. P.	Spear, Edwin W.	Waring, C. H.
Hearne, Samuel B.	Stanley, Charles H.	Wilson, Aquilla.
Hucorn, John F.	Stevers, James C.	Willis, T. N.
Hearne, B. G.	Scaggs, J.	Wright, Sol.

COMPANY C.

Captain, Robert C. Smith.
First Lieutenant, George Howard.
Second Lieutenant, T. Jeff. Smith.
Second Lieutenant, T. J. Green.
Second Lieutenant, Graeme Turnbull.
Second Lieutenant, James D. Watters.
First Sergeant, Illinois Caruthers.

Sergeant, George Smith Norris.
Sergeant, E. Clarence Neale.
Sergeant, William F. Dorsey.
Sergeant, Hamilton Lefevre.
Corporal, Richard Knox.
Corporal, Richard C. Smith.
Corporal, Lafayette Hause.

Privates.

ANDERSON OSCAR.	GLENN, CLEMENT.	MCWILLIAMS, HUGH.
BARBER, CHRISTOPHER.	GLENN, ELIAS.	MCBRIDE, THOMAS C.
BARBOUR, OSCAR.	GLENN, FRANCIS.	MCCOURT, JAMES R.
BREHM, JOHN P.	GEORGE, THOMAS.	MCCLEARY, PETER H.
BILLOP, CHRISTOPHER.	GROGAN, J.	MCKEE, JAMES.
BIAYS, GEORGE.	GRAHAM, JESSE.	MAGILL, DAVIDGE.
BROWN, ROBERT.	HAYWARD, HENRY.	MAGILL, WILLIAM D.
BULL, ELIJAH.	HANCE, JAMES J.	MITCHELL, LEVIN.
BATEMAN, H.	HARTIGAN, JOHN J.	MACATEE, I. J.
BARNES, RICHARD.	HAYWARD, HENRY.	MACATEE, S. E.
BOWIE, HARRY.	HEIMILLER, HERMAN.	MACATEE, HENRY.
BYRNE, ———.	HOLBROOK, JOHN.	MAKOMER, MATHIAS.
CHISILDINE, W. C.	HOWARD, R. MCG.	MACKALL, LEONARD.
COOK, GEORGE.	HOWARD, CARROLL C.	MYERS, CLINTON.
CLAUDE, HAMMOND.	HOWARD, JOHN E.	NEALE, WILFORD.
CRETIN, JOHN.	HERRON, GEORGE.	NORRIS, ALEXANDER, JR.
CRITTENDEN, C.	HOLLYDAY, GEORGE.	OATES JAMES F.
CHAMBERS ROBERT M.	HAGER, JOHN.	POOL, WILLIAM C.
CAREY, MICHAEL.	HARRY, JOHN.	PUE, W. H.
CRANE, WILLIAM.	HUDGINS, CHARLES.	POST, JOHN E. H.
CLEMENTS, WILLIAM.	HUME, J. R. F.	PALMER A.
DALL, H. MCPHERSON.	HARRY ALBERT.	PUE, ARTHUR.
DOUGHERTY, JAMES.	INLOES, CHARLES E.	RILEY, JOHN P.
DITTUS, JOHN F.	JONES, WILLIAM O.	RIDGELY, JOHN.
DANCE, E. SCOTT.	JONES, G. W.	ROGERS, SAMUEL.
EMORY, DANIEL G.	JENKINS, POLAND.	ROGERS, JAMES P.
ELDER, GEORGE H.	JENKINS, GEORGE C.	ROGERS, PHILIP.
ELDER, LAWRENCE.	KREBS, CHARLES.	ROSE, PORTER E.
EDWARDS, WILLIAM.	KETTLEWELL, CHARLES.	REACH, JOHN.
FOLEY, DAVID R.	KIMBALL, H.	REDWOOD, A. C.
FLANEGAN, JOHN.	LURMAN, GUSTAV W.	REDWOOD, J. W.
GILL, WILLIAM H.	LEMMON, W. S.	RAPHAEL, EUGENE.
GOUGH, CHARLES E.	LIAMBAUGH, WILLIAM C.	STONEBRAKER, JOSEPH R.
GROGAN, ROBERT R.	LATROBE, R. STEUART.	SANDERS, HILLEN T.
GRAY, HENRY L.	LYON, SAMUEL H.	SHROFF, PETER F.
GOODMAN, OTHO.	LEAZEY, JOSEPH H.	SPENCER, JERVIS.
GILES, WILLIAM F.	LUMKIN, JAMES T.	STONE, JOSEPH.
GROVE, THOMAS.	LEVERING, THOMAS H.	SMITH, WILSON C.

SULLIVAN, FRANK.
SLATER, WILLIAM J.
SHORB, DONALD M. M.
SNOWDEN, JOHN.
STREET, JAMES.
SHIPLETT, P.
SCOTT, J. E.

TENNANT, T.
THOMAS, RALEIGH C.
TOWLES, J. C.
VALENTINE, GEORGE.
WILLIAMS, AUGUST A.
WELCH, JOSEPH C.
WUNSTEN, HENRY.

WILLIS, CHARLES W.
WOOD I. J.
WHARTON, WILLIAM F.
WEBER, EDWARD.
WILLIAMS, THOMAS P.
WIEL, GEORGE.
YOUNG, WASHINGTON.

COMPANY D.

Captain, WARNER G. WELSH.
First Lieutenant, W. H. DORSEY.
Second Lieutenant, STEPHEN D. LAWRENCE.
Second Lieutenant, MILTON WELSH.
First Sergeant, PHINEAS I. DAVIS.
Sergeant, UPTON L. DORSEY.

Sergeant, ALBERT JONES.
Sergeant, LEWIS W. TRAIL.
Corporal, GEORGE R. SIMPSON.
Corporal, EDWIN SELVAGE.
Corporal, GEORGE R. CATHER.
Corporal, RICHARD H. NORRIS.

Privates.

BROMWELL, THOMAS C. S.
BROMWELL, HENRY H.
BROMWELL, JOSIAH R.
BRASHER, THOMAS P.
BUTLER, CYRUS S.
BOYLE, CHARLES B.
BAUGHMAN, L. VICTOR.
BARRICK, WILLIAM.
COLE, CHARLES N.
CARTER, GRAFTON.
CORCORAN, THOMAS W.
CLARKE, CHARLES H.
CLARK, JOSEPH.
CLEARY, VACHEL T.
CRISSWELL, JOHN O.
CHESLER, HENRY.
CLAGETT, ROBERT.
DADE, WILLIAM F.
DELASHMUTT, WILLIAM H.

DAVIS, EVAN.
DAVIS, THOMAS S.
DOOMANDY, JOHN.
EWING, HARVEY S.
EWING, WILLIAM F.
ENSOR, ZADOCK.
EBBERT, ———.
FEARHAKE, ADOLPHUS.
FITZGERALD, THOMAS.
FLINT, JOSEPH.
FUNK, CHARLES D.
GABRILL, ABRAHAM W.
GRIMES, CORNELIUS.
GEASEY, JAMES W.
GEASEY, CHARLES H.
GIBSON HENRY.
GRIMES, HARRY.
GEIGER, JOHN.
HAMMOND, DENTON.

HAMMOND, OLIVER B.
HOYLE, NATHAN L.
HARRISON, WILLIAM.
HERGESHEIMER, DAVID.
HERING, FRANK.
HILLARY, THOMAS.
JONES, EDWARD C.
JONES, SPENCER C.
KEMP, CHARLES.
KNAUFF, GEORGE W.
LAMBDEN, CHARLES.
LICKLE, JOHN D.
McDANIEL, JOHN.
MERCER, SAMUEL B.
MILES, GEORGE T.
McLANAHAN, WILLIAM H.
MERRYMAN, JOSEPH.
MYERS, THOMAS.
MAYNARD ALBERT.

MacKubbin, James B.
McSherry, Edward L.
Matthews, H. H.
Maguire, Joseph E.
Neal, Frank.
Neal, Harry.
Obendorfe, John.
O'Leary, Jerry.
Ott, George W.
Price, James E.
Pope, William H.
Placide, Robert.
Raitt, Charles H.
Radcliffe, Edward.
Raborg, Christopher.

Raborg, William.
Rosan, Charles W.
Roley, Thomas.
Shafer, Cornelius L.
Steres, Christopher.
Simons, Albert.
Stevenson, Dawson.
Stephenson, Thomas H.
Shultz, William.
Steele, John.
Sollers, William O.
Snook, Jerome.
Shafer, Thomas H.
Shower, George.
Sisson, Christopher.

Shessler, Henry.
Shell, Horace.
Taylor, Charles J.
Tyler, John B.
Tyler, George.
Tyler, Albert.
Traphall, Joseph.
Thomas, William.
Worthington, George E.
Woodward, Columbus O.
Weaver, Hiram.
Wilson, Frederick.
Welsh, Luther.
Wilson, Robert.
Warfield, ———.

COMPANY E.

Captain, W. I. Rasin.
First Lieutenant, S. B. Burroughs.
Second Lieutenant, Nathaniel Chapman.
Second Lieutenant, Joseph K. Roberts, Jr.
First Sergeant, Townley Robey.
Sergeant, John Savage.
Sergeant, Solomon Wright.
Sergeant, Thomas H. Gemmill.
Corporal, George T. Hollyday.
Corporal, Benjamin J. Turton.
Corporal, Henry C. Wallis.
Corporal, John W. Slaven.

Privates.

Booker William T.
Bourne, James B.
Baden, William A. H.
Brawner, T. M.
Brooke, George W.
Brooke, Clements.
Boone, W. C.
Bryant, George H.
Bryan, W. C.
Baker, H. W.
Cox, James B.

Connick, Robert.
Cockey, John P.
Chesley, Daniel S.
Cator, Benjamin.
Crawford George I.
Cadle, James R.
Cleary, Paul W.
Conley, Martin V.
Disharoom, John.
Duvall, James E.
Davidson, Robert.

Ewen, W. T.
Edelin, Jesse R.
Ferguson, John.
Field, George W.
Gilroy, Thomas.
Glenn, James S.
Green, William B.
Goodloe, William.
Hollingsworth, Wm. T.
Harkins, James.
Hunt, Charles W.

HAMBLETON, T. E.
HARWOOD, RICHARD.
JONES, ROBERT.
JENKINS, JAMES W.
JUMP, CHARLES M.
JOHNSON WILLIAM.
JARVOE, WILLIAM F.
KRAUS, CHARLES M.
KEATING, EDWARD.
LEFFINGER, ISAAC.
LUM, BENJAMIN F.
LANCASTER, SAMUEL G.
LOYSDEN, N.
LARKINSON, N.
MCCLERNEY, GEORGE S.
MURRAY, ED. C.
✓ MITCHELL, ROBERT S.
MERRICK, GEORGE C.
MULLIN, C. S.
MOISE, A. W.
METTAM, H. C.

MAGRUDER, ED W.
MORRIS, EDWIN.
MORRIS, LEWIS.
NEWKIRK, JOSIAH.
PACA, E. T.
PUMPHREY, JOHN T.
PUMPHREY, GEORGE W.
✓ PRICE, WILLIAM C.
POLLITT, ALEXANDER.
PRUITT, JOHN.
PUSEY, O. C.
PEELER, MALLARD T.
QUINN, J. H. V.
RICH, EDWARD R.
ROE, SAMUEL.
RATCLIFFE, EDWARD R.
RIDGWAY, M. J.
ROLPH, GEORGE W.
ROBERTS, RICHARD.
SIMPSON, JOHN T.
STALLINGS, C. L.

SCHAKLEY, H. B.
SPENCER, JOHN C.
SWEENEY, GEORGE.
SLINGLUFF, JOHN A.
TURTONS, M. G.
THOMPSON, CHARLES R.
THOMPSON, WILLIAM B.
VANDIVER, GEORGE.
WARRING, THOMAS G.
WELCH, A. J.
WATERS, JOHN A.
WORTHINGTON, H. T.
WEST, JOSEPH, JR.
WOOTERS, ALEXANDER.
WOOD, FRANCIS M.
WHEELER, JAMES R.
WYNN, JOSEPH.
WYNN, JAMES A.
WILSON, CHARLES.
WRIGHT, CLINTON.
WARD, ARCHER.

COMPANY F.

Captain, AUGUSTUS F. SCHWARTZ.
First Lieutenant, C. IRVING DITTY.
Second Lieutenant, FIELDER C. SLINGLUFF.
Second Lieutenant, SAMUEL G. BOND.
First Sergeant, JOSIAH H. SLINGLUFF.

Sergeant, HOWARD H. KINSEY.
Sergeant, HENRY A. WISE.
Corporal, WILBUR J. ROLPH.
Corporal, JOHN W. LATHAM.
Corporal, JOSEPH C. SHORB.

Privates.

ALTWATER, J. W.
ASHBY, R. W.
BERMER, AUGUST.
BITCHEL, FRED. F.
BEASTON, GEORGE M
BREED, HY. L.

BARNES, JOHN.
BROWN, THEOPOLUS.
BROWN, GEORGE.
CARROLL, J. C.
CHAPLIN, CHARLES.
CUNNINGHAM, GEORGE W.

CHAPMAN ISAAC.
CALLAN, OWEN.
CASLOW, JAMES.
DEAVER, JOHN R.
DOOLEY, THOMAS.
DUNN, JOHN.

EIGER, JOHN H.
FLANNIGAN PATRICK.
FLOYD, WILLIAM S.
GREEN, WILLIAM.
GARDNER, J. J.
GREEN, HUGH T.
HUMMER, JOSEPH.
HAMMETT, JOHN H.
HANNIGAN, WILLIAM.
HAMPTON, THOMAS.
HEARD, JOHN L.
JOHNSON, HY. B.
JOHNSON, GEORGE.
JOHNSON, JOHN.
JOHNSON, JOHN.
KELLEY, DANIEL.
KELLY, JOHN.
KELLY, RICHARD.

KONIG, HY.
KIMBALL, LEWIS.
KAUFFMAN, CARL.
LESLIE, JOHN W.
LUCAS, H. C.
LLOYD, JOHN L.
LUSBY, JAMES.
MITCHELL, JAMES.
MEAGHER, JAMES.
MONTERAY, ANDREW.
MINNIHAN, THOMAS.
MEISTER, CHARLES.
METTEE, CHARLES.
McMULLIN, CHARLES.
ORMES, NATHAN.
PERVILLE, LEIGHTON.
PATTON, JAMES W.
PIERCE, ALFRED.

PITTS, WILLIAM.
POOLE, WILLIAM.
REMIE, LOON.
RUSHING, JOHN.
ROSAA, STERLING.
ROSE, JESSE.
SHERRY, CHARLES.
SMITH, THOMAS.
SLEIGHTON, BENJAMIN F.
THACKER, ALBERT.
TYLER, WINFIELD.
WILLIAMS, D. H. S.
WELLS, WILLIAM.
WILNE, J. S.
WEBER, PHILIP.
WEISHARD, MICHAEL.
WARD, JOSEPH.

CHANGES IN THE FIRST MARYLAND BATTALION OF CAVALRY DURING THE WAR.

The following changes took place among the officers in the battalion during the war :

GUSTAVUS W. DORSEY, Lieutenant-Colonel commanding, vice Lieutenant-Colonel Ridgely Brown, killed June 1, 1864.

MAJOR ROBERT C. SMITH, having been permanently disabled by wounds received in battle at Greenland Gap, April 25, 1863, and retired from active service with the rank of Lieutenant-Colonel, no one was commissioned to fill vacancy.

JOHN E. H. POST, promoted Adjutant, with rank of First Lieutenant, vice George W. Booth, promoted Assistant Adjutant-General.

COMPANY A.—Thomas Griffith, promoted Captain, vice Captain F. A. Bond, disabled in battle at Hagerstown, July, 1863 ; retired from active service with rank of Major.

J. A. V. Pue, First Lieutenant, vice Griffith, promoted.

Otis Johnson, private, commissioned Second Lieutenant, vice Edward Beatty, died in prison.

COMPANY B.—Third Lieutenant Blackiston, killed August 12, 1864. No one commissioned to fill vacancy.

COMPANY C.—Thomas Green, promoted Second Lieutenant, vice W. S. Turnbull. Died in campaign of 1863.

James D. Watters, private, commissioned Third Lieutenant, vice Green, promoted.

COMPANY D.—Milton Welsh, promoted Second Lieutenant, vice Stephen D. Lawrence, resigned. No one commissioned to fill vacancy.

COMPANY E.—No change.

COMPANY F.—C. Irving Ditty, promoted Captain, vice A. F. Schwartz, died from effects of wounds received in battle May 9, 1864.

Fielder C. Slingluff, promoted First Lieutenant, vice Ditty, promoted.

Samuel G. Bonn, Second Lieutenant, vice Slingluff, promoted.

COMPANY K.—N. C. Hobbs, promoted Captain, vice Gustavus W. Dorsey, promoted Lieutenant-Colonel.

Edward Pugh, First Lieutenant, vice Hobbs, promoted. No commission to fill vacancy.

LIEUT. COL. HARRY GILMOR.
SECOND MARYLAND CAVALRY.

SECOND MARYLAND CAVALRY.

IT is impossible to write a history of the Second Maryland Cavalry, for no records concerning it, of its organization, or of its exploits can be found after careful search of the Bureau of War Records in Washington. Harry Gilmor left in his " Four Years in the Saddle " a rattling, head-over-heels, sabre-to-sabre tale of adventure and of exploits which is, in the main, true. Told from the standpoint of an actor in them, sometimes the perspective is a little out of proportion, and shows things in somewhat different relations to each other than other actors in the same scenes saw them ; but this is usual and natural in all descriptions of action. Men see things differently, from different points of view.

The Second Maryland Cavalry was Gilmor's Battalion, and Gilmor's Battalion was Harry Gilmor, and no account of one can be given without including the other. It was affectionately known among the men as " the band." It has not left a muster roll — that is, I have not been able to find any.

Kyd Douglas says of Gilmor's commission : " He was just as likely to use it to light a pipe as to have preserved it or taken any care of it."

Early in 1862 (April 21) the Confederate Congress passed " an act to organize bands of partisan rangers," whereby the President was authorized to commission such officers as he may deem proper with authority to form bands of partisan rangers, in companies, or regiments, either as infantry or cavalry.

These partisan rangers, after being regularly received into service, were " to receive the same pay, rations and allowance as regular soldiers. They were to be paid for stores or arms captured from the enemy and delivered to any quartermaster at such places as may be designated by a commanding general."

Under this law many " bands " of partisan rangers were raised, but so irregularly was the service conducted that no records exist of most of them.

The most illustrious were " Mosby's men," who, under their able and gallant leader, taught a new lesson in war, of how efficient irregular troops may be made, for Mosby and his men, never exceeding three hundred in ranks or on rolls, kept thousands of Federal troops guarding the railroads and lines of communication of the army with its base, their bridges or culverts, and chasing the phantom guerrilla through the passes of the Blue Ridge and over the hills of Fauquier or Loudoun.

But " Gilmor's band " did efficient work over in the Valley. Not a wagon train could pass up the Valley pike weakly guarded but that "the band" would dash in, disperse the guard, relieve the wagons of whatever was portable or valuable, and be off like shadows before the cavalry, galloping up from the next camp, could get within firing distance.

The Baltimore and Ohio Railroad was the object of their unremitting and ardent devotion. They had scouts in Martinsburg or Harper's Ferry. News frequently came from Baltimore or Washington of the starting of a quartermaster or paymaster with a great sum of money for army use. That train would be run off the track by tearing up rails, stopped in a defile or deep cut and unloaded. Frequently the passengers would be relieved of their watches and pocket-books. Paymasters always met with the rough chivalry of the border; women were always respected.

Harry Gilmor enlisted as a private soldier in Colonel Turner Ashby's regiment in August, 1861, in Captain Frank Mason's company. In a few weeks Ashby made him sergeant-major. By March, 1862, he had organized a company and attached it to the Twelfth Virginia Cavalry, Colonel Arthur Harman.

This company was the nucleus of Gilmor's Battalion, and by a series of dashing exploits and gallant adventures soon occupied a conspicuous position and attracted other enterprising spirits, not in the army.

Gilmor was at McDowell with Jackson in May, 1862, when he defeated Milroy, and was sent by Jackson to follow up the routed and fugitive Federals. He was then sent with his company over the Shenandoah mountain to watch Fremont.

He gave Jackson the first information that Fremont was closing in on his only line of retreat up the Valley, for Fremont was moving down the Wardensville pike to Strasburg, while Jackson was at Charlestown and Shields marching on Front Royal. Gilmor's information was undoubtedly valuable to Jackson, for if Fremont at Strasburg and Shields at Front Royal had got into communication with each other the Valley would have been hermetically sealed, and Jackson bottled up. But Harry Gilmor's report of Fremont's movements gave Jackson warning, and he held the "Pathfinder" back with one hand at Strasburg while he passed his trains or prisoners behind his line to the rear, drew him and Shields back to the head waters of the east fork of the Shenandoah, whipped Fremont June 8 at Cross Keys, routed Shields just across the river June 9 at Port Republic, and then went into camp and rested.

He had fought and whipped four armies, each of superior numbers, trying to surround and concentrate on him, taken four thousand prisoners, many miles of wagon trains, and during this historic campaign Gilmor did most efficient service and was warmly thanked by Stonewall, who never forgot him nor his fidelity.

After the death of Ashby (June 6, 1862,) Gilmor in a measure took his place in the Army of the Valley.

The commander of the department kept him constantly near the enemy, and to a large extent he was the eye and ear of the Army of the Valley.

By September, 1863, he organized a battalion of six companies of partisan rangers, and it is but fair to say that a braver, more daring and reckless band never followed the flag of a free companion in the Middle Ages. They were rough and ready ; they pervaded the enemy's rear, behind his lines, captured his wagons and couriers carrying dispatches from headquarters to a general in the field, and harrassed the enemy without ceasing by day and by night. In 1864, when Early moved into the Valley, he offered to make Gilmor Colonel of one of the Virginia cavalry regiments. But Gilmor asked that instead of promotion, two of his men then in guardhouse be released. They had fired on the provost guard, and would certainly have been severely punished, if not shot, for their offenses. Early released them.

In the campaign of 1863 Gilmor straggled off east of the Blue Ridge in search of some of his men, who had strayed into Fauquier and Loudoun. Whenever a fight came off he volunteered for the hottest place.

Brigadier-General Fitz Lee, in his report of March 23, 1863, says : " Captain Harry Gilmor, Twelfth Virginia Cavalry, volunteered for the occasion on the staff of the Major-General. I commend him for his marked bravery and cool courage."

Major-General J. E. B. Stuart, in his report (March 25, 1863,) of the battle of Kelly's ford, says : " I was especially indebted to Captain Harry Gilmor, Twelfth Virginia Cavalry, who accompanied me as volunteer staff officer."

At Kelly's ford Gilmor bore off the field the body of the " gallant Pelham."

In the year 1864 an attempt was made to assemble all the Marylanders in the armies of the Confederacy into the Maryland Line. Colonel Bradley T. Johnson was assigned to the command of all the Maryland troops and companies in the service, and directed to rendezvous them at Hanover Junction. Major-General Arnold Elzey was ordered to assemble all the unassigned men at Staunton and organize them into regiments.

Colonel Johnson collected the First Maryland Cavalry, Lieutenant-Colonel Ridgely Brown ; the Second Maryland Infantry, Captain I. Parran Crane (Lieutenant-Colonel James R. Herbert and Major W. W. Goldsborough absent, having been wounded at Gettysburg and prisoners) ; First Maryland Artillery, Captain William F. Dement ; Second Maryland Artillery (Baltimore Light), Captain William H. Griffin ; Fourth Maryland Artillery (Chesapeake), Captain Winfield Scott Chew. The Third Artillery, under Captain Latrobe and subsequently Captain William L. Ritter, was serving with great distinction in the Army of the Southwest, and was never assembled with the command, though it always ranked as belonging to the Maryland Line.

The following general order indicates that Gilmor was expected to report with his command to General Elzey at Staunton. He did not report, however, and the effort to organize the Marylanders at that point failed entirely :

Special Orders No. 105.

ADJUTANT AND INSPECTOR-GENERAL'S OFFICE, RICHMOND, VIRGINIA, May 5, 1864.

Major H. W. Gilmor's Battalion Partisan Rangers will be immediately mustered into the service of the Confederate States as cavalry. Major Gilmor will then proceed by highway with his battalion of cavalry to Camp Maryland, Staunton, Virginia, and report to Major-General A. Elzey, commanding Maryland Line, for assignment. Citizens of other States who are enlisted in any company of this battalion may, if they desire it, be transferred to companies from their own State.

BY COMMAND OF SECRETARY OF WAR.

JOHN WITHERS,
Acting Adjutant-General.

In June, 1864, Early was sent to the Valley after driving Hunter from Lynchburg into the mountains and defiles of West Virginia. He sent Gilmor and the band to hang on and harrass his rear.

In the movement on Winchester Gilmor, with Holmes Conrad, subsequently Assistant Attorney-General of the United States under President Cleveland's Administration, captured a company of infantry and marched them into camp, and the same evening the same pair of free riders took prisoners a troop of fifty-eight men of the First New Jersey Cavalry, with their horses, arms and equipments.

Such an exploit rang through the army, and Gilmor and Conrad received the plaudits of all and the thanks of " old Jubal."

In June Colonel Bradley T. Johnson was promoted Brigadier and assigned to the command of the cavalry brigade of General W. E. Jones, who had just been killed at the battle of New Hope.

Colonel Gilmor was ordered to report with his battalion to General Johnson, who consolidated the First and Second Maryland Battalions and put Gilmor in command.

Since the preceding January General Lee had been contemplating an expedition under Colonel Johnson with the Maryland Line from Hanover Junction to release the Confederate prisoners at Point Lookout. When Early crossed the Potomac in the early part of July General Lee sent him an order by a staff officer to send Johnson with his command to attack Point Lookout on the morning of the 12th. Early on the night of the 8th ordered Johnson with his cavalry to make a detour around Baltimore, destroy all the railroad bridges leading north from Baltimore, and then move rapidly so as to attack Point Lookout on the morning of the 12th. Johnson told Early that horse flesh couldn't make the ride. The prescribed route was over four hundred miles, and a thousand horse could not make the march. Nevertheless, he left Frederick at daylight of the 9th, covered Early's left flank during the battle of the Monocacy with Wallace, and then struck across the country to Cockeysville, north of Baltimore. He there burned the bridges on the Northern Central Railroad, leading to Harrisburg ; and seeing it would be impossible to keep his rendezvous for Point Lookout for daylight of the 12th if he moved farther east to the Gunpowder, he detached Gilmor with his command to burn the bridges over the Gunpowder on the Philadelphia, Wilmington and Baltimore Railroad, while he moved through Howard County to cut the railroad between Baltimore and Washington.

Gilmor accomplished his part of the programme with his wonted efficiency. Johnson's orders were to release the prisoners and enable them to join Early before Washington, and he ordered Gilmor to report to him there. At Beltsville, however, Early ordered Johnson to rejoin him at once. He had learned that Washington had been reinforced by two corps from Grant's army, and he at once withdrew into Virginia. Johnson joined him at Rockville as Gilmor reported at Poolesville.

Subsequently Early sent McCausland and Johnson into Pennsylvania to burn Chambersburg in retaliation for the burning by Hunter of Governor Letcher's house at Lexington, and of those of Alexander R. Boteler, Edward I. Lee and Andrew Harter near Shepherdstown.

On the advance Gilmor's command was the advance guard. Just across the river he met a Federal force at Clear Spring. Gilmor had two hundred men in his two Maryland battalions. He was confronted by two full regiments, but he charged and drove them five miles toward Hagerstown, and held them while the whole column passed up into Pennsylvania.

After the burning of Chambersburg the command was pursued into Virginia and attacked at daylight at Moorefield, where it was badly routed, the Marylanders suffering severely.

On the return to the army in the Valley Johnson's brigade was employed in picketing the front and covering it from Sheridan. In the daily combats between pickets and patrols the Maryland command was constantly engaged until in one of them, at Bunker Hill, Gilmor was badly wounded.

From this wound he did not report for duty until October, 1864. On February 4, 1865, he was captured in his quarters in Hardy County by Major Young, of Sheridan's staff, who had been sent out with a special detail to take him. He passed the remainder of the war in Fort Warren.

Some fragments of muster rolls have been collected from the recollection of survivors and detached fragments of rosters. The roster of officers is supposed to be accurate and complete. The whole is appended as the record of the Second Maryland Cavalry — as brave, as reckless and as faithful a band as fought under the Bars and Stars!

Honor to their exploits and their memory!

※

ROSTER OF SECOND MARYLAND CAVALRY.*

FIELD AND STAFF.

Lieutenant-Colonel,	HARRY GILMOR.
Adjutant,	HERMAN F. KEIDEL.
Sergeant-Major,	EDWARD WILLIAMS.
Quartermaster-Sergeant,	WILLIAM ALLEN.
Quartermaster-Sergeant,	N. GORSUCH.
Quartermaster,	N. W. OWINGS.

COMPANY A.

Captain, NICHOLAS BURKE.
First Lieutenant, W. W. McKAIG.
Second Lieutenant, JOHN B. WELLS.
Second Lieutenant, MEREDITH GILMOR.
First Sergeant, JOSEPH STANSBURY.
First Sergeant, ALONZO TRAVERS.

Privates.

BROOKS, ROBERT S.
BYAS, PHILIP.
DOBBS, ———.
NORWOOD, WILLIAM.
NORWOOD, LEWIS.
PENDLETON, FRANK.

COMPANY B.

Captain, EUGENE DIGGS.
First Lieutenant, ——— HARRISON.
First Lieutenant, GEORGE M. PURNELL.
Sergeant, ——— LEVY.

---

*No official muster rolls of this command have been found. A partial list of officers and men in the respective companies has been made from memory.

COMPANY C.

Captain, DAVID M. ROSS.
First Lieutenant, R. T. GILMOR.
Second Lieutenant, GEORGE FORNEY.
Second Lieutenant, WILLIAM H. KEMP.
First Sergeant, FREDERICK BAKER.

Sergeant, M. TODD.
Sergeant, ——— FIELDS.
Sergeant, JOHN BOSLEY.
First Corporal, WILLIAM H. TODD.
Corporal, JOHN EMMERICK.

Corporal, HENRY BUSHBAUM.

Privates.

ALCOCK, C.
BROTHERTON, DAVID.
BROGDEN, J. SELLMAN.
BRANDEBURG, JESSE.
CLARKE, DUNCAN.
DISNEY, WILLIAM.
DEBRILL, CHARLES.
DORAN, WILLIAM.
DANIELS, WILLIAM.
DEVRIES, WILLIAM.
DAVIS, MOSCOW.
EMMART, GEORGE.

FORD, ———.
FREEBURGER, WILLIAM.
GILMOR, WILLIAM, OF WM.
GORSUCH, N.
GILMOR, HOFFMAN.
GLOCKER, THEODORE.
HANCOCK, H. H.
HARDING, ———.
HEIMILLER, WILLIAM.
KAHLER, CHARLES P.
MURPHY, FRANK.
MURPHY, GEORGE.

MARTIN, DR. HUGH.
MILLER, HENRY.
PULLEN, HENRY.
PHILLIPS, JOHN.
POWELL, GEORGE.
STOCKSDALE, GEORGE W.
SNODGRASS, ———.
STRASBURGER, ———.
TALBOT, J. F. C.
WILLIAMS, PAT.
WEAVER, H.

COMPANY D.

Captain, JOHN BURKE.
First Lieutenant, POLK, BURKE.
Second Lieutenant, ——— BILLINGS.

COMPANY E.

Captain, JOHN E. SUDLER.
First Lieutenant, GEORGE RATCLIFFE.

Second Lieutenant, ——— BILLINGS.
Sergeant, J. C. HOLMES.

Privates.

FEAST, LOUDON.
HOBBS, WILLIAM H.

KELTON, C. B.
SCHAFFER, GEORGE W
TRAVERS, J. M.

*TURPIN, THOMAS L.
UPSHUR, L.

COMPANY F.

Captain, JAMES L. CLARK.
First Lieutenant, W. H. RICHARDSON.
Second Lieutenant, WILLIAM DORSEY.
Second Lieutenant, E. HURST.
Second Lieutenant, JAMES McALEESE.
First Sergeant, J. A. STINE.
Sergeant, J. SPRIGG.

Sergeant, L. McMULLIN.
Sergeant, R. HAHN.
Sergeant, ———— KEMP.
Sergeant, T. KIDD.
Corporal, J. ANDRE.
Corporal, C. J. STEWART.
Corporal, S. C. MAGRAW.

Privates.

ALLEN, JOHN.
BRUBAKER, R.
BURNS, IGNATIUS.
BENNETT, WILLIAM.
BERRITT, J. T.
BOSLEY, J. R.
BUCHANAN, THOMAS.
BOYLE, PHILIP.
CHERRY, JAMES.
CASTLEMAN, C. W.
CASTLEMAN, THOMAS.
CHAPMAN, WILLIAM.
CRUGHAN, MICHAEL.
CALLAM, JOHN.
COOLEY, AMBROSE.
CAMBLE, THOMAS.
CARLISLE, GEORGE.
DUNEGAN, PHILIP.
DENMEAD, AQUILLA.
DORSEY, ALBERT.
DEVRIES, JOHN.
FAVOUR, C. R.
FISHER, C. D.

FIPPS, S.
FITZPATRICK, DANIEL.
FOMAN, PERRY.
FOMAN, CHARLES.
GILLEN, STEPHEN.
GAULT, C.
GILMOR, C. G.
GILMOR, ARTHUR.
GILMOR, H.
GLENN, W. Y.
HORN, H.
HAMMOND, C.
HOBBS, J.
HALPIN, S. P.
HOOK, R. B.
HAMILTON, WILLIAM.
HARDING, JOHN.
HAGAN, R.
KENNEDY, WILLIAM.
LOVEDAY, CHARLES.
LAKINS, CHARLES.
LOGSDEN, NIMROOD.
LAMAR, ROBERT.

MURRAY, GEORGE.
MITCHELL, JAMES.
MARTIN, GEORGE.
MOULTON, WILLIAM.
MOOG, JAMES R.
MOOG, JACOB J.
NEWKIRK, J. V.
PETTIS, A.
PEREGOY, H.
REILY, F.
REED, WILLIAM.
SNIVELY, G.
SCULLY, P.
STINE, JOSEPH.
THOMPSON, GEORGE.
TALBERT, F.
TILGHMAN, JOHN.
TRAVERS, J. H.
WARFIELD, ADOLPH.
WINDER, S.
WOOD, CHARLES S.
ZIMMERMAN, WILLIAM.

COMPANY K, FIRST VIRGINIA CAVALRY.

❦

AMONG the first, if not the very first, Maryland cavalry organizations effected in Virginia was Company M, First Virginia Cavalry. Although it was late in the war transferred to the First Maryland Cavalry, so distinguished had been its services prior to its transfer that the author deems it but just that it should have a separate chapter in this book.

This company was organized at Leesburg, Virginia, on May 14, 1861, and comprised seventy-five fine young men, mostly from the Western Shore counties, and every man a horseman.

In the selection of officers George R. Gaither was elected Captain, George Howard First Lieutenant, and Samuel W. Dorsey Second Lieutenant.

At this early stage of the war there was but little organization in the cavalry arm of the service, and the different companies were often operated separately, and in many instances they moved when and where they pleased.

Captain Gaither's company was not altogether an exception, and it was not even mustered into the service of the Government until several months after its organization.

The first service the company did was to picket at Edward's Ferry, on the Potomac River, at which place and at Leesburg it remained until about the 15th of June, 1861, when the company was sent to Winchester and reported to Colonel Angus McDonald, with whom it marched to Romney, having been united with Captain Turner Ashby's company. McDonald scouted and picketed in the vicinity of Romney until July 15, when he returned to Winchester with his command, and reported to General Joseph E. Johnston, then commanding an army at that place of about ten thousand men.

On July 18, when General Johnston started from Winchester to the relief of Beauregard, who had been attacked at Manassas, Captain Gaither was ordered to Berryville with his company, there to remain until the last of the infantry had crossed the Shenandoah River, when he was to report to Colonel J. E. B. Stuart, in command of the First Virginia Cavalry, and Captain Gaither joined Colonel Stuart at Piedmont, and then the company became known as Company M, Colonel Stuart having so designated it.

The First Virginia reached Manassas at noon of July 21, and took a conspicuous part in the battle fought that day and in the subsequent pursuit of the Federal Army.

Two days after the battle of Manassas the company was sent on picket duty to Falls Church, and made a reconnoissance on July 24 and occupied Mason's Hill, and upon Captain Gaither's report Colonel Stuart (who was at Fairfax Court House in command of the cavalry and infantry advance of the army) immediately marched the First Maryland Infantry and First Virginia Cavalry from Fairfax Court House and took possession of Mason's and Munson's Hills, two important points, each of which overlooked Washington City.

After this, Company M was constantly on picket duty from Lewinsville to the Great Falls of the Potomac, and skirmishes with the enemy's cavalry were of almost daily occurrence. But the enemy finally occupied Lewinsville in force, and Colonel Stuart was compelled to bring a considerable body of troops to drive them out. A severe fight ensued before the place was reoccupied by the Confederates, in which the First Virginia Cavalry, as usual, took a conspicuous part.

About this time Lieutenants George Howard and Samuel W. Dorsey resigned from the company, and upon an election for Lieutenants Ridgely Brown was chosen First Lieutenant, Frank A. Bond Second Lieutenant, and Thomas Griffith Third Lieutenant. The company as thus reorganized was then regularly mustered into the First Virginia Cavalry, for the first time, at Fairfax Court House on August 1, 1861.

The regiment had now undergone a change of commanders, Captain William E. Jones having been promoted to the Colonelcy, vice Colonel J. E. B. Stuart, who had been made a Brigadier-General.

During the fall and winter of 1861-2 the regiment saw much hard service on picket duty in advance of the army of General Joseph E. Johnston, which was at Centreville and Manassas. Heavy skirmishing was of frequent occurrence, until General Johnston finally fell back to the Rappahannock, and during that retreat the First Virginia brought up the rear. In all these operations Company M was conspicuous for its gallantry, and was more than once complimented by the Colonel commanding.

We next find the First Virginia with the army on the Peninsula, under command of Colonel Fitz Hugh Lee, Colonel Jones having been promoted in the meantime. By order of Colonel Lee, the initial of the company was changed from M to K, and to show his appreciation of its services he gave it position on the right of the column.

The history of the First Virginia Cavalry embraces the whole period of the war, and if we should go into detail of its operations up to the time Company K was transferred it would fill a large volume. In all these operations Company K bore a prominent part. We will, therefore, briefly enumerate the actions in which the regiment participated up to the transfer of Company K to the First Maryland Cavalry .

On May 5, 1862, the company was reorganized, its term of service having expired. In this reorganization there was considerable change in its officers. Lieutenants Brown, Bond and Griffith being desirous of going to Richmond, and if possible raise a battalion which was to be distinctively a Maryland command. Therefore, in their stead Gustavus W. Dorsey was elected First Lieutenant, N. C. Hobbs Second Lieutenant, and Rudolphus Cecil, Third Lieutenant. George R. Gaither was re-elected to the Captaincy.

The First Virginia was next stationed at Bigler's wharf, on the York River, until after the battle of Williamsburg, when it acted as rear guard until the battle of Elthau's Landing.

At Statesville the regiment was heavily engaged, and was the rear guard until the army crossed the Chickahominy. It was engaged at Seven Pines, and a portion of Company K, under Lieutenant Hobbs, was detailed to accompany General J. E. B. Stuart in his raid around McClellan's army. The regiment was engaged in the Seven Days' Battles before Richmond, and after the retreat of McClellan's army it was sent to Mount Carmel Church, near Fredericksburg, where it remained until General Robert E. Lee marched to Gordonsville. It was in several skirmishes, and particularly at Jerrold's Mill, where it charged and broke the Third Indiana Cavalry and drove them to the protection of their infantry. In the fight at Catlett's Station the First Virginia, with Company K always at its head, made a glorious charge.

An incident worth relating happened at Catlett's, and proved how much confidence General J. E. B. Stuart had in the First Virginia. The cavalry were drawn up on ground with which they were not familiar, and the night was very dark. Stuart had come upon the enemy's camp-fires somewhat unexpectedly, and he determined to charge toward those fires and ascertain what was there. The Ninth Virginia Cavalry was selected as the leading column in the charge, that to be followed by the First Virginia. After moving a short distance down a steep hill, the Ninth suddenly encountered a stiff fence, and there it stopped, nor could the entreaties of its officers induce the men to put their horses to that fence. Stuart was immediately apprised of the fact, and excitedly exclaimed : " I know a regiment that will ! Tell Colonel Drake to bring up the First and charge the enemy, even though there were a dozen fences before him !"

It is needless to say that the First went over the fence, followed by the Fifth, Company K leading, and they were soon in the midst of the enemy's infantry, where a stubborn fight ensued, but the Federals were badly beaten and five hundred prisoners taken. It proved to be Pope's headquarters, and that General lost his personal baggage, horses and other property. General Stuart felt that he had been fully avenged for the loss of his cloak and hat, captured a few days before at Verdiersville by a sudden dash of a small body of the enemy's cavalry while he and Von Boerck were quietly enjoying the hospitalities of a Virginia family.

The First Virginia accompanied Stonewall Jackson on his march to Manassas, being left at Buckland to protect his rear. It participated in the second Manassas and captured a large body of regular cavalry at Stewart's Tavern the day before the battle of Ox Hill. It was the advance guard in the Maryland campaign, and was engaged in all the battles up to and including Sharpsburg, and it covered the retreat of the Army of Northern Virginia across the Potomac.

The First Virginia remained in the Valley, being always with General Stuart, and it accompanied him in his Chambersburg raid, and when returning the Federals cut off General Stuart's retreat, it charged over the line of battle and opened the way to the river.

The First Virginia was with General tuart in his retreat through Loudoun, and was daily engaged until it reached Culpeper Court House. It was on the extreme right of the army at Fredericksburg and skirmished all day.

In February, 1863, it participated in General Stuart's Falmouth raid and the battle of Kelly's Ford. It was engaged at Brandy Station in June, 1863, and in General Stuart's raid around Hooker's army. It was engaged at Bristow Station and at Annandale, and on the invasion of Maryland and Pennsylvania by the Army of Northern Virginia in June, 1863, the First Virginia was engaged at Westminster and Hanover. Arriving at Gettysburg on July 2d, it was heavily engaged in the great cavalry battle on the left of General Lee's army.

The First Virginia was the rear guard in the retreat by the Cashtown road, and was then hurried forward to the protection of the wagon trains at Williamsport, and when the Federals were driven off, the regiment was sent to Funkstown, on the Boonsboro road, where it fought for two days, holding in check the enemy's advance, but was driven back foot by foot to General Lee's lines around Falling Waters and Williamsport.

The First Virginia was engaged at Kearneysville and covered the retreat of the army to the Rapidan River. It was also engaged at Raccoon Ford, charging across the river, and driving the enemy from the bank.

During Meade's retreat from Mine Run, the First was actively engaged, and was in all the cavalry engagements during the winter of 1863-64.

In the spring of 1864, when Grant entered the Wilderness, the First Virginia was ever active, and at Yellow Tavern, when the noble Stuart fell mortally wounded, he fell into the arms of Captain Gustavus W. Dorsey, Captain of Company K.

The fight at Yellow Tavern was a very severe one. Sheridan, with twelve thousand cavalry, was moving on Richmond, when General Stuart interposed by attacking his flank at Yellow Tavern. About 4 o'clock the enemy suddenly threw a brigade of cavalry upon his extreme left, and at the same time attacked along the whole line. General Stuart hastened to the point where was the greatest danger. The charge of the enemy was irresistible, and two guns of the Baltimore Light Artillery were captured, along with Captain Griffin and several of his men, but not until he had inflicted fearful destruction in the ranks of the Michigan cavalry. Captain Dorsey, with Company K, was stationed on the Telegraph road, where eighty or ninety men were assembled. Among these General Stuart threw himself, and as the enemy passed in their headlong charge they received their fire in flank and rear. But the First Virginia was in their path, all save Company K, as has been stated. The enemy was driven back some distance. As they retired a dismounted cavalryman, running to escape, discharged his revolver at the General, and inflicted the fatal wound. Captain Dorsey had witnessed the act, and immediately rushed to his assistance. Captain Dorsey took him from his horse and placed him against a tree. General Stuart then expressed the belief that he was mortally wounded and could be of no further use, and then ordered Dorsey to go back to his command. But this Dorsey declined to do, until he saw him safely off the field. Calling to Private Wheatly, they placed him upon a horse and led it to a place of safety, when an ambulance was procured, and supported in the arms of Wheatly the ambulance was driven off. The death of Stuart a few hours later (May 12, 1864,) was a severe blow to the Confederacy. He was one of the greatest cavalry generals the world ever saw, and one of the most beloved of men. His soldiers worshiped him, and the public loved and honored him.

A few weeks after the death of General Stuart Company K was transferred to the First Maryland Cavalry, when Captain Dorsey was made Lieutenant-Colonel of the battalion, and how the gallant soldier acquitted himself the reader has seen in reading the sketch of the First Maryland Cavalry.

ROSTER OF COMPANY K, FIRST VIRGINIA CAVALRY.

Captain, GEORGE R. GAITHER.
   Resigned.
Captain, GUS W. DORSEY.
Captain, N. C. HOBBS.
First Lieutenant, GEORGE HOWARD.
   Captured at Lewinsville.
Second Lieutenant, SAMUEL W. DORSEY.
Second Lieutenant, GEORGE HOWARD.
Second Lieutenant, RIDGELY BROWN.
Second Lieutenant, THOMAS GRIFFITH.
Second Lieutenant, FRANK A. BOND.
Second Lieutenant, E. H. D. PUE.

First Lieutenant, RUDOLPHUS CECIL.
   Killed at James City Landing.
First Sergeant, ROBERT FLOYD.
Sergeant, W. H. WRIGHT.
Sergeant, GEORGE BUCKINGHAM.
Sergeant, IRA ALBAUGH.
Sergeant, W. W. BURGESS.
Corporal, F. LEO WILLS.
Corporal, WILLIAM BARNES.
Corporal, B. H. MORGAN.
Corporal, ROBERT BRUCE.
Corporal, JAMES OLIVER.

Privates.

ALBAUGH, JOHN.
   Killed.
ARCHER, ROBERT.
   Promoted to Lieutenant-Colonel of Fifty-fifth Virginia Regiment.
ARNETT, WILLIAM.
BARNES, WILLIAM.
   Killed at Kelly's Ford.
BARRY, DANIEL R.
BEATTY, EDWARD.
   Killed.
BETTS, SAMUEL.
   Wounded at Jarald's Mill.
BOND, FRANK.
BOUDLIN, CONSTANTINE.
   Wounded at Falmouth.
BOWIE, ALBERT.
BRADY, EUGENE.
   Wounded and captured at Spottsylvania.

BRANDT, ALEXANDER J.
BROWN, CHARLES.
   Wounded.
BROWN, J. WESLEY.
BROWN, LOUIS.
   Wounded at Charlottesville.
BROWN, HENRY.
   Killed at Earlysville.
BRUCE, ROBERT.
   Killed at Bunker's Hill.
BUCKINGHAM, GEORGE.
   Wounded.
BUMP, GEORGE C.
BURGESS, WILLIAM.
   Wounded at Bunker's Hill.
BOWLING, C. A.
BOWIE, H. B.
BIGGER, JOHN.
BLAKELY, W. H.
BOWLMAN, M.

CLARK, IGNATIUS.
CONRADT, C. J.
CLINTON, DEWITT.
   Wounded.
CLAGETT, H. H.
CUNNINGHAM, R.
CALBRETH, JOHN.
CAMPBELL, WILLIAM.
   Captured.
CARROLL, HARPER.
CHILDS, WILLIAM.
   Killed.
CLARK, RODY.
   Wounded three times.
CLEMENTS, FRANK.
COOK, RUDOLPHUS.
CECIL, RUDOLPHUS.
   Promoted Lieutenant. Killed at James City Landing.
CONRAD, EPHRAIM.

DURKIN, JOHN.
DAVIS, H. B.
DORSEY, C. R.
DORSEY, WILLIAM.
   Killed at Spottsylvania Court House.
DUSENBERG, B.
DAVIES, WILLIAM.
   Killed at Falmouth.
DITTY, IRVING C.
DORSEY, C. H.
DORSEY, HAMMOND.
DORSEY, JOHN.
DORSEY, PUE.
D'ALL, RASH.
DORSEY, GUSTAVUS W.
   Promoted as Captain. Wounded at Bunker's Hill.
ELLIS, THOMAS.
EVANS, BENJAMIN.
EDWARDS, DOCTOR.
FITZGERALD, W. BOLTON.
   Captured three times at Leesburg.
FORRESTT, PITT.
FLOYD, ROBERT.
   Killed at Kelly's Ford.
GILL, G. M.
   Killed in the Valley of Virginia.
GRIFFITH, RICHARD.
GARDNER, J.
GLONDELL, JOHN.
   Killed.
GAIGING, MICHAEL.
GAITHER, WASHINGTON.
   Killed at Gettysburg.
GIBSON, WILLIAM.
GITTINGS, HARRY.
   Killed at Winchester.

GREY, ———
   Killed.
GRIFFITH, FRANK.
GRIFFITH, GEORGE.
HAYDEN, A.
HOLLAND, J. J. J.
   Captured and died at Point Lookout.
HOLLAND, P. R.
HARTMIER, R.
HOLLAND, JOHN.
   Killed.
HOBBS, JARRETT.
HURLEY, OTHO S.
HOPKINS, H.
HARDING, JOHN.
   Killed at Beaver Dam Station.
HAYDEN, REV. HORACE E.
HAYDEN, WILLIAM.
   Wounded and captured.
HEWES, WARNER.
HOLLAND, MITCHELL.
HOBBS, TOWNLEY.
   Captured and took the oath.
HOBBS, N. CHEW.
   Promoted Lieutenant.
ISAACS, WILLIAM.
JACKINS, WILLIAM.
JAMESON, FRANK.
JENKINS, E. D.
JAMESON, JAMES.
JENKINS, HENRY.
   Wounded and captured.
JOHNSON, JOHN Q. A.
KUHN, JOHN.
KEENE, ROBERT.
KELBAUGH, WILLIAM.
   Killed at Raccoon Ford.
KENLEY, RICHARD.

LEPPER C. V.
LOGAN, ALEXANDER.
   Killed at Martinsburg.
LINTHICUM, JOHN.
LAMBERT, WILLIAM.
LANGLEY, THOMAS.
LEE OTHO S.
   Detailed at General Fitzhugh Lee's headquarters.
LEMAITS, JAMES.
MERRITT SAMUEL.
MCCUBBIN, E.
MAGUIRE, H. A. W.
MCGINNIS, FRANK.
MAYNADIER, JOHN H.
   Captured and sentenced as a spy. Pardoned by President Lincoln.
MAYNADIER, J. M.
   Detailed on Signal Corps. Wounded at Fairfax C. H.
MERCER, E. W.
MCNULTY, JAMES.
MCSHERRY, RICHARD.
MACKALL, ROBERT.
MCCABBE, GEORGE.
   Badly wounded.
MAXWELL, JOHN.
MCCLOUD, HENRY.
MORTON, THOMAS.
MURDOCK, CAMPBELL.
OWINGS, J. H.
   Detailed at General Fitzhugh Lee's headquarters.
O'BRIEN, E.
OFFUTT, WILLIAM.
   Captured and took the oath.
OLIVER, JAMES.
   Wounded and captured.
O'NEAL, JOHN H.

OFFUTT, JOHN.
  Captured and took the oath.
PITTS, FRED.
  Captured and escaped from Fort McHenry.
PITTS, JOHN W.
PITTS, WILLIAM.
PURNELL, W. S.
  Captured and escaped from Fort McHenry.
PITTS, EMORY.
PLUMMER, JOHN B.
PUE, FERD.
PUE, VENTRESS.
PUE, EDWARD H. D.
  Promoted as Lieutenant. Held No. 1 right of the line of First Virginia Cavalry for three years. Wounded at Gettysburg, Spottsylvania, Ream's Station, and in the Valley of Virginia.
RIDGELY, SAMUEL.
RENCH, J. V.
RIDER, WILLIAM.
  Killed at Gettysburg.
RIGGS, JOSHUA.
ROBY, TOWNLEY.
SMOOT, JOSEPH.
SMITH, C. W.
SHOW, JOSEPH.
SLATER, GEORGE.
SMALL, GEORGE.
SHERWIN, THOMAS.
SMITH, JOHN.
SCAGGS, ROBERT.
SMITH, JOHN.
SAKERS, JOHN.
SISSON, O. B.
SHRIVER, MARK O.
SCHULL, JOHN.
SEIGNOR, THOMAS.
SELLMAN, JOHN.
SMITH, THOMAS.
  Killed.
STEWART, ROBERT.
  Killed at Slatersville.
THOMAS, DANIEL.
TREACKLE, ALBERT.
TONGE, RICHARD.
TURNER, THOMAS.
  Detailed with Mosby.
  Killed at Harper's Ferry.
WHEATLEY, CHARLES.
WALSH, THOMAS.
WITZLEBBEN, A.
  Captured.
WATERS, GREEN.
  Died at Fort McHenry.
WATERS, T. J.
WILSON, A. S.
  Captured.
WEEKS, H.
WILSON, CHARLES.
WILSON, LUTHER.
WAGNER, HY.
WHEATLY, FRANK.
  Killed at Raccoon Ford.
WALTERS, JOHN.
  Killed.
WEBSTER, WILLIAM S.
WHEATLEY, WALTER.
WRENCH, JOHN.
  Wounded.
WILSON, WILLIAM B.
WILLS, LEO.
WRIGHT, WILLIAM.
WALTERS, E. H.

SECOND MANASSAS, AUGUST, 1862.

Capt.
William F. Dement
1st Maryland Light Artillery.

Collection of E. Philip Schreier III

FIRST MARYLAND ARTILLERY.

CHAPTER I.

NO battery of artillery in the Confederate Army won more distinction during the four years of the war than did the First Maryland Artillery, or, as it was more commonly known, "Dement's Battery." Composed of young men from eighteen to twenty years of age, they were imbued with a spirit of patriotism that overcame all sense of fear, and made them invincible upon the field of battle, and it was one of the very few batteries in the Army of Northern Virginia that never lost a gun, and no battery in that army saw more hard fighting or lost more men.

The young men of this battery were from lower Maryland, the Eastern Shore and Baltimore City. They started out with the intention of forming a cavalry company under Colonel Jennifer, and rendesvouzed at Fredericksburg, where the citizens supplied their wants and turned over to them the theatre for quarters. The reason they had determined to go into the cavalry was that many of them were from Charles County, and belonged to the Charles County Volunteer Cavalry.

Whilst waiting at Fredericksburg for Jennifer they were joined by other Marylanders from day to day, and also by Frederick Y. Dabney, himself a Mississippian, with a few Virginians. One day R. Snowden Andrews came along with a few men, and he proposed they should raise an artillery company. The men had become restless at the non-appearance of Jennifer, and they told Andrews they would accede to his proposition, provided W. F. Dement was made First Lieutenant, to which Andrews agreed.

The men then procured transportation to Richmond and were given quarters at the Reservoir, where, on the tenth day of July, they were mustered into the service, when R. Snowden Andrews was made Captain, William F. Dement First Lieutenant, Charles S. Contee Second Lieutenant and Frederick Y. Dabney Third Lieutenant.

After overcoming many difficulties, Captain Andrews succeeded in procuring from Governor Letcher four Napoleons and four Parrotts. The Parrotts were, however, discarded after the Seven Days' Battles. The men were now put to hard drilling under the instruction of Lieutenant Dabney, who was proficient in the artillery drill, and the battery was soon ready to take the field.

The First Maryland was ordered to Fredericksburg, to which place it was transported by rail. From Fredericksburg the battery was sent to Brooks Station, near Aquia Creek, where it remained until October, when it was sent to the Potomac batteries blockading that river. Whilst stationed here the battery was busily engaged for awhile mounting guns at the Ship Point Batteries. The boys had altogether a pretty good time here, and they improved their practice wonderfully, for many a saucy craft tried to run the blockade, and came to grief from the accurate fire of the First Maryland Artillery.

The battery remained on the Potomac until the following March, and when Johnston fell back from Manassas it was sent to Fredericksburg, and encamped on the south side of the Rappahannock.

The battery was now attached to General Pettigrew's Brigade, and in a review by General Joseph E. Johnston he paid it a high compliment for its neat and soldierly appearance.

From Fredericksburg the battery was sent to Ashland, and in a few days after to Yorktown, where it remained until the evacuation of that place. From Yorktown the First fell back to Williamsburg, and from there was sent to assist Hood at West Point, but was held as a reserve battery. From there the battery went to Poor's farm, near Richmond, and when the terrible battle of Seven Pines took place, part of the First was actively engaged.

At Mechanicsville, on June 26, the First Maryland had the first opportunity to show of what material it was composed. The battery was hotly engaged, and lost heavily in men and horses. The gallant Andrews was severely wounded, but did not leave the field. That battle won for Captain Andrews his star, and for the battery most honorable mention in official reports.

The glorious Dement now assumed command of the battery, with which he was destined to carve out a name, and his command a reputation, second to no commander and no artillery command in the service.

We next find the battery, on the following day, at Gaines' Mill, in the hottest of that dreadful battle of the Seven Days' series, when blood flowed like water ; and next at Frazier's Farm, and then at Malvern Hill.

Oh ! those were seven fearful days, and brave men willingly died by thousands ; but a great sigh of relief went up throughout the South when it was announced that McClellan and his vast array had been driven to the shelter of his gunboats on the James, and the siege of Richmond was raised.

After the battle of Malvern Hill Lieutenant Dement received his commission as Captain, and at the same time there was assigned to the battery by the War Department Lieutenant John Gale, who subsequently proved himself to be a most efficient officer.

The author has forgotten to state that the brigade to which the battery was attached was now commanded by General Pender, General Pettigrew having been wounded at Seven Pines. To these brave officers the men of the battery were much attached, and the attachment was mutual. General Pettigrew rendered up his life at Falling Waters, on the retreat from Gettysburg, and the gallant Pender died in that great battle.

After the Seven Days' Battles the battery was ordered to Gordonsville. Here Lieutenant Dabney, who had been a civil engineer, was detached and sent to Port Hudson. This necessitated the election of two Lieutenants, for the vacancy occasioned by the promotion of Lieutenant Dement had not been filled. William I. Hill was made Second Lieutenant and J. H. Stonestreet Third Lieutenant. It proved a happy selection, for there were no more gallant and efficient officers in the artillery service of the Confederacy.

Whilst at Gordonsville the battery was ordered to join Jackson near Orange Court House, and were attached to Lawton's Georgia Brigade at the battle of Cedar Run. The First suffered severely in this battle, both in men and horses. Among the killed were Theodore Jenkins, of Laurel, Maryland, and Doctor J. W. F. Hatton. So terrible and accurate was the fire of the First that the battery to which it was opposed was literally cut to pieces, and fell into the hands of the infantry. In a timber chest was found a note signed by a Lieutenant, which read thus : " Take this gun, and make as good use of it as I have." Here Major Andrews received a fearful wound.

After the battle of Cedar Run Jackson took up his line of march in the direction of Warrenton Springs, where his command arrived in the afternoon of the next day, when Early's Brigade and the First Maryland and Chesapeake batteries were thrown across the river. That night a terrific rainstorm came up, and next morning Early found himself cut off, as the rain had so swollen the Rappahannock that it was not fordable.

This was an unlooked-for catastrophe ; but that grand old hero was equal to the emergency. Placing his infantry and artillery in position, and spreading them out as much as possible to deceive the enemy as to his force. Early calmly awaited the attack which he knew must speedily come, for he was in the presence of the greater part of Pope's army.

And he had not long to wait, for presently the enemy advanced his infantry in force, and his artillery opened, but so destructive was the fire of the two Maryland batteries that he was speedily driven back. Again and again he essayed, but cautiously, for he fortunately believed Lee's whole army was in his front.

But Jackson across the river was fully alive to the dangers that beset this little band, and set to work with might and main to build a bridge across the river higher up. All day long this unequal struggle continued, when, at nightfall, the bridge being completed, the grand old soldier marched his command across it and re-joined Jackson.

Jackson now changed his line of march, and at Bristow's the two contending armies met, when a severe fight ensued. But Jackson was on his way to Manassas Junction, and he meant to get there. Disengaging himself, he again changed his course, and when Pope next heard of him he was in his rear and playing sad havoc with his stores at Manassas.

After leaving Manassas, Jackson moved around to Centreville, and thence to the old battle-field of Manassas. On the 28th of August Pope made his attack on Jackson, and Dement's battery fired the first shot by order of General A. P. Hill in person. In the desperate struggle that ensued, the battery was fought with the utmost desperation. The conduct of Lieutenant Hill in command of a section of the battery was particularly noticeable. As the enemy pressed on in overwhelming numbers he would limber his pieces to the rear for a hundred yards, halt, and renew the fight. This he did several times, until at length the enemy was driven back with heavy loss.

The next day and the day after the battery was heavily engaged, and lost severely in men and horses.

At Chantilly the battery was not engaged owing to the wooded nature of the country, but during that severe engagement it was under a hot fire.

As the Army of Northern Virginia was now on its way into Maryland, we will carry the reader across the Potomac at Shepherdstown, and thence to Loudoun Heights, from which elevation the First Maryland battery, in conjunction with the Chesapeakes, hurled their iron hail into the devoted ranks of Miles' command, many hundred feet below.

After the surrender of that unfortunate command, Dement made a forced march to Sharpsburg, but arrived too late to become engaged.

But little of interest occurred until December. After the unfortunate invasion of Maryland, Early's Division, to which the First was still attached, moved to Martinsburg, where it remained awhile, thence to Bunker Hill, to White Post, and in November, 1862, crossed the Blue Ridge near Newmarket, and proceeded to Fredericksburg, and camped below Hamilton's Crossing. On the 12th of December it moved up and took position at the crossing.

Dement was placed on the ridge to the left of Early, and as the enemy charged a long way to their right on the 13th, the battery participated but little in that action, owing to their having Napoleons, though it was under a severe fire both days.

From Fredericksburg the battery was sent to Bowling Green, where it went into winter quarters, and the time was spent pleasantly enough until the first of May, when camp was broken, and Dement was ordered to Fredericksburg.

At Fredericksburg the battery was placed in Andrews' battalion. Sedgwick was there in force, threatening an attack upon that portion of General Lee's line under Early, for Fredericksburg and Chancellorsville was really one battle, though Early was somewhat detached from the main army.

Sedgwick attacked Early with great vigor, and after a stubborn resistance he carried Mayre's Heights, capturing several guns and a portion of Barksdale's command.

The First Maryland was here, as more than once before, handicapped by their short-range guns, and the Chesapeake and Pogue batteries were sent to their assistance, and both suffered severely in getting into position, but when the enemy's infantry got within closer range, the fire of the Napoleons was very destructive. When the enemy overran Mayre's Heights the left fell back some distance. But Sedgwick's success was of short duration.

Colonel Andrews massed his battalion near the Telegraph road, and as the battalion was somewhat concealed when the enemy came suddenly upon him he opened with twenty pieces at short range. The execution was fearful, and the enemy fell back in great confusion beyond Lee's Hill.

General Early then sprung the brigades of Hays, Gordon and Walker to the charge, and Sedgwick was driven across the river, only to meet with a still more disastrous defeat at the hands of General Wilcox at Salem Church.

Colonel Andrews received much credit for the part he played in this engagement.

In the battle of Fredericksburg the First Maryland suffered severely, and after the battle it moved to Holliday's farm to repair damages.

CHAPTER II.

When the Army of Northern Virginia left Fredericksburg in June, 1863, on its invasion of Pennsylvania, Ewell's Corps, to which Colonel Andrews' battery belonged, moved by way of Front Royal to Winchester, at which place the battalion was assigned to General Edward Johnson's Division.

General Early had diverged from Ewell on the march, and his column struck the Valley turnpike near Newtown on the morning of the 13th of June, where, uniting with the Second Maryland Infantry and Baltimore Light Artillery, he advanced upon Winchester, skirmishers from the Second Maryland Infantry leading the way. These encountered the enemy at Kernstown, and soon after General Gordon charged on the left and drove Milroy's troops into their fortifications, the main one of which General Harry Hays, with his Louisiana Brigade, assaulted and carried the next evening in a most gallant manner. All day of the 14th the Maryland skirmishers kept pegging away so as to distract the enemy's attention from the real point of attack, and Hays' assault was a genuine surprise.

On the evening of the 14th General Ewell, believing that Milroy would steal away during the night, ordered General Johnson to take the Stonewall, Nicholls' and three regiments of Steuart's Brigades, and W. F. Dement's battery, with sections of Charles I. Raine's and J. C. Carpenter's (the whole under Lieutenant-Colonel Andrews) to proceed to a point on the Martinsburg pike about two and a half miles from Winchester.

General Ewell had calculated well, for during the night Milroy did evacuate the place and was intercepted by that portion of Johnson's Division sent for the purpose.

General Johnson marched by the way of Jordan's Springs to Stephenson's Depot. Just as the head of the column reached the railroad, two hundred yards from the Martinsburg road the enemy were heard retreating down the road towards Martinsburg.

General Johnson immediately formed his line parallel with the pike behind a stone wall, Steuart on the right and the Louisianians on the left, altogether twelve hundred men. Milroy attacked at once with his cavalry and infantry (he had left his artillery at Winchester), and made repeated efforts to cut his way through, but was as often repulsed with heavy loss. Milroy then attempted to turn both flanks simultaneously, but was met on the right by General Walker, who had just arrived, having lost his way, and by two regiments of Nicholls' Brigade, which had been held in reserve, when in a few minutes the greater part surrendered — two thousand three hundred in number.

And what was Dement's battery doing all this time ? The following extracts from the official reports of General Ewell, Colonel J. Thompson Brown, General Edward Johnson and the brave boy, Major Latimer, beloved by all, will show :

General R. S. Ewell thus speaks of the section of Dement's battery commanded by Lieutenant C. S. Contee :

Lieutenant C. S. Contee's section of Dement's battery was placed in short musket range of the enemy on June 15, and maintained its position till thirteen of the sixteen men in the two detachments were killed or wounded, when Lieutenant John A. Morgan, of the First North Carolina Infantry, and Lieutenant R. H. McKim, aide-de-camp to Brigadier-General George H. Steuart, volunteered and helped to work the guns till the surrender of the enemy. The following are the names of the gallant men belonging to this section :

FIRST GUN — Sergeant John G. Harris, Corporals William P. Compton, Samuel Thompson, Privates Robert Chew, William Koester, Welsh Owens, Charles Pease, A. James Albert, Jr., William T. Wootton, John R. Yates, Jr., H. J. Langsdale and John R. Buchanan.

SECOND GUN — Sergeant John E. Glasscocke, Corporals William H. May and Charles Harris, Privates Thomas Moore, William Gorman, F. Frayer, William W. Wilson, Samuel Thomas, R. T. Richardson, William Sherburne, James Owens, William Dallam and Joseph Mockabee.

Colonel Brown, acting chief of artillery, recommends Lieutenant Contee for promotion to the Captaincy of the Chesapeake Artillery, vice Captain W. D. Brown, a most gallant and valuable officer, killed at Gettysburg.

Extract from official report of Colonel J. Thompson Brown, Chief of Artillery :

On the morning of the 15th Lieutenant-Colonel R. S. Andrews, with Dement's and sections from Raine's and Carpenter's batteries, had a sharp engagement with the enemy's infantry, who were retreating on the road toward Charlestown, by Jordan's Springs. Great credit is due the officers and men for the spirited and determined manner with which they fought the enemy's infantry at close quarters. Especial credit is due Lieutenant C. S. Contee, of Captain W. F. Dement's battery, and the section under his command. Lieutenant Contee is recommended for promotion to a Captaincy for gallantry on this occasion, and I ask that he be ordered to the command of the Chesapeake Artillery, made vacant by the death of Captain W. D. Brown. Sergeants John G. Harris and J. E. Glasscocke, and Corporals William P. Compton, Samuel Thompson and William H. May, of this section, are much to be praised for their coolness and bravery on this occasion. . . . . Lieutenant-Colonel Andrews and Lieutenant Contee were both wounded. The battery lost five killed and fourteen wounded.

General Edward Johnson says:

Before closing this report, I beg leave to state that I have never seen superior artillery practice to that of Andrews' battalion in this engagement, and especially the section under Lieutenant C. S. Contee of Dement's battery, one gun of which was placed on the bridge above referred to, and the other a little to the left and rear. Both pieces were very much exposed during the whole action. Four successive attempts were made to carry the bridge. Two sets of cannoneers (thirteen out of sixteen) were killed and disabled. Lieutenant-Colonel Andrews and Lieutenant Contee, whose gallantry calls for special mention, fell wounded at this point. Lieutenant John A. Morgan, First North Carolina Regiment, and Lieutenant Randolph H. McKim took the place of the disabled cannoneers, rendering valuable assistance, deserving special mention.

Major J. W. Latimer says:

The conduct of the officers, non-commissioned officers and men serving the right section of Captain Dement's battery cannot be spoken of in terms of praise sufficiently high. The stern determination with which they stood up to their guns is proven by the fact that the gun at the bridge was worked with terrible effect until six men were disabled, and, on account of the difficult position which the gun occupied, the two cannoneers who were left were unable to work it. Finding the other gun detachment becoming weak, the Sergeant and Corporal, with the two men, went over to its assistance. In a few minutes the latter detachment had suffered as great loss as the former, but owing to the superiority of the ground the gun could be worked with diminished numbers.

I desire to bring to your immediate notice on this occasion the names of Lieutenant C. S. Contee, commanding the section; Sergeant Harris, Corporals Compton and Thompson, of the first gun; Sergeant Glasscocke and Corporal May, of the second gun.

Ah! here's a record to be proud of!

After Winchester General Ewell directed his steps toward the Potomac, which he crossed at Shepherdstown, and the boys of Dement's battery were happy that day, for it had been many months since they had set foot on the soil of their native State.

After crossing the Pennsylvania line, Johnson's Division directed its steps toward Carlisle by way of Chambersburg, where, after spending a day in the vicinity of that city, it was ordered to retrace its steps to within five miles of Chambersburg. Turning to the left at Greenvillage, the division went into camp on the evening of June 30, near Fayetteville, and resumed its march on the morning of July 1, in the direction of Gettysburg.

But little more than half the distance had been accomplished when the sound of cannon ahead caused the division to hasten its steps. Johnson got there too late, but it was no fault of his. Had General Ewell taken the division direct to Gettysburg from Carlisle, instead of sending it there by a most circuitous route, there would have been no second or third days' battles at Gettysburg. This General Ewell freely admitted and regretted afterward.

Passing through the outskirts of the town, Johnson formed his line of battle along the Hanover road, and that night the troops laid upon their arms.

The sun rose on the morning of July 2d clear and beautiful. Alas! how many saw it rise for the last time!

In the absence of Colonel Andrews, wounded at Winchester, the noble Latimer was in command of the artillery battalion to which the First Maryland was attached.

About 4 o'clock in the afternoon Major Latimer was ordered to take position on Benner's Hill, the best position that could be obtained for artillery, but completely commanded by Cemetery Ridge.

Fiercely did the gallant fellow fight his guns (or rather what was left of them after the first hour) until near dark, when he received a wound that laid him in a soldier's grave a few days after.

And how fared the First Maryland in this fierce battle? The battery was doing its duty nobly, as it had done before, and as it did afterward. It suffered with the rest, and among those who died was the gallant Sam Thompson, who was killed by the explosion of an ammunition chest which was struck by one of the enemy's shells.

Poor Sam Thompson! And who in Baltimore did not know the handsome fellow before the war? Noble, generous and brave, he was the life of every social gathering he attended. Sam Thompson was one of the happiest men on earth, and he was happiest when making others happy. No soldier in the Confederacy left a better record, and none were more beloved by his comrades. Peace to his ashes!

Wearily and sadly the Army of Northern Virginia dragged its shattered body back to Williamsport, and there recrossed the Potomac. At Hagerstown Colonel Andrews reported for duty and resumed command of the battalion.

After reaching Virginia the battalion moved to Martinsburg, and thence to Bunker Hill, to Liberty Mills, and finally to the vicinity of Charlottesville, where it remained until called upon to march to Mine Run to resist the advance of Meade; and here it was heavily engaged. In this battle George Scott, of the First, said to be one of the best gunners in the Confederate Army, was among the killed.

After Mine Run the battalion was sent to Frederick's Hall, where it was turned over to Colonel Braxton, Colonel Andrews being compelled, owing to the terrible wound he received at Cedar Run, to relinquish the command.

In March the First Maryland and Chesapeake Batteries were transferred to the Maryland Line, then in winter quarters at Hanover Junction.

But their stay was destined to be of short duration, for when Grant began his march through the Wilderness the following month the First was ordered to join Breckinridge.

Nor was it long inactive. Slowly but surely Grant was nearing Richmond; it is true it was by a circuitous route and at an awful sacrifice of human life.

The Army of Northern Virginia was assembling at Cold Harbor to administer one more crushing blow to his vast hosts, and Breckinridge was there with it. The enemy was uncomfortably near, and he called for Dement to throw his battery to the front and hold him in check until he could form his line of battle. The gallant Dement brought his battery up on the run, unlimbered, and in an instant was pouring cannister into the ranks of the enemy. Breckinridge formed his line to the right and left of the battery and proceeded to throw up his breastworks. General Breckinridge afterward declared it to have been one of the most beautiful movements he had ever witnessed.

In Grant's grand assault next morning, June 3, the First Maryland contributed its share to the general slaughter, its Napoleons firing nothing but cannister, and before night set in over ten thousand Federal soldiers lay weltering in their blood, while the loss of the Confederates was trifling.

The battery had also been engaged skirmishing heavily along the Totopotomoy for two or three days prior to Cold Harbor.

When Grant moved from General Lee's front, the latter crossed the James, and the First Maryland went into position near Wilcox's Run. After remaining there some time it was placed in one of the fortifications near Petersburg.

On June 22d Mahone's Division of the Third Corps moved out of the works to attack the enemy's left. Lieutenant-Colonel McIntosh, to whose battalion the First Maryland had been transferred, accompanied him with Dement's battery, under Lieutenant Gale. The batteries on the line were directed to co-operate by a combined fire upon the enemy's batteries and on his troops in the woods.

At the proper time Dement's battery moved rapidly forward, took position near the enemy's works, and opened, when the infantry, under cover of this fire and of that from the batteries on the Confederate line, rushed forward and carried the enemy's entrenchments, capturing a large number of prisoners and four pieces of artillery.

Lieutenant Gale and the men of the battery were highly complimented for their gallant behavior in this affair.

The First Maryland made a narrow escape at the explosion of Burnside's mine. It was stationed in such close proximity to the mine that many of the men of the battery were wounded by the falling debris. And then began one of the most terrible artillery duels of the war, for simultaneously with the explosion Grant opened with every gun. Never before had the First Maryland been under such a fire, to which it replied with their accustomed vigor.

But the First Maryland had been seen upon the field for the last time. For awhile it was in the fortifications around Petersburg, firing an occasional shot, until, in January, the guns the boys loved so well were taken from them, and they were sent to man the heavy guns at Drury's Bluff, from which they never fired a shot.

But the end was fast approaching, and when General Lee evacuated his works around Petersburg, the noble men who had braved so much for nearly four long years, followed in his wake with muskets in their hands.

At Sailor's Creek they were engaged in a severe fight, when Harry Pennington gave up his life for the cause he loved so well — the last man of the battery to be killed.

The First Maryland Artillery surrendered at Appomattox.

ROSTER OF THE FIRST MARYLAND ARTILLERY.

R. SNOWDEN ANDREWS, *Captain.*
W. F. DEMENT, *Captain.*
W. F. DEMENT, *First Lieutenant.*
CHARLES S. CONTEE, *Second Lieutenant.*
JOHN GALE, *Second Lieutenant.*
W. I. HILL, *Second Lieutenant.*
FREDERICK Y. DABNEY, *Third Lieutenant.*
J. H. STONESTREET, *Third Lieutenant.*
DE WILTON SNOWDEN, *First Sergeant.*
J. HARRIS FORBES, *First Sergeant.*

GRATIAL C. THOMPSON, *First Sergeant.*
F. W. BOLLINGER, *Corporal.*
THEODORE JENKINS, *Corporal.*
GEORGE T. SCOTT, *Corporal.*
E. C. MONCURE, *Corporal.*
P. A. L. CONTEE, *Corporal.*
J. G. HARRIS, *Corporal.*
JOHN F. RANSON, *Corporal.*
SAMUEL THOMPSON, *Corporal.*

Privates.

ALBERT, A. J., JR.
ALDRIDGE, JOHN.
BOARMAN, RICHARD T.
BOWIE, THOMAS D.
BROWN, W. B.
BUCHANAN, W. J.
BOSWELL, RICHARD T.
BUSK, JEROME.
BRIAN, E. H.
BYRNE, SAMUEL E.
BOTELER, WALTER P.
BROMLEY, GEORGE W.
BRISCOE, JOHN H.
BRADFORD, T. G.
BOWIE, H. C.
BASFORD, G. W.
BOWEN, W. H.
BROOKS, THOMAS.
BRYAN, R. S.
BOWLAND, S. G.
BEALE, JAMES S.
BLUMENAUER, M.

BROUGHTON, THOMAS.
BARRY, M. C. Y.
BUCHANAN, J. R.
BALLARD, W. W.
BURTLES, C. H.
BERRY, E. R.
BRYAN, ROBERT S.
COOMBS, G. G.
COMPTON, W. P.
CHILES, W. L.
COOKE, GEORGE A.
COVINGTON, JESSE H.
COALE, WILLIAM A.
CRAVEN, B. L.
CAMPBELL, JOHN.
CROWLEY, JAMES.
CAWOOD, E. M.
CHEW, R. B.
CONNER, WILLIAM.
CAPERTON, JAMES M.
CLEARY R. E.
CLAYTON, G. W.

CONLEY, MICHAEL.
DAVIS, JOHN T.
DAMAR, JOHN S.
DUVALL, P. B.
DUVALL, S. F.
DORSEY, EVAN L.
DOUGHERTY, G. A.
DIGGS, J. T.
DORSETT, J. H.
DRYDEN, R. J.
DORSEY, DANIEL B.
DUNLOP, S. O.
DAFFIN, FRANCIS D.
DEAN, WILLIAM H.
EDELIN, PHILIP F.
EDGE, J. G.
FORBER, MARSHAL A.
FORD, JAMES E.
FIELD, EDWARD W.
FRANKLIN, J. F.
FREAYER, FREDERICK.
FELLINS, J. W.

GARDENER, J. B. W.
GARDENER, J. B.
GLASCOCK, J. E.
GALE, FRANK.
GALE, G. G.
GLASS, RICHARD C.
GERMAN, M. P.
GUMBY, JOHN W.
GILPIN, JOHN.
GARDNER, A.
GORMAN, W. H.
GOUGH, J. H.
GARNER, J. H.
GOLDSBOROUGH, CHARLES.
HATTON, J. W. F.
HARRIS, C. H.
HATTON, R. H. S.
HOWELL, GUSTAVUS.
HOWARD, WASHINGTON.
HANNON, L. M.
HANNON, S. B.
HANDY, J. C.
HIGGINS, W. G.
HUNTER, FREDERICK.
HILLARY, WASHINGTON.
HATTON, JOSEPH.
HARRIS, JOSEPH.
HOLMEAD, C. H.
HILLEARY, G. W.
HALSTEAD, CHARLES.
HARRIS, JOHN F.
HAWKINS, J. S.
HINES, J. W.
JENKINS, LOUIS W.
JENKINS, W. K.
JENKINS, JOHN.
KEESTER, W. A.
KOONS, ABRAM.
KOESTER, LOUIS.
LEE, J. C.
LEE, RICHARD H.

LANGSDALE, H. J.
LLOYD DANIEL.
McCLINTOCK SAMUEL.
MARRIOTT, GEORGE H.
MACKENHEIMER, C. P.
McWILLIAMS, J. F.
MONCURE CHARLES H.
McGLONE, BARNEY.
MORGAN, THOMAS.
MIDDLETON, EDWARD.
MAGRUDER, EDWARD.
McNEAL, CHARLES.
McLAUGHLIN, E. H.
MANN, CHARLES S.
MAY, W. H.
MOCKABEE, JOSEPH.
MUSGROVE, THOMAS.
MILLER, H. D.
McCORMICK, V. M.
MITCHELL, JOHN.
MUDD, E. M.
NEALE, CHARLES H.
NELSON, FRANCIS F.
NELSON, C. W.
OWENS, JAMES W.
OWENS, WELSH.
PEASE, CHARLES.
PATTERSON, W. W.
POLLITE, NEHEMIAH.
PERRIO, GEORGE W.
PERRIO, ALBERT W.
PHIPP, W. E.
PEARSON, WALTER H.
PENNINGTON, H.
RIDDLE, CHARLES.
ROBEY, WILLIAM S.
RYE, JOHN M.
RICHARDSON, RICHARD.
ROBINSON, G. W.
SANFORD, EDWARD.
STEDHAM, RICHARD.

SLERNAKER, JULIUS.
SINDALL, HARRY S.
SLATER, WILLIAM J.
SHUSTER, J. M.
STENO, JOSEPH A.
STINCHCOMB, J. E.
SLOAN, E. O.
SOMMERS, SAMUEL.
SCHARF, JOHN T.
SUNDERLAND, THOMAS.
SARGEANT, H. D. C.
SHIRBURD, W. L.
SMITH, K. B.
SUTHERLAND, LEIGH.
SCOTT, THOMAS H.
TUCKER, JOHN W.
THOMAS, S. S.
THOMPSON, SAMUEL.
TYLER, GRAFTON, JR.
TRIMBLE, JOHN D.
THOMAS, J. R.
TOLSON, ALBERT.
WADE, JOHN R.
WOOTEN, WILLIAM T.
WINTERS, HARRY S.
WATERS, JAMES F.
WILLS, W. A.
WEEMS, JAMES N.
WORTHINGTON, EUGENE.
WEBB, LEWIS S.
WILSON, G. W.
WILSON, W. W.
WILSON, WILLIAM.
WALLACK, R.
WINGATE, T. C.
WILLIAMS, THOMAS.
WILLSON, A. M.
YATES, JOHN R.
YOUNG, ALEXANDER.

BATTERY IN ACTION.

SECOND MARYLAND ARTILLERY.

(BALTIMORE LIGHT.)

IT was towards the close of a pleasant day in October, 1861, that the First Maryland Infantry dragged its weary length into camp near Centreville, after a long and fruitless expedition to Pohick Church, in search of the enemy. Things seemed much changed, indeed, since their departure, for in their absence a battery of artillery had invaded the sacred confines of their camp, and a scowl was observed upon more than one face, for we were jealous of our rights and dared maintain them. Judge then our surprise when informed it was a battery manned by brother Marylanders, and called the Baltimore Light Artillery. They had just been organized at Richmond, and forwarded to the army at Centreville during our absence. They were welcomed, most heartily welcomed, and it was not long ere we discovered old friends and acquaintances among them.

Before many hours had elapsed we paid our respects to the officers of the battery, and found them to be the true type of the Maryland and Virginia gentlemen. But here they are:

Captain J. B. Brockenborough was a Virginian, a graduate of the Military Institute at Lexington, and a son of Judge Brockenborough, whose name is so well known to the people of the South. He was a young man, not long from college, but in that intellectual face you read more than the ordinary man, and the honor and glory with which he subsequently enveloped his fine command is a matter of history.

His First Lieutenant, W. Hunter Griffin, was also a Virginian, but had been engaged in business in Baltimore for many years. Brave, noble-hearted Griffin; how little I thought, as for the first time I took his hand, we should pass together through so many stirring scenes in the field and prison, for with the mention of his name appears before me all the horrors of the retaliatory dens and dungeons of Morris Island and Fort Pulaski. There we shared between us the wretched pittance given to sustain a bare existence, and there we more than once divided our last dollar.

Second Lieutenant, W. B. Bean, was a Marylander, and a fine officer and brave soldier.

Third Lieutenant, George Wilhelm, was also a Marylander, and during the little while he was with the battery proved himself an efficient officer. On his resigning, the dashing McNulty was appointed to fill the vacancy.

The *personnel* of the men was unsurpassed in the army, and was it a wonder, then, that with such officers and such men the Baltimore Light Artillery should soon become a household word in the Army of Northern Virginia?

During the winter of 1861 and 1862 the battery remained quietly in camp at Manassas, and when the army of General Joseph E. Johnston fell back from that place in March, they were ordered to remain with General Ewell upon the banks of the Rappahannock.

Here about the first of April the enemy for the first time heard the bellowing of their loud-mouthed Blakeleys, which were destined to carry death and destruction into their ranks upon more than one bloody field.

It was a lovely afternoon, and fresh in my memory, that the enemy were observed advancing in force towards the river. Their approach had been long expected, and preparations made to receive them. The Baltimore Light Artillery was posted on the extreme right of General Elzey's Brigade, and supported by the First Maryland Infantry. As the dense masses of the enemy came within range, Brockenborough opened with such accuracy of aim as to attract the attention of Elzey, who upon the spot predicted for them a glorious future. For an hour or two the fight was sharp and severe, and most of the enemy's artillery fire concentrated upon the Maryland battery; but they stood their ground and fought their pieces like veterans of an hundred battles. Late in the evening the enemy retired.

Once or twice after, they advanced in small force towards the river, but Brockenborough was ever ready to receive them, and a shell or two sufficed to drive them back.

On the 19th of April, 1862, the division of General Ewell broke camp, and began the wretched march to Gordonsville, and of which I have spoken in the First Maryland. For three days the rain poured in torrents, making the roads almost impassable, and for three days the officers and men of the Baltimore battery toiled through the mud, into which the wheels sank to the hubs, and at length reached Gordonsville.

After a halt here of three or four days, the division of General Ewell marched to join Jackson at Swift Run Gap.

After the return of that General from McDowell, the whole army advanced upon Kenly's forces at Front Royal, and in the sharp fight which ensued the battery took a prominent part.

Early on the 25th of May, Jackson's army stood in battle array before Winchester, and the engagement soon began. The Baltimore Light Artillery was stationed on the right, and throughout the fight played with much effect upon the enemy's columns. A few days after, at Bolivar Heights, they were engaged for some hours, and finally drove the Federal infantry and artillery from their strong position.

In Jackson's memorable retreat down the Valley from the overwhelming forces of Fremont and Shields, the battery was detailed to support the cavalry under Ashby and Steuart, which was bringing up the rear of the army. Here it was daily engaged with the enemy. At Fisher's Hill a section under Griffin was entirely surrounded and cut off owing to the bad behavior of Steuart's cavalry, which was supporting it, but the gallant fellow drove his pieces through the ranks of the enemy, and reached the main body in safety.

At the battle of Harrisonburg it supported Ashby in his fight with the Pennsylvania Bucktails, and did good service.

On the 8th of June the division of Ewell was drawn up in line of battle at Cross Keys to dispute the enemy's advance, whilst Jackson crossed his prisoners and wagon trains over the Shenandoah at Fort Republic. The ground for the battle had been selected by General Elzey, by order of General Ewell, and a most judicious selection it was, as the result of the fight proved, and for which General Elzey received the thanks of Ewell in his official report.

The Baltimore Light Artillery held the extreme left, supported by the First Maryland Infantry. Theirs was a most exposed position, and upon which was concentrated the fire of several of the enemy's batteries. All day long the battle lasted, and all day long the little battery continued to hurl its shot and shell into the ranks of the enemy. It was a most unequal contest, but stubbornly they held their ground. Generals Elzey and Steuart, who had remained by and watched the battery with painful interest, were both borne wounded from the field. Upon the behavior of that battery perhaps hung the fate of the day, for we were but a handful holding at bay a mighty army. But calmly the officers and men stood to their guns, and although the enemy essayed more than once to drive them from the position, there they remained until night closed upon the combatants, and Jackson's army was saved from the destruction that seemed so imminent.

As a reward for the gallantry displayed in this fight, General Dick Taylor presented the battery with two of the splendid brass Napoleons which his brigade captured next day at Port Republic. " I want you to have them," he said, " for from what I saw of you yesterday, I know they will be in good hands."

After the battle of Port Republic, which closed Jackson's great Valley campaign, the army moved up the mountain, where, upon its summit, it remained two or three days, when it returned and went into camp near Weir's Cave, about five miles from Port Republic. Here the Baltimore Light Artillery was supplied with new harness and fresh horses, and was in a splendid condition for the dreadful fighting about to commence around Richmond, but of which we had not then the slightest conception.

On the 19th of June, 1862, Jackson put his troops in motion for Richmond, and on the afternoon of the 26th the First Maryland Infantry, which had the advance, encountered the enemy in force about ten miles from Gaines' Mills, and a sharp fight ensued, which lasted some time, when Brockenborough was ordered to open fire, which he did with effect, and the enemy retired.

At daylight on the morning of the 27th Jackson resumed his march, but owing to the incompetency of his guides it was late in the afternoon before he neared the point of attack assigned him. But at length everything indicated a rise of the curtain in the fearful drama about to commence. Columns were marching and counter-marching, staff officers dashed hither and thither, while the crash of small arms, and the sullen boom of artillery on the right, told full well that the work of death had begun.

About 4 o'clock Jackson threw out his skirmishers, and moved forward in line of battle, and in a few minutes the enemy were developed in heavy force, and strongly posted, when the fighting became terrific. The artillery was directed to take position in an open field on the left, and were soon heavily engaged. The battle here was very unequal, for the enemy had greatly the advantage in artillery and position, and soon succeeded in disabling a number of Jackson's pieces. In a short time the Jeff Davis Mississippi Battery was torn to pieces and the Baltimore Light Artillery ordered to take its place, immediately under the eye of Jackson himself. Gallantly the Marylanders responded to the order, and dashing at a full run across the field, unlimbered and opened fire.

The author was standing close beside General Jackson when the battery went forward, and he shall long remember the look of anxiety with which he watched it, and well he might, for upon the success of that battery much depended. For a while the air was filled with exploding, crashing shells, and the horses and men fell rapidly before that withering fire, which was directed with almost the precision of a rifle shot. Away went a limber chest high in the air, scattering death and destruction around. "We are not close enough," said the brave Brockenborough. "Limber to the front, forward, gallop!" rung out his sharp command, and in an instant the battery was in position at point blank range. Fiercely those guns were then worked, despite the iron hail that plowed up the ground around them, and in a few minutes Brockenborough had the satisfaction of seeing the enemy retire precipitately, leaving the ground covered with dead and dying men and horses, and shattered carriages and dismounted guns. It was French's famous battery they had encountered, but French's no longer, save in name.

On the morning of the 29th, the battery accompanied Ewell's division to Dispatch Station, on the York River Railroad, where a few shots were exchanged with the enemy, when Ewell retraced his steps, and moved towards Malvern Hill.

In the afternoon of the 1st of July, the battle of Malvern Hill began, and soon raged fiercely. The enemy had been enabled to reach the heights of Malvern, where he posted sixty guns, which swept every foot of ground around. In vain did the heavy masses of infantry rush with desperate valor upon these guns, but it was only to be driven back, leaving the ground covered with heaps of dead and mangled men. In this unequal contest artillery was not available, for not a position was to be had. Two or three times the Baltimore Light Artillery tried it, but was as often compelled to hastily withdraw, and when night ended the conflict, Malvern Hill was not yet won.

Before morning McClellan withdrew to Harrison's Landing, on the James, where he was safe.

The long spring campaign in the Valley and the operations around Richmond had made sad havoc in the ranks of the Maryland Line, and it became necessary for them to recruit and reorganize before again being ready for the field. For this purpose the First Maryland Infantry and Baltimore Light Artillery were ordered to Charlottesville, where they remained a month, when they were once more ordered to join Jackson, who was about to make his great movement to the rear of Pope's army at Manassas. Alas! the two commands did not journey together far, for at Gordonsville an order overtook Colonel Johnson requiring him to at once disband the First Maryland, and the order was reluctantly obeyed.

The separation was affecting to the greatest degree, and the little battery pursued its way with sad and lonely hearts. It was like severing the ties that bind brother to brother, for in the series of battles in which they had participated side by side, the conduct of each had inspired the other with confidence and respect. "With the First Maryland in support," I heard Captain Brockenborough say, "I know I am always safe." And so it was, for one would never desert the other while life lasted.

On the morning of the 19th of August, the battery reached Orange Courthouse, where, much to the joy of all, it was attached to Starke's Louisiana Brigade. An affinity had long existed between the Maryland and Louisiana troops, and they commanded each other's fullest confidence. In fact, they seemed nearer akin, for in both there was that sprightliness, dash and vim not so noticeable in troops from other States.

With three days' rations in haversacks, Brockenborough, on the 21st, moved towards the Rappahannock, where he found the enemy occupying the north bank in force. A severe artillery fight immediately began, and was maintained for some hours. The battery pitted against Brockenborough was Company M, United States Regulars, which, towards nightfall, he succeeded in silencing and driving back with the loss of many men and an exploded caisson.

On the morning of the 22nd, the artillery was thrown across the river, but soon after encountered the enemy in heavy force, and were compelled to recross after a desperate struggle. In this affair the Baltimore Light Artillery suffered a loss of four men killed — Irvin, Cox, Bradley and Reynolds — and several severely wounded.

Brockenborough, finding it impossible to cross at that point, moved up to Hanson's ford, where a crossing was effected, and he then pursued his way through Orleans, Salem and Thoroughfare Gap, and reached Manassas on the 26th, having marched fifty miles in two days, with nothing for his men or horses to eat save the green corn gathered along the road. Here at Manassas, though, was found in the captured trains and sutlers' stores all they could have desired, and for hours they reveled in the good things their new commissary had so bountifully supplied, and over Rhine wine and lobsters forgot for the time the privations of the past few days.

From Manassas, Jackson moved on Centreville, but finding the enemy there in force, he retraced his steps to Manassas, closely pursued, and formed his line of battle about sunset on the 28th, upon the ground occupied by the enemy in the battle of July, 1861.

The engagement immediately commenced, and raged with great fury for some time, but the enemy was repulsed in every assault, and driven back with heavy loss. Colonel Stephen D. Lee then put the several batteries in position along the crest of a commanding hill, and there awaited the attack sure to be renewed next day.

About 2 o'clock on the 29th heavy columns emerged from the woods in Jackson's front and advanced boldly to the attack, but the storm of grape and canister which tore through their ranks was more than flesh and blood could withstand, and they were driven back with dreadful slaughter. But again and again did those devoted columns re-form and return to the attack with undiminished ardor, but the same terrible fire greeted them and strewed the ground with dead and dying.

But nevertheless Jackson's situation was a most critical one. With but a handful of worn and weary troops he was battling with ten times his numbers, which must necessarily soon wear him out and exhaust his ammunition; but as the hearts of his men were sinking within them, they were cheered by the clouds of dust that arose in the distance and heralded the approach of their great chieftain, Lee, with the veterans of Longstreet's corps. At night the battle ceased, and the weary troops threw themselves upon the ground to seek a little repose before the work of death and destruction should be resumed on the morrow.

At the break of day on the morning of the 30th of August, the troops were aroused from their slumbers and ordered to prepare for the great and decisive battle at hand. But hour after hour passed by, and except an occasional picket shot, all else was still. It was, though, but the calm which precedes the storm, for suddenly dense masses of the enemy emerged from the woods and moved at the double quick upon Jackson's lines. It was a grand sight to see those three lines rush forward in the most beautiful order. For a minute a death-like silence prevailed, when the very earth was made to tremble by the roar of Stephen D. Lee's thirty-six pieces of artillery, fired at point-blank range. The slaughter was appalling, and whole ranks melted away in an instant, but the brave survivors closed up their decimated columns, and despite that awful fire pressed on until they encountered the infantry posted in the railroad cut in front, where for a time the fight was waged hand to hand. At length they began to break and to retreat, and the batteries, which had been silent for some time, owing to the proximity of the struggling columns of infantry, again belched forth into the fleeing mass their deadly discharges of grape, which was continued until the fugitives reached the shelter of the woods from which they had emerged.

Of the several batteries under General Lee that day not one was worked more fiercely than the Baltimore Light Artillery, and none contributed more to the defeat and destruction of the enemy.

Long before nightfall the victory was won, and the braggart Pope, with the remnant of his army, was seeking safety in the defenses around Washington.

In the invasion of Maryland, which followed this signal victory, the battery was placed in the advance, and crossed the river at White's ford.

On the 6th of September the battery passed through Frederick City and encamped on the suburbs. Many were the congratulations the brave fellows received from the citizens, and during the three days they remained their wants were abundantly supplied.

Leaving Frederick City, the battery passed through Boonsboro', Middletown, and Williamsport, where they recrossed the Potomac, and on the 12th entered Martinsburg. From thence it moved towards Harper's Ferry, when upon arriving at Loudoun Heights, Brockenborough was assigned a position, from which, at early dawn of the 15th, he opened, along with other batteries, a terrific fire upon the enemy's entrenched position on Bolivar Heights. The batteries were worked furiously for an hour, when just as the Confederate infantry were put in motion to storm the works, a white flag fluttered in the breeze, and Harper's Ferry surrendered with its twelve thousand troops, and artillery and supplies in abundance.

But there was heavy work yet to be done, for General Lee with a portion of his army was confronting the overwhelming masses of McClellan at Sharpsburg, and no time was to be lost in reaching him. The surrender had, therefore, scarcely been effected when the troops were dispatched to his aid. By a forced night march Jackson's artillery reached Sharpsburg on the 16th, and was immediately assigned a position on a range of hills rather northwest of the town.

The morning of the 17th of September found the two armies in position, and ready to begin the work of destruction. For the Confederates the prospects of success seemed gloomy enough, for General Lee had barely forty thousand men with which to meet the mighty army of McClellan, numbering over a hundred and twenty thousand troops. But the vast odds were made almost proportionate by the superior genius of the Confederate Generals. With Lee, Jackson and Longstreet in command nothing seemed impossible to their troops, and, therefore, it was with no feelings of fear for the result that they surveyed the long and glittering lines before them.

Soon after sunrise slight artillery skirmishing commenced along the lines, which increased in volume until the air seemed filled with exploding shells. Upon the position held by the batteries of Brockenborough, Carpenter and Poague, Moody, Raine and Caskie, was opened a terrific fire, which was promptly returned, and the enemy's batteries several times compelled to change position. This continued for two hours, when it became evident that the infantry was massing for a charge. The position was of the most vital importance, for should the enemy succeed in gaining possession of this point and turning Lee's left flank, he would be irretrievably lost. His orders to General Jackson were, therefore, to "Hold the range of hills to the last!"

McClellan's advance upon this point was gallantly met by Jackson's veteran infantry, and for some time the fighting was of the most determined character; but at length the immense superiority of numbers prevailed, and Jackson's troops gradually fell back across the turnpike, past the Dunkard Church, and through the woods, and appeared upon the plain beyond. Most beautifully did the heavy columns emerge from the woods and moved forward upon the batteries quietly awaiting their near approach. "Do not pull a lanyard," said Brockenborough, who was temporarily in command of the whole, "until you get the command." Nearer and nearer those solid columns approached, and amid loud huzzas rushed forward at the double quick. It was a moment of dreadful suspense. On, on, they came! "Will Brockenborough never give the command?" Yes; he now has them at the muzzles of his guns, and the next instant the command, "Fire!" was heard above the exultant cheers of the advancing columns, and twenty-four pieces of artillery, double-shotted with canister, belched forth their deadly contents into the very faces of the assailants.

The scene that was presented as the smoke lifted beggars description. The ground was literally covered — nay, piled — with the slain and maimed of the enemy, and the survivors were in full retreat. They were soon re-formed, however, and again moved boldly to the attack, but only to be again mercilessly slaughtered and driven back. A third time they essayed, but with the same result, when, a disordered mass of fugitives, the survivors sought the shelter of the woods from which they had but a few minutes before emerged, confident of success.

How anxiously the great chieftain, Lee, who was close by, must have watched the dreadful struggle which was to decide the fate of his army, and perhaps of the cause for which he was battling; and how great must have been the relief as he saw the enemy in retreat, and Jackson's shattered columns once more re-formed. Night put an end to the dreadful conflict, and Lee still held his ground, despite the herculean efforts of his adversary to drive him from it, but the day's struggle had cost him thousands of his bravest and best.

The brave Brockenborough that day wan his major's star, and with his battery received special mention in General Lee's official report.

The morning of the 18th broke clear and beautiful, and General Lee was in readiness to renew the fight, which it was not doubted would begin at an early hour. But McClellan's beaten and shattered army required time and rest and reinforcements before again prepared for aggressive operations; and finding this to be the case Lee proceeded to bury his dead, and that night, unmolested, recrossed the river at a point near Shepherdstown.

Soon after the battle of Sharpsburg, the Baltimore Light Artillery, now under command of Captain W. H. Griffin, was ordered to join the cavalry and infantry of the Maryland Line, then in camp near Newmarket, in the Valley of Virginia. Here they passed the fall and winter months quietly in camp, and in early spring were again prepared, with recruited ranks and renewed equipments, to enter the field.

On the 13th of June the infantry and artillery of the Maryland Line, with one company of its cavalry, all under the command of Lieutenant-Colonel James R. Herbert, moved towards Winchester, near which place they were to unite with the division of General Early, which was moving across from Front Royal. Near Kernstown a body of Milroy's cavalry was encountered, but a shot from the battery scattered them in all directions. A short time after, Early came up and proceeded to form a line of battle. The enemy soon made his appearance in force, and opened a severe fire upon Griffin from his batteries, which was vigorously responded to, and in a little while the enemy were driven beyond Kernstown. Early, as soon as he had formed his line of battle, moved forward, and by a spirited charge of Gordon's Brigade, drove him into his strong works to the left of Winchester.

The next afternoon Hays' Louisiana Brigade was moved around to the enemy's right with orders to charge a strong line of works whilst the artillery opened upon him in front. Griffin was posted on a commanding hill a little to the left of the pike, and threw his first shell into the very centre of the Star fort. Finding he had the exact range, he commenced a furious fire, which threw the enemy for a moment into the greatest confusion, and greatly assisted Hays in his movement upon their right. The fire was soon spiritedly returned by the Federal Maryland battery and continued until night, when Milroy evacuated his fortifications and attempted to escape with his army, but in this he was unsuccessful, although he himself succeeded in reaching Harper's Ferry with a few of his troops.

The precision and effect with which the guns of the Baltimore Light Artillery were served upon this occasion elicited the highest praise from General Gordon, to whose brigade it was temporarily attached, and as a mark of the high esteem in which he held the battery, he procured them permission from General Ewell next morning to select from among the captured guns the best pieces, to take the place of their own, which were greatly inferior.

The day after the battle of Winchester, the corps of General Ewell took up its line of march toward the Potomac. The Baltimore Light Artillery was directed by some subordinate officers to report to General Nelson of the *reserve* artillery. The order occasioned the greatest surprise and indignation throughout the command, for always before they had led the advance and covered the retreat. Such an indignity, as they considered it, could not be tamely submitted to, and a protest was immediately drawn up and forwarded to General Ewell, who at once ordered the battery to join Albert G. Jenkins' brigade of cavalry, which was the van of the army in the invasion of Pennsylvania.

The battery crossed the Potomac on the 18th of June, and that day joined Jenkins, when the whole command moved rapidly forward in the greatest good humor. Many were the jokes they practiced, and many the quaint sayings peculiar only to the soldier. "Take them mice out of your mouth," one would bawl out, as an officer with well-waxed mustache rode by ; "Take 'em out, no use to say they ain't thar, for I see their tails stickin' out." And as another came along, but a short time in the service, and wearing a "boiled shirt," and white collar, his ears were sure to be assailed with "Say, mister, how long did you have to soldier afore one of them things growed 'round your neck ?" and a staff officer, with handsome cavalry boots, would be requested by a dozen voices to "Come out of them thar boots, for it's too soon to go into winter quarters."

En parenthase, soldiers are queer beings, and will have their joke, even in the face of almost certain death. At the battle of Malvern Hill, whilst the First Maryland Regiment was awaiting its turn to "go in," and the men were closely hugging the earth to avoid the terrible fire of grape and canister which swept over and around them, I heard an officer of the regiment remark to another at his side, whose face was pressed close to the ground : "Say, Captain, you'll get a scrape down your *back* directly, and you know it's something we don't allow here." and the officer addressed coolly turned over on his back, remarking : "Well, if it will please you better, I'll take it in front."

The command of Jenkins pursued its march rapidly through Maryland, and struck the Pennsylvania line near Greencastle. Thence their way lay up the Cumberland Valley to Shippensburg, where a halt was made for a short time to allow the tired troops to partake of the delicious apple-butter, ham, bread, etc., furnished them in abundance by the startled inhabitants. Whilst thus enjoying themselves to their hearts' content, the cry of "Yanks" wais raised, and in an instant the scene changed. Cavalrymen sprang to their horses, and artillerymen to their guns, but the wary enemy could not be induced to come within range of Griffin's Parrott's, but retired towards Carlisle, followed leisurely by Jenkins.

Upon arriving within sight of that town, the Yankee flag was found defiantly flying from the public buildings, when Jenkins, supposing the enemy to be there in force, prepared to attack. Placing two pieces of artillery in a position to rake the main street, and disposing of his other troops in the most available manner, he demanded the surrender of the town. It was not long before a deputation of the "solid" citizens made their appearance, and surrendered the place, of which General Jenkins at once took possession.

After remaining at Carlisle one day, during which time they were bountifully supplied with provisions and forage by the citizens, the command moved in the direction of Harrisburg. At Mechanicstown a small body of cavalry were encountered, but a shot from Griffin caused them to beat a hasty retreat. Upon reaching the Susquehanna, the Confederate commander found the opposite side of the river strongly fortified, but he at once opened fire from his batteries, which was promptly responded to. This continued until late in the afternoon, when the enemy's infantry advanced in force, and a severe skirmish ensued, which lasted until after night. General Rodes (I have forgotten to mention the fact that Jenkins and Rodes united their forces at Carslisle) having accomplished his purpose, that night withdrew in the direction of Gettysburg.

Upon arriving at Gettysburg the battery was ordered to report to Major Latimer, who assigned it a position a short distance to the left of the Cashtown pike. In the terrible battle that ensued, the Baltimore Light Artillery played its part, and when the retreat commenced it was kept in the rear to assist in covering the passage of the army and wagon trains through the mountain passes.

At a point near Mount Zion the enemy had so stationed his guns as to completely command the road through the gap over which a column of infantry must pass. There was but little time to spare, for the enemy were pressing them hard. Captain Griffin was ordered to place his guns in position, and if possible silence the battery. It seemed a desperate undertaking, but there was no alternative. Quickly the brave fellows ran their guns to within point blank range, and opened a deadly fire. It was promptly returned, and a heavy artillery duel continued for some time, when the enemy's battery was driven from its position, and the infantry and wagon train passed in safety. I have heard it asserted by old soldiers that this was one of the most desperate artillery fights they ever witnessed. And the Marylanders had every reason to be proud of their victory, for it was their old antagonist, Battery M, of the regular artillery, that they had again measured strength with.

At Hagerstown the battery participated in a severe cavalry fight, in which the Confederates were entirely successful.

After the army of General Lee recrossed the Potomac, the battery was ordered to Fredericksburg, where it remained for a few days, and then rejoined the main army at Culpepper Courthouse, and was assigned to the battalion commanded by Major Beckham.

For two weeks everything remained quiet, and well it was, for human endurance had been taxed to the utmost limit in the severe campaign of the summer, and required rest and repose.

On the 10th of September Meade became restive, and General Lee moved forward to give him battle if he desired it. Beckham was ordered to advance and take position with his artillery near Muddy Creek. In a short time the enemy appeared in force, and a sharp artillery fight ensued. The enemy then threw forward his infantry, and compelled Beckham and his supports to fall back to the vicinity of Culpepper Courthouse. The artillery was here ordered to take a position and " hold it." The fighting soon became fierce, and the Baltimore Light Artillery was exposed to the severest part of it, but they gallantly held their ground for some time, despite the fire of six pieces that were playing upon their three. But this could not last long, for all support had been withdrawn, and the enemy's dismounted men were advancing in heavy force. It seemed scarcely possible to save the battery, but the brave fellows had been in such scrapes before, and they determined to hold on to their pieces as long as there was a hope. Retiring through the town, they had nearly accomplished their purpose of escaping, when a body of the enemy charged up a cross street and captured the rear gun, with Lieutenant John McNulty and nine men attached to it. The remaining guns were safely taken off the field.

The next morning the enemy made their appearance in considerable force, and the battery was enabled to repay them for the rough treatment received the day preceding, for as a body of cavalry were engaged in drill, entirely ignorant of the close proximity of the Baltimore battery, it opened upon them with deadly effect at very close range.

After the affair at Mine Run, which soon followed that at Culpepper Courthouse, the battery was detached from the main army, and temporarily assigned to duty with General Young's Brigade of cavalry. On the 9th of October that General crossed the Rapidan, and advanced by way of Madison Courthouse. His progress was slow, as the march was by circuitous and concealed side roads in order to avoid the observations of the enemy. On the 10th Young met the advance of the enemy at James City, without an intimation of his approach, and their bands were regaling the citizens with patriotic airs, when a shot from Sergeant Harry Marston's gun, of the Baltimore Light Artillery, plunged into their midst, and abruptly terminated the musical entertainment for that evening at least. In a short time a battery was brought up, and a severe artillery fight ensued. Soon another made its appearance and opened an enfilading fire upon Griffin, but, notwithstanding, he stubbornly held his position. Whilst this was going on a large force of the enemy's skirmishers attacked the Confederate flank, and threw the cavalry into some confusion by their unexpected onset from this quarter. Griffin at the instant wheeled his pieces, and opened with grape and canister upon this new enemy. This checked them until the supports came up, when the enemy were compelled to retreat precipitately.

On the 12th a sharp engagement took place near Brandy Station, where the enemy were driven across the Rappahannock, and pursued to the vicinity of Cub Run.

After this affair the army retraced its steps to Culpepper Courthouse, when the Baltimore Light Artillery was ordered to proceed to Hanover Junction, and report to Colonel Bradley T. Johnson, who had been directed to assemble the Maryland Line at that point, and keep open General Lee's communication with Richmond.

The battery spent the winter and part of the spring here most delightfully, and by the 1st of May was ready for the field with recruited ranks, for Lieutenant John McNulty and many of the men captured in the battles of the preceding year had returned from Yankee prisons, and were once more ready for the fray.

On the 10th of May, 1864, whilst encamped at Wickham's Park, the battery was ordered by General J. E. B. Stuart, to move up along the Rivanna, and join the forces there awaiting to intercept Sheridan, who was advancing towards Richmond. Reluctantly Colonel Johnson suffered it to go, for during the winter and spring he had reorganized and equipped it with much care; but the exigency of the occasion compelled him to acquiesce, General Stuart assuring him he would " borrow " it for but a few days, and " return it in good condition."

On the 11th the battery took position at Yellow Tavern, and soon after the enemy made his appearance in force. A heavy encounter ensued, when the battery was retired about half a mile. For a time there was a lull in the fighting; but upon the arrival of General Stuart it was again ordered forward, supported by the cavalry, and took position to the left of the Brook turnpike, directly in Sheridan's front. The battle was then renewed with great fury. Sheridan brought three batteries to bear on Griffin at a range of not over eight hundred yards, and the rain of shot and shrapnell became terrific, but the brave fellows never flinched, and served their guns with great effect. Hour after hour this savage fight was waged, but no man faltered at his post, though the groans of the wounded and dying, and the shrieks of maimed and disemboweled horses, were enough to appall the stoutest heart. But General Stuart was there, watching with an anxious eye that little command, upon which so much depended, and they fought on, undismayed, despite the frightful scenes around them. At length the enemy massed a heavy body of cavalry, determined, at any sacrifice, to capture the guns that were making such dreadful havoc in their ranks. A charge was made upon him, when Griffin resorted to grape and canister. At every discharge whole companies melted away, and the enemy fell back in confusion. But again they advanced, and the Confederate cavalry giving away at the instant, the battery was left at the mercy of the enemy, who dashed upon it; but there the brave men continued to stay, determined to remain at their post to the last, for all knew the vital importance of the position; and as the enemy pressed on they were met with that never ceasing hail of canister, until they reached the guns and rode over the men, and sabred and captured them at their pieces. Stuart had witnessed it all whilst rallying his broken cavalry, when seizing the colors of the First Virginia, he rode forward, exclaiming, " Charge, Virginians, and save those brave Marylanders!" Alas! it was his last command on the field of battle, for at the instant he received a pistol shot, and was conveyed mortally wounded from the field, when his men precipitately retreated.

Nevertheless, in the confusion and excitement of the moment, Lieutenant McNulty, with some of the gallant fellows, actually drove two pieces off in triumph, despite the efforts of the enemy to prevent them.

In this desperate battle at Yellow Tavern, the battery suffered the loss of many men and horses, and two guns, and its brave commander was a prisoner in the enemy's hands.

Many were the acts of individual heroism displayed whilst the battle lasted, one of which I will narrate:

During the hottest of the fight Private John Hayden was struck by a piece of shell, and dreadfully mangled, and would have bled to death in a few minutes had not the surgeon of the battery, Dr. Wortham, carried him on his back into the woods and stanched the hemorrhage. In a short time the enemy had possession of the field, but carefully concealing himself and his charge until they had passed on, he that night carried Hayden to a place of safety, where he eventually recovered.

With the two guns saved from the wreck of the battery, Lieutenant McNulty crossed the Chickahominy, closely pursued, and took position on the right of the road, commanding the bridge, where, by a vigorous fire, he checked the enemy's advance and covered the retreat. McNulty then pushed on to Old Church and joined the main body, which had been there reassembled.

On the 13th he was ordered to Hanover Junction, where he joined the army of General Lee, with which he remained until after the battle of Cold Harbor, when he was ordered to Early's command in the Valley of Virginia.

After a march of six days, the battery reached Waynesboro', where four days after it joined Early, *en route* for the Lower Valley. Here the battery (now under the command of Lieutenant W. B. Bean, who had been for some time absent) was attached to General Bradley T. Johnson's Brigade of cavalry, which had the advance.

On the morning of the 4th of July, Johnson approached Martinsburg, when he was charged by about six hundred of the enemy's cavalry, which for a moment created some confusion in his ranks; but a few well-directed discharges of spherical-case from Bean caused them to beat a precipitate retreat.

The command then pushed on and entered Martinsburg, when they came suddenly upon a battalion of women, dressed in their holiday attire, drawn up on the sidewalks, as though bent on preventing Johnson from taking possession of the town, or at least their wagon train, ladened with ice cream, confectionery, etc.; for the fair and unfair dames, damsels and sweethearts of the troopers were about to celebrate the great national holiday by a picnic, when surprised by the naughty rebel Johnson, upon whom they at once opened such a fusilade of invectives in bad and not very choice English as to compel him and his command to retire in disgust, leaving them masters of the field.

From Martinsburg Johnson moved to Shepherdstown, and crossed the Potomac into Maryland, and took position on Catoctin Mountain, where he encountered a force of the enemy with artillery, but Bean soon drove them off, when they retired to Frederick City, closely pursued by Johnson's cavalry. Here, being reinforced, they made a stand within the confines of the city, and opened fire from their battery, protected by the houses. The fire was not returned for some time, as Johnson was loth to open his guns upon defenseless women and children, but finally forbearance ceasing to be a virtue, he opened his battery, and a sharp artillery fight continued until night, when Johnson retired to the mountain to await Early's arrival.

Early having at length come up, Johnson, with his cavalry, and a section of the artillery under command of Lieutenant J. McNulty, proceeded to destroy the railroad bridges at Cockeysville, and this accomplished, he made a rapid move around Baltimore, and struck the Washington branch of the Baltimore and Ohio Railroad at Beltsville, where a large body of the enemy's cavalry was met, which, after a few shots from the battery and a charge from the cavalry, broke and fled towards Washington in the utmost confusion.

The battery, with Johnson's cavalry, covered Early's retreat from Washington, though it was but seldom brought into requisition until the army reached Poolesville, where the enemy made a vigorous attack, but were kept in check by Johnson's cavalry and artillery until the whole army had crossed in safety.

On the 29th of July General Johnson was ordered by General Early to accompany McCausland into Pennsylvania and exact a stipulated sum of money from the citizens of Chambersburg, or in case of their not complying with that demand to burn the town. The Baltimore Light Artillery was attached to the brigade, and the whole crossed at McCoy's Ferry and proceeded on their way. Before day on the morning of the 30th the advance approached Chambersburg, and after feeling the place with a few shells, and finding no enemy, the town was entered and burned.

Retracing his steps to Virginia by way of Cumberland, McCausland arrived at that place late in the afternoon of the next day, and found his situation a critical one. Kelly, with a large force, was in his front, strongly posted behind breastworks, and Averill was rapidly coming up in rear, and to avoid the former he was compelled to move to the left and take a different road from the one he had intended ; but as there was not a man in his command who knew the country, this was not to be easily accomplished. After some delay, Colonel Harry Gilmor settled the question by seizing a Union man who was familiar with the different roads and fords, and with a cocked revolver at his head compelled him to pilot the way. In the night, four miles from Cumberland, McCausland's advance encountered the enemy, who were, after a brisk skirmish, driven back, when McCausland determined to await the morning to ascertain his position.

At the dawn of day the enemy was discovered in line behind the crest of a range of hills between the canal and river, when McNulty was ordered to post his guns, and open the fight, whilst the cavalry dismounted and crossed the canal on a bridge hastily constructed by Captain Welsh of the First Maryland Cavalry, when the enemy retired. But a more formidable obstacle then presented itself in the shape of an iron-clad battery mounted on an engine upon the railroad, whilst the cars to which it was attached were loop-holed for musketry, and the banks of the railroad, which formed an excellent breastwork, was lined with infantry. A very strong block house that commanded every approach to the ford, was also found strongly garrisoned.

Colonel Harry Gilmor was at once ordered to carry the ford, which he attempted in most gallant style, but was unable to reach the opposite bank owing to the dreadful enfilading fire opened upon him.

Lieutenant McNulty was then directed to take position with his pieces, and open on the iron-clad. Quickly moving his guns to an open field, and but two hundred yards from the enemy, he unlimbered at this much exposed point, and called upon his best gunner, George McElwee, to bring his piece to bear upon the formidable looking mass of iron before him. The brave fellow, despite the shower of bullets to which he was exposed, coolly sighted his piece and fired, and when the smoke cleared away McNulty had the satisfaction of seeing the huge monster enveloped in steam, for the shot directed by the unerring aim of McElwee had pierced the boiler, and it lay a helpless wreck upon the track. His next shot was as effective, and entered one of the portholes, dismounting the guns and scattering death and destruction around, when the enemy along the bank broke and fled.

But there was yet the block house to dispose of before the command could resume its retreat, and minutes were becoming precious. An hour was consumed in discussing the matter before anything definite was determined upon, when General Johnson suggested that an attempt be made to get a piece of the artillery across the river. The suggestion was instantly adopted, and under cover of the bank, though subjected to a severe fire, the piece was started over in a full run, and unlimbered in the river, and taken to its bank by hand, when, at the instant, a demand for the surrender of the block house was complied with, and McCausland was safe.

At Moorefield, soon after, McCausland was surprised in camp by Averill, when thirteen men of the Baltimore Light Artillery were sabred and captured at their guns endeavoring to load them, and two pieces were lost.

After this affair the remnant of the battery was ordered to the vicinity of Newmarket, in the Valley of Virginia, to be reorganized and equipped. Here the number of the battery was considerably increased by the transfer of Marylanders who had served three years in Fort Sumter, and also by men from Major Breathed's old battery. Horses and guns were furnished from the reserve artillery, and in a short time Lieutenant McNulty (who had succeeded to the command) found himself in a condition to take the field.

Sheridan was about this time rapidly advancing towards Staunton, and Early, with a small force, had fallen back to Brown's Gap, in the Blue Ridge. McNulty was at once ordered to join him at Port Republic, which he was enabled to do, by making a detour, on the 27th of September. From Port Republic Early moved towards Waynesboro', where the head of his column met that of Sheridan, and after a desperate fight drove him back up the Valley, Early pursuing.

The scenes which these brave men were compelled to witness as they pressed on after the brutal Sheridan and his band of incendiaries were appalling, indeed. Hundreds of poor, helpless women and children were encountered on the road, fleeing to a place of refuge, but knew not where to find it, for other homes as well as their own had been plied with the incendiaries' torch. Piteously they plead for protection and a morsel of food from the rough soldiers, but, alas! it was not within their power to afford them either. Night after night the heavens were illumined by the light of burning farmhouses, barns, mills, etc., and day after day was made dark by the dense smoke that filled the heavens. Surely, Grant and his minion Sheridan will be long remembered by the people of the Valley of Virginia, and their names associated by them and their posterity with all that is bad, brutal and vindictive.

Slight skirmishing ensued between the pursued and pursuers until the former reached Fisher's Hill, where they met their infantry, when Lomax, in command of the cavalry, retired to the vicinity of Woodstock. At daylight next morning, the 8th of October, Lomax and Rosser moved to attack the enemy, who had advanced to Maurytown. Rosser was ordered to attack on the left, and Lomax took the right, forming his troops on both sides of the Valley pike. The Baltimore Light Artillery, under Lieutenant McNulty, was stationed on an eminence north of the town. The fight soon began with great fury, Lomax and Rosser attacking simultaneously, and the enemy were driven back some distance. Heavy reinforcements coming to the support of the enemy, he re-formed his broken columns, and the fight was waged with redoubled fury. Towards noon Rosser, on the left, was overwhelmed, and soon after the heavy columns massed in front of Lomax, attacked furiously, and drove that General back in the utmost confusion.

During this time the gallant McNulty and his brave command were hurling death and destruction into the ranks of the enemy, but to no avail. With the retreat of the cavalry under Lomax, McNulty limbered up and sullenly fell back, unlimbering at every available point, and opening his fire upon the pursuing foe, thus enabling the cavalry to escape. In this manner the village of Woodstock was reached. Still through its streets he continued to pour into the faces of the advancing enemy destructive discharges of grape and canister. But the gallant little battery was doomed, for the enemy pressed upon them in overwhelming numbers, and still they disdained to abandon their pieces. Beyond the town they made one more effort to stay the dense masses which almost enveloped them, but even as the gunners were ramming home the last double charge of canister, they were captured and cut down in the act.

Twenty-three men and the four guns fell into the hands of the enemy. Lieutenant McNulty, who had his horse killed under him, with the balance of his men, fought their way through and escaped.

For his gallantry upon this occasion, McNulty was placed in command of a battalion of artillery, and the command of the Baltimore Light Artillery devolved upon Lieutenant John W. Goodman, Junior Second Lieutenant.

Soon after the disastrous fight at Maurytown, Goodman was ordered to Fishersville, where the little left of Early's artillery were preparing their winter quarters. Whilst here every effort was made to procure guns, horses, etc., for the battery, to replace those lost in their last fight, but without success, for the Confederate Government had none to spare. But the brave fellows were ready for any duty that might be assigned them, and when Sheridan, in March, threatened Lynchburg, they gladly obeyed the summons to repair to that place and assist in its defense in any capacity. But their services were not required, and they were in a few days after ordered to Petersburg, to help man the fortifications there.

When the great crash came, and the little army under General Lee was forced to retreat before Grant's overwhelming masses, along with the rest was to be found the remnant of the Baltimore Light Artillery — one day fighting as infantry, and the next as cavalry, or assisting some battery in trouble. Noble fellows, like their comrades of the Maryland Line, they were true to the cause they had espoused to the last, and, like the infantry and cavalry, were determined to fight on whilst a ray of hope remained. Alas! that last ray disappeared with Lee's surrender at Appomattox Courthouse, and when told they were disarmed, and no more to be led against the enemy, these veterans, who had unhesitatingly faced death in all its dreadful shapes on so many bloody fields, wept like children. Surely Maryland should be proud of her "Young Line" in the Confederate States Army, as she was of her "Old" in the days of the Revolution.

ROSTER OF SECOND MARYLAND ARTILLERY.
(BALTIMORE LIGHT.)

OFFICERS.

Captains.

J. B. Brockenborough.   William H. Griffin.

Lieutenants.

William H. Griffin.	James T. Wilhelm.	John McNulty.
William B. Bean.	William B. Bean.	John W. Goodman.

Surgeon, J. B. Wortham.

Sergeants and Corporals.

W. G. Glenn.	William Wirt Robinson.	Patrick Kirby.
George Poindexter.	Harry A. Marston.	L. T. Talbot.
John F. Hayden.	James T. Morrison.	William H. Kendrick.
John Powers.	Joseph A. Bean.	James O'Grady.
A. J. Byrne.	William J. Ferry.	G. W. McAlwee.
James H. Smith.	William C. Dunn.	W. H. Brockenborough.

William Wallace.   Samuel J. Mattison.

Privates.

Arens, Henry.
Banner, Charles.
Bradley, Thomas J.
Burnett, Charles C.
Bunting, John.
Beane, Martin.
Burgess, John.
Berger, Joseph.
Briscoe, R. C.
Brown, W. H.
Barry, H. C.
Bueke, C. L.
Carr, John C.
Claus, Lewis.
Cleal, Charles.
Clotworthy, G. W.
Cosgriff, James O.
Coffee, M. J.
Charlotte, G. W.
Campbell, William.
Chambers, John E.
Christy, G. W.
Coleman, J. A.
Claiborne, Charles H.
Cox, William H. H.
Cox, George.
Dempsey, Joseph.
Davis, Joshua.
Davis, W. A.
Duvall, W. R.
Duncan, James A.
Dosenberry, H. B.
Edell, Henry J.
Evans, Charles.
Earnest, Thomas J.
Farmer, James.
Fitzpatrick, John.
Forner, William.

Frederick, A.
Fletcher, S. D.
Faucett, James A.
Farr, F. A.
Fitzgerald, R. E.
Gayther, James W.
Grubb, H. C.
Greenwell, Joseph A.
Gatchell, J. G.
Gegan, W. H.
Gordon, W. J.
Gardner, E. F.
Gibson, F.
Gibson, E.
Hammett, Daniel.
Hammer, F. H.
Harrington, J. W.
Hinnick, Marion.
Hunter, Robert.
Hurst, William.
Howard, William.
Hynes, E.
Hottinger, M.
Hart, William.
Hickman, Joshua.
Holland, Albert.
Hands, Washington.
Heron, A.
Hardy, Samuel.
Irvin, Michael.
Irvin, John.
Israel, G. P.
Johnson, O. M.
Johnson, Thomas.
Jones, William.
Jackson, H. J.
Kelly, William.
Knight, John.

Kuble, Adolphus.
King, James A.
Kernan, A.
Knight, L. A.
Knox, William F.
Lanier, James B.
Long, George.
Lucas, William J.
Long, E. J.
Legg, E. A.
Lynch, John P.
Lindenbourne, P.
Ladd, N. E.
Malard, M.
McAviena, Charles.
McLord, M.
Maloney, James.
Mettee, Charles H.
Malone, D.
Moth, E.
Mullan, C. X.
Moran, Michael.
Martin, G.
Monehan, James.
Maccubbin, R. W., Jr.
McAvoy, W. F.
Mackenzie, E. H.
Marston, Fred.
Mudd, John F.
Marshall, P. B.
Mentzer, Samuel.
McClernan, Samuel.
Naylor, W. E.
Neal, Henry.
Neal, Frank.
Oldson, W. H. C.
Owens, J. F.
Paine, William.

Penbroke, George.
Peak, David C.
Peregoy, Charles.
Pohlman, Chris.
Pilert, George.
Quinn, William.
Roane, James.
Robertson, George.
Reilley, John.
Ross, A. P.
Robinson, G. S.
Reiman, H.
Rucker, William.
Richardson, G. W.
Richardson, T. J.
Richardson, H.
Richardson, W.
Rogers, W. C.
Robey, H. A.

Rheim, James I.
Rheim, William G.
Raymond, C. C.
Reynolds, John.
Sanner, Alex. A.
Shaeffer, William.
Shaw, Peter.
Sheil, Michael.
Stout, William.
Shaw, J. C.
Staylor, George W.
Smith, H. C.
Smith, John E.
Smith, W. P.
Schenberger, J. F.
Stinson, R. J.
Shue, J. J.
Sharkey, S.
Shaeffer, Adam F.

Shock, W. A.
Stanbaugh, J. E.
Sullivan, J. H.
Shaeffer, George W.
Stump, George.
Thompson, F. N.
Tarr, William.
Walters, John.
Wysong, Henry.
Walter, John A.
Wilson, T. J.
Wood, W. H.
Warden, William.
Wales, J. C.
Whalen, William P.
Wheeler, Albert.
Watkins, N. W.
Ward, T.
Welch, Martin.

THIRD MARYLAND ARTILLERY.

THE Third Battery of Maryland Artillery served in a wide field and had a varied experience. It was organized at Richmond, Virginia, yet it saw field service in Tennessee, Kentucky, Mississippi, Louisiana, Alabama and Georgia.

Henry B. Latrobe, eldest son of John H. B. Latrobe of Baltimore, received a commission from the Secretary of War at Richmond, Virginia, September 9, 1861, to recruit and organize a company to be known as the Third Maryland Artillery.

The rendezvous was at Ashland, fifteen miles north of Richmond, where recruits were conveyed as fast as enrolled.

John B. Rowan and William L. Ritter joined the company October 24, 1861, and went to camp together.

On November 4 the company (so far as recruited) was ordered to Camp Dimmock for instruction. On the 15th Lieutenant H. A. Steuart started for Maryland to obtain medical supplies and raise recruits for the Third Maryland Artillery, but was captured by the enemy at Millstone Landing on the Patuxent River. He was imprisoned at Washington in the old Capitol for about a year, when he was killed while attempting to escape.

Sergeant McCreary, who went to Maryland about the same time, did not report to the battery on his return.

On December 4 the company was ordered to Camp Lee, at the New Fair Grounds, two miles from the city, where more comfortable winter quarters were to be found. Nothing of importance here broke upon the routine of camp life.

The company was mustered into the service of the Confederate States as the Third Maryland Artillery on January 14, 1862, to serve during the war.

The following is a list of the officers at that time :

Captain, Henry B. Latrobe, of Baltimore, Maryland ; Senior First Lieutenant, Ferd. O. Claiborne, of Louisiana ; Junior First Lieutenant, John B. Rowan, of Elkton, Maryland ; Second Lieutenant, William Thompson Patten, of Port Deposit, Maryland ; Orderly Sergeant, William L. Ritter, of Carroll County, Maryland ; Quartermaster's Sergeant, Albert T. Emory, of Queen Anne's County, Maryland ; First Battery Sergeant, James M. Buchanan, Jr., of Baltimore County, Maryland ; Second Battery Sergeant, John P. Hooper, of Cambridge, Maryland ; Third Battery Sergeant, Edward H. Langley, of Georgia ;

Fourth Battery Sergeant, Thomas D. Giles, of Delaware; Battery Surgeon, Doctor J. W. Franklin, of Virginia.

The company was composed of ninety-two men, exclusive of commissioned officers, a majority of whom were from Maryland and Washington.

The battery consisted of two six-pounder smooth bores, two twelve-pounder howitzers and two three-inch iron rifle pieces, which were received afterwards.

On the 4th of February, 1862, the battery was ordered to report at Knoxville, Tennessee, and arrived there on the 11th. It was quartered first at Temperance Hall, and afterwards at the vacated residence of Mrs. Swan on Main Street. Parson Brownlow was then under confinement as a State prisoner at his own residence, and a detachment of the Third Maryland was detailed to guard his premises from the depredations of the Confederate soldiers. The latter, highly incensed at Brownlow's treasonable opposition to the Confederate Government, could not be relied upon to show him much consideration. The Maryland command was sent to do this duty by reason of the strict discipline under which it had been brought by the exertions of Captain Latrobe; and a detachment under Lieutenant Claiborne, which afterward guarded the prisoner to the depot, received a very complimentary notice in a book which the Parson subsequently wrote upon his experiences in the South.

On the 24th of February two guns were sent to Cumberland Gap, under command of Captain Latrobe and Lieutenant Patten. When, on March 1, Captain Latrobe returned, Lieutenant Claiborne was sent to command the section. On the 16th of March a brigade consisting of the Twentieth and Twenty-third Alabama, Vaughn's Third Tennessee, and the guns of the Third Maryland, under Captain Latrobe and Lieutenant Rowan, the whole commanded by General Leadbetter, made an expedition to Clinch River. The river was first reached at Clinton, whence the brigade continued forty miles down the valley to Kingston, reaching this point about the 28th. Thence on the next day one gun, with a detachment, accompanied General Leadbetter to Wattsburg, where they surprised and captured twenty-one bushwhackers.

Meanwhile Lieutenant Rowan had been ordered to repair to Knoxville to command the detachment left there in March, and now (April 14) Captain Latrobe himself returned, leaving Sergeant Ritter in command of the section. Lieutenant Rowan presently returned with orders to proceed immediately to Lenoir Station, eighteen miles distant, and there embark on the train for Chattanooga, to meet the enemy reported to be marching on that place. It proved to be a false alarm, and the battery marched back to Knoxville, where the right section, which had just returned from Cumberland Gap, was found encamped. During the stay of the right section at the Gap the enemy had assaulted the Confederate works during a snowstorm. The firing was kept up all day with no loss to the battery but a caisson damaged by a Federal shell. In the evening the enemy withdrew, having been repulsed in every assault. On May 1 Holmes Erwin was appointed Junior Second Lieutenant of the battery (having furnished twenty-five Tennessee recruits) and it was made a six-gun battery. About this time two more guns were accordingly received from Richmond. On the 11th orders were received to join General Reynolds' Brigade at Clinton, Tennessee. This brigade consisted of the Thirty-sixth, Thirty-ninth and Forty-third Georgia, and Thirty-ninth North Carolina Regiments.

Again, on the 6th of June, the brigade proceeded to Chattanooga, Tennessee, and thence, after a few days, to Morristown, and then Loudon, in the same State. After a few days a march was made to Blain's Cross Roads, where the brigade remained in camp till the 1st of August. Here the battery received fifty recruits from Georgia.

The next movement was to Tazewell, in East Tennessee, where the enemy was met, defeated and driven back to Cumberland Gap. On the night of the 16th General Reynolds advanced to within four miles of the Gap, driving in the outposts of the enemy, and seizing a range of hills in their front. This position was maintained till the 23d, when General Reynolds received orders from General E. Kirby Smith to march by way of Roger's Gap and Cumberland Ford, and join him in Kentucky. Richmond, Kentucky, was reached two days after the Confederate victory at that place. The enemy had suffered the loss of all their artillery and baggage wagons and the capture of their infantry force. In the subsequent march through Kentucky to the Ohio River, Reynolds' Brigade overtook Smith's advance, and the Third Maryland was the first to enter Lexington. They were greeted on all sides with exclamations of joy and welcome. Great quantities of clothing which had been captured were turned over to the Marylanders and others. The command proceeded thence to Covington, opposite Cincinnati, the whole movement being intended as a feint to draw troops from Louisville, on which Bragg was advancing.

The Confederate advance was ordered back to Georgetown on the 11th of September, and on the 3d of October, at Big Eagle Creek, near Frankfort, there was a review of Reynolds' Brigade by General E. Kirby Smith. When, on the 4th, Governor Hawes was inaugurated Military Governor of Kentucky, at Frankfort, the Third Maryland Artillery was selected to fire the honorary salute of fourteen guns.

That night, however, Frankfort was evacuated, and Smith retired towards Harrodsburg. The battle of Perryville was followed by Bragg's withdrawal to Tennessee, and the Third Maryland battery returned to Knoxville, via Cumberland Gap, where needed repairs were received. On the retreat Reynolds' Brigade closed the Confederate rear. While the Third Maryland was at Knoxville

Lieutenant Rowan served as Judge Advocate in a general court-martial there convened. On the 20th of December the brigade was ordered to proceed to Vicksburg, Mississippi, where it arrived on the 2d of January, 1863. On the 23d three guns of the Maryland battery were sent to Warrenton, a few miles down the river. Two days later one section, under Sergeant Edward H. Langley, was put aboard the steamer Archer, and went down the river, on secret service. At this time Lieutenants Rowan and Patten, who had accompanied the wagon train overland, had not yet come up with the horses belonging to the battery, and Captain Latrobe and Lieutenant Erwin were away on leave of absence. The Archer went up Red River to Fort De Russy, and on the 27th the Third Maryland had the pleasure of firing into the DeSoto. This vessel had been captured by the enemy but a few days previously, while stopping at Johnson's Landing to take on wood.

January 30 a twelve-pound howitzer, with a gun detachment under Sergeant Daniel Toomey, was sent up the Mississippi to General Ferguson's command on Deer Creek. Thus the battery was divided into three parts, scattered up and down the river. Meanwhile Lieutenants Rowan and Patten, having rejoined the battery with the horses, it was now again ready for the field. The guns at Warrenton were at this time placed under the command of Lieutenant Patten. Early on the morning of the 2d of February, the ram Queen of the West passed the batteries at Vicksburg and proceeded down the river. As she passed Warrenton, Patten opened on her without effect, but as she returned on the 4th, Sergeant Ritter hailed her with about sixty rounds of shot and shell, eliciting the compliment from her commander that "those guns at Warrenton annoyed him more on his return than the siege pieces at Vicksburg." A few days later the Queen of the West again passed down (during the night) and went up Red River to Fort De Russy, where she was captured by the Confederates. Sergeant Langley's section was now transferred to the Queen of the West from the Archer, and immediately after the former, with the Grand Era and the Webb, proceeded up the river to Grand Gulf, where (on the 24th) they captured the iron-clad Indianola. The latter was a formidable craft, armed with eight and eleven-inch guns, and had just run the blockade at Vicksburg.

Captain James McCloskey, of General Richard Taylor's staff, commanded the Queen. The entire fleet was commanded by Major J. L. Brent.

A correspondent, speaking of this affair, says:

In closing, we cannot refrain from mentioning specially the command of Edward H. Langley, of the Third Maryland Artillery. He had detachments for two guns (thirteen men) on the Queen, and was in command of the two Parrott guns. He himself took charge of the eighty-six-pounder bow gun, with which he remained during the action, neither he nor his men for a moment leaving their much-exposed position. While the bow of the Queen was yet resting against the side of the Indianola, his guns were still manned and fired, though he and his men were completely exposed. Aside from the courage thus shown, his skill and judgment in manoeuvring his piece in so contracted a space is certainly deserving of the highest commendation.

The officers and crew of the Indianola were made prisoners, and the vessel formed a valuable addition to the small Confederate fleet on the Mississippi. Her subsequent career, however, was a brief one, as she was fired and abandoned by a Lieutenant of infantry, who, with a small detachment, was in charge of her. The enemy above Vicksburg had devised an imitation iron-clad (made of a coal barge, with pine logs for guns, and turned it adrift.) As it floated down near the Indianola, the Lieutenant in charge became alarmed at the approach of so formidable a craft and decamped, after setting fire to his vessel.

Admiral Porter was much chagrined at the capture of this fine vessel, of which so much had been expected, and thus announced his loss:

UNITED STATES MISSISSIPPI SQUADRON, February 27, 1863.

To Secretary Gideon Welles:

Sir:—I regret to inform you that the Indianola has also fallen into the hands of the enemy. The rams Webb and Queen of the West attacked her twenty-five miles from here and rammed her until she surrendered, etc.

DAVID D. PORTER.

Lieutenant Patten, on March 1, was ordered to Red River to take command of the section of the Third Maryland aboard the Queen of the West. He found her at Shreveport, Louisiana.

Early on the morning of the 14th of April Captain E. A. Fuller, now in command of the Queen, with the Lizzie Simmons as a supply boat, attacked the enemy's fleet on Grand Lake, Louisiana, consisting of the Calhoun, Estrella and Arizona, but before the vessels came within short range, an incendiary percussion shell from the Calhoun penetrated the deck of the Queen, exploded and set the vessel on fire. About twenty minutes afterward the fire reached the magazine, and the career of this celebrated boat was closed. After discovering the boat to be on fire, Lieutenant Patten rolled a cotton bale off the side of the vessel and jumped upon it, but it turned with him and he sank, not being able to swim. Thus perished one of the noblest and bravest of the Marylanders who went South. He was a man of commanding physique, polished manners and rare attainments, a soldier who reflected credit upon the cause he espoused; and in his death the battery sustained an irreparable loss, and the service a gallant, brave and faithful officer. Sergeant Langley and all but four of his men remained upon the Queen, and were lost in the general destruction of the vessel. Captain Fuller jumped off the Queen and was picked up by the men of one of the enemy's boats. The Lizzie Simmons escaped capture.

The losses of the Third Maryland in this disastrous affair were:

Killed in the action or drowned in their endeavor to escape from the burning Queen: Lieutenant William Thompson Patten, Sergeant Edward H. Langley, Corporal Michael O'Connell, Privates Richard Tyson, J. Chafin, J. J. McKissick, Thomas Bowler, Edward Kenn and Joseph Edgar.

Captain Latrobe left the service on the 1st of March, 1863, and Lieutenant Claiborne succeeded to the Captaincy. On the 17th of March Orderly Sergeant William L. Ritter was elected to fill the vacancy occasioned by the resignation of Holmes Erwin, Junior Second Lieutenant. On the 21st of March Lieutenant Ritter was promoted to Senior Second Lieutenant, and Lieutenant Patten to Junior First; at the same time Sergeant Thomas D. Giles was elected Junior Second Lieutenant to fill the vacancy caused by Lieutenant Ritter's promotion.

The battery remained encamped at Jett's plantation until Grant crossed his army at Grand Gulf, when it accompanied Pemberton's army to meet him at Baker's Creek, and was engaged in the battle fought there. On the 18th of May it returned with the army to Vicksburg. Private Henry Stewart was captured by the enemy in this engagement, and died afterwards at Fort Delaware.

During the siege of Vicksburg several men of the battery were wounded. Two were killed — Captain Claiborne and Private John Cosson. Captain Claiborne was struck by a piece of shell, on the 22d of June, and fell without uttering a word. He was a fine officer, and a braver one never drew blade in any cause. In him the South lost a generous, gallant and magnanimous man. He was a native of Mississippi, a grandson of General F. L. Claiborne, of Natchez, well known among the early settlers of Alabama, and a cousin of Ferdinand C. Latrobe, Ex-Mayor of Baltimore.

Lieutenant Rowan, on the 30th of June, was promoted to the Captaincy. At the same time Lieutenant Ritter was made Senior First Lieutenant, Lieutenant Giles was made Senior Second Lieutenant, and Sergeant J. W. Doncaster was elected Junior Second Lieutenant. When, on the 4th of July, Vicksburg fell, three officers and seventy men of the Third Maryland battery fell into the enemy's hands. Five of their guns, one hundred and thirty horses and mules, and all the appliances of a six-gun battery were also surrendered.

Only one gun, under the command of Lieutenant Ritter, remained. To trace its history it will be necessary to return to a point three months previous to the fall of Vicksburg, when, on the 2d of April, Lieutenant Ritter was ordered to the command of Toomey's detachment of the Third Maryland Artillery, previously commanded by Lieutenant T. J. Bates, of Waddell's Alabama Artillery. This section, one of Bledsoe's Missouri battery, and one of a Louisiana battery (Lieutenant Cottonham) were all under the command of Lieutenant R. L. Wood, of the Missouri Artillery, and were a part of a force under General Ferguson, which had for several months been operating along the Mississippi River. Their employment was to harrass the enemy by firing into their vessels of war and transports. When, in March, 1863, Porter's fleet of five gunboats entered Black Bayou in order to flank the Confederate batteries at Snyder's Bluff, General Ferguson met him at Rolling Fork and after an engagement lasting three days drove him back, inflicting considerable loss.

The greatest execution in this battle, strange to say, was done, not by the Confederate artillery, whose shot rolled harmlessly upon the backs of the enemy's iron-plated vessels, but by the sharpshooters. These were mainly Texans, who acted with characteristic daring. They approached the very bank of the stream and fired into the portholes of the iron-clads as soon as these were opened by the Federals for a shot at the Confederate artillery. The enemy labored under the additional disadvantage of being unable to depress their pieces sufficiently to reach their antagonists, so that their shell damaged only the tree tops. Harrassed and annoyed past endurance, they at length withdrew.

During April nothing of special note occurred. Steel's command of Federals employed itself in burning dwellings and gin-houses along Deer Creek, in its usual manner.

On the 29th of April Lieutenant Ritter, with his section of the Third Maryland, was ordered to join Major Bridges' force at Fish Lake, near Greenville, Mississippi. He came up with that command on the 1st of May, and the next day proceeded to the river to fire upon the boats, which were continually passing. The object of the Confederates was to prevent, as much as possible, reinforcements from reaching Grant at Vicksburg. Soon after the arrival of the Maryland section a transport appeared in view, ascending the river. Lieutenant Ritter opened fire on her, some of the shell exploding on her deck and others passing through her. She got by, but cast anchor a few miles up the river to repair damages. A swamp prevented further attack on her at her anchorage.

The firing had scarcely ceased when a gunboat hove in sight. The section took position behind the levee, where it would be sheltered somewhat during the engagement which was now anticipated. Lieutenant Ritter had taken the precaution to cut embrasures in the levee, so that he might thus protect his guns in an emergency. Approaching within range, the gunboat proceeded at once to open fire on the Confederates. The latter replied with shot and shell, and the engagement lasted about half an hour, when the enemy steamed away. It was afterward ascertained that the vessel was iron-plated only about the portholes for the protection of her gunners, and that some of Ritter's shells passed through the monster. About the 1st of May Lieutenant Cottonham's section was ordered to Vicksburg.

On the morning of the 4th one of Major Bridges' scouts brought the news that a transport heavily laden with stores, was coming down the river. *Here was sport!* Lieutenant Ritter took his guns and masked them at a point where the current ran in near the bank on his side and awaited the vessel's approach. Soon the black smoke of a steamer was seen rising above the tree tops, beyond Carter's Bend, a few miles off, and shortly afterwards she came in sight. On the vessel came, rapidly and quietly, anticipating no danger. The Confederates were ordered to their positions, the guns were loaded, and as the boat came within their range the order " Fire ! " was given.

The stillness of the calm summer morning must have seemed to the crew rudely broken, when in quick succession the shrill report of the rifle piece and the loud roar of the twelve-pound howitzer broke upon their ears. The first or second shot cut the tiller rope, and another broke a piston rod of one of the engines. The crew, despairing of escape, hoisted a white flag of surrender, and brought the boat ashore. Major Bridges and Lieutenant Ritter were the first to board the prize, which was found to be the Minnesota. The crew met them at the head of the saloon steps, and politely requested their captors, in true Western style, to " take a drink ! " This was as politely declined, but a revolver which one of them wore at his waist was accepted instead — an article of which Lieutenant Ritter was in special need at that time.

The prisoners — seventeen in number — were ordered ashore, and the Confederates took possession. The boat was found to be heavily laden with sutlers' stores — flour, bacon, potatoes, pickles of all sorts, sugar, coffee, rice, ginger, syrup, cheese, butter, oranges, lemons, almonds, preserves, canned oysters, whisky, wines, mosquito nets, clothing, stationery, smokers' articles, etc. To impoverished Confederates no greater mass of wealth could have seemed conceivable. They sat down to a luxurious dinner, which was in preparation at the time of their attack, and relished it, perhaps, more than those for whom it had been intended. Part of the festivities consisted in breaking a bottle of wine over Black Bess, Lieutenant Ritter's iron twelve-pounder, to a shot from which Major Bridges attributed the speedy surrender of the Minnesota. She had long been familiarly known in the battery by this name, but only now at length on this happy occasion received her formal christening. After everything which would be of service was brought ashore, the steamer was fired. Her value was estimated at $250,000. She was the property of a Yankee speculator.

About 5 P. M. that day the enemy's gunboats appeared, and, without notice to the women and children upon them, began to shell the neighboring plantations.

On the 6th the section was ordered to return to Rolling Fork, and upon its arrival Lieutenant Ritter was complimented by General Ferguson and Lieutenant Wood on his management of his guns. On the 14th both sections of artillery and Major Bridges' battalion of cavalry were ordered to Greenville, and on the 16th proceeded to their old camp at Fish Lake.

The morning of May 18, 1863, dawned with splendid promise. The sun rose bright and clear, laughing away the mist and heavy fog that had hid the face of the Father of Waters, and stirring to activity the Federals and Confederates pitted against each other along his whole course. The Confederates encamped at Fish Lake were still jubilant over their recent success with the Minnesota, and the captured stores enabled them to indulge in luxuries to which they had long been strangers. Grouped picturesquely about their fires, they drank their morning coffee with all the gusto due the genuine berry. Chatting, laughing over the details of their recent exploit, some sitting, and some half-reclining on their elbows, under their bivouac shelters, they slipped the aromatic beverage in complete enjoyment. If their inner man was well-to-do, their outer man had no less reason to be felicitated on his surroundings. Their camp was snugly inclosed on all sides by a deep and primitive forest of cottonwood, magnolia and live oak.

The Marylanders of Major Bridges' command were surrendering themselves to the charms of this romantic situation, when an order was received which made them oblivious of it all. The news had just come in through scouts that lined the river for miles above that a number of transports laden with reinforcements for Grant's army at Vicksburg were coming down, and would reach Carter's Bend that morning. Immediately all was life and bustling activity, and the soldier's peculiar feeling of quiet delight at the approach of danger took the place of the more amiable sentimentality of a few moments before.

Major Bridges' force consisted of one section of artillery under command of Lieutenant Anderson, another under Lieutenant Ritter, each with about twenty-five men, and a small squadron of Texas Rangers, the whole command numbering about two hundred and fifty men.

Getting his command speedily in motion, he proceeded rapidly up the Greenville road, eight miles, to a point above Carter's Bend. The Mississippi here makes a detour of fifteen miles, and then, returning upon itself, forms a peninsula, the neck of which is but one mile across. It was thought best to take this position above rather than the one below the Bend, as in case of success there would be an opportunity to fire a second time below at the vessels that had been disabled in the first attack.

The four pieces of artillery were placed on the river bank unprotected, but masked by the thick brush that grew along the water's edge. The dismounted cavalry, acting as sharpshooters and supporting the Maryland section, were disposed to the right and left along the river. The levee was about a hundred and fifty yards in the rear, and beyond that were the open fields of Carter's plantation. Thus disposed, the Confederates awaited the enemy's approach, beguiling the time by picking the luscious blackberries found here in great profusion.

They had not long to wait, as the Federal vessels soon appeared. The Crescent City, a side-wheeler which had formerly plied between New Orleans and Memphis, led the van. She was now employed as a transport, and was loaded down with troops, the whole vessel being blue with them. They covered the entire hurricane deck and crowded the water deck below, packed and jammed in a way that only pleasure-seekers can tolerate and enjoy. Behind the Crescent City, at a distance of about half a mile, was a gunboat, and following that at regular intervals four more transports. The number of troops aboard the five vessels was estimated at about four thousand infantry and cavalry. As the first transport — its decks a scene of jollity and animation — drew near the Confederate battery, the latter opened on her with a rapid fire of shell and cannister, the effect of which on the Yankees was, of course, startling. They jumped and rushed with pain and fright to the opposite side of the boat, thus careening it fearfully and exposing its hull to the artillerists on shore. The latter proceeded at once to fire shell into it, till the Yankee officers got the men back and righted the boat again.

The infantry aboard returned the fire and wounded three Confederates. As soon as the gunboat came within easy cannister range, the artillery withdrew behind the levee in the rear. While this was going on below, the transports above came to the shore, threw out their stages, and speedily landed a force of three thousand cavalry and infantry to capture the pestilent Confederates. The latter withdrew their artillery at once across the open fields in the direction of Greenville, while Major Bridges, with the sharpshooters, remained at the levee to cover their retreat. To cover his own he ordered Lieutenant Ritter to halt his section of artillery at a bridge across a bayou half a mile in the rear, and await further orders. He himself withdrew by another road over a bridge half a mile farther up the bayou, while the enemy, in line of battle, advanced along both roads. As there was no force to hold the upper bridge, the way was open to Lieutenant Ritter's rear; and yet no "further orders" came. The enemy had actually crossed the upper bridge and were nearing their line of retreat, when the Third Maryland limbered up and passed down the road at a gallop. At the same moment, seeing Lieutenant Ritter's peril, Major Bridges ordered a countercharge of his cavalry, on the other road, and thus held the enemy in check until the section was out of danger of capture.

Passing through a strip of woods into an adjacent plantation, the Confederates drew up in line to await the enemy. They not appearing, the retreat was continued by the artillery. The latter had not proceeded far, however, before a hurried order was received: "Form battery and load with cannister, as the enemy will presently be upon us!" Major Bridges, still lingering in the very presence of their advance, being so close as to be summoned by them to surrender, but emptying his revolver into their faces by way of reply, he then came dashing back to the artillery, which let him pass with his Texans, and then opened on the enemy with eight rounds, sweeping the road clear for the distance of more than three hundred yards. The effect on them was decisive; they were thrown into the greatest confusion, many saddles were emptied and their advance checked.

The artillery limbered up again, and set off at a gallop, not stopping till they had crossed Black Bayou, a distance of six miles. The enemy followed, but at length retired to Greenville, burning the town and neighboring residences, in revenge for their losses in the fight.

The next day Major Bridges learned that the enemy held Haynes' Landing and Snyder's Bluff, and were likely to attempt his capture by sending troops up the Yazoo River in his rear. The same evening orders were received from General Ferguson to leave the Mississippi at once and proceed to Greenwood, on the Yazoo River by the way of Deer Creek, Bogue Phaliah and Moon Lake. At midnight the camp at Fish Lake was broken up, and the command proceeded on its way, and reached the Yazoo on the 24th, after marching a distance of seventy miles. Obstruction in the river prevented the enemy from ascending to the point where Major Bridges crossed. From Greenwood the battery was ordered to Yazoo City, where it arrived on the 1st of June. After one more engagement with the enemy's vessels on the Yazoo, the Maryland section proceeded, on the 12th, to Vernon, Mississippi, where it was attached to General McNair's Brigade of Walker's Division. Six days after it was transferred to Ector's Brigade of the same division. A section of Captain McNally's Arkansas battery, under Lieutenant Moore, was also attached to this brigade, and, as he was the senior officer, he took command of both sections. Walker's Division constituted part of the army which General Joseph E. Johnston was assembling for the relief of Vicksburg.

On the 1st of July the movement toward Vicksburg began. While waiting for the pontoons on which the Big Black River was to be crossed to come up the news was received at headquarters that Vicksburg had capitulated. How great a calamity to the Confederacy this event was, is well known. It was especially painful to the detached section of the Third Maryland, as much the larger part of their battery was lost with the city. As before stated, three officers, seventy men and five guns of the Third Maryland were surrendered. They were paroled on the 12th of July, and on the 26th at Enterprise were furloughed for thirty days, with orders to report at Decatur, Georgia.

Johnston's army reached Jackson on the night of the 7th, and before daylight the next morning was ordered into the trenches west of the town. On the 10th the enemy appeared in front, drove in the Confederate pickets and began to fortify.

The sections of Moore and Ritter were placed in an angle of the line, on the Vicksburg road. The enemy constructed their works in a semi-circle about this point in order to dismount a siege-piece which was situated between Moore's and Ritter's sections. In their works the enemy planted about thirty-six twenty-pounder Parrotts and Napoleons. The Confederates had in the threatened angle the siege-piece, two twenty-pounder Parrotts, two three-inch rifle pieces and three twelve-pound howitzers. For two days the enemy were occupied in perfecting their works, and did not often fire a shot.

Sunday morning, July 12, the sun rose in a cloudless sky, and there was nothing to disturb the unusual stillness, appropriate to the day, except an occasional picket shot echoing among the hills.

The men sat idly here and there along the parapet, when suddenly a terrific fire from all the enemy's batteries was opened upon the exposed angle — a fire that seemed to shake the very earth. To add to the unpleasantness of the situation, the cotton bales, which formed part of the parapet, were knocked off and inflamed by the enemy's shell, and had to be rolled to the rear to save the ammunition from danger. In the midst of the storm of lead and iron, the men were called to action, and returned the enemy's fire with vigor. Lieutenant Whitney was presently wounded and Lieutenant Moore was so seriously injured by a falling bale that he had to be taken to the rear, thus leaving Lieutenant Ritter in command.

The enemy's artillery fire continued with unabated fury for two hours, after which it slackened for the rest of the day.

Thursday night, the 16th, the Confederate works were evacuated and the army fell back to Morton, Mississippi.

The losses of the Third Maryland at Jackson during the seven days it was under fire were as follows:

KILLED—Corporal L. McCurry, Private Henry Gordon.

WOUNDED—Lieutenant Ritter, Sergeant Daniel Toomey, Privates Brown, Emmett Wells and J. P. Wills.

On the 5th of September the section was ordered to Demopolis, Alabama, for repairs. On the 19th of October, 1863, by order of General Joseph E. Johnston, the Third Maryland section was transferred to Decatur, Georgia, where it rejoined the battery under Captain Rowan.

The number of men in the battery had been much reduced by its losses in Louisiana and Mississippi, so that Captain Rowan applied to the Secretary of War for seventy-five conscripts. While at Decatur the guns, horses and equipments of a four-gun battery were received, and Doctor Thomas J. Rogers was assigned to the battery as surgeon.

On October 29 the battery was ordered to Sweet Water, East Tennessee, and on the 5th of November to Bragg's army at Missionary Ridge.

On the morning of the 23d of November, 1863, the enemy, under cover of a heavy fog, moved up and attacked the left wing of General Bragg's army, at the foot of Lookout Mountain, and drove it back rapidly, the line at that point being weak and the attack unexpected. The evacuation of Lookout Mountain followed, and Bragg withdrew to Missionary Ridge. The next day he was defeated, and the army fell back to Dalton. The Third Maryland was held in reserve.

General Bragg was here superseded in the command of the army by Joseph E. Johnston. The Third Maryland went into winter quarters in Sugar Valley, below Dalton, Georgia.

On the 20th of January, 1864, the whole battalion, for easier access to long forage, was ordered to Kingston, where it again built winter quarters.

On the 7th of May the battery was ordered to the front of the line in Crow's Valley, and when, on the 8th, the enemy moved up as if to attack the Confederate works, they were received with so vigorous a fire that they rapidly withdrew. But two men of the Third Maryland were wounded. Again, on the 9th, the enemy charged our works, but were repulsed, with no loss to the battery.

On the night of the 12th the corps fell back to Resaca. Two days later the battery took position on the front, two miles north of Resaca, to the left of the Dalton road, and about a hundred yards to the right of an obtuse angle in the line, at this time occupied by Dent's Alabama battery. The latter held the summit of a ridge, the prolongation of which, in front, it was expected to command, while Captain Rowan was directed to construct his works at right angles with the ridge, so as to command the Dalton road. He saw that in case the enemy seized and held the ridge in front of the angle his battery would be enfiladed, and, therefore, began to construct a traverse for the protection of his men. Before it was completed our skirmish line was driven off the ridge to the shelter of the earthworks, and the battery had to begin firing. Dent's battery was soon withdrawn, as the men were shot down as fast as they took their positions beside their guns. Rowan's battery now became exposed to a raking fire from the left.

The first section, under command of Lieutenant Ritter, was on this occasion on the left, instead of its proper place on the right, of the battery, for a special reason, which it is not necessary to mention ; and it was now consequently the most severely handled. His two guns were speedily silenced, and not long after the other two, under Lieutenant Giles. At the right gun of Ritter's section eight men were killed and wounded within a few minutes, leaving but three at the gun. The moment the gun was silenced, Sergeant Wynn, in charge of the second, was directed to throw his trail to the right and fire over the first. It happened that Lieutenant Ritter was lying just in front of the parapet of the second gun, so that the cannister fired from it passed over and very near his head, covering him with dirt knocked off the parapet by fragments of the missiles fired at the enemy. It was a dangerous position, and the Lieutenant called with no little vigor to the Sergeant to "cease firing." The roaring of the guns and the din of the musketry, of course, drowned his voice, so that he had to lie still where he was ; the enemy in front, his own men behind him, the gun over him scattering its cannister fearfully, while it deafened him with its noise, and suffocated him with its sulphurous smoke. Around him lay the dead and wounded of the first detachments. The peril of his own situation did not prevent him from thinking what would be the fate of these poor men if the enemy charged the works. It was with great delight that he heard Captain Rowan give the order to cease firing.

At dusk the infirmary corps came up to remove the wounded, and, later, during the night, the dead were buried. Captain Rowan left Lieutenant Ritter in command, with orders to remodel the works during the night, while he himself went to look after some horses for the battery. Nine horses had been killed, including Ritter's saddle horse. By daylight the works were completed. In the afternoon the enemy charged our right, passing within three hundred yards of Rowan's battery, giving the latter a fine opportunity to revenge its losses of the day before. Right well did it take advantage of it, opening with terrible effect, strewing the field with dead, and giving occupation to numerous litter-bearers, who presently appeared on the scene to carry off the wounded. The firing continued during the evening at intervals. About 3 P. M. Lieutenant Ritter was wounded by a minnie ball in the right arm above the elbow. The ball passed through the fleshy part of the arm, and lodged in the sleeve.

At night the army fell back, marching across Oostenaula River to Adairsville, which was reached on the 16th. The casualties of the Third Maryland at Resaca were three killed and fifteen wounded, as follows :

KILLED—Corporal Sanchez, Private H. Steward, and a third, whose name is lost.

WOUNDED—Lieutenant William L. Ritter, Sergeant L. W. Frazier, Corporals A. J. Davis and B. Bradford, Privates J. Bushong, W. E. Davis, J. G. Cannon, J. Faulk, B. Garst, J. Isham, J. S. Scales, J. A. Turner, M. P. Talton, W. Pickle and A. P. Wade.

The spokes of the second piece were so shattered by the enemy's minnie balls that false spokes had to be put in before the gun could be removed.

The army continued to fall back until it reached New Hope Church, near Dallas, on the 25th, when a general engagement took place. The enemy moved up and charged the greater part of our line, but were repulsed with heavy loss at every point. The Third Maryland was not engaged till late in the evening, when it did terrible execution in the enemy's ranks, itself having but two men slightly wounded. Again, on the 27th, the enemy charged our right wing, and the Third was ordered to open up on them, which it did with telling effect.

On the 31st, Corporal Jones was killed by a random picket shot, and Private Lee was wounded by the same ball.

When, on the 4th of June, the New Hope line was abandoned for the Lost Mountain line, and that afterwards for the Noonday Valley, the Third Maryland took part in every movement. On the 22nd, at Marietta, the battery was ordered out on the field to join in General Stevenson's famous charge upon the enemy's right wing, but was held in reserve. Stevenson was repulsed with the loss of a thousand men.

The Maryland battery lost none, though under a severe artillery fire the whole time. On the night of the 4th of July the battery was ordered to the Chattahoochee River, thence to Mill Creek road, where, on the 20th an attack was made by the enemy and repulsed. General Johnston was superseded by General Hood on the 14th of July.

The next day the battery was ordered to Atlanta, and on the morning of the 22d was assigned to a position in Peach Tree Street redoubt, at that time an unfinished work. When completed it was circular in form, having a parapet right, left and rear, with five embrasures. In the afternoon the battery began to reply to the enemy, who had moved up within reach, and toward sunset, General Loring coming up, ordered the firing to be made as rapidly as possible, so as to attract the enemy's attention and create a diversion of their forces from the left, upon which the Confederates were making a charge. This movement was a success. About three thousand prisoners, twenty-eight pieces of artillery, and a considerable quantity of ordnance stores were captured.

Our batteries kept up a continuous firing night and day for several days to prevent the enemy from advancing their line. Two thirty-two-pound siege-pieces were now brought up, one of which was planted in Peach Tree Street redoubt, and the other two hundred yards in the rear. Captain Corput (now temporarily in command of the battalion) placed Lieutenant Ritter in charge of these guns, detailing men to work them from Rowan's and Corput's batteries. Several attempts made by the enemy to plant batteries in our front were frustrated by aid of these guns.

On the 20th of August Captain Corput was wounded and Captain Rowan took command of the battalion, which left Lieutenant Ritter in command of the Third Maryland.

On September 1 Atlanta was evacuated, and the army fell back to Lovejoy Station. The enemy followed, and on the 4th we fought them two miles north of that place, to such good purpose that on the 5th they returned to Atlanta.

The movement of Hood's army to Sherman's rear began on the 29th of

September, 1864. The Chattahoochee River was crossed on the 30th, and part of the army proceeded to Lost Mountain for Ackworth and Big Shanty and captured the garrisons at those places. At Cedartown the wagon train, the sick, and the shoeless, and all the artillery except one battery of each battalion were left behind, while the remainder of the army proceeded to Resaca and Dalton. Stevenson's Division started on the 9th of October at noon, and the Third Maryland was the battery chosen to accompany it.

It was the intention of General Stephen D. Lee, who commanded the corps, to capture the garrison at Resaca, and he made forced marches in order to take it by surprise. On the 12th it was surrounded by approaches made from the north and its unconditional surrender demanded. The Major in command of the post refused to yield, however, and General Lee did not think it worth while to compel him, and proceeded on his way.

On the 23d all started for Tennessee, marching across Sand Mountain to Decatur, Alabama, and thence to Florence, on the south bank of the Tennessee River. By the 20th of November all the troops had crossed the Tennessee River, and through rain and snow the advance upon Nashville was renewed. The weather was intensely cold, and the march was rendered the more cheerless by the barrenness and poverty of the country through which it led during the first few days. Rations and forage were very scarce, though the more needed by reason of the bitter weather.

When within a mile and a half of Columbia on the 26th the whole army was put in order of battle, and so advanced till within three-fourths of a mile of the enemy's works. The town was evacuated on the night of the 27th, and the Third Maryland was the first Confederate force to enter the next morning. A section of the battery under Lieutenant Ritter was sent three miles below the town to prevent the destruction by the enemy of the railroad bridge over Duck River, but on its arrival found the bridge in flames.

When, on the 29th, the right section rejoined the left, it was found on the south bank of the river, in the cemetery at Columbus, engaged with the enemy. The Yankees on the other side of the river had massed their artillery upon a hill commanding the town, and were opposing the crossing of the Confederates ; the latter had six batteries replying to them, two of them planted above and four within the town. Meanwhile Pettus' Brigade of Stevenson's Division was thrown across the river, preparatory to a charge upon the enemy's works, and while it was forming under the river bank the Confederate artillery increased the intensity of its fire till it became terrific, and effectually prevented any active movement on the part of the enemy. Pettus charged their works as soon as his formation was completed, and drove the Federals out with but slight loss. Three men of the Third Maryland were wounded in the artillery duel, two of them dangerously.

Colonel Beckham was mortally wounded, and was succeeded in command of the artillery regiment by Major Johnston.

Early on the morning of the 30th the advance in the direction of Franklin was renewed, and when the battery was within six miles of the town, an order was received from General Hood to move up at a trot, as it was only needed to "press the enemy at this point, and the campaign would be over!" The scene of action was reached about 4 P. M., when the battalion was placed in reserve, and did not take part in the attack that followed. It was one of the most remarkable, and certainly one of the bloodiest, battles of the war. Cheatham's and Stewart's Corps charged over an open plain of six hundred yards in width, under a severe fire from the enemy's artillery and infantry, the latter occupying a double line of defenses on the brow of an elevation of some fifteen feet. The charge was a brilliant one and was partially successful, as part of the enemy's line was captured, but it was at a fearful loss on our side.

The loss of the Confederates in officers was unprecedentedly heavy. Eleven general officers were killed and wounded. Among the killed were Cleburne, Granberry, Carter and Lewis. All the field officers remained mounted during the charge.

At daylight on the morning after the fight, Lieutenant Ritter rode over the field, and in the part of the line where Cockrell's Missourians charged the enemy's defenses he found the dead lying thick, piled one upon another, till the earth was hidden by the woeful spectacle. Near this point to the right General Lewis' horse was found lying upon the top of the works, and fifty yards within the enemy's main line of fortifications a single Confederate soldier was found, face down, his head toward the enemy, having penetrated thus far alone before he was shot.

Early on the morning of December 1 the enemy evacuated their works, and crossed Harpeth River, under fire from our batteries.

The Confederate Army followed and arrived before Nashville on the 2d, and immediately commenced to fortify. The Third Maryland occupied a hill on the right of and parallel with the Franklin Pike.

On the morning of the 15th the enemy charged the Confederate right wing, but were repulsed with heavy loss. They next moved a heavy column against the left, with better success, causing the whole army to fall back rapidly for the distance of one mile.

On the morning of the eventful 16th of December the Third Maryland was ordered to a hill in an open field a quarter of a mile to the left of the Franklin pike. Defensive works for the battery were at once commenced, and rails to be used in fortifying were brought from a fence some two hundreds yards in front. The enemy discovering the working party, opened on them with six guns. The horses were without cover and suffered severely till removed to a position behind the hill. On returning to the battery, Lieutenant Ritter, being more experienced in such matters, was sent back to the caissons to relieve Lieutenant Doncaster, and take charge of the men engaged in supplying ammunition to the guns, and instruct them as to the distances for which the fuses should be cut. About this time the enemy planted two more batteries, one on the right and the other on the left, making a total of eighteen, whose fire was concentrated on the Maryland battery. Their fire now became fearfully hot, and Captain Rowan, wishing to return it with the greatest vigor, called on the drivers to assist the " fives " and " sevens " in bringing up ammunition. The nature of the ground was such that the horses could not be effectually sheltered from the enemy's battery on the right, and they were falling rapidly. The drivers were being wounded, and the trees cut down, while the air was resonant with the howl of passing shells, and the lighter whistle of the more searching minnies. Ritter, who for the reason given above, had charge of the drivers, horses and ammunition, asked leave to take the horses to a safer place, but it was not thought expedient to separate them as far from the guns as would be necessary to secure their safety. A Parrott shell passed through the head of a wheel horse near him and exploded, cutting the Lieutenant's sword in two and killing his saddle horse. The men engaged in furnishing ammunition also suffered severely. Major Johnston, now coming up, ordered the horses to be removed, and those that remained were thus saved.

At half past twelve Captain Rowan was struck by a piece of shell, and instantly killed.

At about 3 P. M. the Confederate line of battle gave way, and so rapidly did the troops retreat, and so promptly did the enemy follow, that Lieutenant Ritter saw at once that there would be no chance to bring off his guns. He determined to remain with them and work them to the last.

After driving the Confederates from their works, the enemy poured in on Stevenson's left, and forming a line perpendicular to his, swept along within the defenses toward the Third Maryland. At the same time another line was moving up in front, and both seemed to be aiming to form a junction at the battery to overwhelm it. The men stood to their guns and continued to pour a heavy fire of cannister into the heavy masses approaching in front, till they mounted the works. They mounted first upon the left, planting the United States flag on the left gun and capturing sixteen men.

As they showed their heads above the works, Lieutenants Ritter, Doncaster and Sergeant Pendley — who were upon the right — started and ran down the line fifty yards, and then left it and struck diagonally across the field for the pike. The Federals cried " Halt ! " " Halt ! " to no purpose, and pursued them for three-quarters of a mile, firing at them all the while.

They escaped unhurt, however, and continuing some four miles to the rear, overtook the few horses that were left of the battery.

Captain Rowan was a native of Maryland, and at the beginning of the war resided at Elkton, Cecil County, where he had devoted himself with success to the practice of his profession of the law. Though still young, he had already attained considerable prominence as a public man. His manners were winning; in speech he was easy and graceful; in action generous and manly; and every circumstance of his life promised the success which his character deserved. When the war broke out, true to his noble instincts, he devoted himself to the cause of the South, leaving his profession, home, wife and children — all that he held most dear — to take up arms in defense of the right. Through the many trying phases of military life he passed unscathed. Cool in the hour of danger, serene amid defeat and disaster, kind alike to his fellow-officers and to his men; he was cut off in the flower of his age, before he had seen his thirtieth year. Brave, noble, high-principled, his death in any cause would have hallowed it. Had the lost Confederacy no other title to our love, the remembrance that for it such choice spirits as John B. Rowan fought and died, would be enough to keep it forever warm in our hearts.

The losses of the Third Maryland at Nashville were four killed, eight wounded and sixteen captured, exclusive of Lieutenant Giles and Private Cotter, captured two days before the battle.

KILLED—Captain John B. Rowan, Privates S. Aultman, E. R. Roach and A. Wills.

WOUNDED—A. Dollar, D. Beasley, N. Beverly, W. J. Brown, Tom Early, A. J. Davis, E. M. Herndon and J. Nichols.

The retreat continued through pelting rains, and snows, and high water, flooding the country through which the army had to pass. Many of the men were without shoes, and were but poorly clad, though the weather was so intensely cold as to benumb those who were better provided.

On the 10th of January, 1865, Johnston's battalion went into camp at Columbus, Mississippi. Here, on the 20th, Lieutenant Ritter was promoted to the Captaincy by the following special order:

HEADQUARTERS, COLUMBUS, MISSISSIPPI, January 20, 1865.

Special Order No. 10.

The following promotions are announced, the officers named being deemed competent for promotion : . . . .

First Lieutenant William L. Ritter, of Stephens' Light Artillery, Third Maryland, to be Captain, from December 16, 1864, to fill the vacancy caused by the death of Captain John B. Rowan, killed December 16, 1864, before Nashville, Tennessee.

BY COMMAND OF MAJOR-GENERAL ELZEY.

WILLIAM PALFREY, *Captain and Assistant Adjutant.*

About this time Johnston's battalion was ordered to North Carolina. Ritter's battery was transferred to Cobb's battalion, and on the 2nd of February ordered to Mobile, Alabama. The city was reached on the 5th, and on the 10th Ritter's and Phillip's companies took charge of Battery D, three miles from town. The D Battery contained seven guns — two twelve-pound siege-pieces, four thirty-two pound navy guns, and one army gun of the same calibre. Ritter was in command.

On the night of April 11, 1865, Mobile was evacuated and the troops were conveyed on transports to Demopolis, Alabama ; thence to Meridian, Mississippi, on the cars, where, on the 4th of May, General Dick Taylor surrendered to General Canby. On the 10th the Third Maryland Artillery was paroled.

ROSTER OF THE THIRD MARYLAND ARTILLERY.

Henry B. Latrobe, *Captain.*
*Ferd. O. Claiborne, *Captain.*
*John B. Rowan, *Captain.*
†William L. Ritter, *Captain.*
*William Thompson Patten, *Lieutenant.*
Holmes Erwin, *Lieutenant.*
Thomas D. Giles, *Lieutenant.*
J. W. Doncaster, *Lieutenant.*
Thomas J. Rogers, *Assistant Surgeon.*
Rufus McCeeny, *First Sergeant.*
Albert T. Emory, *Quartermaster.*
James M. Buchanan, Jr., *Sergeant.*
John P. Hooper, *Sergeant.*
*Edward H. Langley, *Sergeant.*
Joseph Lackey, *Sergeant.*
†L. W. Frazier, *Sergeant.*
J. W. Smith, *Sergeant.*
William Fleming, *Sergeant.*
†Daniel Toomey, *Sergeant.*
Edward Wynn, *Sergeant.*
†A. J. Davis, *Sergeant.*
Benjamin F. Weaver, *Corporal.*
S. G. W. Gerding, *Corporal.*

*Joseph Edgar, *Corporal.*
*M. H. O'Connell, *Corporal.*
W. H. Erwin, *Corporal.*
George W. Hancock, *Corporal.*
*Thomas H. Jones, *Corporal.*
John C. Pendley, *Corporal.*
Virgil P. Herron, *Corporal.*
William T. Sykes, *Corporal.*
†William Pirkle, *Corporal.*
†A. G. Cox, *Corporal.*
Solomon Hylton, *Corporal.*
William Buckner, *Corporal.*
John Light, *Corporal.*
†Baldwin Bradford, *Corporal.*
*B. Sanchez, *Corporal.*
M. L. Welsh, *Corporal.*
Jackson Simmons, *Corporal.*
S. R. Sheppard, *Corporal.*
Frederick Geiger, *Bugler.*
*Nicholas Powers, *Blacksmith.*
Patrick McCann, *Artificer.*
Joseph G. Fletcher, *Artificer.*
*W. B. P. Mills, *Farrier.*

* Killed.   † Wounded.

Privates.

ADAMS, J. H.
ARMSTRONG, LEWIS.
†ASHBURN, A. R.
AULTMAN, N.
*AULTMAN, S.
BAILEY, F. M.
†BARNES, ROBERT B.
BARRETT, J. H.
†BEASLEY, D.
BEASLEY, JOSEPH.
BELL, WILLIAM.
BENNETT, WILLIAM B.
BENTON, JOHN.
BERG, JOHN.
†BEVERLY, N. M.
BIRDWELL, D. J.
BLACKBURN, WILLIAM.
BLAKESLIE, CHARLES E.
*BOWLER, THOMAS.
BRADBERY, L. S.
BRIDGES, W.
BROWN, A. H.
†BROWN, W. J.
BROWN, N. M.
BURTON, MICHAEL.
†BUSHONG, J. A.
BUTLER, H. C.
BYRON, TIMOTHY.
CALLOWAY, W. A.
CAMP, GEORGE W.
CAMP, JAMES R.
†CANNON, J. G.
CARBERRY, PATRICK.
CARR, PATRICK.
CARRILL, JOHN.
CARY, G. M.
CAULK, WILLIAM H.

*CHAFIN, S.
CHEASHAM, J.
CHESER, G. S.
CLARK, CHARLES.
CLARK, THOMAS B.
CLARK, T. H.
CONNOR, ALEXANDER.
CONNOR, JAMES.
COOK, CHARLES.
*COSSON, J. S.
COTTER, J. J.
COUSINS, J. H.
COX, JAMES.
CRAIG, EDWARD.
CRANGLE, ROBERT.
CRIDER, J. M.
CRIDER, W. R.
CROWLEY, MICHAEL.
CROZART, J. A.
CURRAN, JOHN.
DAILEY, W. H.
DAVIDSON, E.
†DAVIS, W. E.
DAVIS, W. J.
DEGAN CASPER.
DELANEY, FRANCIS.
DONOHUE, EDWARD.
DOOLEY, FRANK.
DOVE, W. S.
DOWNS, JAMES.
DRISCALL, JAMES.
DUFFAN, HENRY.
DUVALL, CHARLES.
DWYER, MARTIN.
†EARLY, THOMAS.
EATON, J. H.
EDWARDS, FRANK K.

ELDER, HENRY.
ELLICOTT, CHARLES J. F.
FARMER, THOMAS.
†FAULK, S.
FILMER, F.
FLEENOR, A.
FLOWERS, W. H.
FOLEY, DANIEL.
†FOLEY, JOHN.
FORD, JAMES W.
FOWLER, A. J.
FOWLER, E. C.
FULKERSON, J. K. P.
GARRETT, W. A. H.
†GARST, BENJAMIN.
GATES, L. R.
GATES, W.
GLOVER, W. H.
GOLDEN, H. F.
GOLDEN, W.
*GORDON, HENRY.
GORDRIAN, ANTONY.
GORDRIAN, S.
GORMAN, P.
GOUGH, JAMES.
GRAY, J. A.
GRIFFIN, W. B.
GUGENHEIMER, S.
HAIL, FRANCIS.
HAM, JAMES.
HAMMOND, W. H.
HARMAN, VICTOR.
HARRIS, G. M.
HARVEY, J. C.
HARVEY, W.
HATTAWAY, W., SR.
HATTAWAY, W., JR.

* Killed. † Wounded.

Hawley, George W.
Heineman, H.
Helwig, L.
Hendry, W.
Herman, Solomon.
Herron, B. C.
Hinton, Nich. J.
Holbrook, A.
Holbrook, G. J.
Hogan, James.
†Hoffman, J. H.
Holder, J.
Hunter, J. P.
Hunter, W.
Hutton, S.
Hughes, J. O.
Hurley, C.
†Isham, J. H.
Jackson, O.
Jackson, J. C.
Johnson, D. W.
Johnson, G. W.
Johnson, J. W.
Johnson, Stephen.
Johnson, S.
Jones, W.
Jones, S.
Jones, C. A.
Jones, W. J. W.
Jordan, B.
Kelly, John.
Kelly, L.
Kelly, Peter.
Kenn, Edward.
Kerns, G. A.
Kimble, William.
King, William.
Kirby, Joseph A.
Kirkland, J. T.

Kitzmiller, H.
Koberg, Charles.
Laton, J. N.
Lawless, W.
†Lee, A.
Lewis, M.
Lindsey, S. J.
Love, William.
Lowrey, F. M.
†Lynch, D.
McCarthy, James.
McCulley, W.
McDonald, Thomas.
McGovern, J.
McGuire, J.
McKehan, W.
*McKissick, J. J.
McMahon, C.
McMahon, J. C.
McMahon, Hugh.
McMillan William.
McNabb, A.
McWhorter, J. D.
Mack, Thomas.
Mackin, James.
Mann, Samuel.
Markey, M.
Markham, J.
Maroney, Z. T.
†Martin, J. G.
Melton, Samuel.
Miller, Charles.
Miller, George.
Miller, Thadeus.
Miller, Thomas.
Milton, John.
Minter, William.
Mitchell, George.
Montieth, G. W.

Montieth, M.
Morgan, Francis.
Moses, J.
Myers, Henry.
Napoleon, Louis.
Newton, F. M.
Newton, J. W.
Newton, S. M.
†Nichols, J. P.
O'Brian, J.
O'Hanlon, J.
O"Neill, D. P.
O'Neill, G. W.
O'Shields, J. P.
Oliver, J. P.
Owensby, G.
Owings, Joshua.
Parkinson, J. S.
Parker, J. B.
Parker, William.
Parnill, T. A.
Perry, Samuel H.
Perry, W.
Peterson, N.
Powell, H. B.
Powell, J. J.
Powell, W. B.
Preston, John.
Price, Charles.
Price, David.
Pue, R. P.
Purdie, William E.
Quinlin, Edward.
Ray, M.
Reynolds, D.
Reynolds, W.
†Rodriguez, Francisco.
Robertson, J. A. G.
Robinson, Charles.

* Killed. † Wounded.

Robinson, W.
Rogers, J. P.
Rogers, W.
Rowland, D. P.
Ryan, M.
St. Clair, Albert L.
Sailor, M.
Samms, R. J.
Savell, Thomas S.
†Scales, J. S.
Schwan, Francis.
Seawright, W. L.
Shea, Timothy.
Shipley, G. R.
Short, James.
†Silas, D.
Silas, L.
Silver, S. M.
Simms, Willis R.
Simmons, J.
Simpson, G.
Singer, G.
Smith, Francis.
Smith, James.
Smith, J. S.

Smith, J. T.
Smith, Pharis.
Smith, Thomas.
*Smith, William.
Snipes, R.
South, F.
Spengling, P.
Stansbury, John S.
*Steward, Henry S.
Stone, A.
Stone, J. W.
Stunt, Robert.
Sullivan, Andrew.
Sullivan, John, No. 1.
Sullivan, John, No. 2.
†Talton, M. P.
Taylor, J.
†Telyea, John.
Thomas, George H.
Thornton, ———.
†Tinley, John.
Tompkins, E. A.
Tomlinson, T. M.
†Turner, J. A.
Tyler, Charles.

*Tyson, Richard.
Ussery, D.
Wakefield, ———.
Ware, R.
Watkins, E.
Weaver, John.
†Wells, Emmit.
Wells, W.
Welsh, Daniel.
Whalen, John.
Whiting, James.
Wilkins, John D.
*Wills, A.
†Wills, J. P.
Wills, W.
Williams, Thomas.
Willson, Thomas.
Wilson, J. J.
Wilson, John S.
Wilson, W.
Woodward, J.
Wooten, Joseph.
Worrall, W.
Young, H. L.
Zimmerman, Isaac.

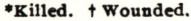

*Killed. † Wounded.

FOURTH MARYLAND ARTILLERY.

(CHESAPEAKE.)

CHAPTER I.

THE Chesapeake Battery was organized by a combination of Maryland volunteers, originally intended for infantry service, under command of Captain Joseph Forest, of St. Mary's County, and Captain William D. Brown, of Baltimore City. The young men composing the battery were from the Eastern and Western counties in about equal proportions, and, as events proved, they were a remarkably fine body of men, and made their mark on more than one desperately fought field. At the time of its organization guns were very difficult to procure, and the consequence was the company was not able to take the field until some weeks after its organization, in the early part of 1861, but they were finally equipped with four pieces of inferior calibre, and sent to Camp Lee for instruction. Here the battery was fully organized by the election of the following officers: Captain, William D. Brown, of Baltimore; First Lieutenant, John E. Plater, of Baltimore; Junior First Lieutenant, Walter S. Chew, of Washington, D. C.; Senior Second Lieutenant, John Grason, of Queen Anne's.

Later on Benjamin G. Roberts, of Queen Anne's, was elected Junior Second Lieutenant, to fill the vacancy occasioned by the death of Lieutenant John Grason, who was killed at Fredericksburg on December 13th, 1862, and Thomas P. La Compte was some time after promoted Junior Second Lieutenant.

At the Camp of Instruction the men rapidly became proficient in the artillery drill, thanks to Martin Harvey and Peter Williams, two young Virginians, who had been detailed from the Richmond Howitzers as instructors, and who remained permanently with the battery, and set an example on the field which the Marylanders were not slow to emulate.

During the Peninsular campaign the battery belonged to the reserve artillery, but was after that attached to Colonel Snowden Andrews' artillery battalion, composed of the Carpenter's Lynchburg, First Maryland and Fourth Maryland (Chesapeake) batteries.

Colonel Andrews won fame at Cedar Run in August, 1862, as he did on many other fields, and so well did the Chesapeake battery acquit itself in this engagement that General Early complimented the men by presenting them with Cushing's regular battery of four ten-pound Parrotts captured in that battle, thus enabling them to discard the old smooth-bores that had prevented the battery from participating more conspicuously in other engagements.

At Warrenton Springs, after the battery had crossed the river at that ford, it became impassable through a sudden storm, thus cutting off their retreat and preventing reinforcements from going to their relief. But so fiercely did the boys fight their guns that time was given to build a bridge, over which they safely recrossed in the very presence of a vastly superior force of the enemy, and then made a forced march by way of Thoroughfare Gap to the second Manassas.

At Bristow's the Chesapeake was actively engaged keeping the enemy in check whilst the immense amount of stores captured at Manassas were being destroyed.

In this action Andrew Egan had his thigh terribly mutilated, and the battery lost a good man, for the poor fellow was rendered a cripple for life. Dad Baker made a narrow escape at the same time, having his clothes partially torn from his body by an exploding shell.

In the midst of the hottest part of the fire, the boys were startled by the sight of Stonewall Jackson, quietly looking on, and evidently much gratified at the execution the battery was doing. Now, there were two things that would always bring a yell from a Confederate soldier, and those were the sight of Jackson or a rabbit. The impulse could not be resisted, and the fire of the battery was stopped and three hearty cheers were given to the grim old soldier. But this was evidently not to his liking, for he instantly ordered the battery to renew its firing, and the way those guns were made to jump was a lesson to the enemy.

But this first day's fight over, the boys sought something refreshing to compensate them in a measure for the danger they had escaped and the severe work they had been compelled to perform ; and even a soldier has his moments of enjoyment, and one of these is a cup of good coffee, something to which the Southern soldier was a stranger for a long period of the war, unless it was captured from the enemy. After a fight, foraging is the first thing in order, and this was not an exceptional occasion. The boys were in luck, and soon a quantity of steaming coffee was being handed around, and that night the camp-fire was enlivened with song and jest at the expense of the enemy.

But these things cannot last forever, for whilst enjoying the agreeable innovation the bugle suddenly sounded the assembly, and the battery was soon thundering away at the enemy in a desperate artillery duel in the night, with nothing to direct their fire but the flash of the opposing guns. Having the advantage of position, the Chesapeake suffered but small loss, whilst, when day broke, the ground where had stood the hostile battery and its supporting infantry was found thickly strewn with dead and wounded men and horses.

And here an incident occurred not so uncommon upon the battle-field as the reader would suppose, that must challenge the admiration of all Christian people. In passing over this ghastly field Lieutenant John Grason, of the Chesapeake, discovered an officer of a New York regiment mortally wounded and dying. This Christian gentleman knelt and prayed with his wounded enemy — not enemy now — whilst the men of the battery stood reverently by until the poor soldier closed his eyes in death.

We next find the Chesapeakes at Harper's Ferry, and there one morning, just as the sun was rising, their Parrotts screamed forth an unexpected surprise to General Miles and the army there in fancied security. Fiercely those guns were worked that day, and one of the last shells fired by the battery cost General Miles his life.

After the surrender of those ten thousand men, the Confederates, under Jackson, were hurried to Sharpsburg, where there was pressing need for their services. A. P. Hill, with his light division, was left at Harper's Ferry to complete the surrender, when he, too, was to follow with all possible dispatch. The reader knows how well Jackson fought that day, and how, happily, in the nick of time, Hill swung his light division into line and saved the army from destruction.

And where were the Chesapeakes? Where were they not on that gory field? First here, then there, those self-same Parrotts, captured at Cedar Run, dealt death and destruction to the enemy, and perhaps never before were those guns so savagely handled. The occasion required that they should be on that dreadful day of the 17th of September.

Shattered and torn by the pounding it had received at the hands of the overwhelming forces of the enemy, the army under General Lee returned to Virginia, after having made the best contested battle it ever did make prior to or subsequently, and the Confederate soldier who fought at Sharpsburg can be proud of the heritage he leaves behind.

After returning to Virginia from the short campaign into Maryland, the Chesapeake moved slowly along the Valley turnpike until Bunker Hill was reached, where it remained for awhile, and crossed the Blue Ridge in November on its way to the Rappahannock in the vicinity of Fredericksburg.

In the fierce engagement at that place on the 13th of December, 1862, the Chesapeake took a prominent part near Hamilton's Crossing, and suffered severe loss. In this battle the lamented Grason fell, as did others equally as brave.

A short time after the battle the battery went into winter quarters in De Jarnette's Woods, in Caroline County, near Bowling Green, where the men had many weeks of much-needed rest.

But spring came at last, and with it came plenty of hard work for the Army of Northern Virginia.

The Federal Army, now under Hooker, occupied a strong position at Chancellorsville. General Lee confronted him with a much inferior army, but he still had Jackson with him, but, alas! it was decreed that it should be for the last time. By a skillful movement Lee, on May 2d, threw Jackson in Hooker's rear and administered to that General a severe blow. Unhappily, that night the great Jackson was fired upon by some of his own men through a mistake, and he died a few days later from the wounds he received.

While these operations were in progress at Chancellorsville, General Early, by skillful manœuvring had detained Sedgwick at Fredericksburg until the 3d, when that General, by a determined advance, forced Early back and carried Marye's Heights, and then proceeded toward Chancellorsville to assist Hooker, who was sorely pressed. But Sedgwick was intercepted at Salem Church by Wilcox, whom General Lee had dispatched for the purpose, and the Federal General suffered a severe defeat.

The Chesapeake battery was attached to Early's command, and therefore was not, properly speaking, engaged at Chancellorsville, although it was rather a continuous line of battle, though in a detached way.

The position occupied by the Chesapeake in this engagement was near Hamilton's Crossing, or nearly upon the same ground occupied by the battery on the 13th of December previous. The accurate firing of the battery attracted much attention, and it did great execution, although it lost heavily itself. Nothing could restrain the enthusiasm of the men. After one of his favorite shots, jumping to the top of the parapet to watch its effect, Tom Carberry had his right leg carried away.

But Dement, close by, was in trouble. His twelve-pound Napoleons were no match for the long-range guns opposed to him, and the Chesapeake was ordered to take his place. It was a position fraught with great danger.

Under cover of their batteries, the Federals crossed the river in great numbers and advanced toward the Confederates. Down to the right was a piece of woods, and in the woods were several batteries. This was unknown to the advancing enemy, who came on with beautiful precision, and not a shot was fired from this woods until they were within short range, when a murderous fire greeted them. To this the Chesapeake contributed its share. The column was staggered, but, recovering, they still pressed on; but human flesh and blood could not withstand that fire, and the column broke. Then General Anderson sent forward his Georgia infantry, and the rout became general, but few of that fated column escaping across the river.

To the left the Confederates were not so successful, and the enemy swept over Marye's Heights and captured several hundred prisoners and a few pieces of the Washington Artillery. This temporary success compelled the Confederate right to fall back some distance, but upon Sedgwick hastily retreating to avoid being crushed between Early, Wilcox and McLaws the artillery advanced and resumed their former positions.

In this engagement the Chesapeake boys worked their guns with their characteristic determination. Many of their comrades had fallen in the first battle upon almost the identical spot they occupied in the second, and it was to avenge Grason, Hopkins, Grahame (dead), and Crowley, Shanahan, Vincent Green, John Green and many others (wounded), that the boys put forth their utmost efforts.

CHAPTER II.

When the Army of Northern Virginia left its position on the Rappahannock in June, 1863, the Chesapeake Artillery was attached to the corps of General Ewell. The Chesapeake did not participate in the battle of Winchester, as there was no occasion requiring their services. Dement's upheld the honor of Maryland upon that occasion and made a bright page in history.

At Gettysburg the Chesapeake was with the gallant Latimer, who was in command of Colonel Andrews' battalion of artillery. By direction of General Edward Johnson, Latimer took position on Benner's Hill, which was directly in front of Cemetery Ridge, a commanding position, crowned by many batteries of the enemy's artillery.

About 4 o'clock Latimer opened fire, and for more than an hour one of the most terrific artillery duels of the war continued. The gallant Captain William D. Brown, of the Chesapeake, was among the first to fall, having both legs shattered, although he survived his dreadful injuries several days. A member of the Chesapeake Artillery who participated in the battle thus describes the terrible ordeal through which the battery passed:

Gettysburg cannot be justly described, as far as our battalion was concerned, which was commanded by the gallant Major Latimer, in the absence of Colonel R. S. Andrews, who had been wounded at Winchester. Benner's Hill was simply a hell infernal. Our position was well calculated to drive confidence from the stoutest heart. We were directly opposed by some of the finest batteries in the regular service of the enemy, which batteries, moreover, held a position to which ours was but a molehill. Our shells ricochetted over them, whilst theirs plunged into the devoted battalion, carrying death and destruction everywhere.

The Chesapeake received the most deadly evidence of that terrible duel. Our gallant Captain, William D. Brown, was the first to fall. Riding to the front of his battery, he enjoined us, for the honor of our native State, to stand manfully to our guns. The words were still upon his lips when he fell, dreadfully mangled by a solid shot. No braver or more unselfish patriot fell upon that blood-soaked field, and none were more beloved by their commands.

There were many deeds of heroism on that field that day, and of these the Chesapeake had its share.

Three of our pieces were silenced, and sadly and with moist eye Sergeant Crowley stood meditatively looking at the wreck around him. Approaching the veteran he pointed, with a trembling voice, to his dead and wounded comrades. There were Doctor Jack Brian, and Daniel Dougherty, and brave little Cusick. They belonged to his detachment. And even while he was deploring their loss, a solid shot struck Thaddeus Parker and literally disemboweled him and killed the two lead horses he was holding.

The fourth detachment was now all that was serviceable of the battery, and it continued to fire. His own piece being disabled, Jacob F. Cook was assigned as No. 2 to Sergeant Phil Brown's detachment, and while inserting a charge in the piece the wheel on the odd number side was hard hit. Sergeant Brown, Smith Warrington, Phil Oldner and Henry Wilson were each severely wounded by this shot. The Sergeant stepped down to Rock Creek, close to our position, bound up his wound, and returned to jack up his gun, put on a spare wheel, and resumed firing. Oldner was suffering at the time from a wound but recently received, and the fresh hurt was more than his system could overcome, and in a short while he was laid in a soldier's grave. And then we lost Lieutenant Ben Roberts and Richard Hardesty, both mortally wounded.

Our loss at Gettysburg was eight killed and eight wounded, and we lost half of our horses. We buried our dead, went into park, repaired damages, and when the retreat began in the direction of the Potomac the Chesapeake was well in the rear.

From Gettysburg to Appomattox the Chesapeake marched and fought, sharing all the vicissitudes of the Army of Northern Virginia.

At Fort Gregg our battery made a most determined defense after all hope had been abandoned. After exhausting our ammunition Lieutenant Chew's gray coat was pressed into service, and we loaded our pieces with such projectiles as could be picked up.

Billy Holtzman, as the columns of Michiganders swarmed over the ramparts, still showed fight. A big fellow seized the boy and seemed intent on distinguishing himself by some sanguinary deed, but a young Lieutenant who divined the brute's intentions, put a stop to it by ordering Holtzman to the rear under a prisoners' guard. Billy couldn't understand why the fellow wanted to wreak summary vengeance upon him until he reached the trench surrounding the ramparts and found it choked with the man's comrades, which he had attributed to the fire of the Chesapeake battery.

Although Pinder was severely wounded in the head, he and Culver fought like tigers at the ramparts. Poor Culver; his young life was sacrificed while fighting with a clubbed rifle, with which he had been doing deadly work, for he was a dead shot, and during intervals of firing by the battery he was busy at the ramparts with his rifle.

ROSTER OF THE FOURTH MARYLAND ARTILLERY.
(CHESAPEAKE.)

OFFICERS.

WILLIAM D. BROWN, *Captain.*
WALTER S. CHEW, *Captain.*
JOHN E. PLATER, *First Lieutenant.*
JOHN GRASON, *Second Lieutenant.*
THOMAS LECOMPTE, *Lieutenant.*
THOMAS LECOMPTE, *First Sergeant.*
ROBERT A. CROWLEY, *Second Sergeant.*
JAMES D. WALL, *Third Sergeant.*
PHILIP H. BROWN, *Fourth Sergeant.*

HENRY C. BUCKMASTER, *Corporal.*
ISAAC J. BLUNT, *Corporal.*
THOMAS A. CARBERRY, *Corporal.*
THOMAS W. MUMMEY, *Corporal.*
JOHN P. HICKEY, *Commissary Sergeant.*
G. B. MCCUBBIN, *Quartermaster-Sergeant.*
DANIEL A. WILKINSON, *Bugler.*
MICHAEL H. BRADY, *Artificer.*
HENRY BAKER, *Veterinarian.*

Privates.

ALSTON, FREDERICK.
ACTON, WASHINGTON.
BROWN, JOHN W.
BARCHUSS, W. W.
BURKE, W. L.
BRIAN, DOCTOR JACK.
CULVER, E. K.
CULVER, WILLIAM.
CUSICK, FREDERICK.
CECIL, JAMES.
CESSLER, HENRY.
CANFIELD, JOHN H.
COVINGTON, ALLEN J.
COTTRELL, EDWARD C.
COOK, JACOB F.
CORRY, H.
DEMPSEY, JOSEPH.
DOUGHERTY, DANIEL.
DAWSON, LAMBDIN T.

DALLAM, CHARLES F.
DEAN, JAMES E.
DEAN, THOMAS.
EMBERT, JOHN.
ENNIS, THOMAS H.
EVERGAU, THOMAS J.
EGAN, ANDREW H.
FAIRBANK, F. M.
FORREST, JOSEPH.
GOLDSBOROUGH, ———.
GRAHAM, ———.
GWYNN, WIZZIE.
GARDENER, JOHN H.
GREEN, VINCENT.
GREEN, JOHN F.
GORE, JOHN W.
GOODHAND, G. W.
GREEN, A.
GRIMES, ROBERT.

HAAS, ISAAC C.
HOPKINS, ALEXANDER.
HARDESTY, RICHARD.
HARVEY, MARTIN.
HILL, JOHN.
HARRISON, P. L.
HARPER, JAMES K.
HOOFF, JOHN J.
HUBER, PAUL.
HOLTZMAN, WILLIAM H. F.
HERMANTROUT, W. F.
IRVIN, JOHN.
JACKSON, THOMAS G.
JONES, ROBERT C.
KIRBY, FRANCIS M.
LUCAS, CHARLES.
LOUD, JOHN J.
LYNCH, CHRISTOPHER G.
LANGLEY, RICHARD E.

Lane, John A.
Lannahan, Thomas.
Maloney James.
Montgomery, John.
Mowbray, John K.
Mason, William H.
McClure, George D.
McCure, Thomas.
McElwee, Andrew J.
Myers, John.
Moore, James T.
Mettee, C.
Maccummins, F.
Oldner, Philip.
Oldson, William.
Pike, Henry.
Poisel, John.
Parker, Thaddeus.
Phillips, George C.
Pratt, James P.
Pinder, William.

Porter, Gustavus.
Peters, Joseph.
Phillips, Samuel W.
Parker, Peter H.
Perry, John G.
Perry, James.
Renshaw, William T.
Richardson, Nicholas T.
Richardson, John D.
Raley, Michael N.
Rice, George.
Russell, Henry.
Randill, J.
Shields, Michael.
Stewart, James P.
Scheesler, Henry.
Shafer, Henry.
Schaefer, William.
Sparks, James S.
Spencer, Bendenfield.
Smith, George A.

Smith, William.
Shannahan, John H. K.
Suit, Norris N.
Stewart, Francis M.
Stansbury, Edward.
Trigger, John.
Tarbutton, William.
Toy, Thomas B.
Tinges, Charles S.
Triggoe, C. P.
Wilson, William.
Willson, James Henry.
Williams, Peter.
Warrington, Lewis.
Warrington, Smith.
Williams, William M.
Webb, Richard Watson.
Young, Benjamin.
Yates, W. F.

KILLED AND WOUNDED AS FAR AS ASCERTAINED.

CEDAR MOUNTAIN.
Private John Shanahan, wounded.

SECOND MANASSAS.
Private Henry Baker, wounded.
Private Andrew Egan, wounded.
Private Frederick Cusick, wounded.

FREDERICKSBURG.
(December 13, 1862.—May 3, 1863.)

Lieutenant John Grason, killed.
Corporal Alexander Hopkins, killed.
Private ——— Grahame, killed.
Sergeant Robert Crowley, wounded.
Corporal Thomas Carberry, wounded.
Private Philip Oldner, wounded.
Private Thomas Toy, wounded.
Private James Stewart, wounded.
Private John Shanahan, wounded.
Private John Green, wounded.
Private Vincent Green, wounded.
Private Richard E. Langley, wounded.

GETTYSBURG.
Captain William D. Brown, killed.
Lieutenant Benjamin Roberts, killed.
Corporal Daniel Dougherty, killed.
Private Doctor Jack Brian, killed.
Private Frederick Cusick, killed.
Private Thaddeus Parker, killed.
Private Philip Oldner, killed.
Private Richard Hardesty, killed.
Sergeant Philip Brown, wounded.
Sergeant Thomas LeCopmte, wounded.
Sergeant James Wall, wounded.
Private Henry Wilson, wounded.
Private Smith Warrington, wounded.
Private James Green, wounded.
Private Henry Parker, wounded.
Private Nich. Richardson, wounded.

FORT GREGG.
Corporal William Pinder, wounded.
Private William Culver, killed.

DEATHS IN HOSPITAL.
Private Edward Stansbury.
Private John Poisal.

ACCIDENTAL.
Private Robert C. Jones, lost an arm at Heathsville, Northumberland County, Virginia.

MARYLANDERS IN THE CONFEDERATE SERVICE.

THE number of Marylanders who were in the service of the Confederate States cannot be accurately determined. General Trimble, who gave attention to the subject, estimated them at twenty thousand.

It is certain that they were represented in every branch of the service on land and sea and in every army. It was impossible to find any considerable organization in which there were no Marylanders.

The distinctive Maryland regiments and battalions only represent a portion of the soldiers who came from Maryland.

Many examples could be given to show that the Marylanders were contented to be in the service, even if not in a State organization — and sometimes whole companies of Marylanders were mustered into other State regiments.

It is a matter of State pride to know that wherever they were they were noted for bravery in action and devotion to duty, which has been always acknowledged by their commanding officers.

The best example of what is said above can be drawn from the records of the Society of the Army and Navy of the Confederate States in the State of Maryland, from which is taken the following list of Marylanders who were not attached to any of the Maryland organizations, and whose names, therefore, do not appear in any of the rosters of them, except in some instances of promotion from the First Maryland Infantry or other commands, and it is taken *only from the roll of the members of the Society*. This list could, of course, be largely increased were other like sources of information available. This list does not embrace the names of those officers who resigned from the United States Army and Navy, and being confined to members of the Society it cannot embrace the names of the many, living and dead, who were not members of that Society:

JOHN F. ALVEY, Major General Echols' Brigade, Department of West Virginia.
GEORGE W. ALEXANDER, Colonel and Assistant Adjutant-General.
WILLIAM G. ATKINSON, Lieutenant Engineer Corps, Army of Northern Virginia.
JAMES ARMOUR, Lieutenant Louisiana Infantry.
J. T. M. BARNES, Major Artillery, Trans-Mississippi Department.
MEYER BLOCK, Private, Border Guards, Hughes' Brigade, Price's Army.
DANIEL A. BOONE, Private, Ashby's Cavalry.
W. JUDSON BROWN, Lieutenant, Poague's Artillery, Army of Northern Virginia.
JOHN L. BRISCOE, Captain and Assistant Quartermaster, Mahone's Division.

E. Sinclair Beall, Sergeant-Major, Otey (Virginia) Battery, Army of Northern Virginia.
T. F. Billopp, Captain, Twenty-Ninth Georgia Infantry.
William Baird, Assistant Adjutant-General.
William H. Baym, Sergeant, Brook Artillery.
Jacob S. Barnes, Private, Seventh Virginia Cavalry.
Luke Tiernan Brien, Colonel, Staff of General W. H. F. Lee.
James Breathed, Major, Steuart's Horse Artillery.
Henry Bowling, Major, Fitz Lee's Staff.
Thomas F. Bowie, Major, Fitz Lee's staff.
William Brengle, Surgeon, Confederate States Army.
———— Burroughs, Lieutenant, Moody's Battery, Army of Northern Virginia.
Frederick M. Colston, Captain of Artillery on Ordnance Duty, Assistant to Chief Ordnance Officer, Army of Northern Virginia.
Alexander G. Cary, Sergeant, Forty-third Virginia Cavalry.
Wilson M. Cary, Captain and Assistant to Chief Quartermaster, Army of Northern Virginia.
Harper Carroll, Lieutenant, Staff of General Ewell.
J. Lyle Clark, Captain of Company B, Twenty-first Virginia Infantry. Lieutenant-Colonel Thirtieth Virginia Battalion of Sharpshooters.
James Cooper, Sergeant of Company C, First Regiment of Engineer Troops, Army of Northern Virginia.
William H. Cole, Surgeon, Hood's Division, Army of Northern Virginia.
Captain George W. Chiswell.
James Carey, Signal Corps.
Lieutenant E. J. Chiswell.
Lieutenant J. R. Crown.
T. O. Chesney, Major, General Elzey's Staff.
Frank Creager, Lieutenant, Texas Infantry.
Vincent Camalier, Captain, Signal Corps.
Charles Cawood, Signal Corps.
Richard Contee, Major, General Elzey's Staff.
P. G. DeGournay, Lieutenant-Colonel of Artillery, General Gardner's Command.
James W. Denny, Private, Thirty-ninth Virginia Cavalry.
H. Kyd Douglass, Colonel and Assistant Adjutant-General, Stonewall Brigade.
Major T. Sturgiss Davis.
Lieutenant Nicholas Dorsey.
Colonel Caleb Dorsey, Missouri Regiment.
John W. Dorsey, Missouri Regiment.
Thomas B. Dorsey, Missouri Regiment.
Eli Duvall, Signal Corps.

John J. Davis, Surgeon, Sixth North Carolina Infantry.
J. W. Drew, Captain, General Imboden's Command.
Richard Emory, Assistant Surgeon, Army of Northern Virginia.
James Emack, Lieutenant of Company F, Seventh North Carolina Infantry.
John Ellicott, Major, Nitre and Mining Bureau.
William H. Fitzgerald, Master's Mate, Confederate States Navy.
Elias Griswold, Major and Assistant Adjutant-General, Staff A, General S. Cooper.
Henry M. Graves, Lieutenant, Engineer Corps, Richmond Defenses.
William B. Graves, Sergeant, Poague's Battalion Artillery.
R. E. Haslett, Captain, Wise's Legion.
A. M. Hawkins, Major of Thirteenth Mississippi Infantry.
Robert W. Harper, Colonel, Army of Tennessee.
James Hooper, Adjutant, First Arkansas Rifles.
George Harrison, Signal Corps.
Thomas A. Jones, Signal Corps.
Meredith Johnson, Surgeon, Confederate States Army.
William C. Kloman, Surgeon, Confederate States Army.
J. Mortimer Kilgore, Captain, Army of Northern Virginia.
R. W. Keyworth, Major, General Van Dorn's Staff.
Thomas W. Hall, Jr., Major and Inspector-General, Department of Mississippi.
A. B. Hardcastle, Colonel, Lowery's Brigade, Army of Tennessee.
J. Monroe Heiskell, Captain, Walker's Battalion.
N. S. Hill, Major and Commissary, Army of Northern Virginia.
R. Curzon Hoffman, Captain, Twenty-first Virginia Infantry.
J. McHenry Howard, Lieutenant on the Staff of General W. H. Stevens.
McHenry Howard, Lieutenant and A. D. C., Stonewall Brigade.
W. Carvell Hall, Major and Assistant Adjutant-General, General Trimble's Staff.
George T. Hollyday of William, Private, Thirty-fifth Virginia Cavalry.
E. Lloyd Howard, Surgeon, Army of Northern Virginia.
A. M. Haskell, Major on General Van Dorn's Staff.
Thomas A. Healy, Surgeon, South Carolina Troops.
Thomas Handy, Lieutenant, Crescent Heavy Artillery.
Henry Hagan, Courier, Staff of General J. E. Steuart.
Charles S. Hill, Lieutenant of Company A, First Virginia Infantry.
Charles Konne, General D. H. Hill's Staff.
Osmun Latrobe, Lieutenant-Colonel and Assistant Adjutant-General, Longstreet's Corps, Army of Northern Virginia.
Otho S. Lee, Sergeant-Major, Steuart's Horse Artillery.
James W. Lyon, Major and Commissary Sergeant.
G. T. Lewis, Surgeon, P. A. C. S.

George Douglass Mercer, Major and Quartermaster, Army of Northern Virginia.
Charles G. W. Macgill, Surgeon, Second Virginia Infantry.
Thomas B. Mackall, Lieutenant, Aide-de-Camp, Staff of General W. W. Mackall.
Charles Marshall, Lieutenant-Colonel and Assistant Adjutant-General, Staff of General R. E. Lee.
Frank Markoe, Lieutenant, General John B. Gordon's Staff.
William McBlair, Master's Mate, Confederate States Navy.
John McWilliams, Sergeant-Major, Thirteenth Virginia Infantry.
Mason Morfit, Major and Quartermaster.
Stirling Murray, Sergeant, Steuart's Horse Artillery.
Charles M. Morfit, Surgeon, Confederate States Navy.
John G. Mason, Surgeon, Confederate States Navy.
I. Stephen Mason, Signal Corps.
William Montgomery, Surgeon, Forty-eighth North Carolina Infantry.
Thomas F. Maney, Surgeon, First Virginia Infantry.
——— McGraves, Major on General Pegram's Staff.
William Norris, Colonel and Chief of Signal Corps, Army of Northern Virginia.
John R. Offalt, Company E, First Virginia Infantry.
George W. Offalt, Company E, First Virginia Infantry.
Z. A. Offalt, Company E, First Virginia Infantry.
David E. Pendleton, Private, Company A, Seventh Virginia Cavalry.
Neilson Poe, Jr., Engineer Corps, Confederate States Army.
William Poole, Major, General Hardie's Staff.
Dennis Poole, General Hardie's Army.
Alfred Price, Captain, Fourth Alabama Infantry.
John E. O'Donnell, Lieutenant, Baltimore Heavy Artillery.
Charles Strahan, Lieutenant on the Staff of General John S. Preston.
John R. Strafford, Assistant Quartermaster, Forty-eighth North Carolina Infantry.
Charles K. Shannon, Captain of Company E, First Virginia Infantry.
William F. Steuart, Surgeon, Confederate States Army.
Samuel D. Smith, Captain, Staff of General Magruder.
D. Bowley Thompson, Captain and Assistant Adjutant-General, Staff of General Wharton.
C. G. Thompson, Captain, Ordnance Department.
W. R. Sinclair, Surgeon, Confederate States Army.
J. Thomas Scharf, Master's Mate, Confederate States Navy.
William E. Stewart, Major, Fifteenth Arkansas Infantry.
Clement Sullivane, Lieutenant-Colonel, Staff of General G. W. C. Lee.
W. Stuart Symington, Major, Staff of General George E. Pickett.
Thomas A. Symington, Captain and Assistant Adjutant-General, General Dearing's Staff.
A. G. Simon, Major, Staff of General Stirling Price.

WILLIAM SCHLEY, Signal Corps, Army of Northern Virginia.

M. M. RASIN, Lieutenant, Moody's Battery, Army of Northern Virginia.

FENWICK ROBERTSON, Assistant Surgeon, Confederate States Army.

JOHN DONNELL SMITH, Captain Battery A, Alexander's Battalion of Artillery, Army of Northern Virginia.

AUGUSTINE J. SMITH, Captain and Assistant Commissary, Department of Eastern Tennessee.

OSWALD TILGHMAN, Captain of Artillery.

G. C. TALIAFERRO, Adjutant, Ninth Virginia Cavalry.

W. T. G. WOODWARD, Secret Service.

FRANK X. WARD, Captain on the Staff of General Elzey.

WILLIAM BOWLEY WILSON, Private, Company K, First Virginia Cavalry.

D. GIRAUD WRIGHT, Lieutenant, Company D, Virginia Regulars.

J. WILLIAM WALLS, Surgeon Stonewall Brigade.

SAMUEL W. WHEELER, Private Company B, Nineteenth Battalion, Heavy Artillery, Army of Northern Virginia.

FRANK A. ZIMMERMAN, Lieutenant Company B, Ninth Virginia Infantry.

THE MARYLAND LINE CONFEDERATE SOLDIERS' HOME.
PIKESVILLE, MD.

MARYLAND LINE CONFEDERATE SOLDIERS' HOME.

THAT there was a division of sentiment in Maryland, upon the causes which led to the war between the States, no one will deny ; yet no intelligent observer, or one at all familiar with the facts, will refuse to admit that the large preponderance of public opinion was heartily in favor of the cause of the South.

Maryland, by reason of her geographical location, close commercial interests with the tobacco and cotton-raising States, similarity of institutions and intimate social and natural relations with the people south of the Potomac, was emphatically a Southern State. Of the same ancestry, prevailing customs and habits, and kept closely welded by intermarriage, with the same views of the character of the Federal Union, and the rights and privileges which were reserved to the States under the Constitution of 1789, it would have been unnatural to have found her people engaging in a fratricidal war of desolation and invasion of those communities, to which she was so bound by historic and sympathetic ties.

The conservatism of her people was pronounced, but the right of self-government had, on this Continent, no firmer supporters and defenders than in Maryland. It did not take long to make manifest the temper and intentions of her people ; and, therefore, by the strong arm of power, and by a most vigorous military despotism, were her legislative bodies dissolved, her leading citizens jailed and sent to dungeons, and the condition of the State reduced to that of an alien principality held by armed forces. The blow fell no less quickly than it did firmly ; but still it did not prevent the young men of the Commonwealth from forsaking the comforts of their homes, and singly, or in small parties, crossing the Potomac and enlisting in the armies of the Confederacy, to battle for the rights of their State, even though she was manacled and helpless. Unable to speak for herself through the regularly appointed methods, the sovereignty of Maryland found representation in the strong arms of the fifteen thousand or more — the flower of her youth, who gave their service to the South, and in the anxious hearts of those who remained at home, and nightly sent up their blessings and prayers for the absent ones, while their daily care was to mercifully assist the unfortunate who, in prison and hospital, were visited and ministered unto, as far as the sufferance of those in power would permit.

The devotion of the women of Maryland, and the insult and indignity to which they were subjected in these merciful ministrations, are of the past ; but no less will the truth of history chronicle their deeds and the oppression under which her people lived during the dreary years of the war. Allusion is only made to these circumstances to explain why it is that we have here in Maryland — a State that was not "out of the Union"— a home for Confederate soldiers. Her sons were in the Confederacy; the hearts of her women were there, and the great body of her people were in sympathy with the cause of constitutional government, with regard to the reserved rights of the States, according to the spirit of the Constitution, and opposed to the action of the Federal authorities in the purpose to coerce the States of the South, who were asserting this right.

As a border community in a sectional quarrel, this feeling could not be unanimous. There were some who were loyal to the Union, and this minority, obtaining control by reason of the bayonets of the Federal power, gave the weight of State authority to their claims, and we find Maryland regiments and Maryland batteries (Maryland at least in name,) responding to the call of the Federal President. The muster rolls of these organizations, in the archives of the State, are not conclusive as evidencing the true feeling of her people. It is conceded that there were those who honestly supported the National authority, and the brilliant record of Maryland soldiers who " wore the blue " is cherished and prized as the common glory of the State, by none more dearly than those of her sons who " wore the gray," and followed the banners of the Confederacy, but they do not admit that the former were the exponents of the great heart of Maryland.

As in the days of the Stuarts, the hearts of the loyalists were " o'er the water with Charlie," so was it in Maryland. Her body bound and shackled, her heart was unchained, and her sympathies were with the followers of Lee and Jackson, beyond the Potomac.

The representation of Maryland in the Southern armies has been variously estimated—there are no positive data to determine the fact. They were found scattered throughout the entire army, in almost every organization and command. This will be understood when it is remembered that only as individuals they could make their way through the lines, and make good their passage to the Confederacy. Many in this way attached themselves to the first Confederate command they met; others sought out old friends, or, perhaps, family connections, and enlisted in the same command with their relatives or friends. A prominent officer, after inspection of the records of the office of the Adjutant-General of the Army in Richmond, estimated that there were twenty thousand Marylanders in the service of the Confederate States. The organizations officially recognized as from Maryland were as follows: First Maryland Infantry, Second Maryland Infantry, First Maryland Cavalry, Second Maryland Cavalry, First Maryland Artillery (Maryland), Second Maryland Artillery (Baltimore Light), Third Maryland Artillery and Fourth Maryland Artillery (Chesapeake).

The above composed the Maryland Line, and were recognized as such by the

APPOMATTOX.

Confederate authorities. It is not within the province of this paper to give the brilliant history and record of these organizations. With the exception of the Third Maryland Artillery, which served with distinguished honor with the army in the West, it is enough to say the history of the Army of Northern Virginia cannot be written without giving the history of these commands of the Maryland Line. From the early days of the war — from Manassas to Malvern Hill, from the Valley to Gettysburg, from the defense of Petersburg to Appomattox — was their valor and efficiency conspicuous. The general orders and reports of the various commanders under whom they served — Johnston, Jackson, Ewell, Stuart, Fitz Lee, Hampton, and the illustrious General Robert E. Lee — are uniform in their praise as soldiers, worthy successors of the " Maccaronies," who, under Smallwood and Gist, on Long Island, held back the British advance and made such heroic sacrifices, while Washington was enabled to withdraw in safety, or of the Continentals, who, with DeKalb at Camden, preserved the honor of the American arms, or who, under Williams and Howard, made possible the after successes of Greene in the Southern campaign.

From the beginning at Harper's Ferry, in 1861, to the end at Appomattox, in 1865, they maintained the same high character and bearing, and the record of their deeds, the reputation of their commanders — of Elzey, Steuart, Johnson, Herbert, Ridgely Brown, Gilmor, Andrews and William Brown — are held in veneration and affection by all familiar with the military history of the Confederacy, and have made for Maryland a name equal, if not above other names, in the admiration of a heroic people.

The State of Maryland can well be proud of its sons of the Maryland Line of 1861-1865, as it has always been of their forefathers of the Revolution and the subsequent wars of 1812 and with Mexico ; and it is but fitting that this feeling of satisfaction should take sensible form in providing for its survivors who, outliving the times of their heroic effort, have at last been made to fall victims of the relentless advances of increasing years and dire poverty, or, perhaps, disabled by wounds received in battle. An honorable, brave people are never forgetful of their veteran soldiers, and the fact that the Federal Government has so generously provided for those of her sons who wore the blue, but makes more pronounced the obligation of our Mother State to care for their unfortunate brothers who, in ragged gray jackets, represented her in the Confederacy, and, to their honor be it said, in this pious purpose the Union citizens of the State have been willing and earnest in their co-operation.

Sad, indeed, was the heart of the poor Maryland Confederate, after the days of Appomattox — the cause to which he had devoted his best years, and for which he had so freely risked his life and shed his blood, had failed — as the tearful good-bye was spoken to his associates, memories of the comrades who had yielded up their lives during the great struggle, came to him ; they happily needed no parole to give them immunity or protection. In the great beyond they had found a rest and a home. The toils of the march, the privations of the camp, and the dangers of the field were over, and with a mighty wail of suffering anguish, the heart of the Confederacy was broken. Like Marius, he gazed on the ruins, as it were alone ; for whither should he now turn ? There was a mockery in the very terms of his parole —" permission to return to his home " ; where was that home ? The vindictive feeling that was then ascendant denied him refuge in the land of his birth, and he was forced to patiently await the ebb of passion and the return of reason. This change was not long coming, and the joys of meeting with loved ones, soothed his wounded heart and gave him fresh courage to meet the stern realities of the hour. Not given over to futile repinings, or idle sorrow, he realized the duties of the present, while not forgetful of the glories of the past, and earnestly engaged in the battle for livelihood — no less fierce than that through which he had recently passed. As his position became assured, although the cares which pressed upon him were severe and trying, he found time to keep up the association of comrades, and determined on an effort to keep fresh the memories of the dead, to assist the disabled and the destitute, and to preserve for posterity a true account of the great struggle and the motives which led him to take up arms. Submitting to the arbitrament of the sword, he appealed to the impartial judgment of the future to justify his past.

The Association of the Maryland Line was formed in 1880, with these objects in view. There was already in existence the Society of the Army and Navy of the Confederate States in Maryland, which was organized in 1871, shortly after the death of General Lee, and it was not proposed to encroach upon, or to displace this organization, but still to cherish it as the parent society, or center of Confederate influence and work. Under the direction of General Bradley T. Johnson, and largely aided by his material assistance, the Association of the Maryland Line made up a fairly complete roster of the various Maryland organizations. In this work they were assisted by the courtesy of the War Department, in permitting access to such muster rolls as were found in the records of the Adjutant-General's office at Richmond, and which were removed to Washington at the close of the war.

Under the auspices of the Society of the Army and Navy of the Confederate States in Maryland, was held in Baltimore in 1885, a most successful bazaar, the proceeds of which, some $31,000, were being devoted to the care of indigent Confederates and the burial of the dead. Through the medium of this fund, and the contributions of generous friends, the duty of ministering to the wants of the unfortunate was faithfully performed, but as the years rolled on it became painfully apparent that the means at hand were not equal to the emergency, and that the applications for assistance were far beyond the ability to meet. It was soon developed that a number of these gallant old soldiers were finding refuge in the almshouses of the State, and not a few instances came to light of the burial of dead in the unhallowed graves of potters' fields. After careful consideration, and appropriate methods for engaging public attention, it was suggested to make an attempt to raise an amount of money sufficient to build a cottage at the Richmond (Virginia) Home to which these destitute veterans could be sent, and to appeal to the General Assembly for proper financial or other aid. This proposition was earnestly canvassed, but after mature deliberation, it was determined to make an effort to establish a soldiers' home in Maryland, and to ask that the property known as the Pikesville Arsenal be devoted to that purpose. To this memorial the General Assembly gave ready ear and took prompt affirmative action, and in February, 1888, the above mentioned property was given by the State to the Association of the Maryland Line, for the purpose indicated, and an appropriation of $5,000 per annum was at the same time voted for the repair of the property and maintenance of the home. This property was singularly adapted to the purpose, by reason of the character of the buildings and convenience of location. The ravages of time and abandonment had, however, sadly marred its fair proportions, and large expenditures were necessary for its rehabiliment. In this connection, it may be interesting to give the history of the establishment of this post, outlining the purposes sought to be accomplished by its location, etc. The following report by Lieutenant Baden, dated United States Arsenal, May 23, 1823, is in the possession of the Home, having been furnished by the War Department in connection with a plat of the property, shortly after the transfer of the same by the State of Maryland to the Association of the Maryland Line :

I will here endeavor to develop in as clear and concise a manner as possible, what I conceive to have been the object of the Government in the erection of this establishment, and its capacity to fulfill the purposes for which it was constructed :

First. It was clearly perceived at the commencement of the late war with Great Britain that our great commercial cities on this seaboard would be proper objects of attack by the enemy, and in many instances would be greatly exposed. Baltimore appears to have been particularly chosen as an object of attack, and from the great extent of the waters of the Chesapeake and the rich and fertile country adjoining, afforded great facility and additional inducement for the enemy to push their operations in that quarter, and the events of that crisis show, from the great deficiency in our military establishment, especially in the Department of Military Supplies, that it was for a length of time before the progress of the enemy could be checked or arrested ; and independent of the causes which have existed, it is believed that in a similar encounter the enemy would renew his design, and as military positions are chosen for general and particular purposes in relation to definite objects, it was found that Baltimore became the natural point for the concentration of the military forces for ulterior operations, and it was determined by the Government to erect an arsenal and depot somewhere in the rear of that city, to afford the facility of supplies to the forces operating in the immediate vicinity, as well as those permanent military posts constructed for the defense of this section of our maritime frontier. In the selection of the site for this establishment, two things presented themselves — the topography of the country, and the means that an enemy might have in operating upon it, and it is believed that on a proper view of the country adjacent to Baltimore, the site for this depot was as judiciously chosen as the nature of the case would admit of ; secondly, it will be seen from the extent of these works (the drawings of which accompany this report,) that they combine in themselves the advantage of an arsenal of construction, as well as a depot of military supplies, and can usefully employ one or two companies of citizens, as the nature of the service may require.

This arsenal is situated on the Reisterstown turnpike road, eight miles from the City of Baltimore. This road is smooth and firm at all seasons of the year, and affords the best land transportation ; it extends back north and northwest of the arsenal and passes through the upper counties of Maryland and into the productive counties of Pennsylvania, and is a great land thoroughfare to Baltimore, thereby presenting to the establishment the advantage of procuring land transportation in time of war with ease and on advantageous terms. The general aspect of the country around the arsenal is remarkable for its fertility of soil, gently rolling and well wooded, and is watered by Jones' and Gwynn's Falls, whose head waters take their rise in the vicinity of the post and present on both sides a number of springs of pure water. The situation is very healthy, the whole country around is remarkable for its salubrious air, and but few local diseases prevail ; these advantages render it a proper position for an encampment of troops and of military supplies. The means by which stores are transported from this arsenal to the permanent posts intended to be supplied from it, are by hauling them to Baltimore, or to the head of the navigable waters of the Severn River and from thence by water. The navigation of the Patapsco is obstructed by ice a part of the months of December and January, but no longer than from twenty to thirty days ; unless the season is unusually cold, it is kept open for commercial advantages. The navigation of the Severn is not usually obstructed by ice, hence this route can be resorted to in case the first fails, and in the event of both these routes being obstructed by the ice, the posts for the interior defense can be supplied by land transportation at short notice, and the fortifications for exterior defense can be readily supplied by taking the stores to Annapolis, where the navigation is scarcely ever known to be closed by ice, and from thence shipped. The distance of this arsenal from Baltimore is eight miles; to Fort McHenry, eleven miles ; to the head of the navigable waters of the Severn River, eighteen to twenty miles, and to Fort Severn and Annapolis, thirty-five miles. The roads are firm and passable at all seasons of the year. The posts on the interior line of defense can be supplied with stores at all times : the nearest to the arsenal, three and a half hours or four hours : the most remote, from about eighteen to twenty-four hours. The fortifications on the exterior line of defense can be supplied at all seasons of the year within from thirty-six to forty-eight hours. Annexed is a sketch showing the relative position of the arsenal to the principal cities, towns and water courses in the vicinity, and also the roads to and from the arsenal.

N. BADEN,
First Lieutenant on Ordnance Duty.

Shortly after, or during the late war, the arsenal was abandoned as a military post, and in 1880, the Federal Government relinquished the same to the State of Maryland. The commandant in 1860, just preceding the commencement of the war, was that distinguished soldier, Major (afterwards Lieutenant-General) Huger. The State, after taking possession of the property, made no practical use of it; in fact, it was an item of expense for several years, by reason of the salary of a custodian. No repairs had been placed on the property for a period of some twenty years, and the condition at the time of the transfer to the care of the Maryland Line was little short of that of a ruin. Work was at once commenced to rescue it from this sad plight in April, 1888, and on June 27, in the same year, had so far progressed as to admit of the formal opening and dedication. Appropriate exercises were held, with a large attendance of citizens from Baltimore and the neighboring country. Addresses were made by Hon. George William Brown, who presided; General A. H. Colquitt, United States Senator from Georgia; General Charles E. Hooker, member of Congress from Mississippi; Hon. Ferd. C. Latrobe, Mayor of Baltimore City; Hon. C. Ridgely Goodwin, State Senator from Baltimore City; General Bradley T. Johnson, and others. Every year since, reunions and like celebrations have taken place, which have been frequently graced by the attendance of distinguished Confederates, many of whom have, since the war, been prominent in the national councils of the country.

The administration of the Home rests with the board of governors of the Association of the Maryland Line, and is under the immediate supervision of a board of managers, who are largely aided in their duties by the labors of a board of visitors, which is made up of well-known ladies, who give the benefit of their counsel and are untiring in their efforts in caring for the sick and ministering to their wants. The command of the Home is intrusted to a superintendent, Mr. W. H. Pope, a gallant soldier of the Maryland Line, who, with his devoted wife, have faithfully given their entire services to the institution.

It was determined from the first to make the institution in fact, what it was in name — a home for those who sought its sheltering care, and this view was held in the furnishing of the rooms, and the rules enacted for the government of the inmates. These last have been framed so as to insure the least restraint possible with the maintenance of proper discipline and decorum. The separate buildings have been named after distinguished Maryland Confederate soldiers or sailors, and the rooms have been furnished as memorials by the friends or relations of some loved one who gave his life for the cause, or who was conspicuous for his gallantry or devotion. These rooms have been furnished in a substantial manner, with many of the comforts and elegancies found in private homes, and at an estimated cost of ten thousand dollars, which expense has been defrayed by the generous friends undertaking this important and interesting feature. As a result, the management have been relieved almost entirely of the great expense incident to the furnishing of the Home, and their means made available for the necessary repairs of the property and the purchase of proper equipment and supplies required by an institution of this character.

The State has continued to make increased appropriations, which, supplemented by generous private contributions, both in money and material, have enabled the management to maintain the high standard of comfort originally had in view, and at the same time there has been due regard to proper economy.

The total admissions, from the opening in June, 1888, to October 1, 1898, a period of over ten years, have been 235. Of this number 70 have died. The number borne on the roster in October, 1898, was 111.

The medical administration is in the hands of the surgeon, Dr. W. P. E. Wyse, who daily visits the Home and is most attentive to the wants of the inmates.

The library is supplied with many valuable and interesting books and periodicals, the gift of friends, and the newspapers of the States regularly mail their issues without charge.

A cordial invitation is extended to the public to visit the institution.

Here will be found a noble charity, creditable to the honor of our State and the public spirit of our citizens. It is a comfort to the old veterans, who feel that if adversity proves too strong for them in their declining years, a haven of rest is here provided, to which they may retire and find refuge, and, at the same time, lose none of their self-respect, nor suffer in the estimation of those whose experience in life is more fortunate ; and it is a standing illustration to the young that our loved Commonwealth reveres manliness and courage, and is proud of the military record of the past and not unmindful of its heroes in their old age.

THE COURT — LOOKING NORTH.

THE COURT — LOOKING EAST.

DESCRIPTION OF MEMORIAL AND OTHER ROOMS IN THE RESPECTIVE BUILDINGS.

1. TRIMBLE BUILDING.
2. BUCHANAN BUILDING.
3. LITTLE BUILDING.
4. TILGHMAN BUILDING.
5. ARCHER BUILDING.
6. SEMMES BUILDING.
7. ELZEY BUILDING.
8. WINDER BUILDING.
9. MACKALL BUILDING.
10. JACKSON BUILDING.

THE MAJOR-GENERAL ISAAC R. TRIMBLE BUILDING contains the relic hall, also a bathroom, and the following memorial rooms: Captain R. B. Buck, Frank H. Sanderson, First Maryland Artillery, Zollinger and Colonel Harry Gilmor.

General Trimble was born May 15, 1802. Cadet at West Point, 1818; graduated, 1822; resigned, 1832; entered the Confederate service May, 1861, and appointed Colonel of Engineers; and September 3, 1861, ordered to command of river batteries at Evansport; November 13, 1861, relieved from duty at Evansport, and assigned November 16, 1861, to command of Third Brigade, Second Division, Army of Northern Virginia; November 22, 1861, assigned to command of Fourth Brigade, Second Division, Army of Northern Virginia; October 26, 1862, recommended by General Lee to be promoted to Major General to command Jackson's Division; January 19, 1863, promoted to Major-General; May 28, 1863, assigned to command of Shenandoah Valley; engaged at Cold Harbor, Gaines' Mill, Malvern Hill, Westover, Winchester (1863), Port Republic, Cross Keys, Slaughter Mountain, Cedar Run, Hazel River and capture of Manassas Junction, August 26. 1862, and Gettysburg. At Cross Keys, General Ewell in his report says: "Trimble's Brigade had the brunt of action and is entitled to most thanks." August 26, 1862, General Trimble, with a force of five hundred men, was voluntarily detached from Jackson's army, and, in co-operation with a portion of Stuart's cavalry, captured a vast quantity of quartermaster's commissary and ordnance stores at Manassas Junction, which was then far in the rear of the Federal Army. His loss was but fifteen men wounded, and the capture amounted to eight guns and three hundred prisoners, besides the immense stores. General Trimble was twice severely wounded — once at the second battle of Manassas, and at Gettysburg, where he was taken prisoner. At Gettysburg he commanded Major-General Pender's Division.

MEMORIAL ROOM TO CAPTAIN RICHARD B. BUCK.—This room is furnished in oak with four beds, dressing case, wardrobes, tables, rockers. woven wire springs, and hair mattresses for the beds. A beautiful china toilet set, a rich drugget and rugs, also lace curtains at the windows ; furnished by Mrs. R. B. Buck.

MEMORIAL ROOM TO FRANK H. SANDERSON.—In this room a fine picture of this brave and handsome youth hangs on the wall. and underneath is a tablet, which reads thus :

IN MEMORIAM

On the fourth day of July, 1863, after receiving a fatal wound the day previous, at that ever memorable battle of Gettysburg, Frank H. Sanderson yielded up his young life in the cause he loved so well. He enlisted in Captain William H. Murray's Company A, Second Maryland Infantry, August 26, 1862. In September of the same year his command was ordered to Winchester, and under the command of General W. E. Jones, experienced a great deal of very hard service, in all of which Frank H. Sanderson was an active participant.

The room was furnished by his brother, W. Cook Sanderson, of Baltimore City.

FIRST MARYLAND ARTILLERY ROOM.—This was one of the best known and most efficient artillery organizations in the Army of Northern Virginia. The room has been furnished through the liberality of Lieutenant-Colonel R. Snowden Andrews, who was the first captain, and who was succeeded by that gallant soldier, Captain William F. Dement. Captain Andrews was distinguished for his skill and soldierly conduct and bearing. He was promoted to the rank of Lieutenant Colonel of Artillery and was severely wounded at Mechanicsville, Cedar Mountain and Jordan Springs.

ZOLLINGER MEMORIAL ROOM.—In memory of Lieutenant William P. Zollinger and his brother, Jacob E. Zollinger. This room is furnished very handsomely and its wants are always kept supplied by Mrs. Charles A. Oakford, Mrs. William P. Zollinger, and Mrs. W. G. Power.

William P. Zollinger enlisted in the Confederate service, Company H. First Maryland Infantry, June 18. 1861 ; discharged. August. 1862 ; again enlisted in Company A, Second Maryland Infantry. August 20. 1862, and elected Second Lieutenant ; was wounded on the Weldon Railroad, also at Pegram's farm.

Jacob E. Zollinger enlisted August 20. 1862. in Company A, Second Maryland Infantry; was severely wounded at Gettysburg, July, 1863, from effects of which he eventually died.

LIEUTENANT-COLONEL HARRY GILMOR ROOM.—This room was furnished by the survivors of Colonel Gilmor's old command, and is one of the handsomest in the Home.

Colonel Gilmor enlisted in the Confederate service August 31, 1861, as a private in Captain Frank Mason's Company G, Ashby's Regiment of Cavalry; March 27, 1862, was elected Captain; May 7, 1863, was commissioned Major and subsequently Lieutenant-Colonel in command Second Maryland Cavalry.

THE RELIC HALL.—In the relic hall is to be found a most interesting collection of relics, consisting of battle flags and regimental colors, pictures of distinguished Maryland Confederate soldiers and sailors, engravings of battle scenes and incidents, arms and uniforms, making in all one of the most complete collections of Confederate relics extant, and well worthy of inspection and study by those who are interested in these reminders of the glorious past. Among the most valuable of these articles is the camp chair of General Robert E. Lee, used by him in his campaign with the Army of Northern Virginia.

ADMIRAL FRANKLIN BUCHANAN BUILDING.—This building, in memory of that distinguished naval commander, contains four memorial rooms — Jenkins, Gill, Brown and Murray.

Franklin Buchanan was born in Baltimore, Maryland, September 11, 1800; he entered the United States Naval Academy January 28, 1815; became a Lieutenant January 13, 1825; Master Commander September 8, 1841; First Superintendent of the Annapolis Naval Academy 1845; Captain September 14, 1855; in charge of Naval Yard at Washington, 1861; resigned his commission, and on the fifth of September, 1861, entered the Confederate service and was assigned to duty as Chief of Orders and Details; ordered to the command of the Virginia (old Merrimac) February 24, 1862; Flag Officer of the James River squadron, March, 1862; in the battle between the Virginia and Monitor, March 8, 1862, he was seriously wounded; Admiral, August 21, 1862; assigned to the naval force at Mobile June, 1863; wounded and taken prisoner August, 1864, at Mobile Bay.

JENKINS ROOM.—This room was furnished by George C. Jenkins, Esq., in memory of his brother, John Carroll Jenkins, who lost his life October 11, 1861, in his country's cause. This room is in oak, very tastefully furnished with everything comfortable. It contains a very quaint old chimney and fireplace.

J. C. Jenkins was a member of Maryland Guards, which company was in the Twenty-first Virginia Infantry.

George C. Jenkins, who furnished this room, also served the cause faithfully in Company C, Maryland Cavalry.

GILL ROOM.—Furnished by Mr. John Gill, in memory of his brother, Sommerville P. Gill, who was killed at Pegram's Farm, Virginia. He was a member of Company A, Second Maryland Infantry. This room is furnished in cherry, and contains four beds, wire springs, hair mattresses, wardrobe, dressing case, stove, lamp and table. The floor is covered with a large rug, rocking chairs, and all that goes to make a room comfortable. Mr. John Gill was also a Confederate soldier; he served in Company H, First Maryland Infantry, and afterwards in the Signal Corps of the Army of Northern Virginia.

RIDGELY BROWN ROOM.—Was furnished through the efforts of Mrs. John F. Hunter, by subscriptions of money and donations of articles suitable. This room contains four beds, wire springs, hair mattresses, dressing case, wardrobes, and everything to add to the comfort of its occupants. The room is in the memory of the gallant Lieutenant-Colonel Ridgely Brown, of Montgomery County, Maryland, who lost his life on the South Anna, Virginia, June 1, 1864, on the field of battle. He was Lieutenant-Colonel of the First Maryland Cavalry, and was one of Maryland's best and bravest soldiers. His picture adorns the wall of this room; also a copy of the general order published at the time of his death.

Colonel Brown went to Virginia on the first of June, 1861; was Lieutenant in Company K, First Virginia Cavalry; afterwards (in 1862) made Captain of Company A, First Maryland Cavalry, which was the nucleus of that organization, and to which he was promoted Major and subsequently Lieutenant-Colonel commanding.

MURRAY ROOM.—This room is furnished by the Murray Association in memory of their Captain, William H. Murray, of Anne Arundel County, Maryland. He entered the service of the Confederate States June 18, 1861, and was killed at Gettysburg in July, 1863. His picture hangs on the wall; also a picture of his monument at Loudon Park Cemetery. This room is in oak, and contains four beds with woven wire springs and hair mattresses. The floor is covered with a large rug, and the other furniture consists of wardrobes, washstand, dressing case, tables, toilet set and various other articles which enure to the comfort of the members. Captain Murray was a most lovable character, modest and unassuming in disposition, pure and chaste in his conversation, tender and considerate for those under his charge; no one occupied a warmer place in the affections of their men than did this gallant soldier. His soldierly qualities were as marked as was his personal character unblemished. He will ever live in the memory of those who knew him, and their sorrow over his early fall is just as keen today as it was thirty years ago. To their children will his character be handed down as an example worthy of emulation, as a Maryland soldier who reflected the honor of his State and whose private life was bright with Christian virtues.

THE ENTRANCE.

THE SUPERINTENDENT'S HOUSE.

BRIGADIER-GENERAL HENRY LITTLE BUILDING.—This building contains a bathroom and memorial rooms as follows : Virginia, McKim, Baltimore Light Artillery, Little, Colston, Marshall, Stonebraker, Goodwin and Chantilly.

General Little was born in Baltimore, March 19, 1817. His record is as follows :
United States Army.—Second Lieutenant Fifth Infantry, July 1, 1839 ; First Lieutenant Seventh Infantry, April 18, 1845 ; brevet Captain for gallant conduct at Monterey, Mexico, September 23, 1846 ; Captain Seventh Infantry August 20, 1847 ; resigned May 7, 1861.
Confederate States Army.—Colonel and Adjutant-General, staff of General Price, May, 1861 ; Brigadier-General April 16, 1862 ; Brigadier-General in command of Confederate forces in the vicinity of Rienza, on the Mobile and Ohio Railroad, April 22, 1862.

General Henry Little was engaged in the battles of Pea Ridge, or Elkhorn Tavern, Arkansas, March 6-8, 1862 ; killed at battle of Iuka, Mississippi, September 19, 1862, commanding First Division, Army of the West.

In a letter from General Earl Van Dorn to General Beauregard, dated April 27, 1862, he says : " I want Little as Major-General."

General Van Dorn, in his report of the battle of Pea Ridge, or Elkhorn Tavern, says : " To Colonel Henry Little my especial thanks are due for the coolness, skill and devotion with which for two days he and his gallant brigade bore the brunt of the battle."

General S. Price, in his report of the same battle, says : " The brunt of the action fell during the early part of the day upon my right wing, consisting of General Slack's and Colonel Little's brigades ; they pushed forward gallantly against heavy odds and the most stubborn resistance, and were victorious everywhere."

General S. Price, in his report of his retreat from Missouri, says : " Colonel Henry Little, commanding the First Brigade, . . . covered the retreat from beyond Cassville and acted as the rear guard. The Colonel commanding deserves the highest praise for unceasing watchfulness and the good management of his entire command. I heartily commend him to your attention."

General Sterling Price, in his report of the battle of Iuka, says : " It will thus be seen that our success was obtained at the sacrifice of many a brave officer and patriot soldier. Chief among them was Brigadier-General Little, commanding the First Division of this army. Than this brave Marylander no one could have fallen more dear to me, or whose memory should be more fondly cherished by his countrymen. Than him, no more skillful officer, or more devout patriot, has drawn his sword in this war of independence. He died in the day of his greatest usefulness, lamented by his friends, by the brigade of his love, by the division which he so ably commanded, and by the Army of the West, of which he had from the beginning been one of the chief ornaments."

Brigadier-General Louis Herbert, in his report of the same battle, says : " Early in the action, when the main charge had been ordered, Brigadier-General Little was instantly killed by a minnie ball, and the command of the division devolved on the undersigned. The fall of the General was immediately known throughout the lines, but far from creating consternation, panic or confusion, every officer and every soldier seemed to become animated with new determination. The leader whom they had learnd to love and esteem, and in whom they had full confidence, had fallen — the foe who had deprived them of him was in front, and revenge was within their grasp. The First Division of the Army of the West will ever remember and venerate the name of Henry Little."

VIRGINIA ROOM.—The Virginia room was furnished through the efforts of Mrs. Martin B. Brown, by subscriptions, in honor of old Virginia. This is a beautiful room, and contains two beds and is furnished in walnut. The appointments are of the first class. The toilet china is inscribed with the name " Virginia " in gilt.

McKIM ROOM.—Furnished by Mrs. William Reed, in memory of her brother, Robert B. McKim, who was a member of the Rockbridge Artillery. He entered the Confederate service April 20, 1861 ; was engaged in the battles of Manassas, Kernstown and Winchester, where he was killed May 25, 1862, aged eighteen years. The furniture of this room is in oak, with two beds, and is very tastefully furnished.

THE BALTIMORE LIGHT ARTILLERY ROOM.—This room is most tastefully and comfortably furnished by the surviving members of that battery, the Second Maryland Artillery, in memory of their deceased comrades. Its surviving members have been as true to each other in the latter days of peace, as were they in the trying scenes which proved their manhood and courage. They have maintained the memories of the past by forming a social organization, and the furnishing of this memorial room is but one of the fruits of their love and appreciation of the cause for which they so nobly fought, endured privation, and for which so many of their number died.

The Baltimore Light Artillery was one of the best-known batteries in the artillery arm of the Confederate service, and no one organization did more to maintain the honor of our State and her fair fame than did this body of young Marylanders. The battery was formed in the early part of the fall of 1861, and was ordered to report to General J. E. Johnston, then in command of the army at Centreville, Virginia. The intelligence of its commanders— the gallantry and skill with which their guns were handled — soon attracted the attention of all, and from the actions in the Valley, under Jackson, the severe battles around Richmond, to the culmination of their active operations in 1862 at Sharpsburg, their valor and devotion were most conspicuous. After the return to Virginia, the battery was directed to report to General W. E. Jones, in command of the Valley District, who had also under his command the First Maryland Cavalry and the Second Maryland Infantry. From this time on the battery served with the cavalry corps. In this service they added to the high reputation they had already achieved, and no service was too arduous for them to undertake — no danger too great for them to face, and in no instance did they ever prove unworthy of the confidence which was reposed in them by those in whose support they were so frequently called upon to take positions of greatest peril. Under the gallant Brockenborough, Griffin and McNulty, they achieved a fame second to no similar organization.

GENERAL HENRY LITTLE ROOM.—Furnished by Mrs. Little in memory of her husband. This room is handsomely furnished with oak furniture, contains two beds with woven wire springs and hair mattresses. The pillows in this room were made of the feathers from the game which General Little shot during his life-time. A fine picture of the General adorns the wall of the room. There are also portraits of Lee and Jackson, the charge of the First Maryland Infantry, and the prayer in Stonewall Jackson's camp.

MARSHALL ROOM.—In memory of two brothers — Robert I. Taylor Marshall, a member of the Washington Artillery, killed at Beverly's Ford, August 23, 1862, and James Markham Marshall, of the Black Horse Company, of the Fourth Virginia Cavalry, who died for his country September 5, 1862. The room contains oak furniture, and was furnished by their brother, Colonel Charles Marshall, of General Robert E. Lee's staff.

STONEBRAKER ROOM.—This room is substantially furnished by Joseph R. Stonebraker, who was a member of Company C, First Maryland Cavalry, as a memorial to his brother, Edward L. Stonebraker.

GOODWIN ROOM.—Furnished by C. Ridgely Goodwin, Esq., in memory of his brother, Frank Greenwood Goodwin. This room is furnished in oak and is very comfortable.

Frank Greenwood Goodwin, tenth child of Robert Morris Goodwin, of Maryland, was born in Savannah, Georgia, November 13, 1846. He was at school at Chattanooga, Tennessee, early in 1861. In April, 1861, he joined the Oglethorpe Light Infantry, of Savannah, and with that company went to Virginia, under command of Captain Frank Bartow, taking part in the first battle of Manassas (Bull Run). The company became a part of the Eighth Georgia Regiment, G. T. Andrews' Brigade, Hood's Division, Longstreet's Corps. At the battle of Seven Pines he was shot through the arm, went to his home, and within a month returned to his command. Participating in all the battles of the Army of Northern Virginia, Frank Goodwin gave his life to his country at Gettysburg, July 3, 1863, aged seventeen years.

CHANTILLY ROOM.—This is a small hall room, with a single bed, and furnished by Mr. H. F. Going, who has been active and helpful in all matters connected with Confederate work. Chantilly was an estate on the picket line, while the army was encamped at Centreville, in the autumn of 1861, and is associated with pleasant recollections by members of the First Maryland Infantry.

WILLIAM E. COLSTON ROOM.—This room was one of the first furnished and presents an attractive and comfortable appearance. The room was furnished by Captain Frederick M. Colston, Assistant to Chief Ordnance Officer, Army of Northern Virginia, a brother of William E. Colston.

William E. Colston was born in Washington March 24, 1839, but his early years were spent in Virginia, the home of his ancestors. He came to Baltimore about 1857, and was among the first to go to Virginia when the war broke out. On June 1, 1861, he enlisted as a private in Company B, Maryland Guard, attached to the Twenty-first Virginia Infantry, but when the First Maryland Regiment was formed, was transferred to Company H, Captain William H. Murray, June 18, 1861. In this company he served in all the campaigns and battles of the year, and at the battle of Cross Keys, June 8, 1862, in Jackson's Valley campaign, he was desperately wounded, being shot through the body. He was permanently injured by this wound and disabled for a long time, but as soon as able to ride, he was appointed volunteer aide to Major-General Trimble. General Trimble being wounded and left at Gettysburg, Colston then volunteered into Mosby's command, and was killed in the night attack on Harper's Ferry, January 10, 1864. He is buried in the Confederate lot at Loudon Park with his old comrades of Company H.

BRIGADIER-GENERAL LLOYD TILGHMAN BUILDING.—This building contains the Colonel James R. Herbert Room, which is furnished with hard wood furniture, in keeping with those in the other buildings. Mr. M. J. Block, Mr. Thomas W. Morse and Mr. Thomas McNulty solicited subscriptions sufficient to furnish it. The other room in this building is furnished by the Home temporarily with cots.

General Lloyd Tilghman of Talbot County, Maryland, was educated at West Point. At Fort Henry, February 6, 1862, he held the fort until nearly half his gunners were killed or wounded. When Foote took the fort he had as prisoners General Tilghman and staff, and sixty men. General Tilghman remained as prisoner a few months and was exchanged. In the fall of 1862 he rejoined the Army of the West, then in Mississippi, and was put in command of the First Brigade, Loring's Division. At the battle of Corinth he took a prominent part, and in all subsequent operations of that army, under Van Dorn, and afterwards Pemberton, he bore a conspicuous part up to the time of his death. General Tilghman was killed by a shell on the evening of May 16, 1863, on the battlefield of Baker's Creek, or Champion Hill, Mississippi.

INTERIOR OF ONE OF THE ROOMS.

THE LIBRARY.

BRIGADIER-GENERAL JAMES J. ARCHER BUILDING.—This building contains on the lower floor the Raleigh C. Thomas memorial hall ; on the second floor a store room and servants' sleeping quarters.

General James J. Archer was born in Harford County, Maryland. Colonel of the Fifth Texas Regiment, commanding Texas Brigade at Evansport batteries, March 21, 1862 ; Acting Brigadier-General at West Point, Virginia, May 7, 1862 ; promoted to Brigadier-General, June 2, 1862, and assigned command of Fifth Brigade, Hill's Division ; June 4, 1862, assigned to Hatton's Brigade, Whiting's Division ; June 26 and 28, 1862, engaged in the battles of Mechanicsville and Gaines' Mill ; August 9, 1862, in battle of Cedar Mountain ; August 26, 1862, engagement at Manassas Junction ; August 28, 29 and 30, 1862, second Manassas ; September 1, 1862, Ox Hill ; September 15, 1862, at Harper's Ferry ; September 17, 1862, Sharpsburg ; September 20, 1862, Shepherdstown ; December 11-15, 1862, Fredericksburg ; May 3, 1863, Chancellorsville ; July 1, 1863, Gettysburg, where he was wounded and captured.

General Early in his report said : "The service lost at this time that most gallant and meritorious officer, Brigadier-General Archer, who fell into the enemy's hands." His death resulted from his wounds and his imprisonment on Morris Island, South Carolina, where eight hundred officers were imprisoned in the line of the fire from the Confederate batteries and forts.

RALEIGH C. THOMAS MEMORIAL HALL.—The Thomas memorial hall was furnished by the family and friends of Raleigh C. Thomas, who was a gallant soldier in Company C, First Maryland Cavalry, and who was much beloved by his comrades. This room, which is 50x27 feet, is used as a reading room. It is furnished in old oak with most comfortable and handsome furniture, tables, arm chairs and rockers. The ceiling is of oak, and the equipping of the room involved an expense of about $1,000. It is a handsome tribute to the memory of the deceased, who died in Baltimore in 1887. A fine painting of Mr. Thomas is on the wall. The library contains 1,000 volumes, contributed at various times by kind friends from all over the State, about one hundred newspapers are on file, which are kindly sent free by the press of the State.

ADMIRAL RAPHAEL SEMMES BUILDING.—This building contains the R. E. Lee and Warfield memorial rooms.

Admiral Raphael Semmes was born in Charles County, Maryland, September 27, 1809. He entered the United States Navy as midshipman at the age of seventeen ; was promoted to Lieutenant ten years later, and rose to the rank of Commander at the age of forty-six. During the Mexican war he served on board ship and as an aid to General Worth ; February

15, 1861, at the oubreak, he resigned the Secretaryship of the Lighthouse Board at Washington, D. C., and took command of the Confederate steamer Sumter, at New Orleans, ran the blockade at the mouth of the Mississippi, and in July, 1861, captured a number of American vessels in the Gulf of Mexico. In August, 1862, he took command of the steamer Alabama; he sunk the Hatteras, after a brief action, January, 1863, off Galveston. At the evacuation of Richmond, Admiral Semmes had charge of the James River squadron. He surrendered at Greensboro, North Carolina, May 1, 1865.

The following is a list of vessels captured and destroyed by Admiral Semmes: Abbie Bradford, Ben Danning, Ebenezer Dodge, Joseph Maxwell, Machias, Neapolitan, Alert, Amazonian, Baron de Castine, Brilliant, Clara L. Sparks, Content, Elisha Dunbar, Express, Harriot Spalding, Arcade, Cuba, Golden Rocket, Joseph Parks, Montmorency, Vigilance, Altamaha, Annie T. Schmidt, Ben Tucker, Charles Hill, Conrad, Dorcas Prince, Emily Farnum, Golden Eagle, Hatteras, Albert Adams, Daniel Trowbridge, Investigator, Louis Kilham, Naiad, West Wind, Amanda, Annie, Bertha Thayer, Chastelaine, Courser, Dunkirk, Emma Jane, Golden Rule, Jabez Snow, John A. Parks, Kingfisher, Lauretta, Louisa Hatch, Martaban, Nora, Talisman, Olive Jane, Tycoon, Punjab, Virginia, Sea Lark, Weather Gage, Justina, Lamplighter, Lafayette, Manchester, Winged Racer, Morning Star, Nye, Ocmulgee, Tonowonda, Parker Cook, Union Jack, Sea Bride, Wave Crest, Sonora, Starlight, Kate Cory, Lafayette I., Levi Starbuck, Martha Wenzell, Nina, Ocean Rover, Thomas B. Wales, Palmetta, Union, Rockingham, Washington and S. Gildersleeve.

GENERAL ROBERT E. LEE MEMORIAL ROOM.—This room has been furnished through the liberality of the Brewers' Exchange of Baltimore, as a token of their appreciation of the institution and of their admiration of the character of the great commander. The following tribute to the memory of General Lee is from the late Senator Benjamin H. Hill, of Georgia:

When the future historian comes to survey the character of Lee, he will find it rising like a huge mountain above the undulating plain of humanity, and he will have to lift his eyes high toward heaven to catch its summit. He possessed every virtue of the other great commanders without their vices. He was a foe without hate, a friend without treachery, a private citizen without wrong, a neighbor without reproach, a Christian without hypocrisy, and a man without guilt. He was Caesar without his ambition, Frederick without his tyranny, Napoleon without his selfishness, and Washington without his reward. He was obedient to authority as a servant, and royal in authority as a true king. He was as gentle as a woman in life, pure and modest as a virgin in thought, watchful as a Roman vestal in duty, submissive to law as Socrates, and grand in battle as Achilles.

THE WARFIELD ROOM.—This room has been furnished in memory of Albert

Gallatin Warfield, Jr., and Gassaway Watkins Warfield, both members of Company A, First Maryland Cavalry, Confederate States of America, by their mother and brothers, Joshua N., Edwin, John and Marshall T. Warfield, and sisters, Mrs. M. Gillet Gill, of Baltimore, and Mrs. Herman Hoopes, of Philadelphia.

Albert Gallatin Warfield, Jr., entered the Confederate Army, joining Company A, First Maryland Cavalry, under command of Colonel Ridgely Brown. In the fall of that year he was stricken down with typhoid fever and lay ill at Winchester for many weeks. He was convalescing when the Confederates evacuated the town, but remained in hiding for ten days after the Federals arrived, and tried in vain to escape. He gives in his diary a most interesting account of the experiences of himself and his companion, Clark, in their efforts to elude the Federal soldiers and to escape, but finally, on December 27, they were compelled to surrender. He was marched to Martinsburg, and from thence sent, via the Baltimore and Ohio, to Camp Chase, Ohio. He was exchanged in the spring of 1863, after having been transferred to Fort McHenry, Baltimore, Maryland. He had not been with his regiment long before he was sent on an important scouting expedition with five other picked men from his company, and with them was captured. This proved his greatest misfortune, as he was destined to spend two long dreary years in prison at Point Lookout, and was finally exchanged the last of March, 1865, just before the close of the war.

Gassaway Watkins Warfield was the third son of Albert G. and Margaret G. Warfield. When the Civil War began he was in his fifteenth year. The one desire and ambition of his youth was to be a soldier and fight for the Southern cause. He was sent to Rock Hill College in 1861, and continued there until July, 1864. During his college life he longed to go South, and then decided to do so when an opportunity offered. This came soon after his return home for his summer vacation in 1864, when General Early invaded Maryland. Notwithstanding the fact that the hope of success of the Confederate cause was fast waning, his patriotic ardor won, and he cast his lot with the forlorn hope of the Confederates. On July 11, 1864, he buckled on his sword, donned the gray, bade farewell to home and dear ones, and with a mother's prayers and benedictions, rode off to do battle for the cause that he believed to be right and just. He enlisted in Company A, First Maryland Cavalry, Confederate States Army, at Triadelphia. The gallant company was then under command of Captain Thomas Griffith. Young Warfield's career as a soldier in active service in the field was brief, lasting but twenty-six days, yet it was one filled with exciting incidents, forced marches and almost daily fighting. He was taken prisoner at Moorefield and sent to Camp Chase, Ohio. The exposure and hardships of prison life soon told upon his youthful constitution, and he was stricken down with a fatal fever in October, and, after long suffering, he died January 14, 1865, a martyr to the cause he loved and for which he freely gave up his life.

MAJOR-GENERAL ARNOLD ELZEY BUILDING.—This building contains the Quartermaster's Department, pharmacy and the Superintendent's office.

This distinguished officer was Captain of the Second Artillery, and in command of the United States Arsenal, Augusta, Georgia, when he resigned in the early part of 1861. On June 19, 1861, he was commissioned Colonel of the First Maryland Infantry. Upon the disablement of General E. Kirby Smith, at the head of this regiment, July 21, 1861, moving into position on the memorable field of Manassas, the command of the brigade devolved upon Colonel Elzey, who successfully continued the movement and assailed the enemy with such vigor as to cause them to give way; this retreat soon became a panic, and the result was the complete rout of the Federal Army. At this moment President Davis rode over the field and, meeting Colonel Elzey, saluted him as "General," remarking, "You are the Blucher of the day."

General Elzey remained in command of this brigade until made a Major-General and assigned to command of the defenses at Richmond in December, 1862.

At Cross Keys, in June, 1862, he rendered valuable service, the position occupied by the Confederate forces was of his selection, and General Ewell, in his report, says: "I availed myself frequently during the action of that officer's counsel, profiting largely by his known military skill and judgment; he was much exposed, his horse was wounded early in the action, and at a later period of the day, was killed by a rifle ball, which at the same time inflicted upon the rider a wound that forced him to retire from the field; he was more particularly employed in the centre directing the artillery."

General Elzey was seriously wounded at Gaines' Mill, June 27, 1862, in which battle his brigade took active part and sustained heavy loss. His ability as a soldier was recognized by General Lee, who suggested to the President he should order him to take the field in January, 1863. Again, in May, 1863, General Lee wrote to President Davis that he greatly needed two Major-Generals, and asked that General Elzey be sent to him to command Trimble's Division.

April 25, 1864, General Elzey was ordered to Staunton to establish headquarters as commander of the Maryland Line; September 8, 1864, was assigned to duty as Chief of Artillery in the Army of Tennessee.

OFFICE OF SUPERINTENDENT.—The Superintendent's office contains the usual office furniture, with the following pictures and muster rolls, framed, hanging on the wall: "Prayer in Stonewall Jackson's Camp," "The Charge of the First Maryland Infantry at Harrisonburg, Virginia, at the Death of Ashby," "Last Meeting of Lee and Jackson." "Muster Rolls of Company A, First Maryland Infantry, and Company D, First Maryland Cavalry," "Letter from Jefferson Davis, Camp St. Mary, or Camp of the Maryland Line at Hanover Junction, January, 1864," and several others.

THE MESS HALL.

THE RELIC ROOM.

QUARTERMASTER'S ROOM.—The Quartermaster's Department is fitted up with shelves and such other conveniences as are required. Everything is given out here that is required in the different departments, from a needle up to a uniform. Tobacco day is looked for with fond anticipation. On one side of the room are the bins which hold the linen of the memorial rooms. The linen is brought here and stored until issued for use. There is an inspector, who takes an account of all the linen coming out of the rooms. On Monday morning a clerk takes an account of all going into the laundry ; a perfect system is maintained, so that everything will be properly accounted for.

MEDICAL DEPARTMENT.—*Surgeon to the Home*—William P. E. Wyse, M. D. *Consulting Surgeons*—Dr. Charles G. Hill, Dr. E. E. Jones, Dr. Thomas S. Latimer and Dr. J. J. Chisholm. The surgeon's office, dispensary, and the Stonewall Jackson Infirmary are the chief points of interest in the medical department of the Home. Those patients able to get about report to the surgeon's office, where they are treated. The less fortunate ones, who are too sick to report at the surgeon's office, are sent to the Infirmary, where they are under the care of skilled nurses and visited by the surgeon every day, or oftener, if necessary.

GENERAL E. KIRBY SMITH ROOM (PHARMACY).—The surgeon's office and dispensary are situated on the east end of the Elzey Building, and is one of the prettiest and most attractive places within the walls of the Home, which is due to the liberality and good taste of Mrs. Decatur H. Miller, who fitted up and furnished it at considerable expense. It is carpeted ; the wood work is of highly polished, hand-carved oak ; the medicine case is of the same wood. Under a brass chandelier, a handsome centre table has upon it a silver waiter, ice water pitcher and goblets, which are decidedly useful as well as ornamental, all combine to make the surgeon's office a cheery place of refuge for those who require the aid of the healing art. Mrs. Miller has indicated her wish that this room be named in memory of the late General E. Kirby Smith.

General Smith was an officer of distinguished reputation in the United States Army, when his duty to his State prompted him to resign his commission at the commencement of the war. He was appointed a Brigadier-General, and ordered to report to General Joseph E. Johnston, commanding the Army of the Shenandoah, in July, 1861, and was severely wounded at the first battle of Manassas, leading his brigade into action. General Smith afterwards was made a Major-General and assigned to a division under General Johnston, but was subsequently transferred to the Armies of the West, and finally was in command of the Department of the Trans-Mississippi. The services of General Smith in this command were of great importance, and added to his already high reputation as an able soldier. It devolved upon him to make surrender of the last army of the Confederacy, when he returned to civil life, and, like the immortal Lee, his honored chieftain, devoted himself to the education of the youth of his country. At the time of his death (March 28, 1893,) he was connected with the University of the South, Sewanee, Tennessee. General Smith attained the rank of full General in the Confederate service.

BRIGADIER-GENERAL CHARLES S. WINDER BUILDING.—Contains the mess hall, dish room, commissary and kitchen on the first floor. The E. Bolton Piper room, containing seventeen beds, chairs, lockers, etc ; two small bedrooms, bathroom and linen-room, also quarters for the servants, on the second floor. This room is furnished with proceeds of a bequest from the late E. Bolton Piper. The mess hall was furnished by Lieutenant George W. Wood, of Baltimore. Lieutenant Wood, prior to the war, lived in Louisiana and served with troops from that State. The commissary department occupies two small rooms, and the kitchen is on the same floor and convenient to the mess hall. The old Winder Building was torn down during the summer of 1898, and a new and much enlarged structure erected, at a cost of some $4,000, the expense of which was defrayed out of the receipts from the bazaar held in Baltimore in April of that year.

General Winder was educated at West Point, appointed Second Lieutenant of Infantry and afterwards promoted to be First Lieutenant, and was ordered to the Pacific coast. The steamer San Francisco, on which the troops took passage from New York, was disabled by a hurricane off the Atlantic coast, and drifting helpless for many days before the storm, was reported lost for several weeks. Different vessels rescued the crew and passengers, however, and Lieutenant Winder and his men, whom he refused to leave, were taken to Liverpool. For his conduct on this occasion he was promoted to be Captain in the Ninth Regiment Infantry, being, it is believed, the youngest captain in the army. He was again ordered to the Pacific coast, and with his company took part in Steptoe's campaign against the Columbia River Indians, being present at his defeat and perilous retreat under cover of night. He also took part in Colonel Wright's subsequent successful campaign against the same Indians. Early in 1861 he resigned his command and offered his services to the Confederate Government at Montgomery, and was commissioned Captain in the regular Confederate States Army. Being ordered to Charleston, he was present at the reduction of Fort Sumter. He was afterwards in the command of the South Carolina Arsenal, until commissioned Colonel of the Sixth South Carolina Infantry, arriving with his regiment at Manassas just at the close of the battle of July 21 ; March 4, 1862, nominated by President Davis to be a Brigadier-General ; March 25, 1862, assigned to the command of the Fourth Brigade, Hill's Division, but without taking command, was on the emergency of a vacancy in the command of the Stonewall Brigade, assigned to the same and participated in the Valley campaign of 1862 ; August, 1862, assigned to command of Jackson's Division ; was mortally wounded whilst in command of this division, August 9, 1862, at Cedar Mountain. General Winder was engaged in the battles of McDowell, Gaines' Mill, Malvern Tavern, Winchester, Harper's Ferry, Port Republic, Cedar Mountain and others.

General T. J. Jackson, in his report of the battle of Cold Harbor, says : " In pursuance of the order to charge the enemy's front, the First Virginia Brigade, commanded by General C. S. Winder, moved forward through the swamp, and upon emerging into the open fields, its ranks broken by the obstacles encountered, were re-formed, meeting at that point with the Hampton Legion, First Maryland, Twelfth Alabama, Fifty-second Virginia, and Thirty-eighth Georgia, they were formed upon his line. Thus formed they moved forward under the lead of that gallant officer, whose conduct here was marked by the coolness and courage which distinguished him on the battlefields of the Valley."

General Robert E. Lee, in his report of the battle of Cedar Mountain, says : " I can add nothing to the well-deserved tribute paid to the courage, capacity, and conspicuous merit of this lamented officer, by General Jackson, in whose brilliant campaign in the Valley and on the Chickahominy, he bore a distinguished part."

General T. J. Jackson, in his report of the same battle, says : " He was proceeding to direct, with his usual skill and coolness, the movements of these batteries, when he was struck by a shell, and he expired in a few hours. It is difficult within the proper reserve of an official report to do justice to the merits of this accomplished officer. Urged by the medical director to take no part in the movements of the day, because of the enfeebled state of his health, his ardent patriotism and military pride could bear no such restraint ; richly endowed with those qualities of mind and person which fit an officer for command, and which attract the admiration and excite the enthusiasm of troops, he was rapidly rising to the front rank of his profession, and his loss has been severely felt."

THE BRIGADIER-GENERAL WILLIAM W. MACKALL BUILDING.—This building is to the left of the entrance, and is occupied by the Superintendent and family. It was occupied in 1861 by General Huger, just before he resigned and entered the service of the Confederacy.

General W. W. Mackall, of Cecil County, Maryland, on September 15, 1861, was Lieutenant-Colonel, Acting Adjutant-General, and Chief of Staff of General Albert Sydney Johnson ; March 4, 1862, nominated by President Davis as Brigadier-General ; March 26, 1862, by Special Orders No. 445, Headquarters Grand Division, Army of the Mississippi, dated Corinth, Mississippi, was ordered to the command of the Confederate forces at Madrid Bend and Island No. 10 ; October 14, 1862, by Special Orders No. 240, War Department, ordered to report for duty to Major-General Samuel Jones, commanding Department of Tennessee; December 14, 1862, assigned to the command of the District of the Gulf ; February 1, 1863, Brigadier-General in command of Western Division, District of the Gulf, Major-General S. B. Buckner commanding ; April 17, 1863, by General Orders No. 9, announced as Chief of Staff, Department No. 2, Braxton Bragg commanding ; October 16, 1863, by General Orders No. 2, Department of Tennessee, relieved as Chief of Staff ; November 4, 1863, by Special Orders No. 235, Headquarters Department of Mississippi and East Louisiana, assigned to the command of the brigades lately commanded by Brigadier-General Herbert ; January 26, 1864, by General Orders No. 6, Department of Tennessee, announced as Chief of Staff to General Joseph E. Johnston ; July 24, 1864, by Special Field Orders No. 56, Headquarters Army of Tennessee, relieved from duty as Chief of Staff at his own request.

Brigadier-General W. W. Mackall was engaged in the battle of Madrid Bend and Island No. 10, April 1-6, 1862, at which time he was captured. General Beauregard, in a letter to General S. Cooper, dated Jackson, Tennessee, February 24, 1862, says : " The services of

THE CONFEDERATE LOT — LOUDON PARK.

Colonel Mackall as a division commander I consider indispensable at this critical juncture. My health is such as to make it essential for me to have as many trained experienced officers to aid me as practicable."

General Beauregard, in a letter to Mackall, dated August 22, 1862, says : " I am happy to hear of your safe return to the Confederacy, and hope you will soon receive a command commensurate with your merit. . . . . I hope to report for duty on or about the first proximo, when I would be most happy to have you under my orders should you desire to serve under me again."

General Samuel Jones, in a letter to the Secretary of War, dated October 14, 1862, says : " I telegraphed you on the 12th instant to say that I needed the services of a Brigadier-General to this department (East Tennessee), and that if you thought proper to order Brigadier-General Mackall, who, I understand, is without a brigade, to report to me, I should be glad to have him."

J. G. Shorter, Governor of Alabama, in a letter dated May 6, 1863, to the Secretary of War, says : " I telegraphed you today that the citizens of Mobile desired the assignment of Brigadier-General Mackall to the command in that city. . . . I need not remind you of the vital importance of assigning to such a high position of responsibility an officer of skill and energy, and whose qualifications will command the respect and confidence of the citizens of Mobile and the authorities of Alabama."

In General Orders No. 2, dated October 16, 1863, General Bragg says : " At his request, Brigadier-General W. W. Mackall is relieved from duty as Chief of Staff with the commanding General of the army. He will proceed with his aides and report to General J. E. Johnston, now commanding the department from which he was transferred. With a grateful sense of the distinguished services rendered by this accomplished officer in the high position he has filled, the commanding General tenders him his cordial thanks and wishes him all success and happiness in his future career. The General and the army will long feel the sacrifice made in sparing the services of one so distinguished for capacity, professional acquirements and urbanity."

General Leonidas Polk, in a letter to General J. E. Johnston, dated January 5, 1864, says : " I will return you Forney or M. L. Smith or Mackall with the recommendation of the latter for Major-General."

STONEWALL JACKSON INFIRMARY.—The necessity of a hospital building, detached from the living rooms at the Home, was early demonstrated. A building, which in the days of the Arsenal was used as a laboratory, was made available for this purpose. It is a substantial structure, removed some one hundred yards or more from the other buildings, and was fitted up for hospital use through the efforts of Mrs. J. H. Tegmyer, Mrs. R. B. Winder, Mrs. Harvey Jones, Mrs. J. H. Harris, Mrs. M. B. Brown, Mrs. John Brosius and their associates. The original building has been very considerably enlarged, and is now fitted up with nine beds, hot and cold water, bathroom and water closet, and has been found a great comfort. It has been named after the immortal Jackson, whose military genius was only equaled by his unshrinking faith and consistent Christian character. With him the watchword of life was comprehended in one word, " Duty." Wherever he recognized this principle his devotion was complete, whether it called him to face the dangers of battle in his country's service, or whether it led him to humbler, but no less noble deeds in the service of his God. His submission to the will of his Maker and recognition of Divine Providence in all things, both small and great, was as marked as those great abilities which made him the military hero of the war.

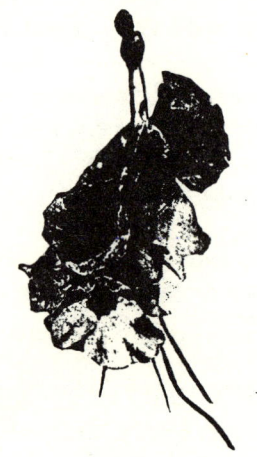

[THE END.]

INDEX to THE MARYLAND LINE IN THE CONFEDERATE ARMY 1861-1865

Originally Published by the State of Maryland
Hall of Records, 1944
and
Reprinted with their Kind Permission

A

Abbott, James, 73, 115, 134, 158
Abel, Charles, 74
Ackhurst, Charles, 73
Ackler, William, 76
Ackworth, 311
Acton, Washington, 326
Adair, William R., 137, 152
Adairsville, 309
Adams, Franklin, 81
Adams, Henry, 77
Adams, J. H., 316
Adams, J. Q., 159
Adams, John S., 81
Adkins, S. E., 115
Agen, Peter, 73
Aisquith, Hobart, 230
Alabaugh, Sergt. Ira, 254
Albaugh, John, 254
Albert, A. J., Jr., 256, 270
Alcock, C., 247
Aldridge, John, 270
Alexander, Col. George W., 329
Alexandria, 187
Allen, James, 78
Allen, John, 146, 248
Allen, Sergt. William, 246
Alston, Frederick, 326
Altwater, J. W., 235
Alvey, James P., 112, 154
Alvey, John F., 329
Amelia Court House, 149, 151
Amey, Charles, 74
Amos, B. F., 142, 156
Anderson, Lt. ———, 304
Anderson, James, 75
Anderson, Leroy, 114, 157
Anderson, Oscar, 232
Anderson, Lt. Gen. R. H., 322
Anderson, Richard T., 134, 155
Anderson, Samuel, 112, 155
Andre, Corp. J., 248
Andre, John A., 73
Andrews, Col. R. Snowden, 259-267, 270, 319, 324, 341, 350
Angell, Thomas, 78
Annandale, 252
Annapolis, 4, 344, 351
Anne Arundel County, 85
Annen, Henry, 76
Applegarth, James B., 138, 156
Appomattox, 89, 133, 147, 150, 151, 221, 223-226, 269, 325, 341
Aquia Creek, 260
Archer, 299
Archer, Brig. Gen. James J., 86, 135, 136, 139, 361
Archer, John R., 77
Archer, Col. Robert, 254
Arens, Henry, 294
Arizona, 300
Armstrong, Joshua, 229
Armstrong, Lewis, 316
Armour, Lt., 329
Arnold, Corp. Charles A., 75
Arnold, Frank A., 75
Arnold, Samuel, 75
Artis, Jeremiah, 154, 229
Ashburn, A. R., 316
Ashby's Gap, 22
Ashby, R. W., 235
Ashby, Gen. Turner, 48-50, 53, 55, 65, 165, 200, 242, 249, 364
Ashe, James, 158
Ashland, 59, 189, 260, 296
Ashton, J. J., 76
Association of the Maryland Line, 342
Atkins, Samuel E., 158
Atkinson, Lt. William G., 329
Atlanta, 310
Atzrodt, Henry, 157
Aubrey, James L., 156
Auburn, 187
Aultman, N., 316
Aultman, S., 314, 316
Averill, Maj. Gen. W. W., 290, 291

B

Baden, J. M., 230
Baden, Lt. N., 343-345
Baden, William A. H., 234
Bagby, Capt. R. H., 190

Bailey, F. M., 316
Bailey, Henry M., 81
Bailey, James T., 154
Bailey, William T., 143, 152
Baird, Asst. Adj. Gen. William, 330
Baker, Dad, 320
Baker, Sergt. Frederick, 247
Baker, H. W., 234
Baker, Henry, 76, 326, 328
Baker, Col. John A., 198, 199
Baker's Creek, 301
Ball, Dionysius, 81, 137, 154
Ballard, W. W., 270
Baltimore, 2-4, 9-12, 34, 44, 85, 197, 203-209, 245, 259, 289, 296, 319, 342, 345, 351, 366-371
Baltimore City Guards, 9
Baltimore Light Artillery, 338, 356, 357
Banks, Maj. Gen. Nathaniel P., 35, 46, 57, 65
Banner, Charles, 294
Bannon, Sergt. John G., 81, 142, 154
Barber, Christopher, 232
Barber, Sergt. John G., 81, 142, 154
Barber, Lt. Joseph W., 86, 88, 112
Barbour, James, 53
Barbour, Oscar, 232
Barchuss, W. W., 326
Barnes, Maj. J. T. M., 329
Barnes, Jacob S., 330
Barnes, John, 235
Barnes, Sergt. Richard M., 161, 232
Barnes, Robert B., 316
Barnes, Corp. William, 254
Barrett, J. H., 316
Barrick, William, 233
Barry, Daniel, R., 75, 254
Barry, Capt. Edmund, 58
Barry, H. C., 294
Barry, M. C. Y., 270
Barry, Michael, 114, 156
Barry, Phillip, 111, 152
Barry, W. D., 230
Bartonsville, 96
Basford, G. W., 270
Batchelder, Col. ———, 109
Bateman, H., 232

Bates, George, 74
Bates, Samuel P., 105
Bates, Lt. T. J., 302
Baughman, L. Victor, 233
Baxley, William G. D., 152
Bayly, James P., 161
Baym, Sergt. William H., 330
Beale, Alexander, 230
Beale, James S., 270
Beall, Sgt. Maj. E. Sinclair, 330
Beall, Robert, 142, 154
Beall, William B., 81
Bean, Lt. Hezekiah H., 31, 56, 81
Bean, Joseph A., 293
Bean, Thomas L., 230
Bean, Lt. William B., 275, 288, 289, 293
Bean, W. M., 230
Beane, Martin, 294
Beasley, D., 314, 316
Beasley, Joseph, 316
Beaston, George M., 235
Beatty, Lt. Edward W., 53, 76, 116, 170, 229, 237, 254
Beauregard, Gen. Pierre G. T., 21, 25, 27, 31, 32, 123, 249, 370
Beaver Dam, 193, 195, 197, 198
Beckett, John M., 229
Beckham, Col. R. T., 285, 286, 312
Becknell, Frederick, 78
Behrens, Barney, 78
Bell, Henry, 229
Bell, Samuel, 158
Bell, William, 316
Belle Isle, 189
Beltsville, 205, 245, 289
Bender, Francis T., 73
Bender, Frank, 229
Benner's Hill, 324
Bennett, Edmund, 77
Bennett, William, 248
Bennett, William B., 316
Benton, John, 316
Berg, John, 316
Berger, Joseph, 294
Bermer, August, 235
Berritt, J. T., 248
Berry, E. R., 270
Berry, John R., 75

Berry, Thomas S., 76
Berryman, John B., 23, 75
Berry's Ferry, 22
Bestor, John Rollin, 161
Bestor, Rollin John, 161
Betts, Samuel, 254
Beverley's Ford, 357
Beverly, N., 314, 316
Beyer, Adam, 78
Biays, George, 232
Big Black River, 306
Big Eagle Creek, 298
Big Shanty, 311
Bigger, John, 254
Bigler's Wharf, 251
Billop, Christopher, 232
Billop, Capt. T. F., 330
Birch, J. A., 230
Bird, Charles E., 76
Birdwell, D. H., 316
Bishop, George W., 72
Bitchel, Fred. F., 235
Bivin, William F., 81
Bivin, Zachariah, 81
Black Bayou, 302, 306
"Black Bess," 303
Blackburn, William, 316
Blackburn's Ford, 23
Blackiston, Lt. Henry C., 166, 178, 179, 212, 230, 237
Blakiston, S. H., 230
Blackistone, George W., 80
Blackistone, Sergt. William J., 110, 152
Blackistone, William T., 80
Blain's Cross Roads, 298
Blair, Lt. Charles W., 14, 73
Blake, Francis T., 77
Blake, John, 78
Blakely, W. H., 254, 276
Blakeslie, Charles E., 316
Blanford, Samuel H., 161
Bledsoe, H. M., 302
Block, M. J., 358
Block, Meyer, 329
Blue Ridge Mountains, 119
Blumenauer, John M., 143, 151, 155, 270
Blunt, Corp. Isaac J., 326
Blunt, Robert, 79
Boarman, J. N., 230
Boarman, Richard T., 270
Bobeth, Charles, 73
Bogue, Phaliah, 306

Bolivar Heights, 46-48, 276, 281
Bolling, John W., 80
Bolling, Thomas B., 111
Bolling, Wallace, 111
Bollinger, Corp. F. W., 270
Boman, Joseph, 230
Bond, Corp. Arthur, 229
Bond, B. F., 73, 152
Bond, Gen. Frank A., 48, 59, 90, 92, 165-168, 170, 173, 174, 176-178, 181, 229, 237, 239, 250, 251, 254
Bond, H., 229
Bond, J. W., 230
Bond, James O., 154
Bond, John, 111, 152
Bond, John J., 80
Bond, Lt. Samuel G., 229, 235
Bond, W. W., 229
Bonn, Lt. Samuel G., 166, 237
Booker, William T., 234
Boone, Daniel A., 329
Boone, W. C., 234
Boonsboro, 177, 252, 281
Booth, Adj. Gen. George W., 14, 59, 66, 68, 72, 76, 122, 166, 170, 181, 201, 210, 228, 237
Booth, John, 159
Bosley, Sergt. John R., 248, 277
Boswell, Josiah T., 138, 157
Boswell, Richard T., 270
Boteler, Mrs. Alexander R., 98
Boteler, Alexander R., 98, 207, 214
Boteler, Walter P., 270
Bottom's Bridge, 63
Bouldin, Constantine, 254
Bourne, James B., 234
Bourner, John, 77
Bowdoin, Lloyd, 152
Bowen, Cornelius, 73
Bowen, W. H., 270
Bowers' Hill, 97
Bowie, Albert, 254
Bowie, H. B., 254
Bowie, H. C., 270
Bowie, Harry, 232
Bowie, Thomas D., 270
Bowie, Maj. Thomas F., 330
Bowland, S. G., 270

Bowler, Thomas, 301, 316
Bowley, William H., 111, 152
Bowling, Alexander, 230
Bowling, C. A., 254
Bowling, Charles F., 152
Bowling Green, 198, 262, 321
Bowling, Maj. Henry, 330
Bowling, Nicholas, 230
Bowling, Wallace, 152
Bowlman, M., 254
Boyd, Andrew, 229
Boyd, David, 161
Boyd, Hamilton, 76
Boyle, Charles B., 233
Boyle, Peter, 74
Boyle, Philip, 248
Boyles, Daniel, 115, 158
Bracco, Edward, 229
Bradbery, L. S., 316
Braddock, Charles S., 111, 152
Bradford, Gov. Augustus W., 204
Bradford, Corp. Baldwin, 309, 315
Bradford, T. G., 270
Bradley, J., 230
Bradley, Thomas J., 279, 294
Brady, Eugene, 254
Brady, John H., 161
Brady, Michael, 79, 326
Bragg, Gen. Braxton, 298, 308, 371
Brandeburg, Jesse, 247
Brandt, Alexander, 77, 78, 114, 156, 254
Brandy Station, 122, 185, 252, 287
Brannock, Charles S., 137
Brannock, Thomas S., 158
Brannock, Corp. Wallis, 137
Brannock, William L., 138
Brashears, Benton T., 79
Brasher, Thomas P., 233
Brawner, John J., 81
Brawner, T. M., 234
Brawner, William, 157
Brawner, William F., 156, 157
Braxton, Lt. Col. C. M., 267
Breathed, Maj. James, 216, 291, 330
Breckinridge, Gen. John C., 125-128, 133, 205, 208, 268
Breed, Hy L., 235
Brehm, John P., 232

Brener, John L., 74
Brengle, Dr. William, 330
Brent, George T., 230
Brent, Maj. J. L., 299
Breslin, Edward W., 115, 158
Bressner, John, 77
Brian, E. H., 270
Brian, Dr. Jack, 324, 326, 328
Briddell, Edward J., 115
Briddell, Corp. James E., 158
Briddle, James, 76
Bride, Samuel, 73
Bridgeport, 173
Bridges, Maj. ———, 302, 306
Bridges, W., 316
Brien, Col. Luke Tiernan, 330
Brighthaupt, Lt. George, 142, 158
Briscoe, Chapman B., 80
Briscoe, David S., 80
Briscoe, Girard, 81
Briscoe, Henry, 80
Briscoe, John H., 270
Briscoe, Capt. John L., 329
Briscoe, Marshall, 81, 157
Briscoe, P. T., 230
Briscoe, R. C., 294
Bristow, 121, 122, 256, 261, 271
Bristow, Col. B. H., 261, 327
Broadfoot, Lt. William J., 15, 78, 87, 113, 156
Brockenborough, Col. J. B., 44, 55, 275, 276, 278-282, 293
Brockenborough, W. H., 293, 357
Brogden, J. Sellman, 80, 247
Bromley, George W., 270
Bromley, Oram J., 74
Bromwell, Henry H., 233
Bromwell, Josiah R., 233
Bromwell, Thomas C. S., 233
Brook, John P., 157
Brooke, Clements, 234
Brooke, George W., 234
Brooke, John B., 88
Brooks, Robert S., 246
Brooks, Thomas, 270
Brosius, Mrs. John, 371
Brotherton, David, 247
Broughton, Thomas, 270
Brown, Gen., 95
Brown, ———, 307

Brown, A. H., 316
Brown, C. C., 229
Brown, Charles, 254
Brown, Charles A., 77
Brown, George, 235
Brown, George William, 345
Brown, Henry, 254
Brown, Col. J. Thompson, 138, 157, 265
Brown, J. Wesley, 254
Brown, James, 159
Brown, James A., 113, 156
Brown, John, 114, 143, 156
Brown, John R., 229
Brown, John W., 73, 326
Brown, Louis, 254
Brown, Mrs. Martin B., 356, 371
Brown, N. M., 3
Brown, Sergt. Phil., 325
Brown, Sergt. Phillip, 328
Brown, Philip H., 326
Brown, Colonel Ridgely, 163, 165, 166, 169-171, 174, 178, 188, 195, 196, 199-201, 202, 212, 226, 228, 237, 243, 251, 254, 341, 351, 352
Brown, Robert, 232
Brown, Theopolus, 235
Brown, W. B., 270
Brown, W. J., 314, 316, 329
Brown, William, 76
Brown, Capt. William D., 265, 319, 324, 326, 328, 341
Brown, William H., 294
Brown's Gap, 57, 291
Browne, Gustavus, 154
Brownlow, Parson, 297
Brubaker, R., 248
Bruce, Corp. Robert, 254
Bruce, William, 81, 110, 152
Bruner, Hamilton, 74
Bryan, C., 230
Bryan, Edmund, 152
Bryan, Henry B., 158
Bryan, Robert S., 270
Bryan, W. C., 234
Bryan, W. L., 230
Bryant, George H., 234
Buchanan, Admiral Franklin, 349, 351
Buchanan, Sergt. James M., Jr., 296, 315
Buchanan, John R., 265, 270

Buchanan, Thomas, 248
Buchanan, W. J., 270
Buck, A. Kirkland, 161
Buck, Capt. Richard B., 349, 350
Buck, Mrs. Richard B., 350
Buckhannon, 173, 174
Buckingham, Sergt. George, 254
Buckingham, George, 254
Buckland, 187, 188, 252
Buckmaster, Corp. Henry G., 326
Buckner, Corp. William, 315
Buford, 185
Bull, Elijah, 232
Bull, John E., 76
Bullen, R. B., 230
Bull Run, 68
Bump, George C., 254
Bunker Hill, 21, 208, 209, 211, 212, 245, 262, 267, 321
Bunting, John, 294
Burch, John H., 152, 230
Burgess, John, 294
Burgess, Sergt. W. W., 254
Burke, C. L., 294
Burke, Capt. John, 247
Burke, John M., 80
Burke, Michael, 114, 156
Burke, Capt. Nicholas, 245
Burke, W. L., 326
Burling, D., 230
Burnett, Charles C., 294, 295
Burns, Ignatius, 248
Burnside, Maj. Gen. Ambrose E., 134, 135, 198, 268
Burrough, Lt. ———, 330
Burrough, Lt. John B., 166
Burrough, Lt. S. B., 234
Burst, George T., 230
Burtles, C. H., 270
Burton, Michael, 316
Burttes, Charles H., 81
Burttes, Thomas W., 81
Bush, George W., 73
Bush, William P., 159
Bushbaum, Corp. Henry, 247
Bushong, J. A., 309, 315
Busk, Jerome, 270
Bussey, Capt. J. Thomas, 87, 92, 120, 130, 138, 159
Bussey, Capt. Thomas J., 75
Butler, Gen. Benjamin F., 4

Butler, Cyrus S., 233
Butler, Elisha, 138, 157
Butler, H. C., 316
Butler, Sergt. Thomas C., 129, 151, 156
Byas, Phillip, 246
Byers, William, 79
Byrne, ———, 232
Byrne, A. J., 293
Byrne, Samuel E., 270
Byron, Timothy, 316
Byus, Charles C., 156
Byus, Charles E., 114, 129
Byus, S. M., 138, 156
Byus, Lt. W. R., 87, 97, 138, 149, 156

C

Cadle, James R., 234
Cadwallader, Gen. George, 4
Cain, Corp. John, 74, 113, 138, 156
Calbreth, John, 254
Calhoun, William H., 133, 158
Calhoun, ———, 300
Callahan, John, 151, 158
Callam, John, 248
Callan, Capt. ———, 120
Callan, John, 73
Callan, Owen, 78, 235
Calloway, W. A., 316
Camalier, Capt. Vincent, 330
Camble, Thomas, 248
Camden, 341
Cameron, Rev. Stephen J., 72
Camp, George W., 316
Camp, James R., 316
Campbell, John, 270
Campbell, William, 254, 294
Camper, Lt. Charles, 43
Camper, Napoleon, 77
Camp Lee, 89
Canby, Benjamin, 229
Canby, Maj. Gen. Edward R. S., 315
Canfield, John H., 326
Cannon, J. G., 229, 309, 316
Cantrell, John, 138
Cantwell, Michael, 79
Caperton, James M., 270
Carberry, Patrick, 316
Carberry, Corp. Thomas, 322, 326, 328

Carey, Constance, 31
Carey, Hettie, 31
Carey, James E., 111, 152, 330
Carey, Jennie, 31
Carey, Michael, 74, 232
Carey, Timothy, 73
Carlin, 94
Carlin, Laurence, 159
Carlisle, 101, 176, 178, 266-268, 284, 285
Carlisle, George, 248
Carpenter, Capt. J. C., 264, 265, 282, 319
Carr, John C., 294
Carr, Patrick, 316
Carr, Thomas, 78
Carr, Wilson C. N., 80, 161
Carrick, John, 73
Carrill, John, 316
Carroll, Harper, 254
Carroll, Lt. Harper, 330
Carroll, J. C., 235
Carroll, James P., 159
Carroll, Gov. John Lee, 181, 204
Carroll, Laurence, 159
Carroll, M. Philip, 161
Carroll, R. G. Harper, 181
Carroll, Gen. S. S., 54
Carroll, T. Stapleton, 161
Carter, Grafton, 233
Carter, Col. J. E., 312
Carter, R. W., 229
Carter, William H., 161
Carter's Bend, 178, 303, 304, 305
Carusi, Samuel P., 161
Caruthers, Sergt. Illinois, 231
Carvell, Corp. Robert, 170, 230
Cartwell, James, 157
Cary, Sergt. Alexander, 330
Cary, G. M., 316
Cary, John B., 229
Cary, Capt. Wilson M., 330
Cashtown, 178, 285
Caslow, James, 235
Castle, James L., 155
Castleman, C. W., 248
Castleman, Thomas, 248
Cather, Corp. George R., 233
Catlett's Station, 187, 251
Catoctin Mountain, 289
Cator, Benjamin, 234

Cator, W. B., 115, 158
Caufield, James, 161
Caulk, William H., 316
Cavanaugh, Francis C., 159
Cawood, Charles, 330
Cawood, E. M., 270
Cecil, James, 326
Cecil, Lt. Rudolphus, 167, 251, 254
Cedar Creek, 93, 167, 168, 174, 187
Cedar Mountain, 328, 350
Cedar Run, 65, 167, 168, 174, 176, 187, 261, 267, 319, 321, 349
Cedar Town, 311
Cedarville, 96
Cemetery Ridge, 267, 324
Centerville, 31-34, 121, 250, 262, 275, 280, 289, 356, 358
Cessler, Henry, 326
Chafin's Bluff, 134
Chafin, J., 301
Chafin, S., 316
Chambers, John E., 294
Chambers, Robert M., 73, 232
Chambersburg, 98, 100, 178, 207-209, 214, 245, 252, 264, 266, 289
Chancellorsville, 262, 322
Chandler, William S. J., 74, 111, 152
Chantilly, 155, 158, 262, 358
Chapalin, George, 81
Chapin, Charles, 78
Chaplin, Charles, 235
Chapman, Isaac, 235
Chapman, Lt. Nathaniel, 166, 234
Chapman, William, 248
Charles Co. 31, 259
Charlestown, 48, 211, 242, 256
Charlotte, G. W., 294
Charlottesville, 65, 66, 216, 217, 267, 279
Chattahoochee River, 310, 311
Chattanooga, 297, 298
Cheasham, J., 316
Cheat River, 172
Cheatham, 312
Chenoweth, Joseph, 74
Cherry, James, 248
Chesapeake, 261, 263
Chesapeake, 322

Chesapeakes, 262, 321-325, 338
Cheser, G. S., 316
Chesler, Henry, 233
Chesley, Daniel S., 234
Chesney, Maj. T. O., 330
Chestney, Asst. Adj. Gen. T. O., 193
Chew, Robert B., 265, 270
Chew, Capt Walter S., 169, 319, 325, 326
Chew, Capt. Winfield Scott, 92, 93, 122, 169, 188, 243
Chickahominy, 60, 191, 251, 288
Chilcot, Joshua, 156
Childs, Buck, 182
Childs, Soper, 182, 229
Childs, W. H., 229
Childs, William, 254, 270
Chiles, W. L., 270
Chilton, R. H., 100
Ching, Garrett, 154
Chisholm, Dr., J. J., 367
Chisidine, W. C., 232
Chiswell, Lt. E. J., 330
Chiswell, Capt. George W., 330
Christian, Brig. Gen. William A., 136
Christy, G. W., 294
Christy, William, 159
Chiswell, Lt. E. J., 330
Chuckatuck, 12
Chunn, John H., 112, 137, 154
Cincinnati, 298
Cissell, James T., 81
Clagett, G. W., 151
Clagett, George H., 114, 157
Clagett, H. H., 254
Clagett, John, 229
Clagett, John W., 157
Clagett, Robert, 233
Clagett, William, 129, 151, 155
Claggett, Edward L., 157
Claggett, John H., 142
Claggett, John W., 142
Claiborne, Charles H., 294
Claiborne, Lt. Fred O., 296, 297, 301, 315
Claiborne, Gen. F. L., 301
Clark, Corp. Bazil, 229
Clark, Charles, 316
Clark, Ignatius, 254
Clark, Capt. J. Lyle, 9, 10, 12,

160, 161, 248, 300, 330
Clark, James, 159
Clark, John E., 81, 154
Clark, Joseph, 233
Clark, Rody, 254
Clark, T. H., 316
Clark, Thomas B., 316
Clark, William A., 154
Clarke, Charles A., 115, 158
Clarke, Charles H., 233
Clarke, David, 229
Clarke, Duncan, 247
Clarke, John, 229
Clarke, Joseph, 157
Clarke, William, 229
Claude, Hammond, 232
Claus, Lewis, 294
Clayton, Corp. C. M., 143, 155
Clayton, G. W., 270
Clayville, Moses, 11, 152
Cleal, Charles, 294
Clear Springs, 208, 245
Cleary, Paul W., 234
Cleary, R. E., 270
Cleary, Vachel T., 233
Cleburne, Maj. Gen. P. R., 312
Clements, Francis, 81, 157
Clements, Frank, 254
Clements, William, 232
Cleveland, Pres. Grover, 244
Clinch River, 297
Clinton, 297, 298
Clinton, DeWitt, 254
Clinton, Lewis R., 77
Close, James, 161
Clotworthy, G. W., 294
Clough, Robert H., 112, 155
Cloverdale, 226
Coakeley, Philip A., 80
Coale, William A., 270
Cobb, Brig. Gen. Thomas R. R., 315
Coburn, Col. John, 230
Cochran, G. M., 20
Cockey, Sergt. Charles R., 229
Cockey, John P., 234
Cockey, Sprigg, 229
Cockeysville, 204, 245, 289
Cockrell, Brig. Gen. F. M., 312
Codd, W. M., 75
Coffee, M. J., 294

Cold Harbor, 59, 126, 133, 134, 139, 268, 288, 349
Cole, Charles N., 233
Cole, Dr. William H., 330
Coleman, J. A., 294
Collins, Corp. John W., 76, 155
Collins, Richard, 159
Colquitt, Gen. A. H., 345
Colston, Capt. Frederick M., 258, 330, 358
Colston, Brig. Gen. Raleigh E., 92
Colston, William E., 80, 161, 358
Columbia, 39, 311
Columbus, Miss., 314
Combs, Edgar, 112, 154
Company B., Twenty-First Virginia Infantry, 160-162
Company K., First Virginia Cavalry, 249-256
Compton, Corp. William P., 265, 266, 270
Condell, Samuel, 78
Confederate Soldiers' Home, 355-371
Conely, Martin V., 234
Conely, Michael, 270
Conn, William G., 76
Connelly, Edward T., 76
Conner, William, 270
Connick, Robert, 234
Connolly, Edward, 77
Connolly, William, 78
Connor, Alexander, 316
Connor, James, 316
Conrad, Ephraim, 254
Conrad, George, 73
Conrad, Holmes, 244
Conradt, Christian J., 75, 254
Contee, Lt. Charles S., 259, 265, 266, 270
Contee, Corp. P. A. L., 270
Contee, Maj. Richard, 330
Cook, Lt Adolphus, 166, 169, 179, 181, 230
Cook, Charles, 316
Cook, George R., 80, 232
Cook, Jacob F., 325, 326
Cook, Brig. Gen. Philip, 146
Cook, Rudolphus, 254
Cook, William, 73
Cooke, George A., 270

Cooke, William, 161
Cooksey, Thedodore, 137, 155
Cooley, Ambrose, 248
Coombs, Charles, 79
Coombs, G. G., 270
Cooper, Sergt. James, 330
Cooper, Gen. Samuel, 68, 370
Cooper W. T., 230
Corcoran, Thomas W., 233
Cornwell, Charles C., 158
Corput, Capt. ——, 310
Corry, Henry, 81, 97, 154, 326
Corry, James B., 154
Cosgriff, James O., 294
Cosson, John S., 301, 316
Costello, Lt. Thomas, 14, 74
Costigan, Dorsey T., 80
Cotter, ——, 314, 316
Cottonham, Lt. ——, 302, 303
Cottrell, Edward C., 326
Cousins, J. H., 316
Covington, 298
Covington, Allen J., 326
Covington, Jesse H., 229, 270
Cox, Corp. A. G., 315
Cox, George, 294
Cox, Maj. Gen. J. D., 279
Cox, James, 316
Cox, James B., 234
Cox, William H. H., 294
Coyle, Patrick, 76
Craig, Edward, 316
Crane, Brent, 229
Crane, Capt. J. Parran, 85, 86, 97, 104, 109, 111, 127, 137, 154, 234
Crane, William, 232
Crangle, Robert, 316
Craven, B. L., 270
Crawford, George I., 234
Crawford, H. H., 137, 155
Crawford, H. V. D., 230
Crawford, Thomas, 229
Creager, Lt. Frank, 330
Creamer, Jacob I., 76
Crenshaw, William, 74
Crescent City, 305
Cretin, Andrew L., 157
Cretin, Henry, 157
Cretin, Hillary, 142, 157
Cretin, John, 232
Crider, J. M., 316
Crise, George, W., 161

Criswell, John O., 233
Crittenden, Churchill, 215, 232
Cropper, Thomas E., 230
Cross, Lt. Alexander, 15, 79
Cross Keys, 54, 56, 242, 277
Crowley, James, 270
Crowley, Michael, 316
Crowley, Sergt. R. C., 323, 324, 326, 328
Crown, Lt. J. R., 330
Crow's Valley, 308
Croyeau, Edward A., 161
Crozart, J. A., 316
Crughan, Michael, 248
Crummer, Armstrong, 156
Cub Run, 287
Culbreth, John, 75
Culpeper, 35, 65, 66, 121, 184, 185, 252, 285, 286, 287
Culp's Hill, 93, 105
Culver, E. K., 326
Culver, William, 325, 326, 328
Cumberland Gap, 297, 298
Cumberland, Md., 208, 209, 210, 289, 290
Cummins, Daniel, 78
Cunningham, Lt. Col. ———, 64
Cunningham, George W., 235
Cunningham, R., 78, 254
Curran, John, 316
Cushing, Lt. John, Jr., 14, 77
Cushing, Robert H., 77, 112, 155
Cusick, Frederick, 74, 324, 326, 328
Custer, Gen. George A., 194, 199, 202, 216
Cutshaw, Maj. W. E., 46

D

Dabney, Lt. Frederick Y., 67, 259, 261, 270
Dabney's Ferry, 190, 198, 200
Dade, William F., 233
Daffin, Francis D., 270
Dahlgren, Col. Ulric, 47, 189-193, 200
Dailey, W. H., 316
Dall, H. McPherson, 161, 232
Dall, Rash, 255
Dallam, Charles F., 326
Dallam, William, 265

Dallas, 309
Dalton, 308, 311
Damar, John G., 270
Dammen, Joseph, 74
Dance, E. Scott, 232
Daniel, Brig. Gen. J., 73
Daniels, William, 247
Darksville, 21, 119
Dashield, George H., 76
Davidson, Gen. ———, 216
Davisdon, E., 316
Davidson, Robert, 234
Davidson, Thomas H., 77
Davis, Corp. A. J., 309, 314, 315
Davis, Evan, 233
Davis, George W., 152, 156
Davis, H. B., 255
Davis, Howard I., 77
Davis, Col. J. Lucius, 181
Davis, Jacob N., 111, 152
Davis, Jacob W., 137
Davis, Lt. James A., 80, 89, 115, 158
Davis, Pres. Jefferson, 25, 189-195, 278, 364
Davis, John G., 145
Davis, Dr. John J., 331
Davis, John S., 158
Davis, John, T., 270
Davis, Joshua, 294
Davis, Michael, 112, 155
Davis, Moscow, 247
Davis, P. A., 231
Davis, Sergt. Phineas, I., 233
Davis, Maj. T. S., 330
Davis, Thomas S., 233
Davis, W. A., 294
Davis, W. E., 309, 316
Davis, W. J., 316
Davis, William, 225
Davis, William F., 81
Davis, William H., 80
Davis' Brigade, 135, 146
Dawson, John, 79
Dawson, Lambdin T., 326
Dawson, Levin G., 157
Dawson, Robert A., 157
Dawson, Robert M., 113, 155
Deakins, Corp. J. R. H., 230, 231
Deale, Theophilus N., 137, 152
Dean, James E., 326
Dean, Thomas, 326

Dean, William H., 270
Deas, Lt. Col. George, 10
Deatore, Corp. George, 141
Deaver, John R., 235
Debrill, Charles, 247
Decatur, 306, 307, 311
Deep Bottom, 134
Deer Creek, 299, 302, 306
Deering's Brigade, 134, 221, 222
Degan, Casper, 316
DeGourney, Lt. Col. P. S., 330
De Grey, Lewis F., 159
DeJarnette's Woods, 321
De Kalb, Gen. Johann, 341
Delaney, Francis, 316
Delashmutt, William H., 233
Delevie, Jacob, 75
Delozier, George, 154
Delozier, J. J., 137
Delozier, John, 154
Delozier, Thomas J., 112, 154
Dement, Benjamin F., 81, 114, 157
Dement, Sergt. Maj. Frank, 151
Dement, John H., 81
Dement, Capt. William F., 122, 124, 188, 243, 259-262, 264-266, 270, 322, 324, 350
Dement, William G., 157
Demopolis, 307, 315
Dempsey, Joseph, 294, 324
Demmead, Aquilla, 248
Demming's Crossroads, 29
Dennis, James, 77
Denny, James W., 330
Dent, ———, 308
Dent, Clay H., 154
Dent, George H., 81
Dent, M., 231
Denton, Corp. George, 80, 152
Deppish, Lt. Edward, 15, 79
Deppish, Frank, 79
DeSoto, 299
Devitt, Edward, I., 76
Devries, John, 97, 156, 248
Devries, William, 247
Dickerson, L. T., 229
Diggs, Lt. Eugene, 31, 81, 246
Diggs, J. T., 270
Disharoom, John, 234

Disney, William, 74, 247
Dispatch Station, 278
Dittus, John F., 232
Ditty, Capt. C. Irving, 166, 192, 196, 212, 229, 235, 237, 255
Dix, William T., 231
Dixon, Corp. James H., 138, 157
Dobbs, ———, 246
Dode, Samuel, 156
Dollar, A., 314
Donahue, Joseph, 159
Doncaster, Lt. J. W., 301, 313, 315
Donohue, Edward, 316
Donohue, John, 159
Donohue, Thomas, 77
Dooley, Bernard, 130, 157
Dooley, Frank, 316
Dooley, Robert, 81
Dooley, Thomas, 235
Doomandy, John, 233
Doran, William, 247
Dorsett, J. H., 270
Dorsey, Albert, 248
Dorsey, Andrew, 229
Dorsey, C. H., 225
Dorsey, C. R., 225
Dorsey, C. W., 229
Dorsey, Col. Caleb, 330
Dorsey, Daniel B., 270
Dorsey, Capt. E. R., 9-14, 19, 29, 40, 46, 72, 75, 160
Dorsey, Evan L., 270
Dorsey, Sergt. Ezekiel S., 80, 97, 152
Dorsey, Lt. Col. Gustavus W., 167, 168, 212, 213, 218-220, 225-229, 237, 251-253, 255
Dorsey, Hammond, 177, 255
Dorsey, Harry, 229
Dorsey, I. G., 229
Dorsey, Q. M. Ignatius, 166
Dorsey, J. Pembrook, 229
Dorsey, James E., 155
Dorsey, John, 229, 255
Dorsey, John W., 330
Dorsey, Lloyd, 229
Dorsey, Lt. Nicholas, 330
Dorsey, Pue, 229
Dorsey, Pulaski, 229
Dorsey, Richard B., 80, 161

Dorsey, Lt. Samuel W., 170, 249, 250, 254
Dorsey, Thomas B., 330
Dorsey, Sergt. Upton L., 229, 233
Dorsey, Lt. W. H. B., 73, 166, 167
Dorsey, William, 255
Dorsey, Sergt. William F., 231
Dosenberry, H. B., 294
Dorsett, James A., 81
Doswell, Maj. Thomas, 125
Dougherty, Cornelius, 78
Dougherty, Corp. Daniel, 74, 324, 326, 328
Dougherty, James, 232
Doughlas, Bernard, 161
Doughlass, Jackson, 80
Douglass, Col. H. Kyd., 241, 330
Dove, Samuel B., 151
Dove, W. S., 316
Dover Mills, 189
Downing, John L., 81
Downing, Corp. John Z., 137, 154
Downs, James, 316
Doyle, John, 79
Doyle, Sergt. Joseph T., 53, 77
Doyle, Philip, 114, 157
Drake, Col. J., 251
Drew, Capt. J. W., 331
Drewry, Charles, F., 151
Driscoll, James, 159, 316
Dropman, Charles, 74
Drury, Charles T., 154
Drury, William C., 154
Drury's Bluff, 219, 269
Dryden, R. J., 270
Duck, Henry R. S., 75
Duck River, 311
Duffan, Henry, 316
Dugan, Hammond, 161
Dugan, Pierre C., 161
Duke, John F., 154
Dulaney, Jeremiah, 112, 155
Dulany, Col. R. H., 168-171
Dunahue, Joseph, 159
Duncan, Rev. ———, 122, 123
Duncan, James A., 294
Dunegan, Philip, 248
Dunkard Church, 282
Dunlop, Joseph L., 229
Dunlop, S. O., 270

Dunn, John, 235
Dunn, William C., 293
Dunnington, Lemuel, 114, 130, 157
Durburrow, J. C., 229
Durham, James, 77
Durkin, John, 74, 255
Durner, John T., 152
Durst, John, 78
Dusenberg, B., 255
Dusenberry, H. Bowie, 161
Dutton, J. W., 231
Dutton, S. S., 231
Duvall, Charles, 316
Duvall, Daniel, 112, 137, 155
Duvall, Eli, 330
Duvall, Evans, 151, 155
Duvall, Capt. Ferd C., 86, 88, 97, 120, 129, 140, 141, 149, 155
Duvall, Franklin, 151, 155
Duvall, James E., 234
Duvall, John, H., 158
Duvall, Leonidas, 161
Duvall, P. B., 270
Duvall, Ridgely, 76
Duvall, S. F., 270
Duvall, Samuel, 155
Duvall, Tobias, 112, 155
Duvall, W. R.,294
Dwyer, Martin, 316
Dyer, A. M., 231
Dyser, Luke, 79

E

Eagan, Peter, 158
Eagan, Thomas T., 159
Eagger, Henry, 79
Eareckson, F. G., 231
Earle, James T., 231
Early, Maj. Gen. Jubal A., 68, 93-96, 98, 133, 176, 203, 204, 206, 207-209, 211, 219, 220, 224, 243-246, 261-264, 283, 288-289, 319, 322, 361
Early, Tom, 314, 316
Earnest, Thomas J., 294
Eaton, J. H., 316
Eastern Shore, 259
Ebbert, ———, 233
Ebert, Charles, 231
Eckhart, August, 74
Eckhart, Charles, 79, 231

Echols, Brig. Gen. J., 126-128
Ector, Brig. Gen. M. D., 306
Edelen, John D., 138
Edelin, Alex W., 77
Edelin, Capt. Charles E., 10, 11, 14, 74
Edelin, Francis, D., 158
Edelin, Jesse R., 234
Edelin, John D., 158
Edelin, Philip F., 270
Edelin, William J., 111, 137, 151, 152, 229
Edell, Henry J., 76, 294
Edgar, Corp. Joseph, 301, 315
Edgar, Thomas, 112, 152
Edgar, William, 126
Edge, J. G., 270
Edwards, Dr. ———, 255
Edward's, Ferry, 249
Edwards, Frank K., 316
Edwards, W. E., 19
Edwards, William, H., 76, 232
Egan, Andrew H., 320, 326, 328
Eiger, John H., 236
Eisenberger, George, 78, 233
Elbert, ———, 233
Elder, George H., 232
Elder, Henry, 316
Elder Lawrence, 232
Elder Philip L., 161
Ellicott, Charles J. F., 316
Ellicott, Maj. John, 331
Elligett, Michael, 142, 158
Elliott, G. M., 231
Elliott, J. T., 231
Elliott, Joseph W., 77
Ellis, Thomas, 155, 255
Elkton, 314
Elthau's Landing, 251
Elzey, Maj. Gen. Arnold, 7, 11, 14, 22-26, 28, 29, 32-34, 39, 54, 72, 192, 193, 243, 244, 276, 277, 314, 341, 364
Emack, Capt. George W., 166, 168, 178, 180, 181, 192, 226, 230
Emack, Lt. James, 331
Embert, J. R. H., 231
Embert, John, 326
Emmart, George, 247
Emmerick, Corp. John, 247
Emmitsburg, 178, 179
Emory, Albert T., 111, 152,
 296, 315
Emory, Daniel G., 232
Emory, Dr. Richard, 331
Ennis, Thomas, 77, 326
Eno, Charles E., 74
Ensor, Zadock, 233
Enterprise, 306
Ernull, A. W., 161
Erwin, Lt. Holmes, 298, 299, 301, 315
Erwin, Corp. W. H., 315
Essender, William, 77
Estrella, 300
Ecthison, W. L., 138, 158
Evans, Benjamin, 255
Evans, Charles, 294
Evans, Dallas, J., 154
Eveline, John, 78
Evergau, Thomas J., 326
Ewell, Gen. Richard S., 33-35, 39, 44, 45, 50, 53-57, 59, 63, 93, 95, 96, 100-103, 119-122, 165, 176-180, 181, 188, 264-267, 276-278, 284, 324, 341, 349
Ewen, W. T., 234
Ewing, Harvey G., 233
Ewing, William F., 233

F

Fairbank, F. M., 326
Fairfax Court House, 28-31, 250
Fairfield, 178
Fairmont, 173
Falconer, Edward, W., 75
Falling Waters, 20, 252, 261
Fallis, Edward, 144, 157
Fallon, James, 114, 157
Falls Church, 250
Falmouth, 252
Farmer, James, 294
Farmer, Thomas, 316
Farmville, 222, 223
Farr, Francis A., 78, 294
Farr, Joseph R., 80
Farrell, James, 79
Farrell, William, 79
Fassitt, William P., 161
Faucett, James A., 294
Faulk, J., 309
Faulk, S., 316
Fauquier, 241

Favour, C. R., 248
Fayetteville, 266
Fearhake, Adolphus, 233
Feast, Loudoun, 75, 247
Federal Hill, 4
Feige, Charles, L., 152
Fellins, J. W., 270
Fenton, Sergt. Daniel A., 138, 147, 149, 151, 158
Fentswait, J. R., 115
Fenwick, Corp. Albert, 112, 154
Fercoit, Corp. Charles, 79
Ferguson, John, 81, 229, 234
Ferguson, Brig. Gen. S. W., 299, 304, 306
Ferrall, John A., 81
Ferrall, J. Thomas, 231
Ferrell, J. Thomas, 76
Ferry, William J., 293
Feuthswait, J. R., 158
Fiege, Charles, 77
Field, Edward W., 270
Field George W., 234
Fields, Sergt. ———, 247
Fillis, Edward, 77
Filmer, Edward, 316
Fink, Henry, 79
Finnegan, Brig. Gen. Joseph, 126, 128
Finney, R. H., 150
Fipps, F., 248
First Maryland Artillery, 259-271, 338
First Maryland Cavalry, 165, 197, 198, 211, 212, 236, 237, 253, 338
First Maryland Infantry, 9-81, 338, 358
Fish Lake, 302, 304, 306
Fisher, C. D., 248
Fishpan, Sergt. Eli, 79
Fitzgerald, John E., 137, 152
Fitzgerald, R. E., 294
Fitzgerald, Thomas, 233
Fitzgerald, William B., 75, 255
Fitzgerald, William H., 331
Fitzpatrick, Daniel, 248
Fitzpatrick, John, 294
Flack, Thomas, J. A., 75
Flanagan, John, 232
Flannigan, Jefferson, 74
Flannigan, John, 159
Flannigan, Patrick, 236

Fleenor, A., 236
Fleming, Sergt. William, 315
Fletcher, F. D., 294
Fletcher, Joseph G., 315
Fletcher, S. D., 294
Flint, Joseph, 233
Flood, Peter, 159
Florence, 311
Flowers, W. H., 316
Floyd, Sergt. Robert, 254, 255
Floyd, William S., 236
Foley, Daniel, 316
Foley, David R., 232
Foley, John, 316
Foman, Charles, 248
Foman, Perry, 248
Foos, George W., 78
Forber, Marshal A., 270
Forbes, Sergt. J. Harris, 270
Ford, ———, 247
Ford, C. S., 129, 155
Ford, Clement, 77
Ford, Henry, 112, 151, 154
Ford James, E., 270
Ford, James W., 316
Foreman, Valentine, 73
Forest, Capt. Joseph, 319
Forner, William, 294
Forney, Lt. George, 247, 371
Forrest, Lt. Davis C., 87, 157
Forrest, Joseph, 326
Forrest, Zachariah, 79
Forrestt, Pitt, 255
Fort Delaware, 301
Fort De Russy, 299
Fort Gregg, 325, 328
Fort Harrison, 139
Fort McHenry, 4, 344
Fort Pulaski, 275
Fort Republic, 277
Fort Severn, 344
Fort Sumter, 2, 291
Fort Warren, 245
Foster, James H., 161
Foster, Michael, 229
Foster, Robert E., 161
Forsyth, A. M., 161
Forsyth, Henry, 229
Fourth Maryland Artillery, 319, 338
Foutain, W. B., 115, 158
Fowler, A. J., 316
Fowler, E. C., 316
Foxwell, Charles J., 142, 154

Frankfort Ky., 298
Franklin, 48
Franklin, J. F., 270
Franklin, Dr. J. W., 297
Franklin, Lt. James S., 87, 129, 138, 156
Franklin, Maj. Gen. William B., 204
Frayer, F., 265
Fraizer, Sergt. L. W., 309, 315
Fraizer's Farm, 260
Freayer, Frederick, 270
Frederick, A., 294
Frederick City, 4, 10, 34, 71, 177, 189, 204, 245, 281, 289
Fredericksburg, 189, 197, 198, 251, 252, 259, 262-264, 285, 321, 322, 329
Freeburger, Willliam, 247
Freeland, Thomas E., 158
Freeman, Bernard, 111, 151, 152
Freeman, Sergt. F. Z., 81, 111, 137, 154
Freeman, J. Marion, 137, 161
Freeman, Lewis, 161
Freeman, R. M., 161
Freeman, Sergt. Thomas S., 81, 111, 154
Fremont, Maj. Gen. J. C., 47, 48, 57, 242, 277
French, Maj. Gen. F. S., 12
Front Royal, 40, 43, 44, 54, 95, 242, 264, 276, 283
Frye, Brig. Gen. B. D., 133
Fulkerson, J. K. P., 316
Fuller, Capt. E. A., 300
Fulton, Alexander, 111, 129, 152
Funk, Charles D., 233
Funkstown, 252
Funsten, Col. O. R., 91, 92, 168, 169

G

Gabrill, Abraham W., 233
Gadd, W. F., 161
Gaiging, Michael, 255
Gaines' Mill, 61, 64, 126, 188, 260, 277, 349, 369
Gaither, Capt. George R., 212, 249-251, 254
Gaither, Washington, 255

Gale, Frank, 271
Gale, G. G., 271
Gale, Lt. John, 260, 268, 270
Gallagher, Howard L., 137, 152
Gannon, William, 77, 152, 153
Gardener, J. B., 271
Gardener, J. B. W., 271
Gardiner, Benjamin, 159
Gardiner, William F., 80, 111
Gardner, A., 271
Gardner, E. G., 294
Gardner, J., 255
Gardner, James, 151, 157
Gardner, John H., 326
Gardner, William F., 152
Garner, J. H., 271
Garnett, Brig. Gen. Robert Selden, 13, 160
Garrett, John W., 206
Garrett, W. A. H., 316
Garrison, Robert D., 155
Garst, Benjamin, 309, 316
Gassaway, Samuel, 75
Gatchell, J. G., 294
Gates, L. R., 316
Gates, W., 316
Gault, C., 248
Gavin, Thomas, 78
Gavin, William, 74, 151, 157
Gayther, James W., 294
Geary, Maj. Gen. John W., 105, 116
Geasey, Charles H., 233
Geasey, James W., 73, 233
Gegan, W. H., 294
Geiger, Frederick, 315
Geiger, John, 233
Gemmill, Sergt. Thomas H., 234
George, Thomas, 232
Georgetown, 203, 298
Georgia, 296, 298
Gerding, Corp. S. G. W., 315
German, M. P., 271
Gephart, Sol. A., 73, 229
Gesdon, Walter, 79
Gettysburg, 26, 101, 102, 104, 109, 116-119, 134, 176-179, 181, 188, 252, 256, 261, 265, 266, 267, 285, 324, 325, 328
Gevin, Peter M., 159
Gibbons, John, 157

Gibbons, Col. S. B., 23
Gibson, E., 231, 294
Gibson, F., 294
Gibson, Henry, 233
Gibson, John E., 231
Gibson, Sergt. George G., 161
Gibson, S., 231
Gibson, W. C., 135, 155, 255
Giles, Lt. Thomas D., 297, 301, 308, 314, 315
Giles, William F., 232
Gilham, Col. William, 160
Gill, G. M., 255, 351, 352
Gill, John, 80, 229, 352
Gill, Mrs. M. Gillet, 363
Gill, Corp. Sommerville P., 137, 141, 152, 352
Gill, William H., 232
Gillaird, Dr. E. S., 72
Gilland, Stephen, 248
Gillen, Stephen, 248
Gilmor, Arthur, 248
Gilmor, C. G., 248
Gilmor, C. J., 161
Gilmor, Col. Harry W., 95, 174, 177, 178, 204, 209, 211, 212, 241-248, 290, 341, 348, 351
Gilmor, Lt. Richard T., 15, 80, 247
Gilmor, William, of Wm., 247
Gilpin, John, 271
Gilroy, Thomas, 234
Girvin, John, 78
Gist, Mordecai, 341
Gist, Washington I., 80
Gittings, Harry, 255
Glass, Richard C., 271
Glasscocke, Sergt. John E., 265, 266, 271
Glaudel, John, 75
Glenn, Clement, 232
Glenn, Elias, 232
Glenn, Francis, 232
Glenn, James S., 234
Glenn, Samuel T., 111, 152
Glenn, Sergt. W. G., 293
Glenn, W. Y., 248
Glenon, John, 74
Glenville, 173
Glocker, Theodore, 247
Glondell, John, 255
Glossner, Hanas, 78
Glover, W. H., 316

Going, H. F., 358
Golden, John, 78
Golden, H. F., 316
Golden, W., 316
Golder, Hamilton, 75
Goldsborough, ———, 326
Goldsborough, Charles, 271
Goldsborough, Eugene Y., 73
Goldsborough, N. Lee, 73, 147, 156
Goldsborough, Maj. W. W., 14, 29, 33, 40, 65-68, 73, 75, 89, 92-97, 110, 147, 152, 158, 243
Goldsmith, John W., 80
Goode, Demetrius, 80
Goodhand, G. W., 326
Goodloe, William, 234
Goodman, Lt. John W., 292, 293
Goodman, Julius D., 77
Goodman, Otho, 232
Goodwin, C. Ridgely, 345, 357
Goodwin, Frank Greenwood, 355, 357
Goodwin, John, 79, 141, 152
Goodwin, R. M., 357
Gordon, Henry, 307, 316
Gordon, Lt. Gen. J. B., 68, 94, 97, 198, 205, 208, 220, 263, 264, 283
Gordon, John H., 79
Gordon, W. J., 294
Gordonsville, 35, 65, 217, 251, 276, 279
Gordrian, Antony, 316
Gordian, S., 316
Gore, John W., 326
Gorman, P., 316
Gorman, W. H., 271
Gorman, William, 265
Gorsuch, Sergt. N., 246, 247
Gosgriff, James O., 294
Gossom, J. H., 115, 158
Gough, Charles E., 231, 232
Gough, J. H., 271, 316
Gover, Sergt. Edwin, 156
Gowdey, James, 161
Grace, William, 142, 151, 155
Grafton, 203
Graham, ———, 229, 326
Graham, George H., 78
Graham, Jesse, 78, 232
Graham, Thomas, 159

Grahame, ———, 323, 328
Grammer, Frederick L., 152
Granberry, ———, 312
Grand Era, 299
Grand Gulf, 299, 301
Grand Lake, 300
Grant, John, 138, 157
Grant, Gen. Ulysses S., 126, 128, 133, 139-145, 198, 205, 206, 214, 218, 220, 223-225, 269, 291, 301, 302, 304
Grason, Lt. John, 319-323, 326, 328
Graves, Lt. Henry M., 331
Graves, Sergt. William B., 331
Gray, Henry L., 232
Gray, J. A., 316
Gray, Joseph, 157
Gray, William R., 76
Grayson, James B., 80
Grayson, Spence M., 152
Great Falls, 250
Green, A., 326
Green, Charles, 79
Green, H. Barton, 77
Green, Hugh T., 76
Green, J. F., 161
Green, James, 328
Green, John, 323, 325, 328
Green, John F., 326
Green, John T., 157
Green, Lewis, 113, 156
Green, Matthew, 76
Green, Brig. Gen. Thomas, 105
Green, Corp. Thomas I., 81
Green, Lt. Thomas J., 206, 237
Green, Vincent, 323, 326, 328
Green, W. O., 231
Green, William, 236
Green, William B., 234
Greencastle, 101, 284
Greenfield, William, 79
Greenland Gap, 169-174, 178, 181, 213
Green Spring Valley, 204
Greenvillage, 266
Greenville, 302, 304-306
Greenwell, Joseph A., 161, 294
Greenwell, Thomas W. H., 80
Greenwood, 306
Gregg, David McM., 20
Grey, ———, 255
Griffin, George C., 229
Griffin, Lt. Joseph, 14, 74

Griffin, Capt. W. Hunter, 92, 94, 134, 200, 243, 253, 254, 275, 283-287, 293, 316, 357
Griffith, David, 229
Griffith, Edward, 77
Griffith, Sergt. Frank, 229, 255
Griffith, George, 255
Griffith, Greenberry, 79
Griffith, Richard, 255
Griffith, Capt. Thomas, 165, 166, 229, 237, 251, 254
Grimes, Cornelius, 233
Grimes, Harry, 233
Grimes, Robert, 326
Griswold, Maj. Elias, 331
Grogan, Charles E., 80
Grogan, J., 232
Grogan, James J., 152, 161
Grogan, Kennedy, 75, 170
Grogan, R. R., 170, 232
Groshon, Sergt. John F., 73
Groshon, Lt. John F., 73
Grove, Louis, 73
Grove, Thomas F., 154, 232
Groves, Thomas F., 81
Grubb, H. O., 294
Gugenheimer, S., 316
Guillette, Lt. G. G., 89, 130, 138, 158
Guise, Andrew, 75
Gumby, John W., 271
Gunpowder, 204, 245
Guy, G. N., 151
Guy, George W., 157
Guyther, Sergt. W. H. W., 230
Guyther, William, 161
Gwynn, Capt. A. J., 86, 87, 114, 130, 142, 157
Gwynn, James J., 80
Gwynn, William, 143
Gwynn, Wizzie, 326

H

Haas, Isaac C., 326
Haase, T. H. B., 161
Haffey, Corp. John, 74
Haffey, Corp. William, 74
Hagan, Henry, 331
Hagan, John, 78
Hagan, R., 248
Hager, John, 232
Hagerstown, 99, 177, 181, 184, 204, 208, 237, 245, 267, 285

Hagley, Alphonsus, 157
Hahn, Reuben H., 73, 248
Hail, Francis, 316
Halbig, J. S., 114, 157
Hall, Edward, 229
Hall, Maj. Thomas W., 331
Hall, Maj. W. Carvel, 331
Haller, John E., 155
Hallohan, Sergt. Michael, 142
Halpin, S. P., 248
Halpin, Thomas, 79
Halstead, Charles, 271
Ham, James, 316
Hambleton, J. P., 231
Hambleton, T. E., 235
Hamilton, Beale D., 112, 155
Hamilton, Edward, 73
Hamilton, Jacob, 78
Hamilton, Samuel H., 112, 155
Hamilton, William, 248
Hamilton's Crossing, 332, 262
Hammell, Edward, 73
Hammer, F. H., 294
Hammett, David, 142, 156, 294
Hammett, John H., 236
Hammett, John M., 81
Hammett, John T., 153
Hammett, Sergt. Whittingham, 142, 154, 316
Hammond, Charles, 112, 143, 155, 229, 248
Hammond, Denton, 233
Hammond, Edgar, 112, 155
Hammond, Oliver B., 233
Hampton, Thomas, 236
Hampton, Lt. Gen. Wade C., 63, 185, 187, 188, 191-193, 202, 203
Hance, James J., 80, 232
Hance, William A., 141
Hance, William H., 153
Hancock, Md., 209, 210
Hancock, Corp. George W., 139, 315
Hancock, H. H., 247
Hancock, Maj. Gen. Winfield S., 139
Hands, Corp. Washington, 76, 294
Handy, J. C., 270
Handy, Lt. Thomas, 331
Hanley, J. Stephen, 157
Hanley, James, 138, 157

Hanley, Thomas, 79
Hanna, George, 77
Hanna, John, 78
Hannaway, William, 229
Hannigan, William, 236
Hannon, L. M., 271
Hannon, S. B., 271
Hannon, Corp. T. L., 81
Hanover, 122-125, 127, 188, 189, 195, 197-200, 243, 244, 252, 258, 288, 364
Hanson, John D., 81
Hanson, Notley, 111, 153
Hardcastle, Col. A. B., 331
Hardcastle, William H., 155
Hardesty, John W., 110, 153
Hardesty, Lt. Richard, 325, 326, 328
Harding, ———, 247
Harding, Maj. Charles R., 122
Harding, Capt. Charles W., 72, 73
Harding, Corp. John, 229, 248, 255
Hardy, Samuel, 294
Hardy, William, 130
Hargey, William, 138, 158, 159
Harkins, James, 234
Harley, Job, 156
Harman, Victor, 316
Harmon, Col. Arthur W., 172, 173, 242
Harney, Daniel, 156
Harper, James K., 326
Harper, Lloyd, 77
Harper, Col. Robert W., 331
Harper's Ferry, 10, 11, 20, 47, 68, 208, 242, 281, 283, 321, 341
Harpeth River, 312
Harrington, J. W., 294
Harris, C. H., 271
Harris, Charles, 265
Harris, G. M., 316
Harris, Mrs. J. H., 371
Harris, John F., 271
Harris, Sergt. John G., 265, 266, 270
Harris, Joseph, 271
Harris, William E., 53, 80
Harrisburg, 101, 165, 173, 245, 277, 285
Harrison, Lt. ———, 246
Harrison, C. H., 229

Harrison, George, 331
Harrison, J. W., 161
Harrison, P. L., 326
Harrison, Thomas D., 129, 153
Harrison, William, 233
Harrison, William H., 153
Harrisonburg, 49, 54, 56, 90-92, 165, 277, 364
Harrison's Landing, 64, 65, 279
Harrodsburg, 298
Harry, James, 229
Harry, John, 232
Hart, William, 294
Harter, Andrew, 245
Hartigan, John L., 215, 232
Hartley, William B., 79
Hartmier, Richard J., 75, 255
Hartz, David, 78
Harvey, J. C., 316
Harvey, Martin, 319, 326
Harvey, W., 316
Harwood, Richard, 235
Haskell, Maj. A. M., 331
Haslett, Capt. R. E., 331
Hastings, Hugh, 73
Hatcher's Run, 134, 145
Hattaway, W., Jr., 316
Hattaway, W., Sr., 316
Hatton, Dr. J. W. F., 261, 271
Hatton, Joseph, 271
Hatton, R. H. S., 271
Hause, Corp. LaFayette, 231
Hawes, Gov. ——, 298
Hawkins, Maj. A. M., 331
Hawkins, J. S., 271
Hawley, George W., 317
Hayden, A., 255
Hayden, Charles G., 81
Hayden, George, 111, 154
Hayden, Rev. Horace E., 229, 255
Hayden, John A., 112, 154
Hayden, John F., 288, 293
Hayden, Richard A., 75
Hayden, William, 255
Hayne's Landing, 306
Hays, Gen. Harry, 64, 95, 97, 125, 263, 264, 283
Hays, J. G., 159
Hays, John, 113, 156
Hayward, Henry, 232
Haywood, Sergt. Charles E., 161

Hazell, Patrick, 73, 154
Head, John L., 236
Healy, Dr. Thomas A., 331
Heaphy, Sergt. William, 142, 156
Hearne, B. G., 231
Hearne, Samuel B., 231
Hearne, William H., 157
Hebb, Henry J., 80
Hebb, Thomas A., 80
Hecht, Robert H., 73
Heck, Jacob, 73, 158
Heck, Robert, 158
Heenan, H., 153
Heenan, Corp. Patrick, 142
Heidlersburg, 176
Heighe, John M., 229
Heimiller, Herman, 74, 232
Heimiller, William, 76, 247
Heineman, H., 317
Heiner, Charles M., 161
Heiskell, Capt. J. Munroe, 331
Helwig, L., 317
Hemston, Alexander T., 79
Henden, Thomas, 229
Henderson, Gaither, 229
Henderson, George, 79
Henderson, Peter, 158
Henderson, William, 158
Hendorg, Frederick, 76
Hendry, W., 317
Henry, Sergt. Algernon, 138, 158
Henry, John C., 129, 137, 153
Herbert, Charles F., 155
Herbert, J. R., 154
Herbert, Gen. James R., 10, 11, 14, 26, 40, 50, 76, 83, 85-97, 104, 110, 129, 152, 243, 283, 341, 358
Herbert, John P., 81
Herbert, Brig. Gen. Louis, 355
Herbert, William, 81, 97, 143, 154
Hergesheimer, David, 233
Hering, Frank, 233
Herman, Solomon, 317
Hermantrout, W. F., 326
Herndon, E. M., 314
Heron, A., 294
Herron, B. C., 317
Herron, George, 232
Herron, Corp. Virgil P., 315
Herster, Frederick, 77

Heth, Maj. Gen. H. C., 133, 135, 139-141, 148
Hewes, James, 73
Hewes, Warner, 255
Hickey, E. P., 231
Hickey, J. F., 231
Hickey, Sergt. John P., 326
Hickman, Joshua, 294
Hidden, Lt. ——, 33
Higdon, Sergt. F. L., 81, 151, 152
Higdon, Corp. Francis L., 81
Higgins, Eugene, 161
Higgins, John P., 161
Higgins, W. G., 271
Hildt, John, 73
Hill, Gen. A. P., 23, 121, 133-136, 148, 262, 321
Hill, Benjamin H., 362
Hill, Dr. C. G., 367
Hill, Lt. Charles S., 331
Hill, J. P., 231
Hill, John, 326
Hill, John A., 73
Hill, John O., 151
Hill, Maj. N. S., 331
Hill, William, 76
Hill, Lt. William I., 261, 262, 270
Hillary, Thomas, 233
Hillary, Washington, 271
Hilleary, G. W., 271
Hines, J. W., 271
Hines, Michael, 130, 158
Hines, Thomas J., 113, 156
Hinnick, Marion, 294
Hinton, Nicholas J., 317
Hircht, Albert, 74
Hissey, John, 74
Hitzelberger, Charles T., 76
Hobbs, Jarrett, 248, 255
Hobbs, Capt. N. Chew, 237, 248, 251, 254, 255
Hobbs, Townley, 255
Hobbs, William H., 247
Hoblitzell, Fetter S., 80
Hodge, Charles A., 143, 157
Hodges, Benjamin, 114, 157
Hodges, Lt. Charles W., 86, 88, 112, 137, 145, 155
Hodges, Sergt. Robert T., 137, 155
Hodges, Sergt. Thomas O., 145, 157

Hodson, E. Payton, 161
Hoerster, Frederick, 129, 153
Hoffman, George, 78
Hoffman, J. H., 317
Hoffman, Capt. R. Curzon, 161, 331
Hoffman, William, 129, 153
Hogan, James, 317
Hogan, Thomas, 77
Hogarthy, William, 113, 156
Hoge, Charles A., 157
Hoke, Maj. Gen. R. F., 95
Holbrook, A., 317
Holbrook, G. J., 317
Holbrook, John, 232
Holbrook, John F., 76
Holbrook, Capt. Thomas, 10
Holden, Robert, 114, 157
Holder, J., 317
Holland, Albert, 294
Holland, J. J. J., 255
Holland, John, 255
Holland, Mitchell, 255
Holland, P. R., 255
Holland, Thomas, R., 77
Holliday, Henry, 151
Hollingsworth's Mill, 94
Hollingsworth, William T., 234
Holloway, Michael, 159
Hollyday, George, 232
Hollyday, Corp. George T., 234, 331
Hollyday, Henry, 153
Hollyday, Lamar, 111, 153
Hollyday, William H., 80, 129, 153
Holmead, C. H., 271
Holmes, Sergt. J. C., 247
Holohan, Sergt. Michael, 158
Holtzman, William H. F., 325, 326
Hood, George, 79
Hood, Gen. J. B., 310
Hood, John M., 155
Hooff, John J., 236
Hook, R. B., 248
Hooker, Gen. Charles E., 252, 321, 322, 345
Hooper, James, 331
Hooper, Sergt. John P., 296, 315
Hoopes, Mrs. Herman, 363
Hopkins, ———, 323
Hopkins, Corp. A., 326, 328

Hopkins, Henry H., 75, 158, 255
Hopkins, Samuel J., 111, 153
Hoppell, George W., 73
Horn, H., 248
Horner, Frank, 229
Hottinger, M., 294
Hough, Gresham, 80, 229
Hough, Lt. Richard D., 33
Hough, Samuel J., 229
Hough, Lt. William D., 15, 78
Howard, C. C., 232
Howard, Charles, 76
Howard, D. Ridgely, 111, 137
Howard, David R., 153
Howard, Dr. Edward L., 33, 75
Howard, Capt. George, 166, 199, 231, 249, 250, 254
Howard, Lt. James McHenry, 75, 331
Howard, Capt. John E., 72
Howard, Q. M. John E., 98, 152, 232
Howard, Capt. McHenry, 63, 80, 88, 331
Howard, R. McG., 232
Howard, Ridge, 137
Howard, Roberts, 81
Howard, Washington, 271
Howard, William, 294
Howard, Lt. William Key, 14, 76
Howard Co., 205, 245
Howell, Gustavus, 271
Hoyle, Nathan L., 233
Hubball, Bernard, 153
Hubbard, Alexander 72, 73
Hubbard, John L., 157
Hubbard, William H., 141
Hubbard, William L., 153
Hubble, Bernard, 111
Huber, Paul, 326
Hucorn, John F., 231
Huey, Brig Gen. Pennock, 178
Huffington, John, 157
Huger, Lt. Gen. Benjamin, 345
Hughes, Alexander, 153
Hughes, J. O., 317
Hughes, Patrick, 79
Hull, John, 161
Hume, Frank, 231
Hummer, Joseph, 74, 236
Hunt, Charles W., 234

Hunter, Andrew, 203, 204, 207, 214
Hunter, Maj. Gen. David, 98, 203, 204, 207, 244, 245
Hunter, Frederick, 271
Hunter, J. P., 317
Hunter, Mrs. John F., 78, 352
Hunter, John I., 153
Hunter, John J., 151
Hunter, Robert, 294
Hunter, Thomas, 229
Hurley, Abel, 142, 157
Hurley, C., 317
Hurley, James, 129
Hurley, Jobe, 156
Hurley, Otho S., 255
Hurst, Lt. E., 247
Hurst, William, 294
Huster, Frederick, 141
Hutchins, Joseph, 158
Hutchinson, John T., 158
Hutchinson, Joseph, 79
Hutchinson, Thomas, 78
Hutton, Charles, 168, 229
Hutton, S., 317
Hyland, Lt. John G., 75, 87, 114, 157
Hylton, Corp. Solomon, 315
Hyne, E., 294

I

Iglehart, I. James, 153
Iglehart, James, Jr., 110
Iglehart, W. T., 161
Imboden, Brig. Gen. J. D., 91, 208
Independent Grays, 9
Indianola, 299, 300
Inglehart, Edward, 78
Inloes, Alfred, I., 75
Inloes, C. E., 232
Inloes, Charles E., 80
Irvin, John, 294, 326
Irvin, Michael, 279, 294
Isaacs, William, 79, 255
Isham, J. H., 309, 317
Israel, G. P., 294
Iverson, Brig. Gen. Alfred, 68
Ives, Leonard W., 111, 153

J

Jackson, 307, 370

Jackson, Andrew J., 229
Jackson, H. J., 294
Jackson, J. C., 317
Jackson, O., 317
Jackson, Thomas G., 326
Jackson, Lt. Gen. Thomas J., 10, 12, 33, 39, 40, 41, 44-48, 54, 57-60, 65-69, 93, 105, 121, 165, 188, 189, 206, 208, 216-218, 227, 252, 261, 262, 277-282, 306, 320-322, 338, 341, 349, 356, 357, 364, 367, 371
Jackins, William, 225
James, Edwin, 153
James, Sergt. Edwin, 151, 152
Jameson, Frank, 255
Jameson, James, 255
Jamison, Francis, 81
James City, 286
James River, 103, 260, 351
Jarvoe, William F., 235
Jeffers, W. H., 231
Jenkins, Brig. Gen. Albert G., 93, 174, 176, 284, 285
Jenkins, E. Courtney, 161
Jenkins, E. D., 255
Jenkins, George C., 232, 351
Jenkins, Henry, 255
Jenkins, James E., 154
Jenkins, James W., 235
Jenkins, John, 271
Jenkins, John B., 81
Jenkins, John Carroll, 162, 351
Jenkins, Louis W., 271
Jenkins, Poland, 232
Jenkins, Corp. Theodore, 161, 261
Jenkins, W. K., 271
Jenkins, Sergt. William, 76, 113, 138, 156
Jennifer, Col. ———, 259
Jennings, Benjamin R., 76, 145, 153
Jerrold's Mill, 251
Johannes, Martin J., 75
Johnson, Brig. Gen. Bradley T., 10-14, 29, 34, 37, 40, 43, 45-53, 56, 58, 59, 63-68, 70-73, 89, 92, 93, 117, 121-125, 189-193, 195, 197-202, 211, 213, 243-245, 279, 287-290, 341, 342, 345

Johnson, Mrs. Bradley T., 19, 20, 31, 66, 123, 125, 188
Johnson, D. W., 317
Johnson, Edward, 229
Johnson, Maj. Gen. Edward, 96, 104-106, 109, 17, 119, 172, 179, 264-267, 324
Johnson, Sergt. Maj. Edward, 228
Johnson, Corp. Edward, 80
Johnson, G. W., 317
Johnson, George, 236
Johnson, Hy B., 236
Johnson, J. N., 229
Johnson, J. W., 317
Johnson, John, 138, 156, 229, 236
Johnson, John Q. A., 255
Johnson, John W., 75
Johnson, Dr. Meredith, 331
Johnson, O. M., 294
Johnson, Lt. Otis, 229, 237
Johnson, P. G., 150
Johnson, Philip P., 75
Johnson, Dr. Richard P., 66-68, 72, 122, 152, 173, 174
Johnson, Richard P., 75
Johnson, S., 317
Johnson, Stephen, 317
Johnson, Thomas, 294
Johnson, William, 235
Johnson's Landing, 299
Johnston, John J., 77
Johnston, John R., 77
Johnston, Gen. Joseph E., 10, 11, 13, 20-22, 25-27, 31-33, 146, 226, 249, 250, 260, 276, 296-314, 341, 356, 371
Jones, Corp. ———, 310
Jones, Sergt. Albert, 233
Jones, C. A., 317
Jones, Dr. E. E., 367
Jones, Edward C., 233
Jones, George W., 156
Jones, Mrs. Harvey, 371
Jones, Brig. John R., 64, 66, 71, 89, 90, 95, 168
Jones, John, 76, 229, 231
Jones, John T., 76, 155
Jones, Corp. Pembrooke, 230
Jones, Robert, 235
Jones, Robert C., 326, 328
Jones, S., 317
Jones, Gen. Samuel, 371

Jones, Spencer C., 233
Jones, Thomas A., 331
Jones, Corp. Thomas H., 315
Jones, W., 317
Jones, Brig. Gen. William E., 86, 88, 167-171, 173, 174, 180, 203, 244, 250, 256
Jones, W. J. W., 317
Jones, William 74, 294
Jones, William O., 232
Jordan, B., 317
Jordan, Brig. Gen. Thomas, 123
Jordan's Springs, 264, 265, 350
Joy, J. E., 97, 154
Joy, Joseph I., 137, 153
Jump, Charles M., 235
Judge, Edward S., 155
Junger, John H., 142, 154

K

Kahler, Charles P., 247
Kane, Bernard, 156
Kane, Col. George P., 144
Kane, James C., 75
Kane, Lt. Col. T. L., 53, 54
Kane, Brig. Gen Thomas P., 115, 116
Kauffman, Carl, 236
Kavladge, John, 74
Kearneysville, 252
Keating, Edward, 235
Keech, James F., 137
Keech, James H., 112, 154
Keech, Shelton A., 162
Keenan, Corp. Patrick, 159
Keene, Robert, 255
Keene Robert G., 229
Keepers Alexis V., 114, 130, 151, 157
Keesler, Sergt. D. Windsor, 73
Keester, W. A., 271
Keidel, Adj. Herman F., 246
Keim Maj. Gen William H., 4
Kelbaugh, William, 255
Kelley, Daniel, 236
Kelley, James, 159
Kelley, John, 159
Kelley John, L., 159
Kelley, Stewart, 74
Kelly, James S., 76
Kelly, John, 236, 317
Kelly, L., 317

Kelly, Peter, 317
Kelly, Gen. R. M., 209, 210, 289
Kelly, Richard, 236
Kelly, William, 294
Kelly's Ford, 243, 252
Kelton, C. B., 247
Kelton, John, 76
Kemp, Charles, 233
Kemp, Sergt. ———, 248
Kemp, Lt. William H., 247
Kendrick, William H., 293
Kenley, J. R., 43, 229
Kenley, Richard, 255, 276
Kenly, Col. John R., 40, 43, 44
Kenn, Edward, 301, 317
Kennedy, Arthur T., 73, 110, 153
Kennedy, McPherson, 229
Kennedy, Samuel A., 78
Kennedy, William, 248
Kennerly, William R., 157
Kenney, Bernard, 74, 112
Kenney, Patrick, 78
Kent Court house, 122
Kentucky, 2, 296, 298
Keppleman, John, 142
Kernan, A., 294
Kerneysville, 98
Kerns, Cornelius, 113, 156
Kerns, G. A., 317
Kernstown, 94, 96, 97, 167, 264, 283
Kettlewell, Charles, 232
Kettelwell, E. R., 229
Key, D. Murray, 76, 180
Key, John R., 76, 180
Key, Richard H., 180, 192, 231
Keyser, Herman, 79
Keyworth, Maj. R. W., 331
Kidd, ———, 210
Kidd, Sergt. T., 248
Kilgore, Capt. J. Mortimer, 331
Killman, Richard G., 113, 138, 156
Kilpatrick, Maj. Gen. Judson, 178-180, 185, 187, 189-193, 200
Kimball, H., 232
Kimball, Lewis, 236
Kimble, William, 317
King, Sergt. Edward S., 76
King, James A., 294

King, John, 79
King, R. K., 192
King, Walter, 76
King, William, 198, 317
Kingston, 297, 308
Kingwood, 172
Kinsey, Sergt. Howard, 235
Kirby, Francis, M., 326
Kirby, Joseph, A., 317
Kirby, Patrick, 293
Kirk, Sergt. Samuel, 79, 129, 143, 156
Kirkland, J.T., 317
Kirwin, Maj. ———, 175
Kitzmiller, H., 317
Klemkiewiez, T. A., 111, 153
Klenkivitz, Benjamin, 81
Kliser, August, 74
Kloman, Dr. William C., 331
Knapp, Henry, 78
Knauff, George, W., 233
Kneller, Jacob S., 76
Knight, John, 294
Knight, L.A., 294
Knott, M. T., 157
Knott, Minion, F., 114
Knox, James, 76
Knox, Corp. Richard, 231
Knox, Richard, 46, 48, 74
Knox, William F., 294
Knoxville, 297, 298
Koberg, Charles, 317
Koester, Louis, 271
Koester, William, 265
Kohlhepp, John, 74
Konig, Hy, 236
Konne, Charles, 331
Koons, Abram, 271
Koppleman, John, 157
Kraus, Charles M., 235
Krebs, Charles, 162, 232
Kretzer, Hiram, 73
Kries, George, 74
Kuble, Adolphus, 294
Kuhn, John, 255
Kyle, Maj. George E., 60, 122

L

Lackey, Sergt. Joseph, 315
Lacy, James A., 81
Lacy, Robert, 81
Lacy's Springs, 169
Ladd, N. E., 294

Laird, Adj. Winder, 136, 137, 152
Laird, James W., 80
Laird, Willaim H., 80, 111, 151, 153
Lake, Craig, 111, 153
Lake, John C., 153
Lakins, Charles, 248
Lamar, Robert, 248
Lamates, Sergt. James, 74, 138
Lamb, John, 113, 156
Lamden, Charles, 169, 233
Lambert, William, 255
Lambson, James B., 154
Lancaster, Albert, 81
Lancaster, Samuel G., 235
Lane, John A., 327
Lane, William B., 155
Langford, George W., 134, 158
Langley, Sergt. Edward H., 296, 299, 301, 315
Langley, Richard E., 326, 328
Langley, Thomas, 229, 255
Langsdale, H. J., 265, 271
Lanham, Benjamin, L., 112, 155
Lanier, James B., 294
Lannahan, Corp. Daniel, 73, 158
Lannahan, Thomas, 327
Larabee, George S., 76
Larabee, H. Clay, 162
Larkinson, N., 235
Latham, Corp. John W., 235
Latimer, George S., 75
Latimer, Maj. W., 265-267, 285, 324
Latimer, Dr. Thomas S., 72, 75, 367
Laton, J. N., 317
Latrobe, Ferdinand O., 150, 301, 345
Latrobe, Capt. Henry B., 243, 296, 297, 299, 301, 315
Latrobe, Lt. Col. Osmun, 331
Latrobe, R. Steuart, 232
Laurel, 261
Laurence, Lt. Stephen D., 233, 237
Law, Edward, 77
Law, Grays, 9
Law, J. G. D., 80
Lawless, W., 317
Lawn, Edward, 151, 157

Lawrence, Lt. Stephen D., 166
Lawson, James A., 73, 112, 155
Lawton, Brig. Gen. A. R., 60, 64, 261
Leadbetter, Brig. Gen. D., 297
League, John S., 76
Leazey, Joseph H., 232
LeCompte, Sergt. Thomas, 326, 328
LeCompte, Lt. Thomas P., 319, 326
Lechilder, George, 73, 229
Lechilder, Thomas G., 73
Leddard, Bernard, 77
Lee, A., 317
Lee, Hon. Edmund J., 98, 207, 214
Lee, Edward I., 245
Lee, Col. Fitzhugh, 167, 184, 185, 187, 198, 217, 218, 220, 223, 224, 250, 341
Lee, Brig. Gen. G. W. C., 193
Lee, J. C., 271
Lee, Sergt. Maj. Otho S., 255, 331
Lee, Richard, H., 271
Lee, Gen. Robert E., 58, 68, 88, 93, 99-103, 117-128, 133-139, 143-146, 150, 160, 179, 184, 185, 187-189, 192, 195, 197, 203-207, 216-227, 251, 252, 261, 268, 269, 280-292, 321, 338, 341, 342, 349, 351, 357, 362, 364
Lee, Gen. Stephen D., 280, 311
Lee, William C., 157
Leesburg, 68, 288, 249
Lee's Hill, 263
Leetown, 184, 203, 211
Lefevre, Sergt. Hamilton, 231
Leffinger, Issac, 235
Legg, E. A., 294
Leigh, William G., 81
Leisher, G. W., 229
Leitch C. C., 156
Leiter, Charles, 229
LeMaits, James, 255
LeMates, James, 114, 157
Lemmon, George, 80
Lemmon, John S., 80
Lemmon, Corp. Robert, 161
Lemmon, W. S., 232

Lemmon, Corp. William S., 80
Leonard, Charles H., 77
Leonard, Michael, 79
Lepper, Charles, V., 75, 255
Leslie, John W., 236
Letcher, Gov. John, 12, 13, 204, 245, 259
Levering, Thomas H., 80, 162, 232
Levy, Sergt. ——, 246
Lewis, Dr. G. T., 331
Lewis, Brig. Gen. J. H., 312
Lewis, M., 317
Lewinsville, 250
Lexington, 226, 245, 298
Liambaugh, W. O., 232
Liberty, 204
Liberty Mills, 267
Light, Corp. John, 315
Lincoln, Pres. Abraham, 1, 2, 203
Lincoln, Rusk J., 229
Lindenbourne, P., 294
Lindsey, S. J., 317
Linkle, John D., 233
Linthicum, Edwin, 229
Linthicum, John, 225
Lipscomb, Frank, 229
Lipscomb, Philip, 113, 138, 142, 156
Little, Brig. Gen. Henry, 355, 357
Little, Mrs. Henry, 357
Littleford, J. S., 115, 158
Littletson, T. P., 162
Lizzie Simmons, 300, 301
Lloyd, C. T., 110, 153
Lloyd, Daniel, 271
Lloyd, John L., 236
Loane, W. T. V., 111
Loane, William, T. J., 153
Locker, Edward, 229
Locker, William, 229
Lockington, James A., 77
Locust Point, 205, 206
Logan, Alexander, 255
Logsden, John, 79
Logsden, Nimrod, 248
Lomax, Maj. Gen. L. L., 184, 185, 187, 198, 211, 212, 216, 217, 291, 292
Long, E. J., 294
Long, George, 294

Long, Jeff T., 154
Longstreet, Lt. Gen. James, 103, 121, 225, 228, 280, 282
Lookout Mountain, 308
Lord, Corp. William, 142, 158
Loring, Maj. Gen. W. W., 310
Lost Mountain, 310, 311
Loud, John J., 326
Loudon, 241, 252, 298
Loudon Park, 370
Loudoun Heights, 262, 281
Louge, John, 788
Louge, Michael, 78
Loughran, Henry, 129
Loughton, Henry, 155
Lousiville, 298
Love, N. L., 151
Love, William, 317
Loveday, Charles, 248
Loveley, John E., 73
Lowndes, James A., 76
Lowe, Daniel W., 74
Lowe, William E., 111, 151, 153
Lowe, Wrightson L., 153
Lowrey, F. M., 317
Lowrey, James, 79
Loysden, N., 235
Lucas, Charles, 326
Lucas, H. C., 235
Lucas, William J., 294
Luchesi, David H., 111, 153
Lum, Benjamin F., 235
Lumkin, James T., 232
Luray, 39
Lurman, Gustav W., 232
Lurtz, Nicholas, 73
Lusby, James, 78, 236
Lutts, Lt. John, 14, 77
Lutz, Conrad, 74
Lyeth, Lt. John McF., 43
Lynch, Christopher G., 326
Lynch, D., 317
Lynch, John, 138, 156
Lynch, John P., 294
Lynchburg, 203, 221, 223-225, 244, 292, 319
Lyon, Maj. James W., 331
Lyon, Sergt. James, 80
Lyon, Samuel, H., 232
Lyons, Burton, 231
Lyons, William H., 157, 158

M

McAleer, Capt. James L., 156
McAleer, Capt. Joseph L., 86, 87, 91, 97, 113
McAleese, Lt. James, 248
McAlwee, G. W., 293
McArdle, Henry A., 162
McAtee, Corp. George W., 156
McAtee, Henry, 156
Macatee, Henry, 232
Macatee, I. J., 232
Macatee, S. E., 232
McAviena, Charles, 294
McAvoy, W. F., 294
McBlair, Master's Mate William, 332
McBride, Thomas C., 232
McCabe, ——, 231
McCabe, George W. E., 75
McCabe, Luke, 77
McCabbe, George, 255
McCaleb, James, 162
McCall, Alexander, 74
McCall, R., 231
McCann, Patrick, 315
McCann, William V., 76, 122, 155
"Maccaronies," 341
McCarthy, Daniel, 78
McCarthy, James, 317
McCaull, ——, 210
McCausland, Brig. Gen. J. C., 207-211, 245, 289-291
McCeeny, Sergt. Rufus, 315
McCevitt, Arthur, 78, 153
McCleary, Peter H., 232
McClellan, Maj. Gen. G. B., 32-34, 58, 64, 65, 160, 179, 185, 260, 270, 281-283
McClernan, Samuel, 294
McClernand, James, 75
McClerney, George S., 235
McClintock, Samuel, 271
McCloskey, Capt. James, 299
McCloud, Henry, 255
McClutchy, John, 78
McClure, George D., 327
McComb, Brig. Gen. William, 144-150
McConnellsburg, 177, 178, 209
McCormick, B. H., 101, 231
McCormick, Henry A., 110, 153
McCormick, John, 78
McCormick, Lewis, D., 153
McCormick, V. M., 271
McCourt, James R., 232
McCourt, Corp. Michael, 78, 153
McCoy, Capt. Harry, 10, 11, 77
McCoy's Ferry, 289
McCready, Corp. John, 156
McCready, Thomas D., 156
McCready, Sergt. ——, 296
McCubbin, E., 255
McCubbin, Sergt. G. B., 326
Maccubbin, R. W., Jr., 78, 294
McCulley, W., 317
McCullough, Lt. Samuel T., 87, 129, 156
McCullough, Sergt. Maj. William R., 151, 152
Maccummins, F., 327
McCure, Thomas, 327
McCurry, Corp. L., 307
McDaniel, John W., 151, 153, 233
McDermott, James, 78
McDonald, Col. Angus, 249
McDonald, Patrick, 78, 153
McDonald, Thomas, 317
McDowell, 369
McDowell, Charles, 229
McDowell, Gen. Irvin, 25, 47, 48, 276
McDowell, Corp. Perry, 73
McElwee, Andrew J., 210, 327
McElwee, George, 210, 327
McGee, Daniel, 74, 114, 157
McGee, George R., 162
McGena, John, 112, 155
McGill, Dr. ——, 99
Magill, Dr. Charles G. W., 332
McGinnis, Frank, 255
McGinnis, James, 77
McGlone, Barney, 271
McGovern, J., 317
McGowan's S. C. Brigade, 140
McGraves, Maj. ——, 332
McGuire, J., 317
McIntosh, Lt. Col. D. N., 268
McIntyre, George W., 110, 153
McIntyre, Joseph, 76
Mack, Thomas, 317
Mackabee, Richard T., 155
Mackabee, W. S., 155
McKaig, Lt. W. W., 246
Mackall, Lt. Charles, 332
Mackall, Leonard, 232
Mackall, Corp. Richard C., 80
Mackall, Robert, 255
Mackall, Lt. Thomas B., 80
Mackall, Brig. Gen. William W., 369, 370, 371
McKea, John, 159
McKee, James, 232
McKehan, W., 317
McKenna, Peter, 76
Mackensheimer, C. P., 271
Mackenzie, E. H., 294
McKim, Lt. Randolph H., 80, 106, 265, 266
McKim, Robert B., 356
McKim, W. Duncan, 80
Mackin, James, 317
McKissick, J. J., 301, 317
McKnew, Lt. M. E., 76, 166, 230
McKnew, Dr. Wilbur F., 166
McKubbin, James B., 234
McLanahan, William H., 73, 233
McLaughlin, E. H., 271
McLaughlin, Martin, 74
McLaughlin, Thomas G., 73, 138, 157
McLaws, Maj. Gen. L. C., 322
McLeod, Harry C., 154
McLeod, W., 231
McLord, M., 294
McMahon, Francis, 73
McMahon, Frank, 157
McMahon, Hugh, 317
McMahon, J. C., 317
McMahon, James, 78
McManus, James, 78
McMillan, William, 317
McMullin, Charles, 73, 236
McMullin, Sergt. L., 248
McNabb, A., 317
McNair, Brig. Gen. E. C., 306
McNally, Capt. ——, 306
McNally, Felix, 78
McNamee, James, 77
McNeal, Charles, 271
McNeil, John H., 172
McNulty, James, 76, 255
McNulty, Lt. John, 210, 275, 286-293, 357

McNulty, Thomas, 358
McSherry, Edward L., 234
McSherry, Richard, 255
McWhorter, J. D., 317
McWilliams, Hugh, 232
McWilliams, J. F., 271
McWilliams, James, 112, 155
McWilliams, Sergt. Maj. John, 332
Madison Courthouse, 276, 286
Madrid Bend, 370
Magil, Thomas, 151
Magill, Davidge, 232
Magill, Thomas F., 112, 154
Magill, William D., 232
Magness, William 78
Magraw, Corp. S. C., 248
Magruder, Edward, 235, 271
Magruder, Zach, 229
Maguire, Sergt. Charles E., 110, 143, 152, 162
Maguire, George W., 73
Maguire, H. A. W., 255
Maguire, James W., 75
Maguire, Joseph E., 234
Mahone, Maj. Gen. William, 59, 135, 218, 268, 329
Makomer, M., 232
Malard, M., 294
Malden, Elias, 79
Mallen, Henry, 73
Malone, D., 294
Maloney, James, 294, 327
Maloney, William, 79
Malvern Hill, 64, 260, 278, 279, 284, 341, 349, 369
Manassas, 1, 13, 19, 21, 22, 25, 27, 28, 31, 33, 34, 58, 66, 89, 93, 121, 122, 147, 256, 262, 276, 280, 320, 341, 349, 356
Maney, Dr. Thomas F., 352
Manly, Joseph, 151, 158
Mann, Charles S., 271
Mann, Samuel, 317
Mannen, Bartley, 74
Manning, George W., 138, 158
Marcus, James T., 78
Marden, George M., 137, 158
Marietta, 310
Markey, M., 317
Markham, J., 317
Marjoe, Lt. Frank, 29, 80, 332
Marney, Sergt. John, 78, 111, 332
Maroney, Z. T., 317
Marriott, George H., 71
Marriott, Henry, 80
Marriott, Joseph G. W., 77
Marshall, Col. Charles, 357
Marshall, James M., 332, 355, 357
Marshall, P. B., 294
Marshall, Robert I. Taylor, 357
Marston, Fred, 294
Marston, Sergt. Harry, 286, 293
Martin, G. 294
Martin, George, 248
Martin, Dr. Hugh, 247
Martin, J. G., 317
Martin, John, 159
Martin, John N., 114, 157
Martin, Joseph, 158
Martin, Patrick, 162
Martin, Corp. Washington, 145, 157
Martin, William P., 79
Martindale, Brig. Gen. ———, 214
Martinsburg, 20, 21, 119, 203, 207-209, 211, 262, 264, 288, 289
Marye's Heights, 322
Maryland Guards, 9, 10
Maryland Line, 5, 92, 93, 167, 197, 338, 341
Marylanders in out of State organizations, 329-333
Mason, Capt. Frank, 242, 351
Mason, I. Stephen, 332
Mason, Dr. John G., 332
Mason, R. R., 230
Mason, William H., 327
Mason's Hill, 29, 31, 250
Matthews, H. H., 234
Matthews, William G., 151, 154
Mattison, Samuel J., 293
Maulsby, ———, 48
Maurytown, 291, 292
Maxwell, John, 255
May, Corp. William H., 265, 266, 271
Mayberry, James P., 73, 158
Mayfield, William, 159
Maynadier, J. M., 255
Maynadier, John H., 255
Maynard, Albert, 233
Maynard, Thomas, 229
Mayre's Heights, 263
Meade, Maj. Gen. George, 117, 118, 121, 184, 189, 252, 286
Meadow Bridge, 190
Meagher, James, 236
Mechanicstown, 285
Mechanicsville, 59, 260, 285, 350
Meister, Charles, 236
Melton, Maj. Samuel W., 92, 317
Melvin, George, 77
Memphis, 305
Mentzer, Samuel, 294
Mercer, E. W., 255
Mercer, Maj. George Douglas, 161, 332
Mercer, Samuel B., 233
Mercersburg, 101
Meridian, 315
Merrick, George C., 235
Merritt, Maj. Gen. Wesley, 199
Merritt, Samuel, 77, 255
Merryman, John, 4
Merryman, Joseph, 233
Merton's Ford, 121
Meshaw, Ebenezer, 157
Messick, Ross, 115, 158
Mettam, H. C., 235
Mettee, Charles, 236, 294, 327
Mewberne, N. H., 73
Michaels, John, 74, 155
Michaels, Joseph, 74
Micou, Thomas, 74
Middle River, 188, 189
Middleton, Edward, 271
Middletown, 28, 44, 46, 168, 174, 204, 281
Mihon, Martin, 78
Miles, George T., 73, 233
Miles, Maj. Gen. N. A., 262, 321
Miller, Andrew T., 151, 153
Miller, Charles, 317
Miller, Mrs. D. H., 367
Miller, George, 317
Miller, H. D., 271
Miller, Henry, 247
Miller, Jacob, 157

Miller, John C., 137, 155
Miller, Thadeus, 317
Miller, Thomas, 317
Miller, William, 77, 230
Miller, William H., 74
Mills, John C., 151, 154
Mills, Lt. Nicolas J., 114, 157
Mills, W. B. P., 315
Mills, William P., 87
Millstead, Joseph H., 154
Millstone Landing, 296
Milstead, Joseph H., 112
Milton, John 317
Milroy, Maj. Gen. R. H., 39, 57, 96, 167, 174, 264, 283
Minch, Christopher, 157
Mine Run, 252, 267, 286
Minnahan, John, 73
Minnesota, 303, 304
Minnihan, Thomas, 236
Minter, William, 317
Missionary Ridge, 308
Mississippi, 296, 301
Mississippi River, 299, 300, 302, 304, 306
Mitchell, George, 317
Mitchell, Lt. Hugh, 31, 81
Mitchell, James, 74, 236, 248
Mitchell, John, 271
Mitchell, Levine, 232
Mitchell, Thomas L., 142, 151, 155
Mitchell, Robert S., 235
Mobile, 315, 371
Mobile Bay, 351
Mockabee, Joseph, 265, 271
Moise, A. W., 235
Moncure, Charles H., 271
Moncure, Corp. E. C., 270
Monehan, James, 294
Monitor, 351
Monmonier, John N. K., 80
Monocacy, 177, 204, 205, 245
Monocacy Junction, 208
Montague, Powhattan, 162
Monteray, Andrew, 236
Monteray Gap, 178
Monteray Springs, 117
Montgomery, John 327
Montgomery, Dr. William, 332
Montgomery, William T., 75
Montgomery Co., 205
Montieth, G. W., 317

Montieth, M., 317
Moody, ———, 282
Moog, Sergt. George, 74
Moog, Jacob J., 248
Moog, James R., 74, 151, 155, 248
Mooney, John, 229
Moon Lake, 306
Moore Lt. ———, 306, 307
Moore, Augustus, 157
Moore, James T., 327
Moore, Philip, 72
Moore, Philip L., 73
Moore, P. M., 113, 157
Moore, Robert, 74
Moore, Thomas, 265
Moore, Warren F., 111, 154
Moorefield, 89, 91, 169, 209-211, 245, 291
Moran, Michael, 294
Moran, Rinaldo J., 154
Moran, William P., 114, 156
Morfit, Dr. Charles M., 332
Morfit, Maj. Mason, 332
Morgan, Corp. B. H., 75, 254
Morgan, Francis, 317
Morgan, Lt. John A., 264, 266
Morgan, Thomas, 271
Morgan, William, 159
Morgantown, 172, 173
Morris, Edwin, 235
Morris, George, 79
Morris, Harry, 79
Morris, Sergt. John, 78
Morris, Lewis, 235
Morris Island, 275
Morrison, Wilbur, 110, 153
Morristown, 298
Morse, Thomas W., 358
Morton, 307
Morton's Ford, 184
Morton, Thomas, 255
Mosby, Col. J. S., 241
Moses, J., 317
Moth, B., 294
Motter, John, 77
Moulton, William, 248
Mount Carmel Church, 251
Mount Jackson, 209
Mount Zion, 285
Mowbray, John K., 327
Mudd, E. M., 271
Mudd, Edwin, C., 81
Mudd, John F., 294

Muddy Creek, 286
Muirhead, Sergt. Philip T., 157
Muirhead, Sergt. R. F., 130
Mulhane, Bernard, 77
Mulligan Brig. Gen. James A., 173, 203
Mulliken, Corp. B. D., 151, 155
Mulliken, Walter, 113, 155
Mullan, C. X., 294
Mullen, Lt. James, 14, 74
Mullin, C. S., 235
Mumford, Corp. Henry A., 145, 158
Mumford, Robert, 142
Mumford, William R., 151, 158, 223, 225
Mummey, Corp. Thomas W., 326
Mummey, Brig. Gen. Thomas T., 88, 165, 221-227
Munson's Hills, 31
Murdock, Augustus, 229
Murdock, Campbell, 255
Murphy, Dennis, 79
Murphy, Edward, 76
Murphy, Frank, 247
Murphy, George, 247
Murphy, John, 79, 159
Murray, Alex, 151, 153
Murray, Lt. Clapman, 80, 85, 86, 137, 152
Murray, Edward C., 235
Murray, George, 248
Murray, John, 74, 157
Murray, Sergt. Stirling, 75, 332
Murray, Thomas, 74
Murray, William, 159
Murray, Capt. William H., 9-11, 14, 19, 75, 80, 85, 86, 97, 104, 106, 109, 110, 152, 159, 160, 231, 350-352, 358
Musgrove, Thomas, 271
Muth, Alfred, 76
Myers, Andrew, 79
Myers, Clinton, 232
Myers, Christeso P., 73
Myers, Henry, 317
Myers, John, 327
Myers, Maj. Samuel B., 92, 174
Myers Thomas, 233

N

Nailor, T. K., 231
Napoleon, Louis, 317
Nash, James, 112, 155
Nashville, 311, 312, 314
Natchez, 301
Naval Academy, 351
Naylor, J. M., 231
Naylor, W. E., 294
Neal, Augustine, 154
Neal, Frank, 234, 294
Neal, Harry, 234
Neal, Henry, 294
Neale, A. W., 129, 151
Neale, Charles H., 271
Neale, Sergt. E. Clarence, 162, 231
Neale, Wilford, 232
Neadham, George, 159
Needhamer, Sergt. Louis, 79
Neenan, N., 137
Nelson, C. W., 271
Nelson, Francis F., 217
Nelson, R. W., 230
New Creek, 209
New Hope, 203, 244, 309, 310
New Kent, 188
Newkirk, J. V., 248
Newkirk, Josiah, 235
Newmarket, 90, 167, 262, 283, 291
New Orleans, 305
Newton, F. M., 317
Newton, J. W., 317
Newton, S. M., 317
Newtown, 44, 93-96, 174
New Windsor, 204
Nicholai, Herman, 110, 155
Nicholas, W. L., 155
Nicholas, Capt. Wilson C., 10, 11, 15, 19, 31, 40, 50, 79, 88, 122, 206
Nicholls, Brig. Gen. F. T., 264
Nichols, John, 159
Nichols, J. P., 314, 317
Nichols, William L., 112
Nicholson, Franklin T., 81
Noel, E., 231
Norfolk, George S., 162
Norfolk, W. H., 75
Nolen, James, 78
Noonan, Michael, 74, 142, 157
Noonday Valley, 310

Norris, Alexander, Jr., 232
Norris, Sergt. George Smith, 231
Norris, Corp. Richard H., 233
Norris, W. Epa, 162
Norris, Col. William, 332
North Anna, 122, 125, 188, 189, 198
North Branch, 43
North Carolina, 2, 19, 22
Norton, John J., 76
Norwood, Lewis, 246
Norwood, William, 246

O

Oakford, Mrs. Charles A., 350
Oakland, 172
Oates, Charles T., 73
Oates, James F., 232
Obendoffer, Augustus, 158
Obendorfe, John, 234
O'Brian, Corp. Dennis, 74
O'Brian, J., 317
O'Brien, Lt. Edmund, 14, 77
O'Brien, Edward, 162
O'Brien, Edwin, 76, 255
O'Brien, James, 145, 159
O'Brien, James H., 113
O'Brien, Sergt. Thomas, 120, 129, 153, 159
O'Bryn, John T., 112, 155
O'Connell, Corp. M. H., 310, 315
O'Connell, Corp. Patrick, 73, 158
O'Donovan, Edward, 151, 153
O'Donnell, Lt. John E., 332
Offalt, George W., 332
Offalt, John R., 332
Offalt, Z. A., 332
Offutt, John, 256
Offutt, William 255
O'Grady, James, 293
O'Hallon, Martin, 142, 157
O'Hanlon, J., 317
Ohio River, 298
Oiltown, 173
Old Church, 190, 192, 388
Oldner, Sergt. Philip, 325, 327, 328
Oldson, W. H. C., 294
Oldson, William, 327
Oldtown, 210

O'Leary, Jerry, 234
Oliver, Corp. James P., 254, 255, 317
O'Loughlin, Corp. John, 75
O'Loughlin, Michael, 76
O'Neal, Andrew, 74
O'Neal, John, 76
O'Neal John H., 255
O'Neal, Patrick, 74
O'Neil, G. W., 317
O'Neill, D. P., 317
Onion, Richard T., 155
Onion, Robert, T., 142
Oostenaula River, 309
Opel, John, 74
Opper, Conrad, 158
Orange & Alexandria Rail Road, 33, 187
Orange Court House, 119, 121, 217, 261, 279
Orleans, 280
Ormes, Nathan, 236
Orr, Peter, 151, 155
Osbourn, James E., 75
O'Shields, J. P., 317
Ott, George, 234
Outten, Sergt. William T., 155, 161
Owens, Henry C., 129, 153
Owens, J. F., 294
Owens, James, 265
Owens, James W., 271
Owens, Samuel A., 73
Owens, Welsh, 265, 271
Owensby, G., 317
Owings, J. H., 255
Owings, Corp. Joshua, 113, 317
Owings, Q. M. N. T., 246
Owings, W. Beale, 142
Ox Hill, 252

P

Pace, E. T., 235
Padgett's Tavern, 29
Page County, 214, 215
Page, Sergt. C. Craig, 137
Page, Charles C., 81
Page Washington, 137
Page, William, 154
Paigo, C. Craig, 154
Paine, William, 294
Palfrey, Capt. William, 314

Palmer, A., 232
Pamplin's Station, 151
Pamunkey, 188-193
Papertown, 178
Pare, David P., 153
Parker, George T., 192, 231
Parker, Henry, 328
Parker, J. B., 317
Parker, John, 134, 151, 159
Parker, Peter H., 327
Parker, Thaddeus, 325, 327, 328
Parker, William, 317
Parkinson, J. S., 317
Parnill, T. A., 317
Parrott, 299
Parsons, James T., 77, 154
Partisan Rangers, 172
Patrick, Charles R., 230
Patrick, James Thomas, 79
Patrick, John, 230
Patten, Lt. William Thompson, 296, 297, 299-301, 315
Patterson, Maj. Gen. R., 20, 21
Patterson, W. W., 271
Pattison ———, 158
Patton, James W., 236
Patton, William, 74
Patuxent River, 296
Paul, William, J., 159
Paxton, Brig. Gen. E. F., 68
Payne, Benjamin, 112, 155
Payne, Brig. Gen. William H., 14, 220, 221
Peak, David C., 295
Pearce, Corp. Alfred, 77
Pearce, John 77
Pearson, Charles, 162
Pearson, Sergt. James F., 137, 152
Pearson Walter H., 271
Pease, Charles, 265, 271
Peddicord, S., 230
Peebles, Dr. ———, 134, 139, 141, 143
Peeler, Mallard, T., 235
Pegram, Maj. Gen. John, 350
Pelham, Capt. John, 243
Pemberton, Lt. Gen. J. C., 301
Penbroke, George, 295
Pender, Maj. Gen. W. D., 260, 349
Pendleton, David E., 332

Pendleton, Frank, 246
Pendley, Sergt. ———, 313
Pendley, Corp. John C., 315
Penn, Capt. ———, 67
Penn, John T., 154
Pennington, Harry, 269, 271
Pennsylvania, 167, 174, 176, 177, 203, 208, 252, 264, 266, 284, 286
Penola Station, 198
Perdue, John, 230
Peregoy, Charles, 295
Peregoy, H., 248
Peregoy, James A., 111, 151, 153
Perkins, L. C., 231
Perregoy, John T., 75
Perrie, I., 231
Perrie, Thomas H., 231
Perrio, Albert W., 271
Perrio, George W., 271
Perry, James, 327
Perry, John G., 327
Perry, O. H., 230, 231
Perry, Oliver, 76
Perry, Samuel, H., 317
Perry, William T., 80
Perryville, 298
Perville, Leighton, 236
Peterkin, Rev. 2·····, 123
Peters, Andrew, 73
Peters, Joseph, 327
Peters, Thomas, 153
Peters, Winfield, 80
Petersburg, 133, 135, 139, 146, 169, 178, 218, 268, 292
Peterson, N., 317
Pettigrew, Brig. Gen. J. J., 260, 261
Pettis, A., 248
Pettus, Brig. Gen. E. W., 311
Phelps, J. R., 137
Phelps, James J., 153
Philadephia, 204, 245
Phillips, Abram, 129, 156
Phillips, George C., 327
Phillips, James C., 79
Phillips, John, 247
Phillips, John J., 80
Phillips, Samuel W., 327
Phipps, W. E., 271
Phyfer, Henry, 153
Pickle, John, 158
Pickle, William, 151, 158

Piedmont, 22, 249
Pierce, Alfred, 234
Pigione, Joseph, 79
Pike, Henry, 327
Pikesville Arsenal, 46, 192, 343-345
Pilert, George, 295
Pilker, Michael, 79
Pindell, Phillip, 111, 153
Pinder, William, 325, 327
Pinder, Corp. William, 328
Pinkney, Campbell, W., 80
Pinkney, William S., 80
Piper, E. Bolton, 368
Pirkle, Corp. William, 315
Pitts, Hosea, 72, 75
Pitts, Emory, 256
Pitts, Fred, 256
Pitts, Frederick L., 80
Pitts, John W., 256
Pitts, William, 236, 256
Placide, Robert, 234
Plater, Lt. John E., 319, 321
Platt, Augustus, 74
Platt, Sergt. John J., 79
Plummer, John B., 256
Poague, Col. William T., 178, 282, 331
Poe, Neilson, Jr., 332
Pohlman, Chris, 295
Pohick Church, 275
Poindexter, Sergt. George, 293
Point Lookout, 204, 205, 244, 245
Point of Rocks, 10, 65
Poisal, John, 327
Poisel, John, 327
Polk, Lt. Burke, 247
Polk, Lt. John W., 87, 138, 143, 149, 157
Polk, Gen. Leonidas, 371
Polk, Samuel, 114, 158, 230
Polk, Truston, 230
Pollard, Lt. James, 190
Pollard's Farm, 202
Pollite, Nehemiah, 271
Pollitt, Alexander, 235
Pool, William C., 232
Poole, Dennis, 332
Poole, Maj. William, 332
Poole, William, 236
Poolesville, 206, 245, 289
Poor's Farm, 260
Pope, Maj. Gen. John, 65,

121, 251, 261, 279, 281
Pope, Sergt. William H., 56, 73, 234, 345
Port Hudson, 261
Port Republic, 48, 54, 57, 58, 249, 277, 291
Port Walthall, 133
Poter, Admiral David D., 302
Porter, Gustavus, 327
Porter, Hugh, 73
Porter, J. J., 230
Porter, John Fitz, 60
Porter, William J., 153
Post, Lt. John E. H., 80, 228, 232, 237
Postley, Charles T., 75
Potomac, 118, 169, 171, 177, 203, 204, 206-209, 249, 252, 261, 262, 267, 281, 284, 285, 289, 325, 337
Powell, George, 247
Powell, H. B., 317
Powell, J. J., 317
Powell, Maj. Gen. R. M., 215
Powell, W. B., 317
Power, Mrs. W. G., 350
Powers, James, 143
Powers John, 159, 293
Powers, Sergt. John J., 159
Powers, Nicholas, 315
Pratt, James P., 327
Pratt, Thomas St. George, 153
Prentiss, William S., 153
Presstman, George R., 162
Preston, John, 317
Pretzman, D. C., 230
Price, ———, 80
Price, Corp. Adrian D., 161
Price, Capt. Alfred, 332
Price, Charles, 317
Price, David, 317
Price, Capt. Frank S., 10
Price, Corp. Frank S., 75
Price, James E., 234
Price, James H., 231
Price, Kennedy, 230
Price, M. A., 230
Price, Gen. S., 355
Price, William C., 225, 235
Prichard's Hill, 94
Probest, Sergt. George, 74, 112, 142, 155
Proudt, Sergt. J. William, 156
Pruitt, John, 235

Pue, Arthur, 232
Pue, Lt. Edward H. D., 254, 256
Pue, Ferd, 256
Pue, Fred, C., 230
Pue, Lt. J. A. V., 165, 166, 170, 197, 299, 237
Pue, R. P., 317
Pue, Ventress, 256
Pue, W. R., 232
Pue, William R., 75
Pugh, Lt. Edward, 237
Pullen, Henry, 247
Pumphrey, George W., 235
Pumphrey, John T., 235
Purdie, William E., 317
Purnell, Lt. George M., 246
Purnell, John J., 158
Purnell, William, 80
Pusey, O. C., 235

Q

Queen of the West, 299-301
Quin, Michael, 78
Quin, William, 78, 294
Quinlin, Edward, 317
Quinn, J. H. V., 235
Quinn, John, 79
Quinn, Lt. Joseph P., 87, 95, 97, 156
Quinn, Michael A., 77, 119, 151, 152, 163

R

Raborg, Christopher, 234
Raborg, Sergt. George C., 77
Raborg, William, 234
Raccoon Ford, 184, 185, 256
Raday, Patrick, 79
Radcliffe, Edward, 234
Radecke, Herman H., 114, 157
Raine, ———, 282
Raines, Charles I., 264, 265
Raisin, Capt. William I., 96, 174, 175
Raitt, Charles H., 234
Raley, James S., 137, 153
Raley, Michael, N., 327
Raleigh, 19, 20
Ramseur, Brig. Gen. S. Dodson, 68, 205, 208
Randall, Sergt. Walter J., 157

Randill, J., 327
Randle, Walter I., 81
Randolph, Lt. George W., 65
Randolph, Lt. Lewis, 67
Ransle, Andrew, 81
Ranson, Corp. John F., 270
Raphael, Eugene, 232
Rapidan, 121, 252, 286
Rappahannock, 101, 184, 187, 188, 216, 250, 260, 261, 276, 279, 289, 321, 324
Rasin, Lt. M. M., 333
Rasin, Capt. W. I., 166, 169, 173-175, 212, 225, 234
Ratcliffe, Edward R., 235
Ratcliffe, George E., 162, 247
Ray, Alexander, 76
Ray, M., 317
Raymond, C. C., 295
Raynor, Kennith, 19
Reach, John, 232
Redd ———, 197
Reddie, Corp. James, 113, 156
Red River, 299, 300
Redmond, George, 80
Redwood, A. C., 232
Redwood, J. W., 232
Reed, Mingel, 231
Reed, Samuel, 79
Reed, Mrs. William, 356
Reed, William, 248
Reed, William S., 130
Reed, William, T., 159
Reeder, Sergt. Philip T., 137, 151, 154
Reilley, John, 295
Reily, F., 248
Reiman, H., 295
Reisterstown, 204, 344
Relay, 4
Relic Hall, 351
Remie, Loon, 236
Rench, J. V., 256
Renshaw, William T., 327
Resaca, 308-311
Reynolds, Gen. John F., 298
Reynolds, D., 317
Reynolds, John, 279, 295
Reynolds, Patrick, 74
Reynolds, W., 317
Rheim, James I., 295
Rheim, William G., 295
Rhodes, George, 74, 77
Rhodes, William Lee, 79

Rice, George, 230, 327
Rich, Edward R., 235
Richards, George, 81
Richardson, G. W., 295
Richardson, H., 295
Richardson, Howard, 230
Richardson, John D., 327
Richardson, Nicholas, 328
Richardson, Nicholas, T., 265
Richardson, R. T., 265
Richardson, Richard, 271
Richardson, T. J., 295
Richardson, W., 295
Richardson, Lt. W. H., 248
Richmond, 9, 12, 13, 19, 21, 33, 34, 58-60, 64-66, 71, 85, 89, 92, 122, 125, 126, 189, 191-193, 197, 200, 201, 212, 217, 219, 251, 252, 257, 260, 277, 296, 298, 338, 342, 343, 366
Rico, George, 230
Riddle, Charles, 271
Riddlemoser, Corp. Alfred, 156
Rider, George J., 159
Rider, Martin L., 73, 138, 159
Rider, William, 256
Ridgel, James, 157
Ridgel, Joseph, 151
Ridgely, Samuel, 256
Ridgley, John 230, 232
Riggs, Joshua, 229, 256
Riggs, Reuben, 230
Riley, John, 77
Riley, John P., 232
Riley Thomas S., 230
Rinaldo, J. Moran, 129
Rinehart ———, 75
Rinehart, William C., 75
Rison, William H., 81
Ritter Corp. William, 73
Ritter, Sergt. William, 155
Ritter, Capt. William L., 243, 296, 297, 310-305, 307-310, 312-315
Rivanna, 287
Rives, Francis S., 80
Roach, E. R., 314
Roane, James, 295
Robbins, William, 115, 159
Roberts, Lt. Benjamin G., 166, 319, 325, 328
Roberts, Edward L., 77

Roberts, Frank, 111, 157
Roberts, George, 155
Roberts, Lt. Joseph K., Jr., 234
Roberts, Richard, 235
Robertson, Dr. Fenwick, 333
Robertson, G. H., 154
Robertson, George, 295
Robertson, J. A. G., 317
Robertson, Brig. Gen. Jerome, 178
Robertson, Capt. Michael Stone, 11, 31, 53, 81
Robey, H. A., 295
Robey, Sergt. Townley, 234, 256
Robey, William, H., 159
Robey, William, S., 271
Robinson, Charles, 317
Robinson, G. S., 295
Robinson, G. W., 271
Robinson, James, 159
Robinson, W., 318
Robinson, W. Wirt, 293
Robinson, William H., 76, 293
Roche, Thomas F., 162
Rock Creek, 109, 117
Rockville, 206, 245
Rodes, Maj. Gen. Robert Emmett, 117, 205, 208, 285
Rodger's Gap, 298
Rodgers, Edward G., 162
Rodgers, J. P., 318
Rodgers, James P., 162
Rodgers, W., 318
Rodgers, W. C., 295
Rodriguez, Francisco, 317
Roe, Samuel, 235
Rogers, Henry C., 76
Rogers, James P., 232
Roders, John C., 75
Rogers, Philip, 232
Rogers, Samuel, 232
Rogers, Samuel B., 80
Rogers, Dr. Thomas J., 307, 315
Rogers, William H., 75
Roley, Thomas, 234
Rolling Fork, 302, 304
Rolph, George W., 235
Rolph, Corp. Wilbur J., 235
Rosaa, Sterling, 236
Rosan, Charles W., 234
Rose Jesse, 236

Rose, Porter E., 232
Rosensteel, James, 73
Ross, A. P., 295
Ross, Capt. David M., 247
Ross, Corp. George, 79
Ross, Sergt. George L., 138, 156
Ross, Messick, 115
Rosser, Maj. Gen. Thomas L., 185, 202, 291
Rowan, Capt. John B., 296, 297, 299, 301, 307-310, 313-315
Rowland, D. B., 318
Rozier, Charles, 230
Ruark, Michael, 77
Rucker, William, 295
Rudden, Thomas, 78
Ruff, Sergt. George F., 76
Ruffin, Chief Justice Thomas, 19
Ruley, James M., 76
Rutter, Elisha, 151
Rutter, Sergt. Wilbur, 151, 156
Rush, Peter, 74, 78, 157
Rushing, John, 236
Russell, Elisha T., 80
Russell, Henry 327
Russell, Thomas, A., 80
Ryan, James, 79
Ryan, James A., 80
Ryan, John, 78, 159
Ryan, Joseph, 78, 79
Ryan, M., 318
Ryan, Patrick, 74
Ryan, Robert S., 76
Ryan, W. H., 73
Ryce, Francis W., 80
Rye, John M., 271

S

St. Clair, Albert L., 318
St. James', College, 208
St. Mary's, 188
St. Mary's Co., 188
Sahm, Joseph, 79
Sailor, M., 318
Sailor's Creek, 269
Sakers, John, 256
Salem, 280
Salem Church, 226, 263, 322
Samms, R. J., 318
Sanchez, Corp. B., 309, 315

Sanders, Hillen T., 232
Sanders, James H., 79
Sanders, Joseph, 81
Sanderson, Frank H., 111, 153
Sanderson, Capt. Frank H., 349, 350
Sanderson, W. Cook, 350
Sandler, William, 77
Sanford, Edward, 271
Sangster's Station, 33
Sanner, Alex A., 295
Sargeant, H. D. C., 271
Savage, Sergt. John, 234
Savell, Thomas S., 318
Saville, Lt. Thomas, 43
Saxton, Gen. R., 47, 48
Scaggs, Edward O., 231
Scaggs, J., 231
Scaggs, Robert, 256
Scales, J. S., 309, 318
Schall, Col. ———, 174
Schaeffer, Henry, 77
Schaeffer, William, 74, 327
Schaffer, George W., 247
Schakley, H. B., 235
Scharf, Col. J. Thomas, 190
Scharf, J. Thomas, Master's Mate, 332
Scharf, John T., 271
Schenberger, J. F., 295
Schessler, Henry, 73, 327
Schley, L. R., 53
Schley, Lake R., 80
Schley, William, 333
Schliephake, Henry T., 80
Scholl, Charles, 79
Scholl, Lt. John H., 229
Schulbak, William F., 162
Schull, John, 256
Schultz, Justus, 113
Schawn, Francis, 318
Schwartz, Capt. Augustus F., 166, 184, 197, 230, 235, 237
Scoggins, Daniel, 159
Scott, Charles A., 75
Scott, George, 230
Scott, Corp. George T., 267, 270
Scott, Corp. Henry C., 75
Scott, J. E., 233
Scott, Sergt. John W., 161
Scott, Thomas H., 271
Scully, P., 248
Seawright, W. L., 318

Second Maryland Artillery (Baltimore Light), 275-295, 338, 356
Second Maryland Cavalry, 241-248, 338
Second Maryland Infantry, 85-159, 338
Sedden James A., 92
Sedgwick, Brig. Gen. John, 263, 322
Seignor, Thomas, 256
Selby, Corp. James, 161, 162
Selby, John, 81
Selby Sergt. Joseph, 161
Sellman, John, 230, 256
Selvage, Corp. Edwin, 66, 76, 233
Seminary Hill, 117
Semmes, F. X., 151
Semmes, H. F., 154
Semmes, Lewis S., 154
Semmes, Admiral Raphael, 204, 361, 362
Septer, John H., 113
Septor, John H., 156
Serpell, Corp. G. M., 230
Severn Pines, 251, 260
Shaeffer, Adam F., 295
Shaeffer, George W., 295
Shaeffer, William, 295
Shafer, Cornelius L., 234
Shafer, Henry, 327
Shafer, Thomas H., 234
Shakelford, George, 162
Shanahan, ———, 323
Shanahan, John, 328
Shanks, Corp. Daniel, 53, 80
Shanley, Thomas E., 153
Shannahan, John H. K., 327
Shannon, Capt. Charles K., 332
Shannon, Michael, 77
Sharkey, S., 295
Sharpsburg, 99, 118, 204, 206, 208, 252, 281, 321, 356
Shaw J. C., 295
Shaw, Peter, 295
Shea, Timothy, 318
Shearer, Lt. George M. E., 14, 19, 73, 204
Sheedy, Daniel, 78, 157
Sheehan, Sergt. Edward, 33, 78, 157
Sheenan, William, 79

Sheil, Michael, 295
Shell, Horace, 234
Shellman, Lt. George K., 14, 73
Shenandoah, 22, 54, 277
Shepherd, R. H., 151, 156
Shepherdstown, 98, 208, 245, 262, 266, 283, 289
Sheppard, Corp. S. R., 315
Sheburne, William, 265
Sheridan, Gen. Philip H., 195-202, 211, 214, 217, 245, 252, 289, 291, 292
Sherman, Maj. Gen. William T., 310
Sherman, Robert T., 74
Sherrington, Henry W., 77
Sherry, Charles, 236
Sherwin, Thomas, 256
Sherwood, Sergt. Issac, 142, 143, 151, 158
Shessler, Henry, 234
Shetkins, John, 159
Shields, Maj. Gen. James, 35, 54, 57, 89, 242, 277
Shields, Sergt. James, 79
Shields, Michael, 327
Shields, Owens, 157
Shierborn, William, 81
Shiplett, P., 233
Shipley, G. R., 318
Shipley, Samuel, 230
Shipley, William A., 112
Shipley, William H., 155
Shippenburg, 178, 284
Ship Point, 260
Shirburd, W. L., 271
Shock, W. A., 295
Shockney, Samuel, 74
Shorb, Donald M. M., 233
Shorb, Corp. Joseph C., 235
Short, James, 318
Shorter, J. G., 371
Shorter, Thomas O., 81
Show, Joseph, 256
Shower, George, 234
Shreveport, 300
Shriver, Mark O., 256
Shroff, Peter F., 232
Shue, J. J., 295
Shultz, William, 74, 234
Shuster, J. M., 271
Shutz, Justus, 155
Silas, D., 318

Silver, S. M., 318
Silver Spring, 205
Simmes, Henry M., 81
Simmes, John, 76
Simmons, Corp. Jackson, 315, 318
Simms, Thomas, 111
Simms, Sergt. Thomas, 154
Simms, W. H., 154
Simms, William H., 112
Simms, Willis R., 318
Simon, Maj. A. G., 332
Simon, August, 76
Simonds, Albert, 77
Simons, Albert, 234
Simpson, Edward, 79
Simpson, G., 318
Simpson, Corp. George R., 233
Simpson, H. A., 79
Simpson, John T., 235
Simpson, Joshua, 57, 76
Simpson, Nathan, 162
Sims, Joseph, 74
Sinclair, Dr. W. R., 332
Sindall, Harry S., 271
Sindall, Samuel W., 80
Singer, G., 318
Sisson, Christopher, 234
Sisson, Oscar B., 75, 256
Skinner, William A., 155
Skinner, William H., 112
Slater, George, 75, 256
Slater, William J., 233, 271
Slaughter's Mountain, 65
Slaven, Corp. John W., 234
Slernaker, Julius, 271
Sleighton, Benjamin F., 236
Slingluff, Lt. Fielder C., 166, 230, 235, 237
Slingluff, John A., 235
Slingluff, Sergt. Josiah, H., 235
Slingluff, Sergt. William H., 76
Sloan, Charles H., 75
Sloan, E. O., 271
Small, C. W., 76
Small, George, 256
Smallwood, Gen. William, 341
Smith, A. Austin, 162
Smith, Capt. Augustine, 333
Smith, C. W., 256
Smith, Daniel, 230

Smith, Gen. E. Kirby, 22-25, 298, 376
Smith, Sergt. Eugene, 158
Smith, Francis, 318
Smith, Frederick, 74
Smith, Capt. George, 43
Smith, George A., 327
Smith, H. C., 295
Smith, H. Tillard, 111, 151, 153
Smith, J. S., 318
Smith, Sergt. J. W., 315
Smith, Capt. J. Louis, 11, 15, 78, 88, 95
Smith, James, 231, 318
Smith, James H., 293
Smith, John, 256
Smith, Capt. John Donnell, 333
Smith, John E., 295
Smith, Sergt. John T., 73, 318
Smith, Joseph, 74, 129, 156, 157
Smith, Joseph E., 151
Smith, K. B., 271
Smith, M. L., 371
Smith, Peter P., 154
Smith, Pharis, 318
Smith, Corp. Richard, C., 231
Smith, Col. Robert C., 14, 29, 75, 166, 170, 212, 213, 228, 231, 237
Smith, Capt. Samuel D., 332
Smith, Lt. T. Jeff, 166, 168, 231
Smith, Thomas, 78, 236, 265, 318
Smith, Thomas J., 75
Smith, W. P., 295
Smith, Lt. William, 124, 318, 327
Smith, William A., 78
Smith, William F., 80, 162
Smith, Sergt. William H., 152
Smith, William S., 158
Smith, Wilson C., 232
Smithfield, 98
Smoot, Joseph, 256
Smyth, Lt. William, 75
Smyth, Sergt. William, 57
Smythe, Lt. William, 29
Snipes, R., 318
Snively, G., 248
Snodgrass, ———, 247

Snook, Jerome, 234
Snovell, D. M., 73
Snowden, Dr. DeWilton, 151, 152, 270
Snowden, J. H., 162
Snowden, John, 233
Snowden, Lt. Nicholas, 14, 53, 76
Snyder's Bluff, 302, 306
Soiskey, Isadore, 76
Sollers, A. J., 111, 153
Sollers, James H., 81, 158
Sollers, Summerville, 80, 97, 137, 153
Sollers, William O., 234
Solon, 39
Sommers, Samuel, 271
Sothron, Marshall, 81
Sothron, Webster H., 80
South, F., 318
South, Howard, 74
South, Anna, 188, 189, 200
South Branch, 122, 125, 209
South Mountain, 177
South River, 57
Sparks, James S., 327
Spear, D. W. C., 231
Spear, Edwin W., 231
Spear, Corp. J. J., 230
Spence, John, 142, 156
Spencer, ———, 169
Spencer, Bendenfield, 327
Spencer, E. N., 162
Spencer, Jervis, 232
Spencer, John C., 235
Spencer, Sergt. Sam B., 179, 230
Spengling, P., 318
Sprigg, Sergt J., 248
Spurrier, Capt. Grafton D., 72
Spurrier, Jay, 76
Squirrel Level, 141, 143
Stallings, C. L., 235
Stanbaugh, J. E., 295
Stanley, Charles H., 231
Stansbury, Edward, 327, 328
Stansbury, John L., 138, 157
Stansbury, John S., 318
Stansbury, Sergt. Jospeh, 246
Stanton, E. M., 47, 48
Stanton, William, 77,
Star Fort, 139
Starke, Brig. Gen. W. E., 279
Starlings, George C., 110, 153

Statesville, 251
Staunton, Va., 47, 58, 89, 167, 203, 216, 291
Staylor, George W., 295
Staylor, Corp. Lewis P., 156
Stedham, Richard, 271
Steel, Maj. Gen. F., 302
Steele, Charles H., 111, 153
Steele, Frank, K., 112, 155
Steele, John, 234
Steele, John H., 73
Steno, Joseph H., 73
Steno, Joseph A., 271
Stephens, John, 74, 159
Stephenson, Thomas H., 234
Steres, Christopher, 234
Stermis, Joseph, 231
Steuart, Brig. Gen. George H., 10, 11, 14, 17, 19, 29-33, 39, 44, 46, 47, 50, 54, 56, 72, 86-88, 96-103, 106, 109, 115, 117, 119, 122, 167, 177, 178, 197, 212, 264, 265, 277, 309, 312, 341
Steuart, Dr. William F., 332
Stevens, Col. ——, 193
Stevenson, Maj. Gen. C. L., 310, 311, 313
Stevenson, Dawson, 234
Stevers, James C., 231
Stewart, Corp. C. J., 248
Stewart, Edward B., 75
Stewart, Francis, M., 327
Stewart, Lt. H. A., 296, 309, 312, 341
Stewart, Henry, 79, 301
Stewart, Henry S., 318
Stewart, James, 328
Stewart, James P., 327
Stewart, Lt. Joseph H., 15, 33, 78
Stewart, Robert, 256
Stewart, Capt. Septimus H., 14, 29, 72, 75
Stewart, Capt. Thomas R., 89, 96, 104, 115, 158
Stewart, Lt. Thomas R., 158
Stewart, Maj. William E., 332
Stewart's Tavern, 252
Stinchcomb, J. E., 271
Stine, Sergt. J. A., 248
Stine, Joseph, 248
Stinson, R. J., 295
Stitler, Charles B., 74

Stockdale, George W., 247
Stone, A., 318
Stone, C., 230
Stone, Henry, 230
Stone, J. W., 318
Stone, Lt. John H., 81, 86, 129, 154
Stone, Joseph, 232
Stonebraker, Joseph, R., 232, 357
Stone Bridge, 26
Stonestreet, Lt. J. H., 261, 270
Stonewall Brigade, 264
Stony Creek, 217, 218
Storm, Francis E., 113, 155
Stout, William, 295
Strafford, John R., 332
Strahan, Lt. Charles, 162, 332
Strasburg, 44, 48, 88, 93, 167, 242
Strasburger, ——, 247
Street, James, 233
Street, John H., 73
Strible, George, 79
Strickland, Jesse, 73
Strong, W., 231
Stuart, Lt. Gen. J. E. B., 21, 28, 31, 63, 101, 184, 185, 196, 202, 243, 249-252, 287, 341
Stump, George, 295
Stunt, Robert, 318
Sugar Valley, 308
Suit, Michael. 79
Suit, Norris N., 327
Sullivan, Andrew, 318
Sullivan, Clement, 162
Sullivan, Frank, 233
Sullivan, J. H., 295
Sullivan, John, 114, 157, 318
Sullivan, John H., 80, 162
Sullivane, Lt. Col. Clement, 332
Summnerville, 173
Sunderland, Thomas, 271
Susquehanna, 285
Sutherland, Leigh, 271
Sutter, 173
Swamley, ——, 169
Swan, George W., 78
Swan, James, 78
Swan John, 81
Sweeney, George, 235
Sweeting, Benjamin F., 78

Sweet Water, 308
Swift Run Gap, 35, 39, 276
Swisher, John, 24, 73
Sykes, Corp. William T., 315
Symington, Capt. T. A., 332
Symington, Maj. W. Stuart, 161, 332
Symington, William H., 162

T

Taliaferro, , Col. A. G., 67
Taliaferro, Adj. G. C., 333
Taliaferro, John R., 76
Talbert, F., 248
Talbot, J. F. C., 247
Talbot, L. T., 293
Talton, M. P., 309, 318
Taney, Roger B., 4
Tappahannock, 198
Tarbutton, William, 327
Tarr, Adj. ——, 43
Tarr, William, 295
Taylor, Corp. ——, 53
Taylor, Charles J., 234
Taylor, George, 81
Taylor, George L., 153
Taylor, Henry G., 114, 158
Taylor, J., 318
Taylor, John B., 73
Taylor, Lt. Gen. Richard, 54, 277, 299, 315
Taylorsville, 189, 191
Tazwell, 298
Tegmyer, Mrs. J. H., 371
Telyea, John, 318
Tennant, T., 233
Tennant, T. M., 162
Tennessee, 2, 149, 296-298, 311, 370
Tennison, Bernard Z., 154
Terrill, Col. ——, 96
Texas Rangers, 304
Thacker, Albert, 236
Thelin, William T., 111, 153
Third Maryland Artillery, 296-318, 338
Thomas, Daniel, 256
Thomas, Daniel L., 75
Thomas, Edward, 179
Thomas, Edwin, 80, 231
Thomas, Col. F. J., 12, 13
Thomas, Capt. George, 15, 80, 85, 86, 96, 110, 129, 141, 152

Thomas, George H., 318
Thomas, Holland, 78
Thomas, J. H., 231
Thomas, J. R., 271
Thomas, J. William, 162
Thomas, Sergt. James W., 80, 110, 137, 152
Thomas, John, E., 231
Thomas, John H., 80
Thomas, Corp. Laurence K., 152
Thomas, Raleigh C., 233, 361
Thomas, Capt. Richard, 86
Thomas, S. S., 271
Thomas, Samuel, 271
Thomas, William, 234
Thomas, Lt. William P., 14, 29, 75
Thompson, Capt. B. Bowley, 162, 332
Thompson, Capt. C. G., 332
Thompson, Charles R., 235
Thompson, Sergt. D. Bowley, 161
Thompson, Dorsey, 230
Thompson, Edward, 230
Thompson, F. N., 295
Thompson, Sergt. G. C., 270
Thompson, G. L., 230
Thompson, George, 248
Thompson, Lt. George W., 43
Thompson, John E., 158
Thompson, John W., 114, 158, 159
Thompson, Corp. Samuel, 265-267, 270
Thompson, William B., 235
Thompson, Thomas M., 81
Thornton, ——, 318
Thornton's Gap, 119
Thornton, Frank A., 71
Thoroughfare Gap, 280, 320
Tiffany, Henry, 162
Tilghman, John, 248
Tilghman, Gen. Lloyd, 358
Tilghman, Capt. Oswald, 333
Tilghman, Richard C., 137, 158
Timble, John D., 271
Timmons, William, 159
Tinges, Charles S., 327
Tingle, D. B. P., 115
Tingle, Davis P. B., 159
Tinley, John, 318

Tippett, George W., 75
Tippett, James B., 80
Tippett, M. A. K., 231
Todd, Sergt. M., 247
Tolby, George, 230
Tolson, A. C., 231
Tolson, Albert, 271
Tolson, Frank A., 155
Tolson, Lt. Thomas C., 88, 129, 148
Tolson, Lt. Thomas H., 112, 155
Tomlinson, T. M., 318
Tompkins, E. A., 318
Tonge, Richard, 256
Tongue, James, 80
Tongue, Richard H., 75
Toomey, Sergt. Daniel, 299, 302, 307, 315
Torsch, Capt. John W., 86, 87, 93, 97, 104, 113, 123, 124, 127, 129, 140, 141, 143, 146, 151, 156
Totopotomoy, 268
Tourney, Sylvester, 77
Towles, J. C., 233
Toy, Joseph D., 153
Toy, Thomas, 328
Toy, Thomas B., 327
Trail, Charles M., 111, 153
Trail Sergt. Lewis W., 233
Traphall, Joseph, 234
Travers, Sergt. Alonzo, 246
Travers, J. H., 248
Travers, John M., 76, 247
Treakle, Albert, 256
Treakle, Emmitt, 230
Tregg, John L., 153
Trevillian, 205
Triadelphia, 205
Trigger, John, 327
Triggoe, C. P., 327
Trimble, Maj. Gen. Issac R., 9, 44, 45, 54, 329, 349, 358
Tripple, Lt. A. C., 11, 122, 153
Tschiffely, Edger L., 230
Tucker, John W., 271
Tunis, John, 231
Tunis, O., 231
Tunis, Theopilus, 231
Tunstill's Station, 190, 193
Turnbull, Lt. Graeme, 231
Turnbull, Lt. W. S., 166, 237
Turner, Sergt. D. M., 80, 230

Turner, Henry, 112, 137, 154
Turner, J. A., 309, 318
Turner, Thomas, 256
Turner, William L., 112, 154
Turpin, Thomas L., 247
Turton, Corp. Benjamin J., 234
Turtons, M. G., 235
Tuttle, Charles, 76
Twilley, George H., 155
Twilly, Corp. Benjamin F., 115, 138, 158
Tyler, Albert, 234
Tyler, Charles, 318
Tyler, Brig. Gen. D., 57
Tyler, Sergt. George, 73, 234
Tyler, Grafton, Jr., 271
Tyler, John B., 234
Tyler, John E., 73
Tyler, William, 74
Tyler, Winfield, 236
Tyson, Richard, 301, 318

U

Uhlhorn, Sergt. John H., 75
Union Church, 54
Unkel, William, 151
Unkles, William F., 157
Upper Marlboro, 205
Upperville, 22
Upshur, L., 247
Upton's Hill, 31
Ussery, D., 318

V

Valentine, George, 233
Valiant, Edward S., 155
Valiant, George E. W., 77
Valiant, Thomas R., 80
Vallandingham, John, 231
Valley District, 39, 40
Vandiver, George, 235
Van Dorn, Gen. Earl, 355, 358
Vaughn, Brig. Gen. John C., 23, 208, 297
Verdiersville, 251
Vernon, 306
Vickers, W. A., 115, 159
Vicksburg, 299-304, 306, 307
Viet, Lewis, H., 133, 155
Virginia, 351
Virginia, 2, 4, 9, 12, 13, 48, 85,

93, 184, 189, 201, 203-206, 214-228, 241-249, 321, 341, 352, 356
Voght, F. E., 78
Volandt's Band (Baltimore), 89
Von Boerck ———, 252
Voss, Franklin, 75

W

Wade, A. P., 309
Wade, Charles E., 158
Wade, George A., 158
Wade, John R., 217
Waddell, Gen. ———, 302
Wagner, Hy, 256
Wagner, J. J., 159
Wagner, John G., 79, 133, 153
Wagner, Sergt. Joseph, 157
Wagner, Sergt. Joseph L., 138
Wagner, Joseph S., 114
Wakefield, ———, 318
Wales, J. C., 295
Walker, Brig. Gen. F. A., 139, 263, 264, 206
Wall, Sergt. James D., 326, 328
Wallace, William, 293
Wallack, R., 271
Wallis, Corp. Henry C., 234
Wallis, William T., 77
Walls, Dr. Samuel W., 333
Walsh, Edward, 159
Walsh, James, 74
Walsh, Thomas, 256
Walsh, Thomas K., 75
Walsh, John A., 295
Walters, E. H., 256
Walters, John 256, 295
Wambersie, J. E., 162
Ward, Archer, 235
Ward, Capt. Frank A., 14, 15, 72, 80, 162, 333
Ward, Corp. John J., 159
Ward, Joseph, 236
Ward, Maurice, 130, 159
Ward, T., 295
Ward, William, 81
Ward, William, 78, 295
Wardensville, 242
Ware, R., 318
Warfield ———, 234
Warfield, A. G., 230

Warfield, Adolph, 248
Warfield, Albert Gallatin, Jr., 363
Warfield, Edwin, 363
Warfield, G., 230
Warfield, Gassaway Watkins, 363
Warfield, John, 363
Warfield, Joshua, N., 363
Warfield, Marshall T., 363
Warhen, Daniel, 75
Waring, C. H., 231
Waring, Edwin, 231
Waring, H. W., 231
Waring, James, 231
Warren, 134, 135, 139
Warrenton, 121, 187, 261, 299, 320
Warring, Henry, 230
Warring, Thomas G., 235
Warrington, Lewis, 327
Warrington, Sergt. Smith, 325, 327, 328
Washington, D. C., 3, 26, 27, 29, 101, 187, 197, 203-206, 216, 241, 242, 245, 250, 281, 289, 296, 297, 351
Washington, Gen. George, 341
Waters, Green, 256
Waters, James F., 271
Waters, Jessie, 142, 159
Waters, John A., 235
Waters, John W., 159
Waters, T. J., 256
Watkins, E., 318
Watkins, John R., 75
Watkins, Lewis J., 230
Watkins, N. W., 231, 295
Watkins, Nicholas I., 80
Watters, Lt. James D., 231, 237
Watts, John, 155
Watts, Joshua, 151, 155
Watts, William, 113, 156
Waynesboro, 178, 217, 226, 288, 291
Weaver, Corp. Benj. F., 315
Weaver, George, 74
Weaver, H., 247
Weaver, Hiram, 234
Weaver, John, 318
Weaver, L. H., 115
Weaver, Lewis H., 159
Webb, 299, 300

Webb, Emmitt M., 113, 156
Webb, George W., Jr., 162
Webb, Lewis S., 271
Webb, Richard Watson, 327
Webb, Thomas J., 142, 158
Webb, William, 230
Webber, Edward, 233
Weber, Edward, 233
Weber, Philip, 236
Weber, William 75
Webster, George, 81
Webster, James R., 112, 154
Webster, W. H., 230
Webster, William, 81
Webster, William S., 256
Weddinger, Ferdinand, 78
Weeks, H., 256
Weeks, Henry, 76
Weems, Charles H., 127, 153
Weems, James N., 271
Wegner, Charles J., 72, 76
Wegner, Henry F., 76
Weishard, Michael, 236
Weitzell, William, 78
Welch, A. J., 235
Welch, Edward, 142, 159
Welch, Corp. Edward A., 113, 137, 155
Welch, John L., 75
Welch, Joseph C., 233
Welch, Martin, 77, 295
Welch, Robert H., 137, 155
Weldon, 134-136, 155
Weldon & Southside Railroads, 137-139
Wells, Emmitt, 307, 318
Wells, Gideon, 300
Wells, Herschel, 76
Wells, Lt. John B., 246
Wells, W., 318
Wells, William, 236
Wellmore, Capt. ———, 10
Wellmore, Edward, 77
Welsh, Daniel, 318
Welsh, Edward, 77
Welsh, Luther, 234
Welsh, Corp. M. L., 315
Welsh, Lt. Milton, 166, 233, 237
Welsh, Capt. Warner G., 166, 178, 180, 181, 233, 290
Wentworth, George, 74
Wentworth, George W., 155
Wentz, Louis, 73

West, Charles 80
West, Edward L., 80
West, George F., 75
West, Joseph, Jr., 235
Westminster, 204
Westover Church, 64
West Point, 260, 349, 358, 361, 368
West Virginia, 203
Wever, Hiram, 73
Weyer's Cave, 57
Whalen, John 318
Whalen, John W., 230
Whalen, William P., 295
Wharton, William F., 233
Wheat, Col. Robert, 40, 49
Wheatley, Charles, 256
Wheatley, Frank, 143, 253, 256
Wheatley, Levi, 138
Wheatley, Levin, 159
Wheatley, Corp. W. F., 81, 111, 137, 154
Wheatley, Walter, 256
Wheatley, William F., 154
Wheeler, Albert, 295
Wheeler, Charles W., 73
Wheeler, James R., 235
Wheeler, Samuel W., 333
White, David D., 75
White, Fisher A., 75
White House, 122, 191, 217
White, James McKenny, 80, 153
White, John G., 112, 137, 155
White, John T., 142
White, Brig. Gen. Julius, 170, 171
White Oak swamp, 133
White Post, 262
White's Ford, 69, 281
Whitely, Robert M., 76
Whiting, Lt. ———, 307
Whiting, James, 318
Whiting, Inspect. Gen. W. H., 11
Wickham, William C., 184, 185
Widner, Gen. Charles S., 368
Widner, Mrs. R. B., 371
Weil, George, 74, 233
Weir's Cave, 277
Wilcombe, Casper, 158
Wilcox, Maj. Gen. C. M., 263
Wilcox's Run, 286

Wilderness, 252, 268
Wilhelm, Lt. George, 275
Wilhelm, Lt. James T., 293
Wilkins, John D., 318
Wilkinson, Daniel A., 326
Wilkinson, William, 129
Wilkinson, William A., 114, 157
Wilks, Thomas M., 231
Williams, August, 80, 233
Williams, D. H. S., 236
Williams, Sergt. Maj. Edward, 73, 246
Williams, John P., 80, 111, 153, 231
Williams, Pat, 247
Williams, Patrick H., 77
Williams, Peter, 319, 327
Williams, T. P., 162, 233
Williams, Thomas, 271, 318
Williams, William M., 327
Williamsburg, 191, 251, 260
Williamson, Capt. George, 80, 106
Williamson, Philip B., 159
Williamsport, 121, 177-184, 207-209, 252, 267, 281
Willis, Corp. Brancock, 152
Willis, Charles W., 233
Willis, R. B., 129
Willis, Robert W., 155
Willis, T. N., 231
Willis, Thomas, 231
Willis, W., 318
Wills, A., 314, 318
Wills, Corp. F. Leo, 254, 256
Wills, J. P., 307, 318
Wills, John W., 112, 154
Wills, James A., 151, 154
Wills, W. A., 271
Willson, A. M., 271
Willson, J. M., 231
Willson, James Henry, 327
Willson, Thomas, 318
Wilne, J. S., 236
Wilson, ———, 74
Wilson, A. S., 256
Wilson, Algernon, 81
Wilson, Aquilla, 231
Wilson, Charles, 235, 256
Wilson, Charles G., 75
Wilson, Frederick, 234
Wilson, G. W., 271
Wilson, Henry, 328

Wilson, Sergt. Henry, 179, 325
Wilson, J. J., 318
Wilson, J. K., 231
Wilson, James, 162
Wilson, Lt. James H., 86, 111, 154
Wilson, John, 78, 97, 153
Wilson, John A., 76
Wilson, John S., 318
Wilson, Luther, 256
Wilson, Robert, 234
Wilson, T. J., 295
Wilson, W. 318
Wilson, Sergt. W. A., 76, 230
Wilson, Corp. William, 229, 271, 327
Wilson, William B., 256
Wilson, William Bowley, 333
Wilson, William W., 256, 271
Winchester, Va., 21, 35, 40, 44, 45, 48, 85-88, 92, 94-96, 119, 134, 167, 174, 176, 177, 184, 211, 249, 264, 266, 276, 283, 284, 324, 349, 350, 365
Winder, Gen. Charles S., 13, 63-65, 88
Winder, Mrs. R. B., 371
Winder, S., 248
Windolph, John H., 110, 153
Wingate, Frederick A., 145, 159
Wingate, T. C., 271
Winters, Harry S., 271
Wise, Lt. Charles B., 80, 86, 127, 128, 143, 149, 154
Wise, Sergt. Harry A., 154, 235
Wisner, John D., 230
Wissman, L. O., 231
Withers, John, 244
Witzlebben, A., 256
Wolf, Joseph, 74
Wood, Charles S., 248
Wood, Francis M., 235
Wood, Lt. George W., 268, 368
Wood, Henry W., 81
Wood, I. J., 233
Wood, Capt. John Taylor, 204
Wood, Lt. R. L., 302, 304
Wood, W. H., 295
Wood, Walter, 151, 154
Woodford, Arthur, 158

Woods, Charles, 77
Woodstock, 90, 291, 292
Woodward, Columbus, 78
Woodward, Columbus O., 234
Woodward, J., 318
Woodward, W. T. C., 333
Wooley, George, 231
Woolford, A., 230
Woolford, J. L., 159
Wooten, Henry E., 230
Wooten, Joseph, 318
Wooters, Alexander 235
Wootten, William T., 162, 265, 271
Wortham, Dr. J. B., 288, 293
Worthington, Charles, 230
Worthington, Eugene, 271
Worthington, George E., 234
Worthington, H. T., 235
Worthington, Joshua, 230
Worrall, W., 318
Wranch, John, 76
Wrea, John, 77
Wrench, John, 265
Wright, Clinton, 235
Wright, Lt. Daniel G., 80, 162, 333
Wright, Joel D., 158
Wright, R. B., 231
Wright, Sergt. Solomon, 231, 234
Wright, Sergt. W. H., 254
Wright, William, 256
Wrightson, Lt. William C., 115, 158
Wrightson, Lt. William H., 89
Wunsten, Henry, 233
Wyndham, Col. Percy, 49, 165
Wynn, Dr. Edward, 315
Wynn, James A., 235
Wynn, Joseph, 235
Wyse, Dr. W. P. E., 346, 367
Wysong, Henry, 295

Y

Yates, John R., Jr., 265, 271
Yates, W. F., 327
Yazoo City, 306
Yazoo River, 306
Yellott, Washington, 80
Yellow Tavern, 191, 197, 252, 287, 288
York Road, 178
Yorktown, 195
Young, Maj. ———, 327
Young, Alexander, 271
Young, Benjamin, 327
Young, H. L., 318
Young, Brig. Gen. W. H., 286
Young, Washington, 233

Z

Zellers, John, 159
Zepp, Charles P., 230
Zimmerman, Lt. Frank A., 333
Zimmerman, Issac, 318
Zimmerman, William, 248
Zollinger, Jacob, E., 111, 153, 350
Zollinger, Lt. William P., 80, 86, 124, 137, 141, 145, 149, 152, 349, 350
Zollinger, Mrs. William P., 350

Some Books Published By
BUTTERNUT PRESS

IN CAMP AND BATTLE WITH THE WASHINGTON ARTILLERY OF NEW ORLEANS, A narrative of events during the late Civil War, from Bull Run to Appomatox and Spanish Fort. By Wm. Miller Owen, First Lieut. & Adjutant B.W.A Boston, 1885, (XV) 467 pp., 4 illus., 8 color maps. Red binding stamped in gold with regimental insignia. "The most read, most relied on, most quoted account of Louisiana's Confederate soldiers" (Harwell). Probably the most famous of all Confederate artillery units, this battalion was a manistay of the Army of Northern Virginia in all its battles. A fifth Company served with the Army of Tennessee from Shiloh through Nashville, finally surrendering at Spanish Fort. D.S. Freeman said this classic is "a standard authortiy .... some documents not found elsewhere."

WITH THE OLD CONFEDS, Actual experiences of a Captain in the Line by Captain Samuel D. Buck, Co. H, 13th Virginia Infantry. Baltimore, 1925. 155 pp., 5 illus., Roster, New Introduction & Index. Known as the "Winchester Boomerangs", Company H was recruited in Frederick County and assigned to then Colonel A.P. Hill's 13th Virginia. After Hill's promotion, their regiment saw much hard fighting in the brigade commanded successively by Arnold Elzey, "Jube" Early, "Extra Billy" Smith, John Pegram, Jim Walker, and at Appomatox, by Henry Kyd Douglas.

RICHMOND HOWITZERS IN THE WAR: Four years Campaigning with the Army of Northern Virginia, By a member of the Company (Frederick S. Daniel). Richmond, 1891. 155 pp. No comparably sized unit produced more memoirs than did the elite, well educated Richmond Howitzers. This is one of the best by a veteran whose "1st Company" served first with Barksdale's Brigade and later in Cabell's Battalion, McLaws' Division.

A BRIEF HISTORY OF THE MILITARY CAREER OF CARPENTER'S BATTERY, From its organization as a rifle company under the name of the Alleghany Roughs to the ending of the War Between the States. By C.A. Fonderen. New Market, Va., 1911. 88 pp., 3 illus, New Introduction & Index. Organized in Alleghany County, this unit served as Company A, 27th Virginia of the Stonewall Brigade at 1st Manassas. Converted to Light Artillery in the fall of 1861, the battery supported Jackson's Old Division through the Valley, Peninsula, and 2nd Manassas, and Maryland campaigns. Gathered into Andrew's, later Braxton's Battalion, they fought valiantly in all II Corps battles through the remainder of the War.

THE MARYLAND LINE IN THE CONFEDERATE ARMY 1861-1865, By Major W.W. Goldsborough 2nd Battalion, Maryland Infantry, P.A.C.S., Baltimore, 1900. 412 pp., 29 illus. Rosters, New Introduction & Index. Blue binding stamped in silver with a Calvert cross. More than any other Confederate soldiers, the sturdy Marylanders in the Armies of Northern Virginia and Tennessee deserved the name "Orphans." From 1st Manassas to Appomattox, in the Valley and on the Peninsula, at Gettysburg and Vicksburg, Maryland Battlions and Batteries served with distinction.

THIS HISTORY OF THE BEDFORD LIGHT ARTILLERY, By Rev. Joseph A. Graves, a veteran of the Battery. Bedford City, 1903. 83 pp. Known also as Jordan's then Smith's Virginia Battery, this unit first saw action as part of Magruder's forces on the peninsula. Subsequently with S.D. Lees' —later Alexander's and Huger's — Artillery Battalion, they served on all major batttlefields of Virginia as well as in East Tennsessee. At Chancellorsville, a shot from their guns rendered the Union General Hooker *hors de combat* for several hours.

HISTORICAL SKETCH OF THE NOTTOWAY GRAYS, Afterwards Co. G, 18th Virginia Regt., Army of Northern Virginia. By Richard Irby, Captain of the Company 1862-63. Richmond, 1878. 48 pp. The 18th Virginia fought at 1st and 2nd Manassas, the Seven Days, Sharpsburg, Gettysburg, Wilderness and Petersburg in Pickett's — Garnett's — Hunton's Brigade. The regiment suffered over 70% casualties on the third day at Gettysburg.

CAMP LIFE OF A CONFEDERATE BOY OF BRATTON'S BRIGADE LONGSTREET'S CORPS, C.S.A., Letters written by Lieut. Lewis of Walker's Regiment, to his Mother during the war. Charleston, 1883. 113 pp. Our reprint of this very rare work contains straightforward, informative letters written by an officer of the 4th South Carolina and subsequently Micah Jenkins' Palmetto Sharpshooters Regiment.

WAR REMINISCENCES, BY THE SURGEON OF MOSBY'S COMMAND, By Aristides Monteiro, M.D. Richmond, 1890. 236 pp. port. Written shortly after the war with a sharp eye for detail, this is the most requested of all books on Mosby's Rangers. Monteiro was Surgeon of the 26th Virginia, Wise's Brigade when Mosby, a fellow student at the University of Virginia, had him transferred to the Rangers.

A HISTORY OF THE SIXTIETH ALABAMA REGIMENT, GRACIE'S ALABAMA BRIGADE, By Lewellyn A. Shaver. Montgomery, 1867. 111 pp. port. Organized in 1862 as Hillard's Legion, the 60th first saw action at Chickamauga. Accompanying Longstreet into East Tennessee and then to Virginia, they served in Anderson's Corps until Appomatox. "Exceptionally accurate". (Freeman).

SHOEMAKER'S BATTERY, STUART HORSE ARTILLERY, PELHAM'S BATTALION, Afterwards commanded by Col. R.P. Chew, Army of Northern Virginia, By Captain J.J. Shoemaker, Memphis, 1908. 108 pp. port. Originally raised in Lynchburg, Virginia, Moorman's then Shoemaker's Battery first served with Huger's and R.H. Anderson's Division. Converted to Horse Artillery late in 1862, they served the balance of the war in that role. The orignial of this interesting book is exceedingly rare.

REMINISCENCES OF THE CIVIL WAR, By Judge W. Stevens, A soldier in Hood's Texas Brigade, Army of Northern Virginia. Hillsboro, Tx., 1902. 213 pp., 1 illus. From Liberty County, Texas, Stevens joined Company K (Polk County Flying Artillery), 5th Texas Regiment in the spring of 1862. First seeing action at Gaines's Mill, he followed the fortunes of his Brigade through 2nd Manassas, Sharpsburg, Fredericksburg, and the Suffolk Expedition until his capture in the Devil's Den at Gettysburg. After exchange from Point Lookout in the fall of 1864, he was appointed to the staff of Brigadier General J.B. Robertson, then commanding the Reserve Forces of Texas.

HISTORICAL SKETCH OF THE PEE DEE GUARDS (Co. D., 23rd North Carolina Regiment), from 1861 to 1865, By Captain H.C. Wall, Raleigh, 1876. 100 pp. The 23rd North Carolina served in Garland's — Iverson's — R.D. Johnson's Brigade and D.H. Hill's — Rodes' Division. In early 1864 they were sent to North Carolina to recruit and arrest deserters but returned to face the final dangers of Petersburg and the retreat to Appomatox.

MOSBY'S MEN, By John H. Alexander, of Co. A, 43rd Battalion, Virginia Cavalry. New York, 1907. 180 pp., 13 portraits. This Neale title has been called "one of the most interesting items of the voluminous literature related to Mosby'y Command (Krick). Rather than writing a formal history of the Rangers, Alexander penned a "a narrative of what the writer saw of the men and their doings, as they impressed him at the time. . .

All reprints are bound in Oxford linen cloth with stamped covers and sewn headbands. Printed on 60lb. acid free paper.

The Butternut Press is dedicated to the preservation, through reprinting, of the finest Civil War memoirs, personal narratives, and regimental histories. We pledge to maintain the highest standards, both in selection and production.

TO ORDER CONTACT: **BUTTERNUT PRESS**
12137 Darnestown Road
Gaithersburg, Maryland 20878
(301) 963-7878

TERMS: Check or Money Order. Visa or Mastercard accepted. Maryland residents must add 5% sales tax. Postage or UPS is $1.50 for each volume. Libraries can be billed. Dealer inquiries welcome.

973.742 GOL
Goldsborough, W. W.
The Maryland line in the Confederate States Army.

EIK